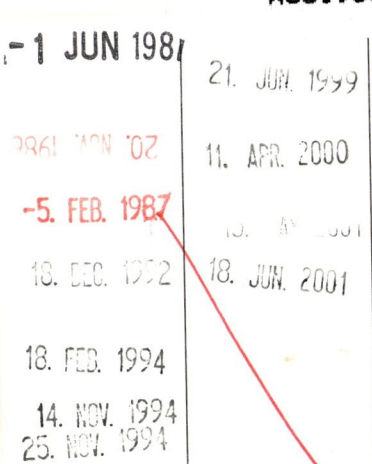

- 1 JUN 1981	21. JUN. 1999
20. NOV. 1986	11. APR. 2000
-5. FEB. 1987	
18. DEC. 1992	18. JUN. 2001
18. FEB. 1994	
14. NOV. 1994	
25. NOV. 1994	
24. APR. 1995	
26. JAN. 1996	
-4. DEC. 1996	
29. JAN. 1997	

943 CAR   005766   CARSTEN, F.L.

ALTON COLLEGE LIBRARY

This book is due for return on or before the last date shown above; it may, subject to the book not being reserved by another reader, be renewed by personal application, post, or telephone, quoting this date and details of the book.

HAMPSHIRE COUNTY LIBRARY

005766   TELEPEN

ESSAYS IN GERMAN HISTORY

ESSAYS IN GERMAN HISTORY

F. L. CARSTEN

THE HAMBLEDON PRESS
LONDON AND RONCEVERTE

Published by The Hambledon Press 1985

35 Gloucester Avenue,
London NW1 7AX (U.K.)

309 Greenbrier Avenue,
Ronceverte, West Virginia 24970 (U.S.A.)

ISBN 0 907628 67 2

History Series 50

© Francis L. Carsten 1985

British Library Cataloguing in Publication Data

Carsten, F.L.
    Essays in German History. – (History series; 50)
    1. Germany – History
    I. Title II. Series
    943   DD89

Library of Congress Cataloging in Publication Data

Carsten, F.L. (Francis Ludwig)
    Essays in German history.

    Includes bibliographical references and index.
    1. German – History – Addresses, essays, lectures.
    I. Title.
DD93.C37   1985   943   85-5538

Printed and bound in Great Britain
by Robert Hartnoll Ltd., Bodmin, Cornwall

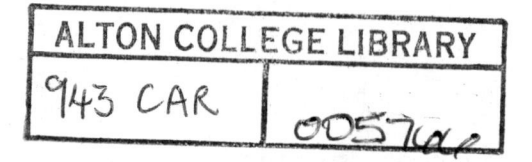

CONTENTS

Acknowledgements		vii
Preface		ix
1	Slavs in North-Eastern Germany	1
2	The Origins of the Junkers	17
3	Social Movements in the Pomeranian Towns from the Fourteenth Century to the Reformation	51
4	The Peasants War of 1525 in East Prussia	63
5	Was there an Economic Decline in Germany before the Thirty Years War?	73
6	The States General and the Estates of Cleves about the Middle of the Seventeenth Century	81
7	The Empire after the Thirty Years War	91
8	The Causes of the Decline of the German Estates	119
9	The Court Jews: Prelude to Emancipation	127
10	Prussian Despotism at its Height	145
11	British Diplomacy and the Giant Grenadiers of Frederick William I	171
12	Britain and Prussia	177
13	From Scharnhorst to Schleicher: The Prussian Officer Corps in Politics, 1806-1933	193
14	The Historical Roots of National Socialism	217
15	Bismarck and the Prussian Liberals	235
16	August Bebel	245
17	The Forerunners of National Socialism in Austria	255
18	Rosa Luxemburg, Freedom and Revolution	271
19	Revolutionary Situations in Europe, 1917-1920	283
20	Arthur Rosenberg: Ancient Historian into Leading Communist	295
21	'Volk ohne Raum': A Note on Hans Grimm	309
22	Radical Nationalist Officers contra Hitler	317
23	Interpretations of Fascism	325
Index		357

ACKNOWLEDGEMENTS

The articles reprinted here appeared first in the following places and are reprinted here by the kind permission of the original publishers.

1   *Economic History Review*, xi (1941), 61-76.
2   *English Historical Review*, lxii (1947), 145-78.
3   *Tijdschrift voor Geschiedenis*, liii (1938), 366-81. Published originally in German under the title, 'Die sozialen Bewegungen in den Pommerschen Städten vom 14. Jahrhundert bis zur Reformationszeit'.
4   *International Review for Social History*, iii (1938), 398-410. Published originally in German under the title, 'Der Bauernkrieg in Ostpreussen 1525'.
5   *English Historical Review*, lxxi (1956), 240-7.
6   *Tijdschrift voor Geschiedenis*, lv (1940), 14-40. Published originally in German under the title, 'Die Staten-General und die Stände von Cleve um die Mitte des 17. Jahrhunderts'.
7   *New Cambridge Modern History*, v (1961), 430-57.
8   *Album Helen Maud Cam* (Louvain and Paris, 1961), 289-96.
9   *Yearbook of the Leo Baeck Institute*, iii (1958), 140-56.
10   *History*, xl (1955), 42-67.
11   *History Today* (November, 1951), 55-60.
12   *Jahrbuch für die Geschichte Mittel- und Ostdeutschlands*, 31 (1982), 26-46. Published originally in German under the title, 'Preussen und England'.
13   *Soldiers and Governments*, ed. Michael Howard (Eyre and Spottiswood, London, 1957), 75-98.
14   *Upheaval and Continuity. A Century of German History*, ed. E.J. Feuchtwanger (London, 1973), 116-33.
15   *History Today* (November, 1961), 760-9.
16   *Soviet Survey*, 55 (1965), 141-50.
17   Lecture given in Vienna on 11 June, 1980.
18   *Soviet Survey*, 33 (1960), 93-9.
19   *Revolutionary Situations in Europe 1917-1922: Germany, Italy, Austria-Hungary. Proceedings of the International Colloquium (March 25, 26, 27, 1976), University of Quebec at Montreal*, ed. Charles L. Bertrand (1976), 21-31.

20 *Journal of Contemporary History*, viii (1973), 315-27. Reprinted in *Historians in Politics* (London, 1974), 315-27.
21 *Journal of Contemporary History*, 2 (1967), 221-7.
22 *Das Parlament*, 15 July 1964, 46-50. Published originally in German under the title, 'Nationalrevolutionäre Offiziere gegen Hitler'.
23 *Fascism: a Reader's Guide*, ed. W. Lacqueur (London, 1976), 457-87. Revised version by Pelican Books (London, 1979).

PREFACE

The essays assembled in this volume deal with very different periods of German history, from the Middle Ages to the twentieth century. Yet there is a continuous thread running through all of them: an attempt to try and discover why the German historical development was so different from that of its neighbours in the west and in the east, why German history seemed to take the 'wrong' turning at every decisive point, why the forces of reaction were so often victorious over those which seemed to open the way to a more promising future. These questions – more easily put than answered – early on induced me to make comparisons with the history of more fortunate countries. As I did my researches and writing outside Germany, it was only natural to draw on the experiences of the countries where I lived, first in Holland and later England.

When I began my historical researches in Holland nearly half a century ago, my interests concentrated on the peculiar phenomenon of early 'Prussia', starting with the German colonization east of the Elbe. The conquest and the intermingling of Germans and Slavs did not seem to account for the characteristic traits of the later Prussia, and the Teutonic Knights did not seem to exercise any traceable influence on the kingdom which inherited their name and colours. More and more I found that the specific 'Prussian' developments – the rise of the Junkers, the subjugation of the towns, the destruction of the powers of the Estates – could only be explained by an analysis of the social changes in late medieval and early modern times. My Oxford thesis of 1942 was exclusively concerned with the agrarian changes which produced the 'Gutsherrschaft' of north-eastern Germany, and this had to be seen side by side with the decline of the once so powerful towns of the Baltic area, in contrast with the development elsewhere in Germany and in western Europe.

In the 1960s my attention began to focus more and more on the enormous mass of documentation which survived the downfall of the Third Reich. Yet, as some of the essays in this volume show, my interest in Prussia and the Prussian army remained as strong as ever. It certainly was no accident that my first book on a topic of the twentieth century was devoted to the role of the German army after 1918, in which the 'Prussian spirit' survived the defeat and the revolution: an army hostile to the world of democracy and the new republican order. My work in this field is surveyed in the essay "From Scharnhorst to Schleicher", first published in a volume edited by Michael Howard. The antecedents and rise of National Socialism and of the Fascist movements were other obvious topics for someone who had lived through the 1920s and 1930s, first in Berlin and then outside Hitler's Germany. Indeed, my interest in these questions was first aroused when I was an active member of the German socialist movement in Berlin; the failure of the revolution of 1918-1919 and of the German labour movement had been some of the first historical problems which aroused my interest as a young student. To return to them in later life was like coming back to my earliest rather immature attempts. If anything, the distance of time and the masses of documents now available had only sharpened my interest. Finding some exciting new document in the archives is one of the great pleasures of the working historian, whether it confirms or contradicts an opinion held over a long time.

My work owes a great deal to the help and advice given by colleagues and friends considerably older than myself. Professor Norbert Elias first encouraged me to embark on what then seemed a very ambitious project of research, which many years later saw its fruition in *The Origins of Prussia*. In the 1930s Professor J.G. van Dillen in Amsterdam was good enough to accept for publication the first results of my work, some examples of which are included in this volume. At Oxford, I owed a great deal to the help which I received from three senior historians, Professor G.N. Clark, Mr. Reginald Lennard and Professor F.M. Powicke, and to the generous financial assistance given by Wadham and Magdalen Colleges. Most of all I owe to my wife from whose help and criticism I have benefited through many years. I am very grateful to Mr. Martin Sheppard and the Hambledon Press for publishing this volume of my selected essays, several of which have previously only been published in German.

F.L.C.

BIBLIOGRAPHY OF F.L. CARSTEN

BOOKS

The Origins of Prussia (Oxford, 1954; German translation, 1968)

Princes and Parliaments in Germany from the Fifteenth to the Eighteenth Century (Oxford, 1959)

Reichswehr und Politik, 1918-1933 (Cologne-Berlin, 1964; English translation, 1966)

The Rise of Fascism (London, 1967; German translation, 1968)

Revolution in Central Europe, 1918-1919 (Berkeley-Los Angeles, 1972; German translation, 1973)

Fascist Movements in Austria: From Schönerer to Hitler (London, 1977; German translation, 1977)

War against War: British and German Radical Movements in the First World War (London, 1982)

Britain and the Weimar Republic (London, 1984)

Britain and the First Austrian Republic, 1918-1938 (Forthcoming)

ARTICLES NOT INCLUDED IN THIS COLLECTION

'Die Judenfrage in der Auseinandersetzung zwischen dem Kurfürsten Friedrich Wilhelm von Brandenburg und den Landständen', *Tijdschrift voor Geschiedenis*, liii (1938), pp. 52 ff.

'De sociaal-historische grondslagen van Pruisen', *Verslag von het vierde congres van Nederlandsche Historici*, The Hague, 31 October 1938, pp. 18 ff.

'Medieval Democracy in the Brandenburg Towns and its Defeat in the Fifteenth Century', *Transactions of the Royal Historical Society*, 4th series, xxv (1943), pp. 73 ff.

'The British Court at Wiesbaden, 1926-1929', *Modern Law Review*, vii (1944), pp. 215 ff.

'The Great Elector and the Foundation of the Hohenzollern Despotism', *English Historical Review*, lxv (1950), pp. 175 ff.

'The Resistance of Cleves and Mark to the Despotic Policy of the Great Elector', *English Historical Review*, lxvi (1951), pp. 219 ff.

'The Failure of the Weimar Republic', *History Today*, vi (1956), pp. 318 ff.

'The Estates of Württemberg', Anglo-American Conference of Historians, *Bulletin of the Institute of Historical Research*, xxxi (1958), pp. 21 ff.

'The German Generals and Hitler', *History Today*, viii (1958), pp. 556 ff.

'A Note on the Thirty Years' War', *History*, xliii (1958), pp. 190 ff.

'Die deutschen Landstände und der Aufstieg der Fürsten', *Die Welt als Geschichte*, 1 (1960), pp. 16 ff. Reprinted in *Die geschichtlichen Grundlagen der modernen Volksvertretung* (Darmstadt, 1974), pp. 315 ff.

'The German Estates in the Eighteenth Century', *Receuils de la Société Jean Bodin pour l'Histoire comparative des Institutions*, viii (1961), pp. 227 ff.

'L'échec des libéraux allemands de 1860 à 1866', *Rasegna Storico Toscana*, viii (April-December, 1961), pp. 295 ff.

'History under Ulbricht', *Survey*, 37 (1961), pp. 90 ff.

'The Reichswehr and the Red Army', *Survey*, 44/45 (1962), pp. 114 ff.

'Die Reichswehr und Sowjetrussland, 1920-1933', *Österreichische Osthefte*, 6 (1963), pp. 445 ff.

'Reports by Two German Officers on the Red Army', *Slavonic and East European Review*, xli (1962), pp. 217 ff.

'Die Entstehung des Junkertums', in R. Dietrich (ed.), *Preussen: Epochen und Probleme seiner Geschichte* (Berlin, 1964), pp. 57 ff.

'What German Historians are Saying', *Encounter* (April, 1964), pp. 106 ff.

'A Bolshevik Conspiracy in the Wehrmacht', *Slavonic and East European Review*, xlvii (1969), pp. 483 ff.

'Die faschistischen Bewegungen: Gemeinsamkeiten und Unterschiede', in *Fascism and Europe*, an International Symposium (Prague, August, 1969).

'New "Evidence" against Marshal Tukhachevsky', *Slavonic and East European Review*, lii (1974), pp. 272 ff.

'Rivoluzione e Reazione nell'Europa Centrale (1918-1920)', in *Rivoluzione e Reazione in Europa 1917/1924*, Convegne storico internazionale (Perugia, 1978), vol. ii, pp. 135 ff.

'Faschistische Bewegungen in Österreich, mit einem Vergleich zu Deutschland', in K. Bosl (ed.), *Die Erste Tschechoslowakische Republik als multinationaler Parteienstaat* (Munich, 1979), pp. 43 ff.

'Die Entstehung der Brandenburgisch-preussischen Monarchie', in O. Büsch (ed.), *Das Preussenbild in der Geschichte* (Berlin-New York, 1981), pp. 53 ff.

'German Refugees in Great Britain 1933-1945', in *Exile in Great Britain* (London, 1982), pp. 11 ff.

'Stresemann im Spiegel der britischen Akten der zwanziger Jahre', lecture to Stresemann-Gesellschaft, 10 June, 1983, Mainz, pp. 1 ff.

'Adolf Hitler im Urteil des Auslandes – in britischer Sicht', in W. Treue and J. Schmädeke (ed.), *Deutschland 1933: Machtzerfall der Demokratie und Nationalsozialistische "Machtergreifung"*, (Berlin, 1984), pp. 97 ff.

FOR RUTH

1

SLAVS IN NORTH-EASTERN GERMANY

THE relation between Germans and Slavs at the time of the medieval German colonisation east of the Elbe and the Saale is one of the most important aspects of this great movement. If it could be proved, first, that the Slavs as a rule were neither killed nor driven into the marshes or farther east, but stayed on, and secondly, that the remaining Slavonic population outnumbered the German immigrants, our whole estimate of the German colonisation, and not this alone, would be changed. This article tries to answer the first of the two questions for one region, namely the north-east of modern Germany. This area was subjected to three different types of colonisation: under the native Slavonic princes, in Pomerania and Rügen, under conquering German princes in the Brandenburg Mark, and thirdly under the Teutonic Order in Prussia.

I

We possess more documents about the colonisation of Pomerania and Rügen than about that which took place in the Brandenburg Mark, and in the former countries the problem is less disputed. The colonisation was carried through chiefly by the monasteries, which had been established since the middle of the twelfth century by the native princes. At a very early date they received estates of unusually large size, were awarded far-reaching rights, and soon began to develop their vast possessions. On these monastic estates German villages sprang up in quick succession, while the Slavonic inhabitants had been handed over to the monasteries with the land. As a rule, at the time of their transfer or soon afterwards, they were freed from their former burdens, and sooner or later placed under the jurisdiction of the village mayors and the *advocatus* of the monastery. Thus their legal position became the same as that of the newly settled German peasants, both entering into the same relationship with the monasteries.

The Slavonic peasants would naturally adapt themselves to the customs of the Germans and intermarry with them when living together in the same village. We have, in Pomerania, various proofs of this from the early thirteenth century. In the district of Tribsees from 1221 onwards the Slavs living together with the Germans in one village paid the tithe like the latter, whilst the Slavs, who had vacated their acres in favour of the Germans and now lived in other villages, gave the *Biscoponiza*, the episcopal tribute.[1] And from 1241 the peasants of the monastery of Eldena were able to defend themselves in court according to their own law, but when they lived in the village of another nationality they had to use its laws.[2] The Slavs living in German villages soon adopted the German standard of agriculture, with the iron plough and the three-field system, as well as their laws and dues. This development spread even to the purely Slavonic monastic villages, as the monks were especially interested in the increase of their revenues resulting from it.

Various monasteries were expressly granted the right of using Slavs for the purpose of colonisation,[3] probably because they could not introduce quickly enough a sufficient number of German peasants into the country. These Slavonic settlements served the same purpose as the German villages, and presumably from the very beginning had a similar constitution. Thus the old Slavonic villages of the bishopric of Cammin in East Pomerania gave the full unfixed tithe (*integra decima*), while the newly founded Slavonic villages had to pay, instead of the tithes, a fixed due from each hide, approximately the same as that given by the German peasants.[4] In 1296 Slavonic peasants of a village belonging to the monastery of Buckow, under the guidance of their *villicus* Volzeko, were apparently acting as assessors in a village court.[5] It may be assumed that amongst the so-called " German " villages many were entirely or partially occupied by Germanised Slavs, the formal bestowal of the *ius teuthonicum* on the Slavonic peasants of a whole monastery[6] being only the seal of a transformation which already had taken place.

After the middle of the thirteenth century the process of Germanisation began to extend to the Slavonic peasants outside the

---

[1] *Codex Pomeraniae Diplomaticus*, edited by K. F. W. Hasselbach and J. G. L. Kosegarten, No. 134, p. 310.

[2] " Si quis vero in villis gentis alterius . . . elegerit habitare, volumus ut illorum iure utatur, quorum contubernium approbavit . . .": *ib.*, No. 400, p. 827.

[3] " Vocandi ad se et collocandi . . . Teutonicos, Danos, Sclavos vel cuiuscunque gentis . . . homines . . .": privileges for the monastery of Dargun of 1174, for the monastery of Eldena of 1209, for the monastery of Neuenkamp of 1231, and for the monastery of Kolbatz of 1272: *ib.*, No. 36, p. 92, No. 88, p. 210, No. 188, p. 427, *Pommersches Urkundenbuch* (quoted as *Pomm.* U.B.), II, No. 963, p. 268.

[4] *Ib.*, II, No. 976, p. 279, alleged to be of 1273. It is significant, however, that the latter rule is missing in the first version of this charter (No. 975, p. 277). It would seem that it was inserted later during the process of Germanisation.

[5] *Ib.*, III, No. 1751, p. 259.

[6] Monastery of Kolbatz in 1247: *Codex Pomeraniae Dipl.*, No. 368, p. 755.

monastic estates. Slavonic villages bought themselves free from the re-surveys undertaken by the princes to increase the number of hides and thereby their dues. At the same time, the villages received the assurance that they would possess their hides in perpetuity.[1] In 1276, John of Gristow, a relative of the princes of Rügen, fixed the boundaries of one of his villages and conceded to its inhabitants the free use of everything within its boundaries, while they were to give him and his heirs the customary dues.[2] Other Slavonic peasants bought the heritage of their hides[3] and freedom from labour services. They also were exempted from the receptions and entertainment of the prince and his officials.[4] In another case, the peasants were granted the right to marry freely and relieved from the duty of maintaining their lords' horses and hounds.[5] Thus the Slavonic burdens were removed. All these charters fixed the yearly dues once and for all, bestowed upon the peasants the right to sell and bequeath, and freed the villages from every re-survey. In 1286, a man with the Slavonic name Bratus was *villicus sive burmester* of the village of Gugulis;[6] and in 1327 one John Pryszlaw was village mayor of Schillersdorf.[7] Thus, throughout Pomerania, Slavonic villages were peacefully transformed into German villages.

In his last will of 1302, Prince Vizlav of Rügen stipulated that the Slavs on his estates should in future enjoy the same freedom as they had had in his lifetime.[8] There is no trace of any discrimination, persecution, or extirpation of the Slavs; neither were they more burdened than were the German peasants: in 1314, Niendorp on the isle of Rügen, a " new " foundation (as its name shows) and one of the few villages with a German name, paid the highest dues per hide of all the villages on the island belonging to the prince.[9]

Germans and Slavs as a rule lived side by side here,[10] and similar

---

[1] The first example to be preserved is from the year 1255, others from 1280 and 1291: *Pomm. U.B.*, II, No. 616, p. 27, No. 1173, p. 432, No. 1181, p. 437, III, No. 1574, p. 125.   [2] *Ib.*, II, No. 1027, p. 319.
[3] Thus 1296, 1307, and 1330: *ib.*, II, No. 1788, p. 294, IV, No. 2351, p. 267, VII, No. 4592, p. 371.
[4] Thus 1290, 1297, and 1324: *ib.*, III, No. 1542, p. 102, VI, No. 3799, p. 240, *Urkunden zur Geschichte des Fürstenthums Rügen unter den eingebornen Fürsten*, edited by C. G. Fabricius, III, No. 447b.
[5] 1300: *Pomm. U.B.*, III, No. 1927, p. 398.
[6] *Ib.*, II, No. 1387, p. 599.   [7] *Ib.*, VII, No. 4262, p. 87.
[8] " Item volo et mando heredibus meis, quod Slavi mei . . . eandem libertatem habeant in omnibus, quam meo tempore habuerunt . . .": *ib.*, IV, No. 2057, p. 68.
[9] According to the roll of the dues of the island: *ib.*, V, No. 2918, pp. 191-9.
[10] C. J. Fuchs, *Der Untergang des Bauernstandes und das Aufkommen der Gutsherrschaften nach archivalischen Quellen aus Neu-Vorpommern und Rügen*, p. 25.

conditions existed elsewhere.[1] According to a Pomeranian chronicle of the sixteenth century, the last woman to speak Wendish on the isle of Rügen died in 1404;[2] only in the east of Pomerania there existed " a few Wends and Kassubs in the country " about 1530.[3]

The Slavonic nobles quickly adopted German economic methods and feudal law, and tried to increase the revenues of their estates by founding German villages and towns. It is significant that while founding the town of Prenzlau in 1235 duke Barnim of Pomerania stated : *Nostris volentes utilitatibus et commodis providere . . . in terra nostra civitates liberas decrevimus instaurare. . . .*[4] Through intermarriage the amalgamation of the German and the Slavonic nobility was very much accelerated. By the end of the thirteenth century it had made great progress, and it is often impossible to ascertain whether a particular family is of German or Slavonic origin.[5]

II

The colonisation of the Brandenburg Mark differed from the peaceful colonisation of Pomerania and Rügen ; a German princely family—the Counts of Ballenstedt of the house of Anhalt, the so-called " Ascanians "—conquered and subjugated the different parts of the Mark during the twelfth and thirteenth centuries. It is said that when Otto, the son of the first margrave Albrecht the Bear, was christened, he was given the county of Zauche by the childless Prince Pribislav of Brandenburg, and that Albrecht became Pribislav's heir on his death in 1150.[6] But possibly the margraves only sought to prove their legitimacy in thus establishing a direct link with the former rulers. This in itself would indicate that there was no wholesale removal or extirpation of the Slavs, not even of the noble upper class. Of course, many a Slavonic nobleman died

[1] In 1327 three peasants of Stoltenhagen were expressly mentioned as *Slavus* : *Pomm. U.B.*, VII, No. 4291, p. 119.

[2] Th. Kantzow, *Pomerania*, edited by G. Gaebel, I, p. 316. J. W. Thompson, *Feudal Germany*, p. 449, n. 2, asserts that " the Slav tongue ceased to be understood in Rügen after the sixteenth century." N.B. This is about two centuries too late.

[3] Kantzow, *Pomerania*, II, p. 153.

[4] *Codex Pomeraniae Dipl.*, No. 219, p. 479.

[5] W. von Sommerfeld, *Geschichte der Germanisierung des Herzogtums Pommern oder Slavien bis zum Ablauf des 13. Jahrhunderts*, pp. 228-9 ; M. Wehrmann, *Geschichte von Pommern*, I, pp. 110-11.

[6] " Heinrici de Antwerpe Tractatus de Captione Urbis Brandenburg," *Monumenta Germaniae Historica*, Script rum Tomus, XXV, p. 483 ; " Cronica Principum Saxoniae," *ib.*, p. 477 ; " Pulcava's Böhmische Chronik," *Codex diplomaticus Brandenburgensis*, edited by A. F. Riedel (quoted as Riedel), DI, p. 3.

in the battles, and others, who would not submit to the new rulers or to baptism, had to emigrate. But the above-mentioned report of the conquest of the town of Brandenburg tells of partisans of the margrave amongst the native nobility. And in 1208 we find the *Sclavi nobiles Heinricus, Prizzlaviz, Pribbezlauz et Andreas fratres* witnessing a charter of the margraves.[1]

Soon the intermarriage between the German and Slavonic nobility increased to such a degree that, as in Pomerania, all authentic indications whether a family was German or Slav are missing.[2] Only in one family of the high nobility, that of the lords of Friesack, can Slavonic origin be proved beyond doubt;[3] while the same has also been alleged of two other families of the high nobility, the lords of Plotho and the Gans von Putlitz.[4] As late as the fourteenth century, many knights had Slavonic Christian names,[5] an almost certain indication of a non-German origin. On the other hand, even after the conclusion of the conquest some Slavonic noblemen, either voluntarily or under pressure, gave up their estates. While the noble family of Friesack seems to have died out after 1290,[6] the noble Jaczko of Salzwedel, in the Old Mark, who in 1235, centuries after the conquest of this district, was mentioned as a witness in one of the documents of the margraves,[7] left the Mark a little later to acquire the county of Gützkow in Pomerania. As late as 1263, the *filii domini Jakeze* held possessions in the Old Mark.[8] Yet another Slavonic lord, John of Havelberg, lost his

---

[1] *Riedel*, III, No. 11, p. 89.

[2] A. F. Riedel, *Die Mark Brandenburg im Jahre 1250*, II, p. 39; L. von Ranke, *Zwölf Bücher Preussischer Geschichte*, Sämtliche Werke. XXV, I, p. 11; B. Guttmann, "Die Germanisierung der Slawen in der Mark," *Forschungen zur Brandenburgischen und Preussischen Geschichte*, IX, 1897, p. 455; W. von Sommerfeld, *Beiträge zur Verfassungs- und Ständegeschichte der Mark Brandenburg im Mittelalter*, pp. 45-6.

[3] *Riedel*, I, p. 269, VII, p. 42, XXVI, No. 244, p. 189.

[4] G. W. von Raumer, "Der Senioriatslehnhof der Freiherren Edlen von Plotho auf Parey bei Burg im Herzogtum Magdeburg," *Allgemeines Archiv für die Geschichtskunde des Preussischen Staates*, IX, 1832, pp. 290-4. *Riedel*, I, p. 277, and von Sommerfeld, p. 23, deny this.

[5] "Yvanus milens residens in Grabove." 1345; "Yvan von Nybede," 1355; "Pribislaus de Wopersnow," 1389; in the family von Redigsdorf occur the Slavonic Christian names Prizbur in 1274 and Ivan in 1317, 1341, 1350, 1352, 1354; in the family von Wartenberg Yvan in 1352, Benesch in 1363, 1373, 1374, Wenzla in 1374, Janekow in 1387, Janco in 1397; in the family von dem Knesebeck recur Yvan in 1338 and 1367, and Paridam continuously until modern times; in the family von Wedel we find the Slavonic Christian name Czulis in 1286, 1291, 1296, 1398. All these examples are taken from *Riedel's Codex*.

[6] The last of their charters belongs to this year: *Riedel*, VII, No. 2, p. 48.

[7] *Ib.*, XXII, No. 6, p. 5.   [8] *Ib.*, XXII, No. 17, p. 95.

estates at about the same time ;[1] but we do not know the reasons for these emigrations.

But apart from these few cases, there is no evidence of any dispossession of the Slavonic nobility. If they submitted to baptism and offered no political resistance, they remained in the country and mingled with the German knights to form a united upper class. Still less could the new masters have any interest in wiping out the Slavonic peasants, as this would have robbed them of their sources of revenue and their farmhands. Many documents show that an extraordinary number of Slavonic peasants remained on their farms. As late as the fourteenth century, many villages were described as *villa slavicalis* or as *Wendish*. Even the religious conversion progressed very slowly. As late as 1235, about two centuries after the conquest of the Old Mark, four villages belonging to the monastery of Diesdorf, in the extreme western part of this district, still retained pagan customs; consequently, a church was to be built to forward the conversion of the peasants. Ten years later, this not yet being achieved, the peasants were warned that *Teutonici catholicae fidei cultores* were to be settled in their place if they still refused to become Christians.[2]

Economic inefficiency was another reason for which Slavs could be expelled, as is shown by an example from the possessions of the Ascanian house. In 1177, the prior of the monastery of Hamersleben besought margrave Otto to dispossess the Slavs of the monastic estates which they had hitherto neglected, and to settle in their place Germans, who as Christians would serve to benefit the monastery. The margrave complied with the request.[3] This shows that such powers were vested in the margrave himself. There are some further proofs that Slavs could be displaced or expelled. In 1173 it was said that two villages of the monastery of Leitzkau were then occupied by Slavs, but should they later on be occupied by Germans they were to pay the monastery one-third of the tithes. In fact, fourteen years later both villages paid the tithe, but one also paid the Slavonic corn tax, the *Vozop*,[4] and was therefore inhabited by Slavs; possibly the other village was occupied by Germans at

---

[1] Between 1256 and 1283 : *ib.*, II, pp. 359-60, No. 1, p. 329, No. 9, p. 368.
[2] *Ib.*, XVI, Nos. 11-13, pp. 400-1.
[3] " Veniens siquidem ad nos dilectus nobis Fridericus, eiusdem loci praepositus, debita sollicitudine postulavit, ut ab eisdem praediis Sclavos, per quos eatenus neglecta erant, mutarem et Theutonicos, qui voluntati et utilitati eorum sub Christiana religione deservirent, subrogarem . . . Proinde ego . . . satisfeci petitioni ipsorum et desiderio . . ." : *Codex Diplomaticus Anhaltinus*, edited by O. von Heinemann, V, No. 553a, p. 297. We do not know if this refers to possessions in the Brandenburg Mark.
[4] *Riedel*, X, Nos. 9-10, pp. 75-6.

this date.¹ At about the same time another Slavonic village was stated to have become deserted (*deserta facta*); many years later twelve hides of its land were given to German peasants.² The monastery of Chorin evacuated Slavs out of one of its villages.³ And in 1426 Margrave John reinstated his Wends of Kalbu, who had been expelled by his stewards, and at the same time reconfirmed all their old liberties, rights, and charters.⁴ The causes of these evacuations are obscure, but it is notable that in none of these latter instances can expulsion in favour of German peasants be proved.

The Germanisation developed rapidly in the Brandenburg Mark. As early as the eleventh century, in villages of the Old Mark belonging to the monastery of Corvey, peasants with German and Slavonic names lived side by side.⁵ In a village of the Havelland *cives and sclavi* lived together in 1302.⁶ In other villages, in the fourteenth century, *duo slavi*, a *Conradus Slavus*, or an *Elizabeth Slava* were specially mentioned,⁷ which indicates that the other peasants were Germans. In many a village, German and Slavonic fields or hides were lying side by side.⁸ As in Pomerania, new Slavonic villages were founded, and Slavonic villages transformed into German ones.⁹ The Slavs, like the German peasants, had to attend the General Assizes, the *Landding*,¹⁰ and in the towns they, like the Germans, stood under the jurisdiction of the mayor.¹¹ The Slavonic villages, like the German ones, had a village mayor,¹²

---

¹ Guttmann, " Die Germanisierung der Slawen in der Mark," p. 448, holds the view that both villages remained Wendish, and that it was the Slavs who paid the tithes in 1187.

² A document of 1201 mentions it as a remote event: *Riedel*, XVII, No. 20, p. 346. Riedel, *Die Mark Brandenburg im Jahre 1250*, I, p. 147, seems to think that the village had become deserted because of a war.

³ In 1274 (?): *Riedel*, XIII, No. 18, p. 217.

⁴ *Ib.*, XVI, No. 55, p. 49. This is the last charter which calls the inhabitants of this village *Wends*. Cp. the various privileges indicating a very favourable legal position of Kalbu of the years 1360-1536: *ib.*, Nos. 22-4, 26, 31, 38, 116, 149, 183, pp. 16-149.   ⁵ Between 1053 and 1071: *ib.*, XVII, No. 9, p. 426.

⁶ *Ib.*, XXIV, No. 38, p. 344.

⁷ *Ib.*, XIV, No. 60, p. 49, II, No. 15, p. 31, XVI, No. 77, p. 438.

⁸ 1271, 1375, and 1491: *ib.*, XXII, No. 12, p. 8, IV, No. 97, p. 142; *Kaiser Karl's IV. Landbuch der Mark Brandenburg*, edited by E. Fidicin (quoted as *Landbuch*), pp. 108, 126, 131.

⁹ e.g. by the chapter of Havelberg Cathedral before 1275: *Riedel*, III, No. 15, p. 93; frequently in the Ucker Mark according to a document of 1274 (?): *ib.*, XIII, No. 18, p. 217.

¹⁰ According to a charter for the district of Havelberg of 1275: *ib.*, III, No. 15, p. 93.

¹¹ Privileges for Salzwedel of 1247, and for Templin of 1320: *ib.*, XIV, No. 5, p. 3, XIII, No. 1, p. 165.

¹² Documents of 1226, 1375, and 1427: *ib.*, VIII, No. 53, p. 140, XVI, No. 26, p. 19, No. 56, p. 49.

who exercised the lower jurisdiction. These Germanised Slavs were considered Germans rather than Slavs. The foundation charter of the monastery of Diesdorf enumerates eight villages *quarum incolae adhuc Sclavi erant*,[1] *adhuc* presumably meaning up to the time of their conversion. A later charter of the same monastery mentions one *Bernardus, filius Slobe, quondam Slavus*.[2] Likewise a medieval chronicle speaks of the Pomeranians as: *Pomerani slavi, nunc Saxones, convertuntur per S. Ottonem*. . . .[3]

It has often been stated that the Slavs were much more burdened with services and dues than the German immigrants. As in Pomerania, the Slavs originally gave the church the full tithes on the field (*more Polonorum* it was called in the New Mark), while the newly settled Germans paid a small fixed due instead.[4] But as early as 1267, the Slavonic and German peasants of the whole district of Pritzwalk gave the same tithes fixed at a low level.[5] As to the dues of cottagers, we have a document from the New Mark according to which Slavonic cottagers were considerably more burdened than the sole German cottager of the village;[6] while, in the Old Mark, *Elizabeth Slava* paid the same dues as the cottagers with German names.[7] Slavonic hides, mentioned in the *Landbuch* of 1375, gave a little more in dues than the German hides in the same village.[8] These few indications certainly do not prove that the Slavs were much more burdened than the Germans.

Presumably most of the class of the so-called *Kossaten* (cottagers) were Slavs. These were smallholders whose land was insufficient for their maintenance and who, therefore, had to work for peasants or noblemen. However, the situation of these cottagers was not unfavourable. Their holdings were called a *heritage*.[9] In 1340, two cottagers in the Old Mark possessed a hide free from any dues whatsoever.[10] In 1362, the cottagers of another Old Mark village, together with the peasants, bought a wood for common use.[11] In 1490, the cottagers of an Ucker Mark village appeared side by side with the peasants as witnesses in their village court.[12] And above

---

[1] 1160: *ib.*, XVI, No. 2, p. 394.   [2] 1341: *ib.*, XVI, No. 50, p. 422.

[3] "Chronicon Theodoricii Engelhusii," *Scriptorum Rerum Brunsvicensium*, edited by G. W. Leibnitius, II, p. 1096.

[4] 1236, 1241, and 1243: Riedel, XX, No. 5, p. 181, XIX, No. 1, p. 124, XXIV, No. 4, p. 3.

[5] *Ib.*, II, No. 15, p. 449.   [6] 1355: *ib.*, XIX, No. 26, p. 78.

[7] *Ib.*, XVI, No. 77, p. 438.   [8] *Landbuch*, p. 108.

[9] 1362: Riedel, V, No. 81, p. 337.   [10] *Ib.*, XVII, No. 19, p. 237.

[11] *Ib.*, V, No. 81, p. 337.   [12] *Ib.*, XIII, No. 85, p. 77.

all, the cottars had to render almost exactly the same services as the peasants.[1]

The Slavonic language and customs persisted the longest in the *Kietze*, villages established originally under the protection of Slavonic castles, and mostly situated near the water. Their inhabitants could be considered as belonging to a certain piece of water and could be sold together with it[2] (presumably an old Slavonic institution), just as the peasants were sold together with the land on which they dwelt. The holdings of the *Kietzer* were likewise called a *heritage*,[3] and as far as we know they had to render restricted services.[4] As with the German villages, the *Kietze* had village mayors,[5] jurymen, and their village court.[6] The *Kietzer*

---

[1] The same services according to documents of 1335, 1360, and 1473 (*ib.*, X, No. 23a, p. 463, Supplementband No. 27, p. 238, XIII, No. 131, p. 292); services of two days yearly in 1477 and 1485 (*ib.*, V, No. 299, p. 454, XI, No. 215, p. 429); of four days yearly in 1439 and in the bishopric of Lebus about 1400 (*ib.*, XXII, No. 289, p. 263; Riedel, *Die Mark Brandenburg im Jahre 1250*, II, p. 261); services of two days as compared with eight of the peasants at the end of the fourteenth century (*Riedel*, I, No. 9, p. 451); of six days as compared with four of the peasants in 1485 (*ib.*, XX, No. 92, p. 86). Only the cottagers of Nachteheide in the Old Mark had to render unlimited services in 1375: " VIII cossati Alberto pro servitio quamdiu vult . . .": *Landbuch*, p. 206.

[2] Documents of between 1321 and 1391: *Riedel*, VIII, Nos. 182, 194, 319, 334, 339, 380, pp. 224-361, VII, No. 28, p. 321, No. 56, p. 341.

[3] 1389, 1450, and 1525: *ib.*, VIII, No. 380, p. 361, IV, No. 107, p. 156; *Landbuch*, pp. 272, 302; H. Ludat, *Die ostdeutschen Kietze*, pp. 164-5.

[4] Exemption of the *Kietzer* of Wriezen from all services with the exception of boating and errands on the water if necessary in 1420 (*Riedel*, XII, No. 27, p. 430); manorial services of eight days yearly of the *Kietzer* of Spandau in 1437 and 1441 (*Codex Dipl. Brandenburgensis Continuatus*, edited by G. W. von Raumer, I, No. 117, p. 139; *Riedel*, XI, No. 141, p. 101); apparently also restricted services of the *Kietzer* of Küstrin in 1412 and 1511 (*Riedel*, XIX, No. 93, p. 60) and of the *Kietzer* of Arneburg in 1441 and 1452 (*ib.*, VI, Nos. 273, 275, pp. 204-6). The first document I know of which stipulates unrestricted services for *Kietzer* is one for the fishermen of Köpenick, Rahnsdorf, and Woltersdorf of 1487 (*ib.*, XI, No. 219, pp. 433-5), repeated in 1516 and 1649. But in 1375 the service of the *Kietzer* of Köpenick was valued at two *frusta* of money (*Landbuch*, p. 21) and thus fixed.

If Guttmann, " Die Germanisierung der Slawen in der Mark," pp. 498-9, and Ludat, pp. 181-2, speak of unrestricted services of the *Kietzer* as an old Slavonic institution and, as proofs, quote documents of the sixteenth to eighteenth centuries (a period of rapid deterioration of the peasants' situation) it shows how lightly such statements are made, the above documents apparently being unknown to them.

[5] 1383, 1420, and 1589: *Riedel*, VIII, No. 351, p. 344, XII, No. 27, p. 430; Guttmann, p. 501, n. 6; Ludat, pp. 162-3.

[6] 1383: *Riedel*, VIII, No. 351, p. 344.

were not necessarily tied to the soil. In 1378 a nobleman stipulated that if he should ever wrong his Wends of Uscz, they were to be allowed to leave and go to another prescribed village, but had to render him, as before, services during the harvest.[1] All this indicates that the situation of the *Kietzer* was not bad, their Germanisation assimilating them to the rest of the country population. By the middle of the fifteenth century the Germanisation of the *Kietze* in the Brandenburg Mark had also been completed.[2]

In the New Mark, to the east of the Oder, and in the bishopric of Lebus, the colonisation started and German law was introduced before these districts came under the rule of the margraves who then proceeded with it without making any fundamental changes. Apparently, even the old Slavonic castle system remained intact;[3] and most of the Slavonic nobles remained on their estates,[4] while the majority of the high noble families, the von Wedel, von Güntersberg, and von Borke, were probably of Slav origin.[5] The immigration of German peasants also does not appear to have been very extensive. As late as 1345, two villages near Lippehne were expressly mentioned as *villae theutunicales*,[6] showing that they must have been comparatively rare. To a large extent Slavs were used as settlers, and very often they lived side by side with Germans.[7] In the bishopric of Lebus the German villages were founded on uncultivated land,[8] no dispossession of Slavs taking place. And in the New Mark German peasants were granted *free years*,[9] which were generally only given to settlers on new land.

[1] 1383 : *Riedel*, VIII, No. 319, p. 318.

[2] Guttmann, pp. 501-2 ; Ludat, pp. 112-4, 123-5.

[3] G. W. von Raumer, *Codex Dipl. Brandenburgensis Continuatus*, II, p. 117 ; *Die Neumark Brandenburg im Jahre 1337 oder Markgraf Ludwigs des Älteren Neumärkisches Landbuch*, p. 52.

[4] Guttmann, p. 495 ; P. von Niessen, *Geschichte der Neumark im Zeitalter ihrer Entstehung und Besiedlung*, p. 391.

[5] As late as 1286 the von Wedel were mentioned as *Hasso, Zulitz, Ludeko* without a family name, and ranking before various German knights (*Riedel*, XIX, No. 1, p. 443) ; the Christian name Czulis frequently recurring in the family is certainly Slavonic. Von Niessen, p. 313, considers the von Güntersberg to be identical with the von Kenstel, who were Poles ; and the von Borke were undoubtedly Slavs (*Riedel*, XVIII, No. 1, p. 100). The von Liebenow had extensive estates as early as the time of the Poles, but were probably of German origin.

[6] *Ib.*, XVIII, No. 32, p. 81.

[7] Von Raumer, *Die Neumark Brandenburg im Jahre 1337* . . ., p. 61 ; P. J. van Niessen, " Zur Entstehung des Grossgrundbesitzes und der Gutsherrschaft in der Neumark," *Programm des Schiller-Realgymnasiums zu Stettin 1903*, p. 19 ; von Niessen, *Geschichte der Neumark* . . ., p. 152.

[8] Charter of 1252 : *Riedel*, XX, No. 10, p. 183.

[9] 1232 and 1261 : *ib.*, XIX, No. 1, p. 1, XXIV, No. 7, p. 5.

These are the only documents of the Brandenburg Mark to give information on this important point. In the whole colonisation area, the iron plough enabled the Germans to break up hitherto untilled soil, while the Slavs could not drain the moors and marshes or clear the forests, which then covered great parts of Northern and Eastern Germany, nor build dykes against flooding by sea or river. Helmold's *Chronicle of the Slavs* expressly says that " the Hollanders received all the swamp and open country " (*terram palustrem atque campestrem*) in the Old Mark near the Elbe.[1]

Many Slavs became burghers of the towns. The foundation charter of the Neustadt Salzwedel of 1247 speaks of the *rustici teutonici sive sclavi* as future citizens of equal rights, both to come under the jurisdiction of the mayor.[2] As early as 1233, one *Wilhelmus Sclavus* was alderman of the important town of Stendal, while in 1266 *Johannes Slavus* became a member of the aristocratic guild of the clothdealers, and in 1287 *Conradus Slavus* was one of its officials. *Jacobus Slavus* was juryman (*scabinus*) of Stendal in 1272, alderman in 1285, and again in 1301 and 1307.[3] In 1332 *Henneke Went* was alderman of the Alstadt Salzwedel, and in 1336 *Johannes dictus Went* was a burgher of this town.[4] The Slavs in the towns mixed very quickly with the Germans and were entirely assimilated.[5] All this shows that in the Brandenburg Mark also the colonisation and the mingling of Germans and Slavs took place in an essentially peaceful manner.[6]

---

[1] Helmold, *The Chronicle of the Slavs*, translated by F. J. Tschan, p. 235; *Monumenta Germaniae Historica*, Scriptorum XXI, p. 81. Thompson, *Feudal Germany*, p. 553, does not see the problem when he states: " The first German incomers into these regions had *naturally* . . . appropriated for themselves the tilled soil of the conquered Wends."

[2] Riedel, XIV, No. 5, p. 3.

[3] *Ib.*, XV, Nos. 9, 27, 41, 62, 69, 112, pp. 10-82.

[4] *Ib.*, XIV, Nos., 104, 108, pp. 75-8.

[5] Guttmann, pp. 504-5; Ludat, pp. 125-6.

[6] There is no documentary evidence whatsoever that " Albrecht's (the Bear's) successors unfortunately abandoned this policy of toleration and the Wends were wantonly hunted down ": thus Thompson, p. 447, n. 3, who refers to A. Hauck, *Kirchengeschichte Deutschlands*, IV, pp. 558, 609, for his assertion. But most of the documents quoted by Hauck are from the time of Albrecht the Bear, but do not concern the Brandenburg Mark. The only one referring to it expressly states that many Slavs still lived in the bishopric of Brandenburg in 1197 (Hauck, p. 609, n. 2; Riedel, VIII, No. 35, p. 122). On p. 578 Thompson states, on the other hand, that " in Brandenburg around Dessau, Wörlitz, and Pratau . . . a ruthless expulsion of the Wends took place under Albrecht the Bear and Wichmann of Magdeburg." But these three places did not belong to the Brandenburg Mark but to Anhalt. E. O. Schulze, *Die Kolonisierung und Germanisierung der Gebiete zwischen Saale und Elbe*, p. 130, asserts without any proofs: " Hier um Dessau, Wörlitz, Pratau fand denn auch

III

If, in any country of the colonisation area, a deliberate policy of segregating the nationalities was attempted, it was in the Prussia of the Teutonic Order. The struggles during the conquest of the country and long-drawn-out revolts during the following decades undoubtedly blotted out a great part of the native nobility and peasantry. Here we may indeed speak of an embittered resistance by the Prussians against the foreign knights during the first decades of their rule.

After the last big revolt of the Prussians, which began in 1261 and lasted for fourteen years, the Teutonic Order divided the Prussians into various classes. Those Prussian noble families who had remained loyal retained their extensive estates, were put on equal footing with the German nobility and speedily Germanised.[1] In particular, noblemen of Prussian origin were engaged, during the fourteenth century, in the colonisation of the eastern *wilderness*, no distinction at all being made between them and the German nobles.[2] The other native Prussians who had remained loyal were likewise tied by very real bonds to the Teutonic Order, becoming an elevated class, the so-called Prussian Freemen; while the disloyal and newly subjugated were made villeins. This was the fate of the majority of the Prussians in many parts of the country.[3]

The *Prussian Freemen* had to render military services as light-armed horsemen, to build new castles and to repair or pull down old ones at the Teutonic Knights' request, as it was regularly laid down in their *Handfesten*, while they were exempt from all other services and paid only a nominal due. In general, they were treated as Germans and were quickly Germanised. In the bishopric of Samland, as early as 1309, the *ius teutonicale* was bestowed upon two Prussians;[4] and thirty years later Prussian Freemen were simply called *Theutonici rustici*.[5]

ebenso wie im Brandenburgischen und um Jüterbock eine rücksichtslose Austreibung der Wenden statt, von der wir sonst in unsern Gegenden nicht hören." Cp. Guttmann, p. 427, n. 4.

[1] E. Weise, *Die alten Preussen*, p. 24; H. Harmjanz, *Volkskunde und Siedlungsgeschichte Altpreussens*, D. 14.

[2] K. Kasiske, *Die Siedlungstätigkeit des Deutschen Ordens im östlichen Preussen bis zum Jahre 1410*, p. 146; H. und G. Mortensen, *Die Besiedlung des nordöstlichen Ostpreussens bis zum Beginn des 17. Jahrhunderts*, I, pp. 63-4.

[3] W. von Brünneck, "Die Leibeigenschaft in Ostpreussen," *Zeitschrift der Savigny-Stiftung für Rechtsgeschichte, Germanistische Abteilung*, VIII, 1887, p. 41; G. Aubin, *Zur Geschichte des gutsherrlich-bäuerlichen Verhältnisses in Ostpreussen von der Gründung des Ordensstaates bis zur Steinschen Reform*, p. 12; R. Kötzschke and W. Ebert, *Geschichte der ostdeutschen Kolonisation*, p. 88.

[4] *Urkundenbuch des Bisthums Samland*, edited by C. P. Wölky and H. Mendthal, No. 211.   [5] *Ib.*, Nos. 302 and 308.

The *Prussian Serfs* could be removed from their farms and transplanted to other manors, but there was no question of a systematic dispossession in favour of the Germans. German villages as a rule were founded on uncultivated or assarted land, as is indicated by the many *free years* which they were generally granted. The serfs either managed their own holdings as peasants, or possessed small properties as *gardeners* (cottagers) and, in addition, worked on a manor, or they served as menials. They had to help the Teutonic Knights to build and repair castles and frontier fortifications, dykes and canals, and to do drainage work, which might take them at times far away from their domicile to the east of the country. Furthermore, they had to serve their lords in the fields, but probably these services were restricted according to the custom of the country.[1] Presumably the Prussian serfs had only a right of usufruct and not of property on the soil on which they dwelt, but their holdings were in practice hereditary. They could certainly freely acquire and bequeath movable goods, as long as they did not belong to the inventory of the farm.[2] The serfs were not tied to the soil and had only to pay a small ransom on leaving their lord.[3] All this indicates that their situation was not so unfavourable. In any case, their economic Germanisation, beginning at the end of the thirteenth century, assimilated them to the German peasants.

First in the west of the country, and a little later in the east also, villages were granted to Polish or Prussian mayors for settlement;[4] while Polish villages were the first ones to be transformed according to German law, *ad utilitatem ordinis* as it was

---

[1] The Prussian Freemen were expressly freed from the mowing of hay and corn, from wood-cutting and wood-carting, *and the like* (*Preussisches Urkundenbuch*, I, 2, Nos. 329, 343, 347, 350). Had the tilling of the field—ploughing, sowing, carting of dung—been part of the Prussian services, it would have been enumerated as well.

[2] See K. Lohmeyer, *Geschichte von Ost- und Westpreussen*, I, p. 196; von Brünneck, pp. 42-3; H. Plehn, " Zur Geschichte der Agrarverfassung von Ost- und Westpreussen," *Forschungen zur Brandenburgischen und Preussischen Geschichte*, XVII, 1904, pp. 434-5; Aubin, p. 14; Elisabeth Wilke, " Die Ursachen der preussischen Bauern- und Bürgerunruhen 1525," *Altpreussische Forschungen*, VII, 1930, p. 41; H. Harmjanz, *Volkskunde und Siedlungsgeschichte Altpreussens*, p. 17.

[3] Charter of 1263 which does not mention any conditions for leaving, and others of 1263-9, 1267, 1277, and 1280 stipulating a ransom of ¼ Mark: *Preussisches Urkundenbuch*, I, 2, Nos. 204, 263, 353, 381, II, 3, No. 732.

[4] e.g. 1295, 1300, 1310, and before 1325: *ib.*, I, 2, No. 650, II, 2, No. 604, II, 1, No. 7; *Urkundenbuch des Bisthums Samland*, No.242.

significantly stated in one case.[1] From now on the inhabitants became in every respect equal to the German peasants, paid their dues, and as a consequence the revenues of the Teutonic Order increased.

Prussians also became peasants in German villages, especially in the bishoprics. In 1326, the German and Prussian inhabitants of a village in the bishopric of Samland were granted by a special act of grace the German hereditary and criminal law.[2] The official who drew up the charter did not find anything remarkable in the fact that Germans and Prussians lived together in the same village; he merely considered it noteworthy that they came under the same law and the jurisdiction of the village mayor. Elsewhere, the jurisdiction over the Prussians in the village was reserved to the *advocatus* of the bishop.[3] In the *Handfeste* of another Samland village German law was bestowed upon the Prussians who acquired a heritage in the village; but first they had to appear before the bishop,[4] probably so that he could ascertain their economic efficiency. According to these charters the German and Prussian peasants had to pay exactly the same dues from their hides, no difference being made between them. An extraordinary number of Prussians were used as settlers in the bishopric of Ermland. Many Prussian mayors were granted villages for settlement, the peasants of which nearly always enjoyed German law.[5] At the foundation of a village Prussian Freemen received hides in them, were submitted to the jurisdiction of the village mayor, and thus admitted into the village community.[6] Prussian

[1] e.g. 1290, 1298, 1303, and 1312: *Preussisches Urkundenbuch*, I, 2, Nos. 569, 700, 729, 801, II, 1, Nos. 73-4; *Urkundenbuch des Bisthums Culm*, edited by C. P. Wölky, No. 247; Codex Diplomaticus Warmiensis, edited by C. P. Wölky and J. M. Saage, I, No. 137; Kasiske, p. 157.

[2] "Omnibus et singulis in memorata villa nostra Medenowe residentibus tam Teuthunicis quam Pruthenis ex speciali favore et gratia contulimus . . . ut in successione hereditaria nec non in excessibus seu violentiis quibuscunque . . . ad officium advocatiae spectantibus iure Theutonico omnes unanimiter gaudeant . . .": *Urkundenbuch des Bisthums Samland*, No. 243.

[3] *Ib.*, Nos. 244-5, 256, 286.

[4] "Pruteni, si qui in eadem villa mansos seu hereditates emere voluerint, praedicto Culmensi iure cum ipsis uniformiter perfruantur, qui tamen, antequam idem ius assecuti fuerint, se nostro . . . conspectui praesentabunt . . .": *ib.*, No. 259 (1327).

[5] *Codex Diplomaticus Warmiensis*, I, Nos. 277, 283, 288, 290, 292, 297, 299, 302; II, Nos. 2-3, 7, 19, 22-3, 50, 68, 85, 89, 97, 99, 101, 103, 106, 127, 133, 148, 159, 165, 187, 217, 247, 262, 279-80, 320, 337, 348, 361, 369, 435, 476, 487b; III, Nos. 48, 102, 167, 191, 311, 477, of the years 1336 ff.

[6] *Ib.*, II, Nos. 138-9, 156, 207-8, 280, 318, 383, 435; III, No. 58; probably also Nos. 402 and 412, of the years 1349 ff.

peasants also remained in newly founded German villages,[1] while Prussian villages were granted Culmic law.[2] Probably the Prussian proportion of the population was very high in all the Ermland villages.[3]

The Teutonic Order itself also founded villages according to Prussian law and granted villages to Prussian mayors for settlement, but at first did not permit Germans to live side by side with less efficient non-Germanised Prussians. When the shortage of settlers became more noticeable in later years, this practice could not be maintained and was relaxed under certain conditions. Then it was stipulated in a number of *Handfesten* that Prussians using the wooden plough in a German village were required to pay the same dues as the Germans paid from their iron plough.[4] This shows that the Order did not in the least object to Prussians living in German villages provided that they worked with the German plough and became economically Germanised and efficient;[5] then they could be trusted with the heritage of a German peasant. It may be safely assumed that amongst the so-called " German " peasants of the later period many were Germanised Prussians, exactly as we know this of many a " German " noble.

Before the end of the Middle Ages, the Germanisation had succeeded everywhere. Only in the Samland, where the Prussian population was at its densest, did their language and customs survive up to the end of the sixteenth century.[6] Thus we see that in Prussia, as well as in the Brandenburg Mark and in Pomerania, the colonisation was accompanied by a process of amalgamation and assimilation. After the political resistance of the Prussians was crushed, nothing was further from the aim of the Teutonic Order than a policy of extirpation or dispossession of the Prussians.

In the whole area dealt with by this article the German villages seem preferably to have been founded on soil hitherto uncultivated

---

[1] 1349 and 1355: *ib.*, II, Nos. 147, 223.
[2] 1379 and 1390: *ib.*, III, Nos. 69, 245, 247.
[3] Kasiske, p. 94.
[4] " Und wer is, das ymant yn dem egenannten dorfe ein erbe mit eyme haken trebe und nicht mit eyme pfluge . . . dy sullen uns thun von dem haken als von eyme duczem pfluge . . .": thus or similarly nine *Handfesten* of the years 1370 ff.: Kasiske, pp. 71, 73, 118; Mortensen, I, pp. 95, 97.
[5] The decrees of the 15th century (a period of increasing shortage of menials and farmhands) which barred the settlement of Prussians on German hides (*Acten der Ständetage Preussens unter der Herrschaft des deutschen Ordens*, edited by M. Töppen, I, Nos. 72, 250, 286, 364) were not due to a policy of discrimination but were to check the desertion of the land and the shortage of menials, as was expressly stated by the Commander of Balga in 1425 (*ib.*, No. 344).
[6] Plehn, p. 401; Kasiske, p. 158; Weise, pp. 22, 34-8.

or claimed from the marshes or woods (*aus wilder Wurzel*). In a thinly populated country, the Slavs and Prussians were too valuable to be annihilated or driven out. The large majority of them remained on their holdings and formed part of the peasant population. They had only to fulfil two conditions: first to adopt the German religion (significantly Christ was called *Teutonicus deus* by the Slavs) and therewith the tithe, and secondly the German methods of agriculture, enabling them to pay higher dues. If they refused to accept this they had to abandon their holdings. If they did comply with it they became Germanised and henceforth might as well be called Germans. This is exactly why the second question asked in the introduction, i.e. what proportion of the local population did the Slavs form, is so very difficult to answer. My personal impression is that the Slavonic or Prussian stock of the population was probably considerably larger than the German part. But much more local research work, geographical, ethnological, and medical, would be required to give any more definite answer.

2

THE ORIGINS OF THE JUNKERS

ALTHOUGH the Junkers of Brandenburg and Prussia only gained prominence in European history in the course of the nineteenth century, the foundations of their political and economic power were laid at a much earlier period. These foundations were: their large estates which were continuously encroaching upon the land of the peasants; the strict serfdom of the peasants and their children which persisted up to the nineteenth century; the rigid division of society into three main classes, nobility, burghers, and peasants, among which the nobility was dominant; the strong influence exercised by the Junkers upon the territorial princes who depended on their political support; their right of filling the higher posts in state and army; the identification of their own interests with those of the state.

It is well known that practically all these characteristics developed in the course of the sixteenth century, and that they were intimately connected with the transformation of the medieval agrarian system, the '*Grundherrschaft*', into a system of large estates producing corn for export, normally called the '*Gutsherrschaft*'. This system came into being only in eastern Germany and Poland during the fifteenth and sixteenth centuries; it not only entailed a complete revolution of the agrarian system, but it caused sweeping social and political changes from which the Junkers emerged as the all-powerful ruling class, the once free peasants having been reduced to serfdom and the towns to a mere shadow of their former wealth and power. Yet this manorial and political reaction has quite rightly been called 'capitalistic farming', or at least 'agrarian pre-capitalism'; [1] for the farming of large estates was more rational from the purely economic point of view than that of small peasant holdings and produced a larger surplus for the market. This in its turn was a precondition of the growth of the cities of western Europe which could not buy sufficient corn from their immediate neighbourhood.

[1] Eileen Power, 'Peasant Life and Rural Conditions', *The Cambridge Medieval History* (1932), vii. 736; Otto Hintze, 'Wesen und Verbreitung des Feudalismus', *Sitzungsberichte der Preussischen Akademie der Wissenschaften, Philosophisch-Historische Klasse* (1929), xix. 328.

The rise of the cities and industries of western Europe thus provided one of the motive powers for the decay of the towns of eastern Europe.

The manorial system of the middle ages, the '*Grundherrschaft*', was very similar in most countries of Europe. Yet from this common starting-point entirely different systems developed in East and West. The famous German sociologist, Max Weber, forty years ago put this problem in the following form: It is an acknowledged fact that the '*Grundherrschaft*' (consisting of peasants paying dues, side by side with landlords who did not have a considerable demesne) was everywhere the older, and in all major characteristics similar form of the manorial system, prevalent in the whole realm of European feudalism; thus the important question arises: how did it come about that this structural similarity led to such diverging developments in East and West?[1] If we consider how deeply this diverging development was to influence the whole course of European history, and how well the causes of agrarian changes have been investigated for many European countries, it seems puzzling that, up to this day, the question put by Max Weber has not been answered satisfactorily, although many detailed studies have been published since.[2]

If we try to find an answer to this question, we can exclude from the outset all parallel developments which took place in western as well as in eastern Germany and Europe. This applies in particular to the main argument of G. F. Knapp and his school, namely that the change of the methods of warfare compelled the knight to find new means of livelihood, to become a farmer himself and to acquire more and more land, hitherto farmed by peasants, for his demesne.[3] For, quite apart from the rights and wrongs of this much discussed opinion, the same force would have been effective in western Germany and western Europe as a whole, and it cannot therefore explain the entirely different development of East and West. This also applies to the more recently advanced theory, that the fall in the value of money caused a

[1] M. Weber, 'Der Streit um den Charakter der altgermanischen Sozialverfassung', *Gesammelte Aufsätze zur Sozial- und Wirtschaftsgeschichte*, p. 510.

[2] For Poland, J. Rutkowski, *Histoire Économique de la Pologne Avant Les Partages*, p. 106, has stated that the reasons for the agrarian transformation of the sixteenth century have not yet been established with the necessary clarity. The same has been stated for Germany by M. Weber, *loc. cit.* p. 510, and by W. Wittich, article 'Gutsherrschaft', in *Handwörterbuch der Staatswissenschaften*, 3rd edn. (1910), v. 210.

[3] Thus G. F. Knapp, *Die Bauernbefreiung und der Ursprung der Landarbeiter in den älteren Theilen Preussens*, i. 37–8, and *Die Landarbeiter in Knechtschaft und Freiheit*, pp. 53–4; F. Grossmann, *Ueber die gutsherrlich-bäuerlichen Rechtsverhältnisse in der Mark Brandenburg vom 16. bis 18. Jahrhundert*, p. 16; S. B. Fay, 'The Roman Law and the German Peasant', *The American Historical Review* (1911), xvi. 251, n. 66; A. Bruce-Boswell, 'Poland and Lithuania in the Fourteenth and Fifteenth Centuries', *The Cambridge Medieval History* (1936), viii. 582.

The Origins of the Junkers

shrinking of the income of the nobleman, which consisted of dues and rents, and thus induced him to increase his demesne.[1] For money economy was far more developed in the West than in the East, where dues were still largely paid in kind, so that the effect of the depreciation of currency must have been more strongly felt in the West.

As the system of 'Gutsherrschaft' only came into being in districts which had been colonized and Germanized in the course of the middle ages and in which Slavonic influences remained more or less strong, it is only natural that many historians should have tried to trace back its origins either to those Slav influences, or to the German colonization and the agrarian system which it created. For example, it has often been stated that not all farmers were granted the favourable conditions of German law at the time of the colonization, but that numerous Slavonic peasants continued to live under the harsher rules of Slavonic law, so that later the landlords were led to reduce the other peasants to the level of those living under Slavonic law.[2] Some writers have even gone so far as to consider the whole social system, and in particular the serfdom of the peasants, as it developed to the east of the Elbe, to be of Polish or Slav origin, and alien to German institutions.[3]

The persistence of Slav influences over a period of several centuries, however, is more than doubtful. For the Brandenburg Mark, which was to become the cradle of the Prussian State, there is no documentary proof whatever of unfavourable conditions among the Slavonic peasants in the fifteenth century. By that time, their Germanization had proceeded so far that all differences between them and the German peasants had disappeared.[4] One document is quoted as a proof to the contrary:

---

[1] Thus H. Maybaum, *Die Entstehung der Gutsherrschaft im nordwestlichen Mecklenburg (Amt Gadebusch und Amt Grevesmühlen)*, pp. 108–16; A. Bruce-Boswell, *loc. cit.* p. 582; W. Maas, ' Zur Entwicklung der polnischen Agrarstruktur vom XV. bis XVIII. Jahrhundert ", *Vierteljahrschrift für Sozial- und Wirtschaftsgeschichte* (1928), xx. 491; H. Rosenberg, ' The Rise of the Junkers in Brandenburg-Prussia ', *The American Historical Review* (1944), xlix. 231.

[2] Thus G. von Below, *Territorium und Stadt*, pp. 24–5; B. Guttmann, ' Die Germanisierung der Slawen in der Mark ', *Forschungen zur Brandenburgischen und Preussischen Geschichte* (1897), ix. 491; P. von Niessen, *Geschichte der Neumark im Zeitalter ihrer Entstehung und Besiedlung*, p. 405; C. J. Fuchs, ' Zur Geschichte des gutsherrlich-bäuerlichen Verhältnisses in der Mark Brandenburg ', *Zeitschrift der Savigny-Stiftung für Rechtsgeschichte, Germanistische Abteilung* (1891), xii. 22; F. Engels, ' Zur Geschichte der preussischen Bauern ', introduction to: W. Wolff, *Die Schlesische Milliarde*, edited by F. Mehring, p. 65; M. Weber, *Wirtschaftsgeschichte*, p. 91.

[3] Thus E. Schmidt, *Geschichte des Deutschtums im Lande Posen unter polnischer Herrschaft*, p. 186; F. Mager, *Geschichte der Landeskultur Westpreussens und des Netzebezirks*, pp. 48–9, 56; F. Schnabel, *Deutsche Geschichte im Neunzehnten Jahrhundert*, ii. 273, and *Freiherr vom Stein*, p. 53.

[4] For all details, see F. L. Carsten, ' Slavs in North-Eastern Germany ', *The Economic History Review* (1941), xi. 67 ff. See above, chapter 1, p. 7ff.

a late fourteenth-century survey of the possessions of the Brunswick monastery of Amelungsborn in the border district between Brandenburg and Mecklenburg. In one village, it was stated in this survey, the *mansi* ' belong to the monastery and not to the peasants, nor are they appropriated to the farmsteads, but only leased, according to Slavonic law, so that they can be taken away from the peasants if they do not satisfy the monastery in paying dues, and can be let out to other peasants. . . '.[1] Of the *mansi* of another village it was said that they ' are not given to the village community to farm but to the more loyal and reliable peasants. . . ' ;[2] but in this case it was not stated that this was a Slavonic custom. The author of this survey obviously thought these conditions so exceptional that they needed special mention ; for no similar remark occurs with regard to the other villages of the monastery. It would be a mistake to conclude from this document that these conditions were typical of the position of the Slavonic peasants of Brandenburg ;[3] for it was expressly stated that these villages belonged to Mecklenburg, and not to Brandenburg.[4]

In Prussia, the distinction drawn by the Teutonic Order between the Prussian (i.e. Slavonic) Serfs on the one hand and the German peasants and Prussian Freemen on the other, was originally much sharper than anywhere else in the colonization area. But here also, before the end of the middle ages the economic Germanization of the Prussian serfs brought them to the same level as the German peasants.[5] Curiously enough, in Prussia the opposite argument could be made : the one district of Prussia where ' *Gutsherrschaft* ' never developed was the bishopric of Ermland,[6] and this is exactly the district where the native Prussians were particularly numerous.[7] This shows to what

[1] ' . . . sunt monasterii et curiae et non villanorum, nec sunt ad areas curiarum villae appropriati, sed simpliciter locati, secundum ius Slavicale, ita sane, cum cultores villae non satisfaciunt in pactis curiae nec sufficiunt tunc mansi possent auferri ab eis licite et locari aliis agricolis pro pactis . . . ' : *Codex diplomaticus Brandenburgensis*, edited by A. F. Riedel (quoted as Riedel), i, no. 9, p. 457.

[2] ' Mansi non dantur communitati ad colendum, sed fidelioribus et certioribus in ipsa villa . . . ' : *ibid.* p. 454.

[3] This has been done by B. Guttmann, *loc. cit.* p. 491, and P. von Niessen, *op. cit.* p. 405.

[4] ' Haec villae et mansi praedicti in dominio terrae Slaviae sunt siti . . . ' : Riedel, i. 458. *Slavia* was, significantly enough, the medieval name of Mecklenburg.

[5] H. Aubin, ' The Lands East of the Elbe and German Colonisation Eastwards ', *The Cambridge Economic History of Europe*, i. 369. For details see F. L. Carsten, above, p. 13 ff.

[6] G. von Below, *op. cit.* p. 91 ; H. Rosenberg, *loc. cit.* p. 229.

[7] H. Aubin, *loc. cit.* p. 369 ; F. L. Carsten, above, pp. 14-15. Already G. von Below, *op. cit.* p. 90, has observed that large estates are most widespread in the predominantly German parts of the area around Königsberg, so that the relation would be exactly opposite to the one usually assumed : the stronger the German influence, the larger the estates !

strange conclusions the whole argument of the comparative importance of Germanic and Slavonic influences can lead; in reality, the national characteristics or institutions of either nationality had nothing whatever to do with the origins of 'Gutsherrschaft'.

There is, however, one other (and apparently much more convincing) argument which also traces back the origin of 'Gutsherrschaft' to the colonization period, basing itself not upon alleged national characteristics but upon economic developments. It runs briefly as follows: from the beginning the estates granted to the immigrating German knights, and those retained by the Slav noblemen, were much larger, and demesne farming was much more prevalent than in western Germany and western Europe as a whole; large-scale production of corn for export by nobles did not only start in the fifteenth century, but much earlier; in short, 'Gutsherrschaft' did not originate in the fifteenth century, but 'was always there'.[1]

When the German colonization to the east of the Elbe started, the manorial system of western Germany and western Europe had already moved far towards the disintegration of the manor and the gradual substitution of demesne farming by peasant farming. This development was intimately connected with the growth of money economy and the towns; it was strongest in their vicinity,[2] as they provided the market for the sale of the peasants' produce.[3] Compact estates had been split up, and in their place 'Streubesitz' (the possessions of a landlord consisting of scattered small pieces of land and rights within a considerable area) had become more and more prevalent. This system could obviously not be introduced in the East where its pre-conditions were lacking; many large and compact estates were granted, and demesne farming was probably rather widespread. For example, in the New Mark in 1337 (that is, not so long after the beginning of the colonization of this district) demesnes covered nearly one-seventh of the total land under cultivation.[4] In the agreement of 1283 between the margraves of Brandenburg and

[1] This argument has recently been put forward very strongly by H. Rosenberg in *The American Historical Review* (1944), xlix. 228 ff. Dr. Rosenberg bases himself mainly on G. Aubin's study, *Zur Geschichte des gutsherrlich-bäuerlichen Verhältnisses in Ostpreussen von der Gründung des Ordensstaates bis zur Steinschen Reform*. But the conditions in the State of the Teutonic Knights were by no means typical of eastern Germany. [2] See Eileen Power, *loc. cit.* pp. 727–8.
[3] M. Weber, *Wirtschaftsgeschichte*, p. 90, and 'Der Streit um den Charakter der altgermanischen Sozialverfassung', *loc. cit.* pp. 510–11; J. Rutkowski, 'La Genèse du Régime de la Corvée dans l'Europe Centrale depuis la Fin du Moyen Age', *Extrait de la Pologne au VI-e Congrès International des Sciences Historiques* (1928), p. 3; F. L. Ganshof, 'Medieval Agrarian Society in its Prime', *The Cambridge Economic History of Europe*, i. 322.
[4] 1733 *Hufen* out of a total of 12,388. These 1733 *Hufen* belonged to 187 estates so that their average size amounted to more than nine *Hufen* (i.e. about two to three peasant farms): C. J. Fuchs, *loc. cit.* p. 20. H. Aubin, *loc. cit.* p. 388, has 8½ *Hufen*.

their vassals, it was assumed that the average size of a knight's demesne was six *mansi*, and that of a squire's, four.[1] But that was only about 50 to 100 per cent. larger than the average peasant farm which, in Brandenburg, comprised two to four *mansi*.[2] It has always been thought that a straight development led from this starting-point to the large demesnes of the sixteenth and later centuries.[3] The main source for Brandenburg, the 'Landbuch' of 1375, indeed shows widespread demesne farming. Their average size in the Old Mark amounted to only 3·7 *mansi*, in the Ucker Mark to 6·2, and in the Middle Mark to 7·6; in the latter, the demesnes covered less than one-tenth of the total cultivated soil.[4] Although these figures were about the same as those of the previous century, it has been presumed that they represent a growth of the demesnes through the absorption of peasant land since the colonization,[5] and that this process then continued into the fifteenth and sixteenth centuries. Thus, from the very beginning the whole development in the East would have been exactly opposite to that in the West.

It can be clearly shown, however, that the development in East and West, up to the fifteenth century, took place along parallel lines, and that, with the growth of the towns, the manorial system disintegrated in the East as well. It is only surprising that, apparently, all these proofs have not been noticed previously.

In the early colonization period demesne farming was undertaken not only by noblemen, but to a considerable extent also by the monasteries, in particular the Cistercian foundations. Their '*grangiae*' were frequently mentioned in the charters of Brandenburg and of Pomerania. The Pomeranian monastery of Eldena alone, in 1280, possessed seven granges.[6] The monks even had the right to convert their villages into granges and to pull down houses for this purpose.[7] Only a few decades later, however,

[1] 'Miles sub aratro suo habebit sex mansos, famulus vero quatuor, et hii erunt penitus liberi, et si plures quidem habuerint, de his dabunt censum praelibatum . . .': Riedel, *op. cit.* C i, no. 9, p. 11.

[2] W. Gley, *Die Besiedlung der Mittelmark von der slawischen Einwanderung bis 1624*, p. 81. In the West, many demesnes were originally considerably larger than a peasant farm: cf. G. F. Knapp, *Die Landarbeiter in Knechtschaft und Freiheit*, p. 47. The *mansus* or *Hufe* was, like the English hide, a variable measure of land, originally considered sufficient to maintain a peasant family; in the colonization area, however, most peasants from the outset received several *Hufen*, as there was a surplus of land.

[3] Thus G. von Below, *op. cit.* pp. 25 ff., and article 'Grundbesitz' in *Handwörterbuch der Staatswissenschaften*, 4th edn., Supplement, p. 442; F. Grossmann, *op. cit.* p. 10; M. Weber, *Wirtschaftsgeschichte*, p. 81; Eileen Power, *loc. cit.* p. 736; H. Aubin, *loc. cit.* p. 389. See further the literature quoted below in footnote 1, p. 154.

[4] F. Grossmann, *op. cit.* p. 7; C. J. Fuchs, *loc. cit.* p. 21; H. Aubin, *loc. cit.* p. 388.

[5] H. Aubin, *loc. cit.* p. 388; J. Schultze (editor), *Das Landbuch der Mark Brandenburg von 1375*, p. xviii.

[6] *Pommersches Urkundenbuch*, ii, no. 1171, p. 430, no. 1221, p. 463.

[7] Privileges for Eldena of 1295, and for Neuenkamp of 1285: *ibid*. iii, no. 1710, p. 228; ii, no. 1322, p. 545. One example: 'Kusiz et iterum Kusiz quae villae redactae sunt in grangiam Kusiz nominatam . . .': *ibid*. ii, no. 1233, p. 473 (1282).

The Origins of the Junkers

the reverse process began. In 1326 the monks of Eldena acquired the right to convert two of their granges into villages;[1] a '*curia*' was transformed into a village in 1357, and a demesne in the immediate neighbourhood of the monastery in 1407.[2] Six granges of another great Cistercian monastery, Kolbatz in eastern Pomerania, were converted into villages about the middle of the fourteenth century.[3] Two Cistercian foundations of the Ucker Mark, Chorin and Himmelpfort, were also granted the right to lease their '*curiae*' or to transform them into villages.[4] A '*grangia*' of the Silesian monastery of Leubus in Brandenburg developed into a village;[5] the same happened to a '*curia*' of the Benedictine nunnery of Spandau,[6] and to a '*hoff*' of the Hospitallers near Berlin.[7]

It could, of course, be argued that what applied to the monastic estates, did not necessarily apply to the demesnes of noblemen; for direct proofs of their conversion into peasant farms are almost entirely lacking.[8] There are, however, many indirect proofs. First of all, there was widespread commutation of labour services in Brandenburg which went on from the fourteenth to the sixteenth century. The labour services of the peasants were no longer needed, and the landlords found it more advantageous to receive quit-rents instead. This movement was particularly strong in the Old Mark, the part of Brandenburg to the west of the Elbe, where the colonization had started earliest, and where town life and trade were further developed than to the east of the river.[9] It may be remembered that in 1375 the demesnes of the

---

[1] *Pommersches Urkundenbuch*, vii, no. 4152, p. 8, no. 4162, p. 16. Unfortunately, the Pomeranian documents have not been published beyond the year 1326.

[2] J. C. C. Oelrichs, *Verzeichniss der von Dregerschen übrigen Sammlung Pommerscher Urkunden*, no. 6, p. 113 (1407); C. J. Fuchs, *Der Untergang des Bauernstandes und das Aufkommen der Gutsherrschaften nach archivalischen Quellen aus Neu-Vorpommern und Rügen*, pp. 19, 287, 303, 309.

[3] 'Annales Colbazienses', *Monumenta Germaniae Historica, Script.* xix, 718 (ad annum 1347); J. C. C. Oelrichs, *op. cit.* no. 12, p. 91 (1356), no. 14, p. 93 (1360).

[4] Riedel, *op. cit.* xiii, no. 64, p. 246 (1335), no. 32, p. 31 (1342).

[5] W. Gley, *op. cit.* p. 110.

[6] 'Quondam fuit curia': *Kaiser Karl's IV. Landbuch der Mark Brandenburg*, edited by E. Fidicin, p. 51.

[7] Riedel, *op. cit.*, Supplement, no. 27, p. 238 (1360).

[8] One exception: as early as 1289 the knight Lodewicus de Sciltberch sold his '*allodium*' near Hardenbeck (Ucker Mark) to the peasants of Hardenbeck: Riedel, *op. cit.* xxi, no. 10, p. 7. This charter was only preserved because Hardenbeck was a monastic village. The lack of more proofs can partly be explained by the scarcity of non-ecclesiastical documents.

[9] In 1375 a number of Old Mark villages paid quit-rents: *Landbuch* (edn. Fidicin), pp. 226-7, 233-4, 236-8. Riedel's *Codex* contains numerous documents according to which quit-rents were paid in the Old Mark: thus v, no. 353, p. 480, no. 361, p. 483, no. 387, p. 494, nos. 393-4, p. 497; vi, no. 435, p. 259, no. 454, p. 275; xvi, no. 626, p. 182, no. 650, p. 276, no. 651, p. 277; xvii, no. 239, p. 207, no. 142, p. 315, nos. 143-4, pp. 317-8; xxii, no. 177, p. 192, no. 179, p. 194; xxv, no. 394, p. 471; Supplement, no. 32, p. 380.

Old Mark were considerably smaller than those in the other parts of Brandenburg; out of a total of 317 villages, only 39 then had one or several demesnes. In the other parts of Brandenburg also, quit-rents were given instead of the services,[1] although it seems to a lesser degree than in the Old Mark; for these districts were economically less advanced and had few important towns. As late as 1540 the Brandenburg nobility complained to the margrave that their pressing need made it necessary to re-commute their peasants' quit-rents into services, but that the peasants refused, and that this attitude was backed by a decision of the margrave's court, the *Kammergericht*.[2] The Pomeranian nobles also demanded services from their peasants instead of the quit-rents which they had previously paid, as they stated themselves in 1585.[3] In both principalities, the subject was so important that the nobles raised it during the negotiations between the estates and the prince. Thus the paying of quit-rents must have been very common as late as the sixteenth century. Even in the early seventeenth century the subject was mentioned several times in decrees, draft regulations, and legal discussions.[4] This indicates a strong tendency towards the disintegration of the manorial system in Brandenburg and Pomerania. In Brandenburg, moreover, we can examine this question from a number of more direct sources.

For the central part of Brandenburg, the Middle Mark, we possess, apart from the '*Landbuch*' of 1375, a number of later surveys, the '*Schossregister*' of 1450, 1480, and 1624, the last of these not only giving data for that year, but also changes in the distribution of holdings during the past fifty years.[5] It is, therefore, possible to examine more closely agrarian developments in this district during a period of 250 years. One of the most striking features of the fifteenth-century surveys is the large number of deserted peasant holdings. Of 6667 peasant *Hufen* in 157 villages

---

[1] In six Ucker Mark villages quit-rents were paid in 1375: *Landbuch* (edn. Fidicin). pp. 135, 142–3, 155–6, 158. Further Riedel, *op. cit.* x, no. 256, p. 358; xii, no. 67, p. 113, no. 46, p. 184; xxiii, no. 417, p. 404; xxi, no. 64, p. 515; xxv, no. 182, p. 148.

[2] *Kurmärkische Ständeakten aus der Regierungszeit Kurfürst Joachims II*, edited by W. Friedensburg (quoted as Friedensburg), i, no. 17, p. 96.

[3] M. Spahn, *Verfassungs- und Wirtschaftsgeschichte des Herzogtums Pommern von 1478 bis 1625*, p. 125, n. 2.

[4] See J. Scheplitz, *Consuetudines Electoratus et Marchiae Brandenburgensis*, i. 660 (edn. 1744); C. O. Mylius, *Corpus Constitutionum Marchicarum*, vi. 3, no. 3, col. 58; F. Grossmann, *op. cit.* p. 14, n. 3.

[5] The '*Schossregister*' of 1450 and 1480 are printed as an appendix to Fidicin's edition of the *Landbuch* of 1375, the figures of that of 1624 as an appendix to F. Grossmann, *op. cit.* As Fidicin's edition leaves a lot to be desired, the *Landbuch* has recently been reprinted by J. Schultze, but unfortunately without the '*Schossregister*'. That of 1480 is very incomplete and can only be used as auxiliary evidence. As these '*Schossregister*' have been published for many years, it seems curious that, apparently, they have never been compared with each other: see Appendix, below.

1953, or more than one-quarter, were deserted and only 4714 occupied in 1450. Nor did matters improve later in the century: for 117 of these villages we possess figures for the year 1480 as well; in these villages the number of deserted *Hufen* had increased from 945 to 1145, and the number of occupied *Hufen* had decreased from 3714 to 3483 in the course of only thirty years. This widespread desertion of the land by the peasants caused a lowering of the standard of living of the landlords, for their income from dues and rents shrank correspondingly. They tried, of course, to find successors to take over the deserted holdings, but these efforts were only very partially successful. As the landlords would not have derived any benefit at all from land lying fallow, they started demesne farming on an increased scale.[1] Again and again the '*Schossregister*' tell us that so and so many *Hufen* were deserted and ploughed by the lords of the manor themselves. Thus very considerable demesnes of $15\frac{1}{2}$, 20, 25, 31, 33, 34, 36, and even 63 and 72 *Hufen* had been formed from deserted peasant land.[2] The large majority of the deserted holdings, however, was not farmed by the manorial lords: of the 1953 deserted *Hufen* mentioned above, only $337\frac{1}{2}$ were listed as demesne land; while the others were apparently lying fallow until somebody could be found to take them over.[3]

As the desertion of the land undoubtedly provided a great stimulus towards increased demesne farming, it could be expected that the figures of 1450 would show considerably more demesne farming than those of 1375. The really surprising fact is that this is *not* the case. We possess data for 291 villages of the Middle Mark for both years. In 155 of them there was no demesne in either year. In the other 136 villages the size of the demesne land [4] had decreased from $1419\frac{1}{2}$ to 1361 *Hufen* in spite of the desertion of the land.* In twelve of these villages the size of the demesne had remained the same; in twenty-nine it had decreased, and in twenty-nine it had increased; in twenty-eight villages a

---

[1] This has already been observed by G. F. Knapp, *Die Bauernbefreiung und der Ursprung der Landarbeiter*, i. 38.

[2] *Landbuch* (edn. Fidicin), pp. 268, 270, 285, 295, 299, 301, 333.

[3] By 1570 about half of them were again occupied: the number of occupied peasant *Hufen* in the 157 villages mentioned above then amounted to at least 5670, that is 956 more than in 1450; while the other 997 *Hufen* had, apparently, remained deserted or become demesne land in the meantime.

[4] Demesne land has been taken here in the widest sense. It does not always imply that the nobleman himself farmed his estate or even lived there, but that the *Hufen* in question were not farmed by the peasants and were tax-free. The expressions used in the *Landbuch* vary: '*ad curiam*', '*mansi liberi ad curiam sub cultura*', '*colit per se*,' '*sub aratro suo*', '*inhabitat*', '*residet*', &c., the first one being by far the most frequent. Already G. von Below, *op. cit.* p. 32, n. 1, has remarked that the exact meaning of some of these terms is doubtful. The '*Schossregister*' also are not always clear on this point.

* See Appendix.

new demesne had come into being where there had been none in 1375; but in thirty-eight villages the demesne, which had been there in 1375, had disappeared altogether. Out of these 291 villages only 98 had a demesne at all in 1450, while all the others were entirely peasant villages. (See appendix, p. 170.) This decrease of demesne farming in a period of increasing economic difficulties for the landlords is perhaps the best proof of the strength of the forces causing a disintegration of the manorial system, in spite of all tendencies to the contrary.

How far was the development of the manorial system in Prussia, under the Teutonic Knights, different from that in Brandenburg and Pomerania ? It has always been assumed that, in Prussia, demesne farming and corn export on a considerable scale, by the Order as well as by private landlords, were a feature of the fourteenth (or even the thirteenth) century, and that from that time an unbroken development led to the period of the 'Gutsherrschaft'.[1] The Teutonic Knights themselves not only sold and exported corn on a very large scale, but also undertook demesne farming. Their manors excelled in their yields and management. Some of them were not larger than a peasant farm, while others were of a medium size, and a few very large. At the end of the fourteenth century, as many as 420, 620, 940, and even 4100 acres were under cultivation on four large manors belonging to the Teutonic Order (including the fallow).[2] But even the Order showed a certain tendency towards selling its demesnes: in the Commandery of Schlochau an 'allodium' was converted into a village in 1350, and two demesnes of six *Hufen* each sold to peasants, in 1381 and 1412 respectively.[3] The same applied to the bishopric of Ermland, where the bishops as well as the cathedral chapter founded villages on their 'allodia' or sold them to burghers or towns.[4]

If we want to find out, however, whether there was 'Gutsherrschaft' in Prussia before the fifteenth century, we have to investigate the extent of the demesne farming undertaken by private

[1] Thus W. von Brünneck, in *Jahrbücher für Nationalökonomie und Statistik*, 1, 1888, p. 370; H. Plehn, 'Zur Geschichte der Agrarverfassung von Ost- und Westpreussen'; *Forschungen zur Brandenburgischen und Preussischen Geschichte* (1904), xvii. 425; (1905), xviii. 86, 107; H. Mauer, *ibid.* (1911) xxiv. 289; G. Aubin, *op. cit.* pp. 62–7; R. Kötzschke, *Grundzüge der deutschen Wirtschaftsgeschichte*, p. 150; W. zur Ungnad, *Deutsche Freibauern, Kölmer und Kolonisten*, p. 149; Eileen Power, *loc. cit.* p. 736; H. Rosenberg, *loc. cit.* p. 229.

[2] G. Aubin, *op. cit.* p. 24: 170, 250, 380, and 1655 *Hektar*.

[3] *Handfesten der Komturei Schlochau*, edited by P. Panske, no. 31, p. 45, no. 133, p. 144, no. 164, p. 171. Unfortunately, the *Handfesten* of the Teutonic Order are only printed up to 1335 (apart from the two Commanderies of Schlochau and Tuchel), so that no further evidence on this important point is available.

[4] *Codex Diplomaticus Warmiensis*, edited by C. P. Woelky and J. M. Saage, i, no. 226, p. 381; iii, no. 125, p. 91, no. 205, p. 164, no. 310, p. 283, no. 422, p. 418, no. 456, p. 458 (from the years 1326 to 1410).

landlords. We know that in the fifteenth century the nobles exported corn on a considerable scale. In the assemblies of the Estates the knights frequently demanded that free corn exports should be permitted;[1] agriculture was their living, as they stated themselves on one occasion.[2] But the fifteenth century was a period of swift changes and, in Prussia also, of increasing desertion of the land. It is thus impossible to draw any conclusions from these documents as to the state of affairs in preceding centuries. We possess very little evidence of private demesne farming in the fourteenth century; it seems likely that it was undertaken (as in Brandenburg), but not on any large scale. All the evidence known so far, interestingly enough, mentions corn exports, demesne farming or sheep farming by burghers, village mayors, or peasants, but not by noblemen.[3]

As to the size of the estates of private landlords in Prussia, at the beginning of the colonization, as well as later on in the so-called 'Wilderness' in the east of the country, the Teutonic Order granted estates of a very large size to private entrepreneurs, wherever its own forces were insufficient to carry out the settlement of the country, that is in particular on the eastern border of the settled territory. Thus, in the thirteenth century, the nobleman Dietrich von Tiefenau was invested with property of about 450 *Hufen*;[4] or the family Stange, members of which had already been working as contractors on a large scale on the settlement of Moravia,[5] were given a thousand *Hufen* (later limited to 665) by the bishop of Pomesanien, as well as other property by the Teutonic Order.[6] Other immigrating landlords received, at least in the thirteenth century, estates of more than a hundred *Hufen*.[7] But in the fourteenth century these estates were divided into many smaller ones through sale, dereliction, division among

[1] G. Aubin, *op. cit.* pp. 57–60; *Acten der Ständetage Preussens unter der Herrschaft des Deutschen Ordens*, edited by M. Toeppen, ii, no. 41, p. 62, no. 152, p. 221, no. 166, p. 236, no. 190, p. 296; iii, no. 6, pp. 10–11, no. 8, p. 13, no. 54, p. 98.

[2] *Ibid.* ii, no. 396, p. 634; similarly iii, no. 31, p. 63.

[3] *Codex Diplomaticus Warmiensis*, i, no. 75, p. 129; *Preussisches Urkundenbuch*, i. 2, no. 688, p. 431; ii. 1, no. 276, p. 176, nos. 306–7, pp. 199–200; ii. 2, no. 678, p. 448, no. 706, p. 469; *Codex diplomaticus Prussicus*, edited by J. Voigt, iii, no. 53, p. 77; *Urkunden der Komturei Tuchel*, edited by P. Panske, no. 34, p. 41 (from the years 1287, 1298, 1320, 1330, 1347, 1350).

[4] *Codex diplomaticus Prussicus*, i, nos. 46, 50, 54, pp. 45–51 (from the years 1236–42); H. Plehn, *loc. cit.* p. 391; C. Krollmann, 'Die Besiedlung Ostpreussens durch den Deutschen Orden', *Vierteljahrschrift für Sozial- und Wirtschaftsgeschichte* (1928), xxi. 289.

[5] C. Krollmann, 'Die Herkunft der deutschen Ansiedler in Preussen', *Zeitschrift des Westpreussischen Geschichtsvereins*, Heft 54, 1912, pp. 24–6, 29–30.

[6] *Preussisches Urkundenbuch*, i. 2, no. 462, p. 297, no. 654, p. 413; *Codex diplomaticus Prussicus*, ii, no. 8, p. 10, no. 29, p. 34; *Codex Diplomaticus Warmiensis*, ii, no. 542, pp. 571–3; C. Krollmann, *loc. cit.* pp. 32–3.

[7] *Codex diplomaticus Prussicus*, ii, no. 18, p. 21; *Codex Diplomaticus Warmiensis*, i, nos. 79–83, pp. 136–49, no. 157, pp. 272–3, no. 96, pp. 166–7, no. 102, pp. 175–7; *Preussisches Urkundenbuch*, i. 2, no. 514, pp. 323–4.

heirs, separation among several joint owners, or settlement.[1] The enormous possessions of the Stanges were split up into many parts in the very next generation.[2] Presumably, these large estates had only been granted for the purpose of dividing them up at an early stage. This, at any rate, can be proved in the case of the grants of very large estates in the ' Wilderness ' during the fourteenth century.

By far the largest tract of land in the ' Wilderness ', 1440 *Hufen*, was granted, in 1321, to three knights 'and some of their friends ', this area being subdivided into six pieces of eighty and twenty-four pieces of forty *Hufen* each.[3] These circumstances alone show that it did not remain one estate, but that in reality a collective assignment, comprised into one charter, was made to a group of entrepreneurs.[4] On these 1440 *Hufen*, twenty-nine independent villages and estates came into being.[5] The other grants of large tracts of land in the ' Wilderness ' were of a similar type ; they were not always taken up : in several instances, they were repeated later on a smaller scale, or the land remained unoccupied for a long time. But even the opposite case did not necessarily mean that the estates were farmed by the owners themselves, for some of them carried out a peculiar speculation : by granting smaller estates with the obligation to render military service, or by founding villages, they succeeded in freeing themselves from the military service as stipulated by the Teutonic Order, for this was now rendered by the owner of the smaller estate or the village mayor.[6] These new owners herewith entered into a direct obligation towards the Order and lost every obligation towards the original landlord, whose estate had become considerably smaller.

Thus the large estates granted at the beginning of the colonization were split up in course of time. In the fourteenth century the average size of a knight's estate [7] was small : twelve *Hufen* in the Culmerland (varying from two to forty *Hufen*), about six *Hufen* in the Commandery of Elbing, and slightly more in the Commandery of Christburg.[8] Not even in the ' Wilderness ' were

[1] L. Weber, *Preussen vor 500 Jahren*, pp. 252–3, 255 ; G. Aubin, *op. cit.* pp. 18–19 ; C. Krollmann, ' Die Besiedlung Ostpreussens durch den Deutschen Orden ', *loc. cit.* p. 289.

[2] K. Lohmeyer, *Geschichte von Ost- und Westpreussen*, 3rd edn., p. 193 ; C. Krollmann, *loc. cit.* p. 291.

[3] *Preussisches Urkundenbuch*, ii. 1, no. 363, pp. 270–1.

[4] C. Krollmann, *loc. cit.* p. 297 ; K. Kasiske, *Die Siedlungstätigkeit des Deutschen Ordens im östlichen Preussen*, p. 77.

[5] H. Plehn, *loc. cit.* p. 392 ; K. Kasiske, *op. cit.* p. 77.

[6] H. and G. Mortensen, *Die Besiedlung des nordöstlichen Ostpreussens bis zum Beginn des 17. Jahrhunderts, Teil I, Die preussisch-deutsche Siedlung am Westrand der grossen Wildnis um 1400*, pp. 65–8, 94, 112–13, 134.

[7] That is an estate from which a knight's service had to be rendered in case of war.

[8] L. Weber, *op. cit.* pp. 253, 453, 458–67 ; G. Aubin, *op. cit.* p. 25.

the average estates much larger;[1] and in the bishoprics they were smaller than in the territory of the Order, as military demands played a less important role.[2] From the fourteenth century the Teutonic Knights, as well as the bishops, even bought out many noblemen's estates and founded villages on them, or let them out anew in small pieces for which peasants' dues had to be paid.[3] In this way they tried to check the rise of a powerful nobility, and at the same time to increase their income. In view of all this, it can fairly be stated that, right up to the first half of the fifteenth century, there was a strong tendency in Prussia towards the splitting up of the large estates, and not towards their consolidation. Exactly as in Brandenburg, the manorial system was disintegrating to a certain extent.

It thus seems certain that the argument that, in the East, 'Gutsherrschaft' 'was always there' is not borne out by the facts. On the contrary, the development in western and eastern Germany was running along parallel lines: towards the break-up of the manor. But eastern Germany was several centuries behind the West, as it was economically less advanced, and as the whole movement had started there much later, so that, in the fifteenth century, the manorial organization of the East was still considerably stronger than it was in the West. The question now arises: what caused a complete reversal of this trend in the East and the manorial reaction of the sixteenth century, while the disintegration of the manorial system continued in the West?

One cause has already been mentioned: the increasing desertion of the land by the peasants. This was not a new development of the fifteenth century. Already in the '*Landbuch*' of the New Mark of 1337 (that is, only a short while after the colonization of this district) there are long lists of completely deserted villages.[4] In 128 (out of a total of 150) villages of the Ucker Mark 2395 peasant *Hufen* out of a total of 4930 were deserted in 1375, this

---

[1] For details see K. Kasiske, *op. cit.* pp. 105-8, 110-11, 116, 122-4; L. Weber, *op. cit.* p. 501; M. Toeppen, *Geschichte Masurens*, pp. 93-4, 100, 105-6; G. Aubin, *op. cit.* p. 26.

[2] L. Weber, *op. cit.* p. 255; G. Aubin, *op. cit.* p. 26.

[3] *Preussisches Urkundenbuch*, ii. 1, nos. 78, 96, 120; ii. 2, nos. 656, 667; *Urkunden der Komturei Tuchel*, no. 101; *Handfesten der Komturei Schlochau*, nos. 107, 158, 167; *Codex Diplomaticus Warmiensis*, iii, nos. 204 and 206; *Das Grosse Aemterbuch des Deutschen Ordens*, edited by W. Ziesemer, pp. 322-4; C. Krollmann, 'Zur Besiedlungs-Geschichte und Nationalitätenmischung in den Komtureien Christburg, Osterode und Elbing', *Zeitschrift des Westpreussischen Geschichtsvereins*, Heft 64, 1923, pp. 23-4; F. Mager, *op. cit.* pp. 28-30. In the fifteenth century, this subject provided the material for one of the standard complaints of the nobility: *Acten der Ständetage Preussens*, i, no. 487, p. 629; ii, no. 30, p. 34, no. 150, pp. 219-20; iii, no. 68, p. 141; iv, no. 23, p. 42.

[4] *Die Neumark Brandenburg im Jahre 1337 oder Markgraf Ludwig's des Aelteren Neumärkisches Landbuch*, edited by G. W. von Raumer, pp. 82, 84-6, 88, 99, 101, 103, 105-6.

being usually attributed to the constant wars between Brandenburg and Pomerania.[1] In the Middle Mark, on the other hand, comparatively few deserted villages and holdings were listed in 1375.[2] Not only in the East, but also in other parts of Germany and Europe, there were many deserted villages and holdings in the late middle ages.[3] It seems, however, that the land was deserted to a much higher degree in the East than in the West. It must be borne in mind that the colonization area still had a relatively small population. When peasants deserted their holdings in the West, it was comparatively easy to find a successor among the sons of other peasants or among the landless labourers in the village. The nobles could lighten the peasants' burdens, commute their labour services and advance their emancipation, in order to induce them to stay on, if repressive measures were of no avail.[4]

All this was much more difficult in the East. Here also deserted holdings were given to other peasants: in the '*Schossregister*' we find peasants with farms of four, five, six, and even eight *Hufen*, as well as peasants of a neighbouring village tilling the fields of a deserted village; but there was an obvious limit to this. Up to the fifteenth century, the position of the peasants in the East was extremely favourable, and there was not much room for new concessions. If they left their farms, they did not do so because of their servile condition,[5] as was frequently the case in the West, but for other reasons. The eastern landlords were more accustomed to demesne farming than those of the West and, if they could not find any new peasants, the easiest way out of their difficulty was to increase their demesne, at least temporarily. In general, the disintegration of the manorial system had not progressed so far in the East as it had in the West, so that it was far easier here to revert to a stricter manorial organization. First, the fields of deserted villages were utilized as a sheep-run, and from the sixteenth century onwards, for corn growing, while single deserted holdings were used for demesne farming on a smaller scale. Increased labour services were required for the growing demesnes. These services the nobles had the right to demand; for in course of time they had acquired the entire jurisdiction on their estates, and labour services were considered to derive from the jurisdiction.[6] The transfer of the jurisdiction

[1] J. Schultze, *op. cit.* p. xviii.

[2] Landbuch (edn. Fidicin), pp. 56, 76, 78–82, 90, 98, 106, 107, 128.

[3] Eileen Power, *loc. cit.* p. 733; H. Nabholz, 'Medieval Agrarian Society in Transition', *The Cambridge Economic History of Europe*, i. 503.

[4] Eileen Power, *loc. cit.* p. 727; H. Nabholz, *loc. cit.* p. 511.

[5] The opposite is assumed for Poland by J. Rutkowski, *Histoire Économique de la Pologne Avant Les Partages*, p. 107, and E. Schmidt, *op. cit.* p. 278.

[6] This is to be seen from many a document: thus Riedel, *op. cit.* v, no. 19, p. 311, no. 97, p. 69; x, no. 23a, p. 463; xi, no. 219, p. 435; xxii, no. 13, p. 495; i, p. 459.

to the landlords, however, did not cause the manorial reaction of the East, as has frequently been assumed,[1] but merely provided the means by which they could enforce their demands.

We do not know for certain why so many holdings became deserted in the fourteenth and fifteenth centuries. This phenomenon has often been attributed to the many wars and feuds of the period.[2] In Prussia, it is true, the depopulation of the countryside seems to have been caused by the continuous wars against Poland and the frightful devastations caused by them, in the years 1409–11, 1414, 1422, 1431–3, 1453–66, 1519–21; the peasants escaped their plight by seeking refuge in the towns or abroad. The Hussites ravaged Brandenburg in 1429 and 1432,[3] and Prussia in 1433. A charter of the bishop of Havelberg of 1409 expressly mentioned the fury of wars and robberies which had lasted for a long time past as the cause of the desertion of the soil.[4] There must, however, have been other and more fundamental reasons for the peasants to abandon their holdings permanently, even when more peaceful conditions had returned. In the fourteenth, and perhaps still in the fifteenth, century the growing towns attracted many peasants. At the peak of the colonization, villages had probably been founded on soil which in the long run did not produce sufficient yields, or they were ill situated, endangered by floods, dearth of water, or soil erosion.[5] The soil of the Brandenburg Mark was, already in the middle ages, known for its poor quality. Perhaps we must rate the achievement of the colonization in general lower than has been done so far. The peasants, even if they did not move into a town, probably found it easier than they would do in modern times to pack up their belongings and to migrate further East

[1] Thus G. von Below, *op. cit.*, pp. 11–12, and *Probleme der Wirtschaftsgeschichte*, p. 51; S. B. Fay, *loc. cit.* p. 251, n. 66; Eileen Power, *loc. cit.* pp. 734–5; H. Rosenberg, *loc. cit.* pp. 15–16.

[2] Thus H. Maybaum, *op. cit.* p. 108; J. Schultze, in *Forschungen zur Brandenburgischen und Preussischen Geschichte* (1927), xxxix. 400; W. Zahn, *Die Wüstungen der Altmark*, p. xxiii; Freiherr von Wintzingeroda-Knorr, *Die Wüstungen des Eichsfeldes*, pp. xxi–xxvi; G. F. Knapp, *op. cit.* i. 38; H. Rosenberg, *loc. cit.* pp. 230–1.

[3] E. Fidicin, *Die Territorien der Mark Brandenburg*, attributes the desertion of many a village to the Hussite invasion of 1432.

[4] 'Et quia saevissima hostilitas guerrarum et latrociniorum a longo retroacto tempore in diocesi nostra plus ceteris partibus continuata dispendia agricultores et colonos . . . disreptis eorum bonis et incendiis devastatis nudos et inopes sua deserere . . . coegerunt, agri ipsorum . . . inculti remanent et deserti . . .': Riedel, *op. cit.* i, no. 16, p. 39.

[5] H. Nabholz, *loc. cit.* p. 503; G. Hertel, *Die Wüstungen im Nordthüringgau*, pp. xviii, xxvi–xxvii; Freiherr von Wintzingeroda-Knorr, *op. cit.* p. xxviii; W. Zahn, *op. cit.* pp. xxi–xxii; E. Blume, 'Beiträge zur Siedlungskunde der Magdeburger Börde', *Archiv für Landes- und Volkskunde der Provinz Sachsen* (1908), xviii. 60; M. Bolle, 'Beiträge zur Siedlungskunde des Havelwinkels', *ibid.* (1909), xix. 59–62; (1910) xx. 8–9; G. Reischel, 'Die Wüstungen der Provinz Sachsen und des Freistaates Anhalt', *Sachsen und Anhalt, Jahrbuch der Historischen Kommission für die Provinz Sachsen und für Anhalt* (1926), ii. 251, 278–9, 343–4.

where colonization and settlement went on without any interruption, exactly as their forefathers had moved into these regions in search of a better living. We have no evidence of this movement, as the peasants were entitled to leave freely and gradually infiltrated into already existing villages farther East. From the sixteenth century onwards, however, we have many proofs : [1] the peasants had been tied to the soil and could only leave with their lord's permission, who was now entitled to complain if any peasant left without it, and could try to recover the fugitive ; many new villages were then founded across the border in Poland.[2] Quite apart from the question of the peasants' destination, there was also a genuine decline of population, caused by pestilence and famine, and in particular by the Black Death of 1348–50.[3] It seems likely that it was a combination of all these factors which brought about the desertion of the land.[4]

To check the increasing desertion of the land, the nobles pressed for measures by which it would become more difficult for the peasants to leave, or by which the towns would be compelled to hand over fugitive peasants. In Prussia the knights demanded, for the first time in 1412, that all peasants who could not prove that they had left with their lord's consent were to be driven out of the towns, a demand which was incorporated into the Statutes published in the same year.[5] Five years later, the Grand Master and Estates agreed that a runaway peasant was to be handed over to his lord, so that he could provide a successor and pay his arrears before he was allowed to quit.[6] In 1445 it was stipulated for the first time, acceding to repeated requests of the nobles,[7] that nobody was permitted to receive a peasant unless he could show a writ from his former lord.[8] The Statutes of 1494 went so far as to decree that no absconding peasant was to be received in any town, castle or manor, that he was to be handed over if his lord caught him, and that his lord could have him hanged, seemingly without any trial.[9] Similar efforts were made in Brandenburg about the same time. In 1484 the assembled lords

---

[1] See E. Schmidt, *op. cit.* pp. 325–8 ; G. F. Knapp, *op. cit.* i. 83 ; ii. 3, 16, 27 ; E. Gohrbandt, ' Das Bauernlegen bis zur Aufhebung der Erbuntertänigkeit und die Kolonisation des 16. Jahrhunderts in Ostpommern ', *Baltische Studien* (1936), xxxviii. 213.

[2] E. Schmidt, *op. cit.* pp. 330–6.

[3] Eileen Power, *loc. cit.* p. 733 ; G. Hertel, *op. cit.* p. xxvii ; W. Zahn, *op. cit.* p. xxiii. G. Reischel, *loc. cit.* pp. 346–7, in particular mentions the pestilence years of 1315, 1348–50 and 1463–4. E. Fidicin, *op. cit.* ii. 2, p. 8, considers the Black Death of 1348 as particularly disastrous for Brandenburg.

[4] G. Hertel, *op. cit.* pp. xxvi–xxviii ; Freiherr von Wintzingeroda-Knorr, *op. cit.* p. xxxi. For a detailed discussion, see in particular G. Reischel, *loc. cit.* pp. 222 ff.

[5] *Acten der Ständetage Preussens*, i, no. 155, p. 199.

[6] *Ibid.* i, no. 250, p. 308.

[7] *Ibid.* ii, no. 152, p. 222, no. 388, p. 627.

[8] *Ibid.* ii, no. 410, p. 666.

[9] *Ibid.* v, no 142, pp. 413–14.

of Brandenburg requested that nobody should receive or harbour any peasant, who had left without his lord's consent, but should hand him over on demand.[1] And in the following year the *Hauptmann* of the Old Mark decreed that no peasant was allowed to leave before he had found a successor.[2] Thus the peasants were gradually tied to the soil. The same happened in Poland at exactly the same time and for the same reasons: fugitive peasants had to be apprehended and handed over; to harbour them became an offence.[3] In Russia, the codes of 1497 and 1550 still recognized the right of the free peasants to depart provided they had paid their dues; but here also economic pressure on the landlords, and in particular the increasing number of deserted holdings and runaway peasants, resulted in their being tied to the soil in the course of the following hundred years.[4]

For the towns, the curtailment of their right to receive newcomers from the countryside was a question of first-rate importance, as their growth depended on it. At least one town, Anklam in Pomerania, resisted a demand of the von Schwerin, in 1458, that one of their peasants, who had sought refuge in the town, should be handed over. This caused a long feud between the nobles and the town. After three years, a peace was concluded according to which the burghers could retain all the booty they had taken, but had to give way on the main issue: they agreed that absconding peasants would no longer be given asylum.[5] The town of Köpenick was forced to do exactly the same twenty years later. This small Brandenburg town was tried, in 1483, for harbouring a fugitive peasant and was ordered to hand him over with all his goods and chattels, the decision as to the fine to be imposed on the town being left to the margrave.[6] We do not know any more details of this case, nor on what grounds the town was sentenced. The towns sided with the peasants,[7] and on the outcome of the struggle between towns and nobles depended the future social and political structure.

[1] Riedel, *op. cit.* C ii, no. 245, p. 303. See also a document of 1470: *ibid.* xv, no. 375, p. 311.

[2] F. Priebatsch, 'Die Hohenzollern und der Adel der Mark', *Historische Zeitschrift* (1902), lxxxviii. 244.

[3] E. Schmidt, *op. cit.* p. 276; A. Bruce-Boswell, *loc. cit.* p. 582; G. Slocombe, *A History of Poland*, p. 106.

[4] B. H. Sumner, *Survey of Russian History*, pp. 148–52; P. Struve, in *The Cambridge Economic History of Europe*, i. 429; B. Pares, *A History of Russia*, pp. 121–2, 149–51.

[5] L. Gollmert, *Urkundenbuch zur Geschichte des Geschlechts von Schwerin*, no. 336, pp. 249–50; Th. Kantzow, *Pomerania*, edited by G. Gaebel (1908), i. 387–8; Valentinus ab Eickstet, *Epitome Annalium Pomeraniae* (edn. 1728), p. 103; J. Micraelius, *Antiquitates Pomeraniae* (edn. 1723), p. 283; F. W. Barthold, *Geschichte von Rügen und Pommern*, iv. 1, pp. 244–5, 261–2; G. Kratz, *Die Städte der Provinz Pommern*, pp. 9–10.

[6] *Codex diplomaticus Brandenburgensis continuatus*, edited by G. W. von Raumer (quoted as Raumer), ii, no. 119, pp. 180–1.

[7] Exactly as they did in other countries: Eileen Power, *loc. cit.* pp. 727–8.

In this conflict, which broke out in the fifteenth century, there was much more at stake than the point whether the towns were entitled to receive runaway peasants. It was a struggle for political supremacy, and simultaneously for economic privileges. Corn exports became so important that the question, whether or not the towns should continue to handle these exports, in accordance with the medieval system of market rights, assumed great prominence. In Prussia, for example, the nobles, in the middle of the fifteenth century, turned against the measures of the towns which restricted the activities of foreign merchants ; they complained that the trade of these merchants was being hampered, and demanded that the latter should be allowed to visit every landlord, to travel up and down the country, and to buy the nobleman's corn and other produce.[1] The Teutonic Order, as long as its power lasted, tried to prevent the rise of a powerful landed aristocracy ;[2] as the Order itself engaged in trade on a large scale, it was interested in restricting the activities of foreign merchants. The rulers of the other principalities of north-eastern Germany were not restrained by any such considerations. They allied themselves openly with the nobility against the towns.

In Brandenburg, the second margrave of the Hohenzollern house, Frederick II, in 1442 used internal strife in the twin towns of Berlin and Cölln to establish his rule over them. They had to cede him their common town hall, a site for the erection of a castle, the jurisdiction they had exercised, and, above all, their rights of staple and toll ; they also lost their right to elect aldermen, as well as their 'unions' with other towns inside and outside Brandenburg, and in particular with the Hanseatic League. All Brandenburg towns were forbidden to send delegates to the Hanseatic Diets. A new rebellion which broke out in Berlin six years later was crushed by the margrave who imposed very heavy fines on the burgher families.[3] From then onwards the opposition of Berlin ceased ; its trade never recovered from the loss of its privileges and from the severance of its links with the Hansa ; it became an unimportant and subservient country town. In 1488 Frederick's nephew, John, in the same way subjugated the towns of the Old Mark, especially Stendal and Salzwedel, economically the foremost towns of Brandenburg. The point at issue was a proposed excise on beer, to which the prelates and nobles had consented, the beer they brewed themselves having been exempted

[1] *Acten der Ständetage Preussens*, ii, no. 323, p. 485, no. 324, p. 488, no. 332, p. 504, no. 396, p. 633 (from the years 1442-4).

[2] See above, p. 29.

[3] For all details, see F. L. Carsten, 'Medieval Democracy in the Brandenburg Towns and its Defeat in the Fifteenth Century', *Transactions of the Royal Historical Society*, 4th series (1943), xxv. 83-5.

from the duty. Beer brewing, however, was a major industry on which the towns' wealth depended; therefore, they resisted vigorously and rose in revolt. An open feud between the Old Mark towns and nobles broke out which ended with a complete victory for the margrave and the nobles. All the Old Mark towns lost their privileges, had to concede the excise, and finally left the Hanseatic League.[1]

The dukes of Pomerania also turned against their towns. Duke Kasimir in 1428 exploited a rebellion of the burghers of Stettin against the aldermen in order to march with the assembled nobles against the town; he was at first defeated by the burghers, but forced his entry, punished the ring-leaders, built a castle in the town and forced Stettin to leave the Hansa.[2] About the middle of the fifteenth century continuous feuds broke out between the dukes and the nobility on the one hand, and on the other hand Stralsund, the most important town of Pomerania, supported by other towns; in this war between towns and nobles neither side was victorious.[3] Duke Bogislav X, however, followed the anti-town policy of the Brandenburg Hohenzollerns and succeeded, at the end of the fifteenth century, in subjugating the towns of Köslin and Stettin; both had to pay heavy fines, and a new castle was built in Stettin.[4] All Pomeranian towns were forced, in 1498, to accede to a three-fold increase of the ducal tolls at Wolgast and Dammgarten. The duke curtailed the independence of the towns, limited their jurisdictional privileges and regulated their internal affairs.[5] Only against Stralsund was his success more limited. A long drawn-out feud between him and the town had no decisive result; but as he was supported by the nobility, the town, in 1512, was compelled to make some important concessions, to pay a fine, and to allow its burghers to appeal to the duke.[6] The Pomeranian towns also lost their power and influence, their trade declined, and they became unimportant country towns without any political ambitions.

Probably the loss of the independence and political power of the towns was not the only reason for their stagnation and decay

[1] For all details, see *ibid.* pp. 87-9.
[2] Th. Kantzow, *op. cit.* i. 347-8, 351-2; J. Micraelius, *op. cit.* pp. 242-3; F. W. Barthold, *op. cit.* iv. 1, pp. 83-5; G. Kratz, *op. cit.* pp. 391-2.
[3] See F. L. Carsten, ' Die sozialen Bewegungen in den Pommerschen Städten vom 14. Jahrhundert bis zur Reformationszeit ', *Tijdschrift voor Geschiedenis* (1938), liii. 371-3; see below, pp. 55-6.
[4] Th. Kantzow, *op. cit.* ii 36-9, 50-1, 86-7; J. Micraelius, *op. cit.* pp. 299-300, 304-6; *Hausbuch des Herrn Joachim von Wedel*, edited by J. Freiherr von Bohlen-Bohlendorf, pp. 15-16; F. W. Barthold, *op. cit.* iv. 1, pp. 428-31, 486-7; iv. 2, pp. 32-3; G. Kratz, *op. cit.* pp. 74, 395-6.
[5] Th. Kantzow, *op. cit.* ii. 82; F. W. Barthold, *op. cit.* iv. 2, pp. 21-3; M. Wehrmann, *Geschichte von Pommern*, i. 241, 244-6, 256.
[6] F. L. Carsten, *loc. cit.* pp. 373-4; see below, pp. 56-7.

which started in the fifteenth century.[1] In any case, it was to have fatal consequences. The weakness of the middle classes, which was to become such a prominent feature of the political life of Germany in later centuries, can be traced back to these events. In the state of the Teutonic Knights the same change was brought about by the cession to Poland, in 1466, of the whole west of the country, including all important towns, with the only exception of Königsberg. What remained to the Teutonic Order was an undeveloped, purely agrarian territory, with only small country towns. In Poland also, the towns, in the course of the fifteenth century, lost their privileges, in particular that of freely electing their aldermen, together with their trading rights.[2] The towns to the east of the Elbe, having been founded considerably later than those of western Europe, never equalled their strength and power; after a short and rapid rise, they were easily subjugated by the combined force of nobles and princes. In none of the countries concerned, was there any longer a force which could have prevented the nobility from becoming the ruling order of society. In spite of the economic boom of the sixteenth century, the towns continued to decay and to shrink, while the Junkers emerged as a strong leading group, united by their victory over the towns and bound together by their common interests.

These developments in themselves did not create the 'Gutsherrschaft' of the sixteenth century. One additional factor was necessary to make demesne farming not merely a solution born of necessity, but an attractive proposition, so much so that it gradually replaced peasant farming: the rising corn prices and growing corn imports of western Europe in the sixteenth century. If these had not occurred at this juncture, it is at least feasible that the vacant peasant holdings would slowly have been reoccupied; in the Middle Mark, for example, about half of them were indeed occupied by 1570.[3] But this was no longer the main aim of the landlords. During the hundred and twenty years from 1450 to about 1570 demesne farming in this district increased only slowly, from 1671 to 1879 *Hufen* (or by about 12 per cent.) in 347 villages for which we possess comparable figures.* During the fifty years from about 1570 to 1624, however, demesne farming in the same villages increased from 1879 to 2890 *Hufen*,* i.e. by

---

[1] H. Rachel, *Die Handels-, Zoll- und Akzisepolitik Brandenburg-Preussens bis 1713* (*Acta Borussica*), pp. 4–5, attributes the decline of the Brandenburg towns also to the rise of the coast towns, above all, Hamburg. H. Croon, *Die kurmärkischen Landstände 1571–1616*, p. 91, on the other hand, dates the economic decline of the Brandenburg towns only from the middle of the sixteenth century, that is, after their subjugation. The agricultural depression of the fifteenth century, however, must have affected the towns as well, as their income and that of their burghers partly derived from dues and rents. [2] E. Schmidt, *op. cit.* pp. 243–4; G. Slocombe, *op. cit.* p. 108.

[3] See the figures above, p. 25, n. 3.

* See Appendix below.

over 50 per cent.¹ Now not only deserted land was ploughed up by the Junkers, but peasants were evicted in large numbers to make room for the growing demesnes. In vain did the towns protest against this '*Bauernlegen*'.²

The foundation of new noble residences on former peasant land was furthered by the abolition of ecclesiastical sinecures through the Reformation; previously many younger sons of the nobility had been provided for by the church.³ Now they had to find a living by other means, and agriculture had become a profitable undertaking. Corn exports, however, undoubtedly provided the greatest stimulus for increased demesne farming. Poland acquired a Baltic port of great importance by the acquisition of Danzig in 1466 (peace of Thorn). Thereafter her corn exports increased by leaps and bounds, and most of the exported corn was produced on private demesnes, which quickly grew up in districts favourably situated for export purposes, mainly along the navigable rivers.⁴ The serfdom of the peasants everywhere developed in proportion to the demand for labour on the demesnes. This demand could only be satisfied by imposing upon the peasants and their families services of several days a week, and later often unlimited services; on account of the great shortage of labourers and menials, the peasants had to bear almost the entire burden. Only where the disintegration of the manorial system had proceeded comparatively far, for example in the Old Mark, did the position of the peasants remain slightly better.

The characteristics of the eastern '*Gutsherrschaft*' not only affected the system of agrarian economy, but also the relations between towns and nobles, in particular in the fields of industry and trade. The Junkers, exploiting their political victory of the fifteenth century, in the sixteenth century succeeded in ousting the towns from their former position. Using the concession of 1488, which allowed them to brew beer free of duty for their own use (but not for sale),⁵ the Brandenburg nobles brewed larger and larger quantities and compelled their peasants and village inns to buy it, to the detriment of the urban brewing industry.⁶ Repeated warnings and orders to stop these practices ⁷ met with

¹ The '*Schossregister*' of 1624 probably does not list all peasant *Hufen* which had become demesne land during the last fifty years, as the nobles had an interest in concealing this fact, since only demesne land proper was exempted from the land-tax. For this reason, the increase up to 1570 must have been slower, and the increase after 1570 more rapid than is indicated by the above figures.

² M. Hass, *Die Kurmärkischen Stände im letzten Drittel des Sechzehnten Jahrhunderts*, p. 145.

³ Thus the nobility itself stated in 1540: W. Friedensburg, *op. cit.* i, no. 17, p. 87.

⁴ J. Rutkowski, *op. cit.* p. 32; G. Slocombe, *op. cit.* p. 105.

⁵ Riedel, *op. cit.* C ii, no. 265, p. 336.

⁶ M. Hass, *op. cit.* pp. 166-7; H. Croon, *op. cit.* pp. 96-7.

⁷ Riedel, *op. cit.* C iii, no. 198, p. 229; Raumer, *op. cit.* ii, no. 17, p. 227; Friedensburg, *op. cit.* i, no. 12, p. 57, no. 16, p. 82, nos. 165-6, pp. 484-5, 491, no. 184, pp. 545-9.

no success. The fact that the Junkers could produce beer cheaper than the towns proved decisive. Nothing occurred so often in the minutes of the estates as the complaints of the towns about the Junkers' brewing.[1] The Junkers further tried to exclude the towns from the corn trade, either by exporting corn themselves, or by selling it directly to foreign merchants.[2] After 1527 they enjoyed freedom from export duty for their own produce ;[3] but here again they used this right to trade in corn other than their own, against the repeated injunctions of the margraves.[4] The beer and corn trades were merely the two most important commercial activities of the Junkers, which extended to many other fields as well : wool, hemp, flax, hides, tallow, suet, fish, poultry, eggs, cheese, butter, honey were bought up and exported by them, and salt and millstones were imported duty-free, ostensibly for their own use, and sold at a profit.[5]

Exactly the same happened in Prussia, in Pomerania, and in Poland. There also the nobles brewed beer in increasing quantities, bought up the peasants' corn and other produce, and sold it inside and outside the country, exploiting their exemption from tolls and urban market rights.[6] In Russia, on the other hand, the 'Grundherrschaft' did not develop into 'Gutsherrschaft',[7] although there were no important towns, and there also the desertion of the land had caused the spread of serfdom : for corn exports played no important role in this inaccessible region.

The towns of north-eastern Germany and Poland declined further and further ; more and more houses were left by their inhabitants and slowly fell into ruins.[8] Too weak to prevent the rise of the Junkers, the towns were confined to endless and futile complaints at the meetings of the estates. The territorial princes

---

[1] See Friedensburg, *op. cit.* i, nos. 9, 16, 103, 141–4, 146, 148, 151–4, 183, 196, 199, 238, 245 ; ii, nos. 303, 305, 309, 315, 322, 350, 366–7, 396, 437.

[2] M. Hass, *op. cit.* pp. 136–9, 162–5 ; H. Croon, *op. cit.* pp. 91–4.

[3] C. O. Mylius, *op. cit.* vi. 1, no. 13, col. 19 ; H. Rachel, *op. cit.* p. 82.

[4] Friedensburg, *op. cit.* i, no. 9, p. 38, no. 12, p. 57, no. 165, p. 483, nos. 183–4, pp. 542–9 ; C. O. Mylius, *op. cit.* iv. 1, nos. 6–7, col. 13–14 ; vi. 1, no. 16, col. 29, no. 36, col. 106, no. 58, col. 156 ; v. 2, no. 10, col. 78 ; H. Croon, *op. cit.* p. 95 ; M. Hass, *op. cit.* pp. 163–4.

[5] Friedensburg, *op. cit.* i, no. 140, p. 409, no. 155, p. 441 ; Mylius, *op. cit.* iv. 4, no. 4, col. 13 ; v. 2, no. 4, col. 8, no. 5, col. 10, no. 6, col. 13, no. 4, col. 210 ; H. Croon, *op. cit.* p. 94 ; M. Hass, *op. cit.* p. 162.

[6] M. Toeppen, 'Zur Geschichte der ständischen Verhältnisse in Preussen', *Historisches Taschenbuch, Neue Folge* (1847), viii. 313–15 ; and 'Der lange königsberger Landtag', *ibid.* (1849), x. 557, 577, 579, for Prussia; M. Spahn, *op. cit.* pp. 164, 173, for Pomerania; G. Slocombe, *op. cit.* p. 106 ; A. Bruce-Boswell, *loc. cit.* p. 583, for Poland.

[7] O. Hötzsch, 'Adel und Lehnswesen in Russland und Polen und ihr Verhältnis zur deutschen Entwicklung', *Historische Zeitschrift* (1912), cviii. 559, n. 3.

[8] As the Old Mark und Prignitz towns stated in 1556: Friedensburg, *op. cit.* ii, nos. 345 f, h, k, pp. 111, 114, 117. In the Prignitz towns, 317 out of 1373 houses were deserted in 1567 : *ibid.* no. 484, p. 564.

were also too weak to resist the demands of the Junkers effectively; they depended on the votes of credit granted by the estates, which thus became more and more powerful and finally dominated the state and the administration. Furthermore, the territorial princes were themselves landowners on a large scale; they ruled over their own estates and peasants in exactly the same manner as the Junkers, and were thus tied to them by the same material interests and many other bonds. They sided with the Junkers, and against the towns, whenever there was a dispute which called for their decision.

By the end of the sixteenth century, the Junkers had become the ruling class in the economic as well as in the political field. They were a closely-knit caste, jealous in defence of their privileged position; they considered themselves the equals of any prince and looked down upon the servile peasants and the burghers of the towns, who had lost their pride and wealth. In course of time they had acquired all state prerogatives on their estates; they became the one and only authority for 'their' peasants and the burghers of 'their' small towns: secure from any outside interference, their possessions formed small states within the state.

In the course of the sixteenth century, the feudal knights and warriors of the fourteenth and fifteenth centuries became peaceful land-owners, whose main interest was agriculture: time and again, in the later sixteenth and early seventeenth century, the nobles of Brandenburg, formerly so bellicose, urged the Hohenzollerns to pursue a peaceful policy and were opposed to alliances and territorial claims, to prevent Brandenburg from being involved in military expenditure and war.[1] This remarkable change was accompanied by a rapid deterioration of the military strength of the nobility. When the elector Joachim Frederick (1598–1608) tried to muster his feudal levies, they amounted to no more than a thousand horsemen.[2]

This change in the social habits of the Junkers coincided with a long period of peace which Brandenburg, and north-eastern Germany in general, enjoyed throughout the sixteenth century, in contrast with most other parts of Europe. In 1493 the interminable frontier wars between Brandenburg and Pomerania, which had contributed so much to the desertion of the land,[3] were terminated by a treaty; by this the Hohenzollerns renounced their claim to the feudal overlordship over the dukes of Pomerania, in exchange for the right of succession if the dukes'

---

[1] H. Prutz, *Preussische Geschichte*, i. 266, 284; O. Hintze, *Die Hohenzollern und ihr Werk*, pp. 135, 152; H. Croon, *op. cit.* pp. 105 ff.

[2] H. Prutz, *op. cit.* i. 276; O. Hintze, *op. cit.* p. 153; A. Waddington, *Histoire de Prusse*, i. 110.

[3] See above, pp. 29-30, 31.

male issue should fail. From then onwards peace reigned in this troubled border region.[1] Up to 1610 Brandenburg did not become involved in any war, and no hostile incursion took place until the Thirty Years' War. In Prussia also, after the disastrous wars of the fifteenth century and the devastating Horsemen's War of 1519–21,[2] peaceful conditions prevailed for the rest of the century. Furthermore, the internal feuds and robberies, which had disturbed Brandenburg and Pomerania for centuries, were ultimately brought to an end: in Brandenburg by the elector Joachim I (1499–1535) who had many disturbers of the peace and robber barons imprisoned or executed,[3] in Pomerania by the dukes Bogislav X (1474–1523) and Barnim X (1523–69).[4] This policy of internal pacification was made possible by the general prosperity and the easy profits which could be made in agriculture and which induced the nobles to take up farming on an increased scale. They thus became interested in the maintenance of peace. In Prussia, under the Teutonic Knights, there had never been any feuds, so that there was no change in this respect. Thus, contrary to what has often been assumed, the Junkers did not rise either as a military caste, or because of the military needs of a frontier region,[5] but as an aristocracy of business-minded and non-military landowners who had shed their feudal armour, and not yet donned the uniform of the Prussian officer.

From the second half of the seventeenth century onwards, political developments in north-eastern Germany and Poland ran along different lines. In Poland the nobles preserved their political supremacy and prevented the rise of a strong government. The same applied, in north-eastern Germany, only to the duchy of Mecklenburg. In the other principalities, the territorial princes, above all the Hohenzollerns, succeeded in establishing their despotism, but only at the cost of guaranteeing and enhancing the privileges and power of the Junkers and granting them a monopoly of posts in the officers' corps. Their importance as a military caste dates only from this period.

The developments leading to the rise of the Junkers in north-eastern Germany and Poland bear, in some respects, a striking resemblance to the developments in England which caused the rise of the gentry. To begin with, in the fifteenth century both

[1] H. Prutz, *op. cit.* i. 175; A. Waddington, *op. cit.* i. 65; R. Koser, *Geschichte der brandenburgisch-preussischen Politik*, i. 169, 171, 181.

[2] See above, p. 31.

[3] H. Prutz, *op. cit.* i. 183–4; A. Waddington, *op. cit.* i. 80–1; O. Hintze, *op. cit.* pp. 108–9, 116; G. Schmoller, *Preussische Verfassungs-, Verwaltungs- und Finanzgeschichte*, pp. 17, 32.

[4] F. W. Barthold, *Geschichte von Rügen und Pommern*, iv. 1, pp. 443–4, 472–4; iv. 2, pp. 94, 233–4; H. Prutz, *op. cit.* i. 174.

[5] Thus, for example, R. H. Tawney, 'The Rise of the Gentry', *The Economic History Review* (1941), xi. 13.

regions experienced an agricultural crisis : an increasing number of vacant holdings, a decline of the agrarian population, a shrinking of the income of the landlords and a severe pressure on their economic existence.[1] The methods also which were adopted by the landlords to overcome their economic difficulties were similar in both cases : they evicted or bought out peasants and expanded their own agrarian and commercial activities ; they enlarged their demesnes, developed their home-farms on commercial lines, enclosed meadows and woods hitherto used as commons, and supplemented their agricultural income by extensive trade.[2] In England, as well as in north-eastern Germany, this led to a decline of the peasantry, but in the former no attempt was made to reintroduce villeinage. This difference can partly be explained by the different needs of wool and corn growing. In England, sheep-farming was the prime mover of agrarian changes, so that labour services were no longer required and the number of peasants could be reduced. In north-eastern Germany and Poland, on the other hand, corn-growing for the market became the landlords' primary concern, the demand for labour services increased correspondingly, and villeinage—unknown during the middle ages—grew up with it. In both regions, the traditional methods of agriculture changed further on account of the rising prices and the widening markets of the sixteenth century. Yet in north-eastern Germany and Poland the rising prices no longer turned the screw on the landowners, as they did in England, where the demesne was usually leased ;[3] but, on the contrary, the Junkers with their growing demesnes benefited enormously from the rise in the price of corn.

There is, moreover, one fundamental difference between the Junkers and the gentry. The rise of the Junkers was caused and accompanied by the subjugation of the towns : this made the introduction of villeinage possible and enabled the Junkers to become the ruling class and to usurp the burghers' position in trade and industry. In England, too, a decline of the corporate towns was caused by the depression of the fifteenth century ; yet the development of the cloth industry brought about the rise of new towns, and London and certain other towns continued to grow and retained their political influence.[4] Above all, there was no clash of interests and no sharp division between gentry and towns, such as existed between Junkers and burghers. In England

---

[1] For England, see M. Postan, 'The Fifteenth Century', *The Economic History Review* (1939), ix. 160 ff.

[2] See R. H. Tawney, *loc. cit.* p. 14. In this respect, the difference between the Junkers and the gentry was, in my opinion, far smaller than is assumed by Professor Tawney.

[3] R. H. Tawney, *The Agrarian Problem in the Sixteenth Century*, pp. 200, 203.

[4] M. Postan, *loc. cit.* pp. 163–4 ; G. M. Trevelyan, *English Social History*, pp. 83–5.

42   *Essays in German History*

'landed and monied interests were often indistinguishable'; [1] no rigid barriers separated the gentry from the urban middle classes from which part of it had originated; its younger sons entered urban professions and trades, while merchants and other urban notables bought estates and joined the ranks of the gentry.[2] Thus the gentry rose in close alliance with, and depended on, the development of urban trade and industry; while the Junkers rose to power on the ruins of the towns' wealth, prevented any recovery of the middle classes and refused to part with any of their political privileges until the nineteenth century. They formed a rigid class which only nobles could enter, and all its members, including the younger sons, looked down with contempt upon the burghers and their occupations. This again seems connected with the difference between the production of wool and that of corn: the corn-growing nobles of eastern Europe could dispense with the services of the towns, while the wool-growing gentry of England depended on the requirements of the cloth industry, on expanding markets, and on the growth of the towns.

APPENDIX

NUMBER OF *HUFEN* HELD IN DEMESNE OR TAX-FREE IN THE MIDDLE MARK

This appendix is to illustrate the development, between 1375 and 1624, of the demesnes and estates of the nobility in the district which later became the core of the Prussian monarchy: in particular, the actual decline of demesne farming between 1375 and 1450, its very slow growth during the following hundred and twenty years (which certainly was slower than is indicated by the figures and may only have been apparent; see above, footnote 1, p. 165), and its rapid growth between 1570 and 1624. The appendix also shows that the large majority of villages, up to the sixteenth century, were pure peasant villages which had neither a demesne nor tax-free *Hufen* (for these terms, see above, footnote 4, p. 153: the exemption from the land tax was a privilege of the nobles to compensate them for their feudal service, but did not necessarily mean, at least not before the later sixteenth century, that the *Hufen* in question were farmed as a demesne; the land registers do not distinguish clearly between the two possibilities). The figures for 1375 are derived from the *Landbuch der Mark Brandenburg* of that year (there are two editions: by E. Fidicin, Berlin, 1856, and by J. Schultze, Berlin, 1940). The figures for 1450 and 1480 are taken from the *Schossregister* of those years, printed, rather un-

[1] G. M. Trevelyan, *op. cit.* p. 84.
[2] R. H. Tawney, 'The Rise of the Gentry', *The Economic History Review* (1941), xi. 2; G. M. Trevelyan, *op. cit.* pp. 84, 86, 125–6; M. M. Postan, 'Some Social Consequences of the Hundred Years' War', *The Economic History Review* (1942), xii. 6–7, 11–12.

satisfactorily, by Fidicin as an appendix to the *Landbuch*. And the figures for 1570 and 1624 are derived from the *Schossregister* of 1624, which also lists changes in the distribution of holdings during the past fifty years; it is printed as an appendix to F. Grossmann, *Über die gutsherrlich-bäuerlichen Rechtsverhältnisse in der Mark Brandenburg vom 16. bis 18. Jahrhundert*, Leipzig, 1890. Unfortunately, none of these four land registers contains a description of all villages of the Middle Mark: a question mark indicates that the particular village is not mentioned in the land register of that year, while a stroke indicates that the village is described, but that it has no demesne or tax-free *Hufen*.

(i) *District of Havelland*

Village.	1375.	1450.	1480.	About 1570.	1624.
Bagow	7	14	?	7	7
Bamme	—	—	—	—	—
Barnewitz	—	—	?	—	—
Bauersdorf	—	—	?	—	—
Berge	—	14	?	7	13½
Börnecke	?	—	—	—	—
Bornim	30	30	27	19	41
Bornstedt	29	7	?	8	8
Bötzow	?	10	?	12	18½
Bredow	10	10	12	15	17
Buchow	—	4	4	5	11
Buckow	—	—	?	—	—
Buschow	14½	9½	10	5	6
Butzow	21	—	?	—	—
Carpzow	11	7	15	6	9½
Cladow	—	—	—	—	—
Dallgow	6	6	—	—	—
Damme	?	7½	?	—	—
Döberitz	—	—	—	—	—
Dyrotz	—	4	3	6	9
Eiche	8 (?)	—	—	—	—
Etzin	13½	—	—	4	4
Fahrland	?	14	18	18	18
Falkenhagen	12	—	?	—	—
Falkenrede	3	2	4	6	6
Ferchesar	—	—	?	—	—
Flatow	?	31	31	5	7
Fohrde	—	8	?	—	—
Garlitz	—	—	?	—	—
Gatow	—	—	—	—	—
Gelte	—	14	10	18	18
Germendorf	?	—	—	—	—
Glienicke	—	6	14	8	8
Gohlitz	?	—	?	—	—
Golm	5	8	12	—	20
Gortz	5	5	8	9	9
Gröningen	—	—	?	—	—
Gross-Bähnitz	—	4	2	—	14
Gross-Zieten	?	34	32	15	19½
Grünfeld	?	—	?	—	2
Gutenpaaren	—	—	4	7½	7½

44   *Essays in German History*

(i) District of Havelland (continued)

Village.	1375.	1450.	1480.	About 1570.	1624.
Hohennauen	?	—	?	16	20
Hoppenrade	8	—	—	—	—
Kartzow	8	7	—	—	8
Ketzür	6	8	8	12	12
Klein-Bähnitz	8	—	?	12	12
Knobloch	18	—	?	7	7
Kotzen	10	14	18	17	21
Landin	8	5	5	6	9
Lietzow	12	5	5	$12\frac{1}{2}$	$12\frac{1}{2}$
Lüchnow	—	7	6	10	10
Markau	21	5 (?)	5	5	10
Markee	15	6	—	10	16
Marquardt	26	12	?	5	5
Marwitz	?	26	25	2	8
Marzahne	—	—	?	—	—
Mögelin	—	—	?	—	—
Möthlow	—	—	—	$8\frac{1}{2}$	$8\frac{1}{2}$
Mützlitz	—	—	?	—	—
Nennhausen	—	18	15	21	21
Niebede	4	—	?	—	—
Nieder-Neuendorf	—	—	3	3	3
Paaren	18	10	10	13	13
					($15\frac{3}{4}$?)
Pansin	?	—	—	—	—
Paretz	—	—	4	13	$18\frac{1}{2}$
Perwenitz	?	7	8	11	18
Pessin	4	15	18	17	25
Premnitz	3	—	?	—	—
Prietzen	?	—	?	—	—
Priort	24	20	22	6	13
Retzow	7	22	18	30	31
Ribbeck	4	11	18	13	$17\frac{1}{2}$
Riewendt	—	—	?	—	—
Rohrbeck	10	—	—	—	—
Roscow	—	—	2	4	8
Saaringen	?	—	?	—	—
Satzkorn	31	31	?	$18\frac{1}{2}$	$21\frac{1}{2}$
Schönwalde	?	—	6	$7\frac{1}{2}$	$13\frac{1}{2}$
Schwante	?	10	21	18	21
Seeburg	—	—	?	—	—
Seegefeld	8	—	3	$4\frac{1}{2}$	$7\frac{1}{2}$
Selbelang	8	10	17	—	32
Semlin	?	—	?	—	—
Spaatz	?	—	?	6	6
Staffelde	?	16	17	13	20
Stechow	8	9	9	11	14
Strodehne	?	—	?	—	—
Tietzow	?	$15\frac{1}{2}$	18	7	7
Tremmen	—	—	?	—	—
Uetz	15	$31\frac{1}{2}$	?	10	13
Vehlefanz	?	43	46	23	$24\frac{1}{2}$
Velten	?	—	—	—	—
Verbitz	?	8	?	22	22
Wachow	?	—	?	$6\frac{1}{2}$	$6\frac{1}{2}$
Wansdorf	?	—	?	7	10

The Origins of the Junkers

(i) *District of Havelland (continued)*

Village.	1375.	1450.	1480.	About 1570.	1624.
Wassersuppe	?	8	7	8	8
Wernitz	7	7	—	—	—
Weseram	—	—	?	—	—
Witzke	?	—	—	2	2
Wustermark	—	—	—	3	3
Zachow	—	—	?	—	—
Zeestow	8	12½	12½	8	12½

(ii) *District of Nieder-Barnim*

Village.	1375.	1450.	1480.	About 1570.	1624.
Ahrensfelde	29	—	—	—	—
Basdorf	—	—	—	—	—
Biesdorf	—	—	?	—	9
Birkholz	—	—	—	5	5
Blankenburg	8	8	8	11	17
Blankenfelde	—	—	—	7	12
Blumberg	—	—	?	6	16
Borgsdorf	?	—	—	—	—
Buch	4	12	12	14	14
Buchholz	8	8	8	—	—
Dahlwitz	14	24	5	15	15
Dalldorf	—	—	—	—	—
Eggersdorf	12	—	13	19	19
Eiche	—	—	—	4	5
Falkenberg	10	—	—	8	16
Fredersdorf	16	18	18	16	24
Friedrichsfelde	—	—	—	32	38
Friedrichsthal	?	—	—	—	3
Glienicke	?	—	—	—	—
Heiligensee	10	18	8	—	—
Hennickendorf	—	—	—	—	—
Hermsdorf	—	—	—	13	17
Herzfelde	—	—	—	—	—
Hohen-Schönhausen	—	10	—	8	8
Hönow	—	—	—	—	—
Karow	6	—	—	4½	4½
Kaulsdorf	4	—	—	—	—
Klosterfelde	?	—	—	—	—
Krummensee	22	24	11	19	19
Lehnitz	?	—	—	—	—
Lindenberg	—	—	—	—	—
Löhme	10	10	?	8	26
Lübars	—	—	—	—	—
Mahlsdorf	5	9	7	10	16
Malchow	—	2	12	17	25½
Marzahn	—	25	?	16	23
Mehrow	—	—	—	—	4
Mühlenbeck	22	11	?	—	—
Neuendorf	—	—	?	—	—
Neuenhagen	—	—	?	4	12
Nieder-Schönhausen	10	—	—	4	11
Pankow	26 (30 ?)	—	—	—	—
Petershagen	—	—	20	14	14
Prenden	16	—	—	—	2
Rehfelde	—	—	—	—	—
Rosenthal	—	—	—	8	12
Rüdersdorf	6	—	7	24	24

46   *Essays in German History*

(ii) District of Nieder-Barnim (continued)

Village.	1375.	1450.	1480.	About 1570.	1624.
Ruhlsdorf	—	—	—	—	—
Schildow	—	—	—	—	—
Schmachtenhagen	?	—	—	—	—
Schönebeck	—	—	—	—	—
Schöneiche	—	—	—	12	21
Schönerlinde	—	—	—	—	—
Schönfliess	4	—	—	11	21
Schönow	2	—	—	—	—
Schwanebeck	—	—	—	—	—
Seeberg	4	—	—	8	10
Seefeld	13	6	6	—	—
Stolpe	16	26	?	16	24
Stolzenhagen	?	—	—	—	—
Tasdorf	—	—	?	—	6
Tegel	—	—	?	—	—
Vogelsdorf	—	11	10	7	7
Wandlitz	?	—	—	—	—
Wartenberg	—	—	—	8	13
Wensickendorf	?	—	—	—	—
Werder	15	—	—	—	—
Woltersdorf	—	—	—	—	—
Zehlendorf	?	32	18	28	30
Zepernick	—	2	—	—	—
Zinndorf	—	—	—	—	—
Zühlsdorf	9	—	—	—	2

(iii) District of Ober-Barnim

Village	1375	1450	1480	About 1570	1624
Batzlow	17	16	18	8	16
Beiersdorf	—	—	?	—	—
Biesdorf	—	—	—	—	—
Bliesdorf	8	4	3	10	10
Bollersdorf	—	—	—	—	15
Brunow	—	36	36	31	49
Buchholz	—	—	—	10	13
Danewitz	—	—	?	—	—
Dannenberg	10	—	—	20	39
Falkenberg	?	—	?	—	—
Frankenfelde	—	—	—	2	7
Freudenberg	—	—	—	—	—
Friedland	—	—	—	20	20
Garzau	—	—	—	5	21
Garzin	38	16	?	4	12
Gersdorf	—	—	—	—	—
Gielsdorf	16	16 (?)	?	16	16
Gross-Barnim	?	—	?	—	—
Grünthal	—	—	—	—	14
Grunow	—	—	—	11 (?)	11 (?)
Haselberg	14	36	36 (?)	5	19
Haselholz	10	30	?	—	—
Heckelberg	—	—	—	—	—
Hegermühle	4	—	—	—	2
Hirschfelde	—	8	4	5	39½
Hohenfinow	?	10	4	24	38
Hohen-Prädikow	—	—	—	12	16
Hohenstein	—	—	—	—	—

The Origins of the Junkers

(iii) District of Ober-Barnim (continued)

Village.	1375.	1450.	1480.	About 1570.	1624.
Ihlow	54	63	?	28	30
Klein-Barnim	?	—	?	—	—
Klobbick	10	14	?	18	24
Köthen	?	10	?	14	14
Kunersdorf	12	15 (?)	17	21	21
Ladeburg	—	—	—	10	10
Lauenberg	— (?)	14	?	28	37
Lewin	?	—	?	—	—
Lichterfelde	15	10	10	12	23
Lüdersdorf	—	—	—	9	13
Medewitz	?	—	?	—	—
Metzdorf	—	—	?	—	—
Nieder-Prädikow	19½	30 (?)	30	24	39
Pritzhagen	14	12	?	12	12
Prötzel	30½	6	6	15	22
Ranft	—	26	26	—	—
Reichenberg	25	20	22	12	16
Reichenow	4	—	—	—	5
Ringenwalde	—	—	—	—	20
Rüdnitz	—	—	—	—	—
Ruhlsdorf	—	—	—	—	—
Schönfeld	—	—	—	—	—
Schöpfurth	—	—	—	—	2
Schulzendorf	—	9	?	13	18
Sommerfelde	—	—	—	—	—
Steinfurth	—	—	—	—	—
Sydow	—	16	?	—	3
Tempelfelde	1	—	—	—	—
Tornow	21½	—	—	—	—
Trampe	22	—	—	17	28½
Trebbin	?	—	?	—	—
Wedigendorf	—	—	—	8	11
Werneuchen	—	—	—	—	—
Wesow	—	—	?	—	—
Wiesenthal	—	—	—	—	14
Wilmersdorf	—	10	—	—	—

(iv) District of Teltow

Village.	1375.	1450.	1480.	About 1570.	1624.
Ahrensdorf	—	—	—	—	—
Blankenfelde	14	30	16 (20 ?)	19	22
Bohnsdorf	8	—	—	—	4
Britz	31	28	18	18	29
Brusendorf	—	—	—	11	14
Buckow	10	9¼	?	—	—
Dahlem	?	10	20	12	12
Dahlwitz	6	6	10	16	18
Diedersdorf	8	31	21	12	16
Genshagen	?	8	?	32	34
Giesensdorf	—	—	7 (?)	—	—
Glasow	5	—	7	—	—
Glienicke (nr. Cöpenick)	32	27	?	29½	29½

48   *Essays in German History*

(iv) District of Teltow (continued)

Village.	1375.	1450.	1480.	About 1570.	1624.
Glienicke (nr. Potsdam)	—	—	?	—	—
Gröben	—	—	—	11	11
Gross-Beeren	12	12	?	11	15
Gross-Beuthen	—	—	?	31	31
Gross-Kienitz	—	4	—	—	—
Gross-Zieten	—	8	15	—	1
Gütergotz	—	—	?	—	—
Heinersdorf	—	—	—	—	6
Hoherlöhme	—	—	—	—	—
Jühnsdorf	5	—	—	—	12
Jütchendorf	—	—	—	—	—
Kerzendorf	?	—	?	—	5
Kiekebusch	—	—	—	—	9
Klein-Beeren	?	—	?	11	14
Klein-Kienitz	—	—	—	4	11
Klein-Zieten	—	5	—	—	4
Lankwitz	—	—	—	—	—
Lichtenrade	—	—	—	—	—
Lichterfelde	—	—	1	—	19
Löwenbruch	?	10	16	12	20
Lützow	—	—	—	—	—
Mariendorf	—	—	?	—	—
Marienfelde	—	—	—	—	—
Miersdorf	—	17	?	17	21
Neuendorf	—	—	—	—	—
Nudow	—	—	—	—	3
Pramsdorf	—	—	—	—	10
Ragow	?	—	?	—	4
Rangsdorf	—	—	?	—	8
Rixdorf	—	—	—	—	—
Rotzis	—	—	?	5	13
Rudow	31 (43 ?)	15	?	8	11
Ruhlsdorf	—	—	—	4	15
Schenkendorf	—	—	—	8	8
Schmargendorf	11	8	—	—	12
Schmöckwitz	—	—	?	—	—
Schöneberg	22	—	—	8	11
Schönfeld	4	9 (?)	16	4	4
Schönow	—	6 (8 ?)	6	8	9
Schulzendorf	12	33	?	12	13
Selchow	—	—	—	5	22
Siethen	—	—	—	13	20
Sputendorf	—	—	?	—	—
Stansdorf	—	—	—	—	—
Steglitz	?	—	—	10	10
Stolpe	—	—	?	—	—
Tempelhof	—	—	—	16	16
Thyrow	—	—	?	10	10
Waltersdorf	—	13 (17 ?)	14	6	15
Wasmannsdorf	11	—	?	—	5
Wilmersdorf	29	38	18½ (?)	15	22
Wusterhausen	4	—	—	—	—
Zehlendorf	—	—	?	—	—
Zeuten	—	—	—	—	—

(v) District of Zauche

Village.	1375.	1450.	1480.	About 1570.	1624.
Barnewitz	—	—	?	—	—
Bliesendorf	—	—	?	—	—
Bochow	—	—	?	—	—
Cammer	—	—	?	5	9
Dahmsdorf	—	—	?	6	6
Deetz	—	—	?	—	—
Derwitz	—	—	?	—	—
Fehben	?	—	?	—	—
Ferch	—	—	?	—	—
Freesdorf	—	—	?	—	—
Glindow	—	—	?	—	—
Göhlsdorf	5	—	?	—	—
Göttin (nr. Brandenburg)	—	4 (?)	?	4	8
Göttin (nr. Potsdam)	—	—	?	—	—
Götz	—	—	?	—	—
Gollwitz	20	4	?	$21\frac{1}{2}$	25
Grebs	—	—	?	—	—
Gross-Damelang	—	—	?	—	—
Grosskreutz	7	5	?	12	16
Jeserig	?	—	?	—	21
Kähnsdorf	—	—	?	—	—
Kemnitz	—	—	?	11	11
Klein-Damelang	—	—	?	—	—
Krahne	—	—	?	16	31
Krielow	—	—	?	—	—
Leest	—	—	?	—	—
Michelsdorf	—	—	?	5	5
Nahmitz	—	—	?	—	—
Netzen	—	—	?	—	—
Neuendorf	—	—	?	—	4
Pernitz	—	—	?	—	—
Plessow	12	9	?	4	6
Plötzin	—	—	?	—	—
Rädel	—	—	?	—	—
Reckahn	—	—	?	—	26
Schmergow	—	—	?	—	—
Schmetzke	—	—	?	—	—
Schwiena	—	—	?	—	4
Töplitz	—	—	?	—	—
Tornow	—	—	?	—	—
Trechwitz	—	—	?	6	10
Wildenbruch	—	—	?	—	—

The two following tables give the consolidated figures for the five districts. The figures for the year 1375 are incomplete, as they are not known for 56 out of the total of 347 villages. These 56 villages are entirely excluded from the first table, but are included in the second.

District.	Number of Villages.	1375.	1450.	About 1570.	1624.
Havelland	73	474	408½	410½	593
Nieder-Barnim	62	301	224	348½	512
Ober-Barnim	56	345½	407	386	668
Teltow	60	255	299½	301½	499½
Zauche	40	44	22	90½	161
	291	1419½	1361	1537	2433½

Havelland	102		638½	609½	844½
Nieder-Barnim	72		256	376½	545
Ober-Barnim	64		427	424	720
Teltow	67		327½	378½	598½
Zauche	42		22	90½	182
	347		1671	1879	2890

NOTE.—The figures for the year 1570 are maximum figures; the number of *Hufen* held in demesne or free of tax for that year was probably considerably lower: see above, footnote 1, p. 37.

3

SOCIAL MOVEMENTS IN THE POMERANIAN TOWNS FROM THE FOURTEENTH CENTURY TO THE REFORMATION

In the towns of the area of German colonization to the east of the Elbe trade was much more important than industry – a phenomenon that can initially be observed in all colonial developments. But the East Elbian lands only outgrew this state of affairs in very recent times. The towns of Pomerania which in the Middle Ages, through their membership of the Hanseatic League, were very important and powerful thereafter became unimportant country towns.

In the larger Pomeranian towns the guilds only slowly acquired a certain influence and the smaller towns remained no more than large villages. The urban administration everywhere was exercised by the mayors and aldermen who also gradually acquired the rights of jurisdiction. Legally the guilds and their masters were not excluded from the urban councils, but in practice these replenished their ranks from the wealthy merchant and patrician families which were linked to the nobility by family ties and common interests as landlords and were often themselves of noble origin.[1] From the beginning of the 14th century the patrician rule was attacked time and again by movements and revolts of the urban Commons, especially in the most important town of Pomerania, Stralsund, one of the leading towns of the Hanse. Yet these movements had little chance of success on account of the overriding importance of trade and the economic backwardness of most of the local towns – in contrast with the contemporary movements in many towns of southern and western Germany.

Influenced by a successful violent uprising against the council which occurred in Rostock in 1312,[2] conflicts between council and guilds broke out in Stralsund in 1313. Finally it was agreed to entrust an elected committee of eight men with the drawing up of new statutes; the aldermen and the masters of the guilds swore in advance to accept its decisions. Their principal content emerges from the fact that henceforth all important resolutions were passed by the aldermen and guild masters together with the Commons,[3] while hitherto this had been done by the aldermen alone. But it seems that this innovation only

---

[1] F. W. Barthold, *Geschichte von Rügen und Pommern*, iii, Hamburg, 1842, pp. 153, 296–7; M. Wehrmann, *Geschichte von Pommern*, Gotha, 1904, i, pp. 157–61, ii, p. 6.

[2] For this, see C. G. Fabricius, *Urkunden zur Geschichte des Fürstenthums Rügen unter den eingebornen Fürsten*, iv 2, Stralsund, 1843, pp. 69–72. In Stralsund a rumour was circulating that the Rostockers would arrive: ibid., p. 50, no. 27 of the *liber de proscriptis* of Stralsund.

[3] The first time in June 1313: Fabricius, op. cit., iv, no. 649.

lasted until 1328. The internal conflicts in Stralsund were used by the ruler, Prince Vizlav of Rügen: through two noble patricians he incited the Commons against the aldermen and sought to foster the suspicion that they planned to kill the leaders of the guilds and secretly collected weapons. The two patricians were in close contact with the prince and his envoys, communicated to them privileges of the town hitherto unknown to him, and informed him of confidential deliberations and decisions of the council, the tax assessments of certain burghers and the contents of other documents. The two were put on trial and their possessions confiscated.[4]

In 1323 the aldermen of Greifswald, together with plenipotentiaries of Anklam and Demmin, stipulated the imposition of the death penalty and a fine of a hundred marks silver for those who conspired against the aldermen and court or instigated a riot against them.[5] During the Rügen succession war (1326–28) a disaffected burgher of Stralsund proposed to the council of Greifswald that five aldermen of his town should be dragged through Stralsund by horses and executed. During the following years this man and the son of a mayor emerged as the leaders of a popular movement in Stralsund. Armed men burst into a meeting of the aldermen with the guild masters, demanded that the captains of the urban forces should be elected by all the burghers and not be appointed by the council. But the move was unsuccessful, and the leaders were banished from Stralsund.[6] In 1387 discontented burghers of Stralsund conspired to murder the aldermen; but these were informed and the conspirators were arrested and sentenced to death. People attacked the wealth of the ruling merchant families, the 'Junkers', who walked about in 'short clothes reaching only to the loins, with long sleeves down to their feet and long peaked shoes', and accused them of making common cause with the robber barons outside the gates. In 1390 new unrest broke out in the town. Aldermen and burghers agreed that two representatives of the Commons were to be added to the council and that no one was to be punished. But soon after one of the new councillors was expelled from the council for having contravened an ordinance prohibiting the export of corn and was later executed for an attempt on the life of a mayor. Yet the disturbances continued, directed above all against the mayor Wulflam and his three sons. Wulflam was forced to give an account of the urban revenues over the past 18 years; his son Wulf was accused of occupying the conquered small town of Tribsees 'like a Junker in community with the robbers'. To save their lives the Wulflams and their partisans had to quit Stralsund, although the duke of Pomerania demanded their

[4] The indictment is printed ibid., iv 2, pp. 50–2; in addition see ibid., text, pp. 81–2, 89–91; Barthold, op. cit., iii, p. 305; Wehrmann, op. cit., i, p. 158, 161.
[5] *Pommersches Urkundenbuch*, vi, Stettin, 1906–7, no. 3677, pp. 164–5.
[6] Barthold, op. cit., iii, p. 306, from the *liber de proscriptis*.

reinstatement. The old statutes and ordinances were repealed and a committee of twelve guildmasters was appointed to assist the new council; two of them and four councillors were to administer the urban finances, and no burgher was permitted to hold a ducal office. The movement was clearly directed against the patrician families as well as the duke. The new popular mayor was Karsten Sarnow who had successfully fought against the pirates (well organized in the form of a brotherhood) and had entered the council in consequence of the reform of 1390. But the change did not last. Already in 1393 the Wulflams were able to return and to regain their position. Sarnow was executed in the market square and the new constitution abrogated.[7]

The popular movement, however, was not stifled. The council was forced to declare the memory of the executed Sarnow untarnished; his body was exhumed and given a solemn funeral. The populist party triumphed once more, helped by battles against the pirates. Yet after only a short time the rule of the old council was restored; the leaders of the rebellion were executed and 48 burghers were expelled. In these years the Stralsunders fought successfully against members of the neighbouring nobility, against the well organized pirates and against the duke who was their ally. But he did not derive any gain from the alliance, only saved himself with difficulty and in 1400 had to reach an agreement with the town.[8]

The 15th century brought new unrest to Stralsund, of a clearly anticlerical character. The ecclesiastical superintendent of the town was a nobleman, Kurt von Bonow. In 1407 he complained about the low offerings the burghers gave to him, quit the town, assembled his noble friends and appeared with 300 horsemen outside the walls. They cut off the hands and feet of burghers whom they found outside, burnt down the farms beyond the walls and departed triumphantly with cattle and other booty; burning villages marked their path. When the priests in Stralsund added their insults and the rumour spread that they supported their leader with arms and money, the burghers, led by the porters' guild, rose against the clergy, imprisoned sixteen of them and then attempted to burn the house where they were confined. The council tried to protect the priests, but the enraged crowd shouted they were all knaves and evildoers, they had helped to fan the fires and therefore they must burn. The master of the porters' guild demanded the death of the three senior priests who were burned in the market place; the others were saved by the council. The news of 'the priests burning at the Sund' (i.e. Stralsund) spread throughout Germany. Then the burghers marched out of the town and pillaged the houses and estates of

[7] Thomas Kantzow, *Pomerania, Eine pommersche Chronik aus dem 16. Jahrhundert*, ed. by G. Gaebel, Stettin, 1908, i. pp. 303–5; Barthold, op. cit., iii, pp. 532–5; Wehrmann, op. cit., i, pp. 162, 172.

[8] Barthold, op. cit., iii, pp. 534–6, 543, 558, 570; Wehrmann, op. cit., i, p. 172.

noblemen who had participated in Bonow's enterprise. The feud between them and the nobility allied with the duke lasted seven years, and several other Pomeranian towns supported Stralsund. All trade languished; burghers venturing outside the walls were killed by the noblemen. In 1410 Stralsund estimated that its commercial damages came to 100,000 gold florins. For many years the town was put under an episcopal interdict and to obtain absolution it had to pay heavy fines. They were paid to the bishop of Schwerin for 22 years, and he used the money to build his cathedral church. There an inscription could be read until the 18th century: 'This vault has been built with the pennies from the Sund in expiation of the death of three innocent priests burnt by them in their market place.'[9] In 1418 followers of the Hussites were discovered in Stralsund, among them a priest who was burnt at Rostock.[10]

About this time the social conflicts in the Hanseatic towns, especially in Lübeck, became so strong that the League – which meant the ruling merchant aristocracies – at a Diet held in Lübeck stipulated the death penalty for burghers who summoned the Commons to take action or agitated otherwise against the council; any member town in which the council was forcibly deposed by the burghers was to lose the Hanseatic privileges and liberties and was not to receive any help from the other towns. Fear had grown to such an extent that it was further ordained no burgher was to appear in front of the council with more than six companions.[11] In a new war between the Hanse and Denmark which began in 1427 the dukes of Pomerania-Wolgast took the Danish side and tried to prohibit their towns from participation in the war. Greifswald and Anklam obeyed, 'for their lords, the dukes, sided with the king [of Denmark], and they could not become their Lord's enemy with honour.' Stralsund, however, declared that they must preserve their alliance with the other Hanseatic towns, an attitude that should not be considered malice. But in the battle between the Hanseatic and the Danish fleets in which the latter was commanded by one of the Pomeranian dukes, the Stralsunders did not take part, perhaps so as not to fight against their own prince. The Hanse was defeated and the defeat caused revolts of the Commons against the council in Hamburg, Rostock and Wismar, where a mayor and an alderman were executed. In Stralsund the guilds of the brewers and the beer porters conspired against the council, encouraged by letters from the king of Denmark to the Commons attacking the council and by their own duke. These two guilds were hit by the blockade of all beer exports to the north and felt aggravated by the council's plan to impose an excise on beer for the

---

[9] Kantzow, op. cit., i, pp. 317–20; Barthold, op. cit., iii, pp. 587–605; iv 1, Hamburg, 1843, pp. 11–12; Wehrmann, op. cit., i, pp. 185–6.
[10] Kantzow, op. cit., i, p. 330; Barthold, op. cit., iv 1, p. 58.
[11] Barthold, op. cit., iv 1, pp. 48–9. The ordinance was renewed in 1487.

duration of the war. But the council was informed of their plans; early in 1428 six ringleaders were arrested and sentenced to death, while others were fined very heavily.[12]

Around the middle of the 15th century, long-drawn-out feuds broke out between the dukes of Pomerania-Wolgast and the nobility on the one side and Stralsund, supported by the Hanseatic towns on the other. In 1452 six burghers, apparently with the support of Duke Wartislaw, conspired to murder members of the council, but their plan was discovered in time. In the following year some burghers were again in secret contact with the duke and his captains, asked them for help against the oppression they were suffering, and promised to admit the duke and his forces through a gap in the walls. The mayor, Otto Voge, summoned the Estates of the duchy to meet in Stralsund, but the duke prohibited the assembly. Yet such was the power and influence of the town that the delegates of Anklam, Barth, Demmin, Greifswald, Grimmen and Wolgast disregarded the prohibition and appeared, as did the majority of the neighbouring nobility, among them surprisingly one of the ducal confidants, Raven Barnekow, the advocatus of the island of Rügen. When Voge was told of the conspiracy between the burghers and the duke and of the presence of the duke near Stralsund, he had Barnekow and the burghers in question arrested; they were tried as traitors and executed. Thereupon the old feud between the town and the duke broke out anew. Conflict also arose within the walls where many disagreed with Voge's radical measures. A moderate party gained the upper hand; ten weeks after the execution of Barnekow, Voge and the leaders of his party had to make their escape from Stralsund. Although the new council tried to satisfy the ducal demands and declared Voge an outlaw, the feud continued. Burghers were taken prisoner when venturing outside the walls, and the merchants were waylaid and plundered. Even after a preliminary peace between the duke and Stralsund its feud with the Barnekows continued with looting, killing and burning. Again the damages Stralsund suffered were estimated at 100,000 florins.[13]

In 1456 Duke Wartislaw signed a treaty with the dukes of Mecklenburg against all disturbers of the peace, in particular against any disobedient towns. When he died in the following year, it is said that he admonished his sons on his deathbed not to allow Voge and the Stralsunders to escape their punishment. A few months later the sons renewed the alliance with Mecklenburg against the 'disobedient towns'. Soon after a conflict with the town of Greifswald erupted on account of

---

[12] Kantzow, op. cit., i, pp. 341–5; Barthold, op. cit., iv 1, pp. 78–83. At that time Pomerania was divided into the two duchies of Pomerania-Wolgast and Pomerania-Stettin.

[13] Kantzow, op. cit., i, pp. 372–7; Barthold, op. cit., iv 1, pp. 164–86; Wehrmann, op. cit., i, p. 202.

the hunting rights on a ducal domain pawned to the town. Within the town a successful revolt of the Commons occurred against the mayor who was forced to leave; apparently it was instigated by Duke Eric. About the same time his knights surprised burghers of Stralsund returning from a fair and led them away into captivity although they had been promised a safe-conduct. In Stralsund the burghers rose against the pro-ducal council and forced it to accept forty additional members from the Commons. The towns of Stralsund, Greifswald, Anklam and Demmin renewed their ancient treaty of alliance, as they were 'pursued by great evil and threatened with oppression'. The war of the towns against the duke and the nobility started. The mayor of Greifswald, Rubenow, was recalled and reinstated. Voge returned after five years of banishment and again became a mayor of Stralsund.[14] At the end of 1462 Rubenow, the popular mayor of Greifswald, was murdered at the instigation of personal enemies within the council. When a deadly enemy of the murdered man was elected in his place by the council new unrest broke out in the town, the Commons accusing members of the council that they were implicated in the murder. The latter appealed to Duke Eric for help and at Easter 1463 admitted him and 400 armed men secretly into Greifswald. The surprised burghers were forced to render an oath of allegiance and loyalty to the duke. He forbade under threat of heavy punishments any rebellion against the council which he declared innocent of Rubenow's murder. But this had little effect; some months later the new mayors were killed by an enraged crowd led by a relative of Rubenow; he started the revolt by shouting that the duke stood outside the gates, the town had been betrayed! Duke Eric was unable to enforce his prohibition and the revolt went unpunished.[15]

In 1478 the two Pomeranian duchies were reunited under Duke Bogislav X. He took as his example the subjugation of the Brandenburg towns by the Hohenzollern Electors Frederick II and Albrecht Achilles.[16] In 1486 he led his forces to help the duke of Brunswick against Hildesheim and other towns; in the following year he supported the dukes of Mecklenburg against the town of Rostock. In 1480 he used an opportunity to subjugate the small town of Köslin in eastern Pomerania. In 1490 and 1502 he turned against Stettin and forced it to pay him higher taxes and fines and to depose its mayor and jurymen, after a blockade of the town by land and water. All Pomeranian towns, with the only exception of Stralsund, in 1498 had to accept a trebling of the princely tolls at the mouth of the Peene at

---

[14] Kantzow, op. cit., i, pp. 376–7, 384–5; Barthold, op. cit., iv 1, pp. 230–43, 343–6; Wehrmann, op. cit., i, p. 202.

[15] Kantzow, op. cit., i, pp. 390–3; Barthold, op. cit., iv 1, pp. 267–73; Wehrmann, op. cit., i, p. 211.

[16] For this, see F. L. Carsten, *The Origins of Prussia*, Oxford, 1954, pp. 137–45.

Wolgast and Dammgarten.[17] Encouraged by these successes and embittered by the opposition of Stralsund, Bogislav then took up the cudgels against his most powerful town. He disputed its ancient privileges of the right of appeal in legal cases to Lübeck, of confiscating the feudal property of noblemen who had lived and died within the walls, and of minting coins. Early in 1504 Bogislav suddenly imposed a blockade on the town and encouraged his men to attack the burghers outside the walls. Stralsund was no longer supported by the other towns of Pomerania but it resisted stoutly; the armed burghers crossed over to the island of Rügen, looted the ducal villages and domains, took noblemen who had not fled prisoner and extracted an oath of loyalty from the inhabitants. The duke in his turn plundered the possessions of the burghers on the mainland but was unable to take the well fortified town. In March 1504 peace was concluded at Rostock. Stralsund was able to retain all its important privileges but had to make one important concession, the payment of the toll at Wolgast.[18]

Soon the undecided battle recommenced. In the war of 1509–11 between the Hanseatic League and Denmark, Bogislav was allied with the Danes; the towns of Greifswald and Stettin did no longer support the League and even helped its enemies, thus obeying Bogislav's orders. Stralsund, however, confiscated Pomeranian ships which continued to trade with the Danes, among them those of Stettin. The Danes devastated villages belonging to Stralsund on the island of Rügen but left the peasants of other temporal and ecclesiastical lords in peace. To take their revenge the Stralsunders stopped ships which the duke sent to the Netherlands, laden with corn and herring, on his own account 'because the prince was not entitled to such trade'. Thereupon Bogislav, with the support of the Estates, attacked the possessions and trade of Stralsund which suffered very severe damage. In June 1512 the town had to seek a settlement which confirmed that of 1504 and contained further important concessions: it had to pay a fine of 3220 florins, to cede to the duke the jurisdiction in seven of its villages, and to permit its burghers the right of legal appeal to the duke or to Lübeck, while hitherto all appeals had gone to Lübeck. Yet Stralsund retained the rights of appealing to Lübeck and of minting coins which Bogislav had disputed.[19] His victory was not complete.

The time of the Reformation brought new severe social conflicts in a number of towns, revolts against the urban authorities as well as against the duke. It is therefore not surprising that both took their stand against any religious innovation, while the lower orders, as in the whole of

[17] Kantzow, op. cit., ii, pp. 36–9, 50–1, 82, 86–7; Barthold, op. cit., iv 1, pp. 428–31, 486–7, iv 2, pp. 21–3, 32–3; Wehrmann, op. cit., i, pp. 244–5.

[18] J. C. Daehnert, *Pommersche Bibliothek*, ii, Greifswald, 1753, pp. 47–52; Kantzow, op. cit., ii, pp. 88–95; Barthold, op. cit., iv 2, pp. 38–47; Wehrmann, op. cit., i, p. 245.

[19] Kantzow, op. cit., ii, pp. 99–101; Barthold, op. cit., iv 2, pp. 76–82; Wehrmann, op. cit., i, p. 245.

northern Germany (and often in the south too), were the protagonists of religious change.[20] At a time of high social tensions, their old hatred of the rich patrician families revived in a religious or temporal garb. This applied in particular to Stralsund, the leading Pomeranian town with the most vociferous Commons and most pronounced social conflicts.

In the spring of 1522 a burgher, Roloff Möller, called the discontented together in St. John's church, explained to them from an old register the taxes and rents of the town, attacked the measures taken by the council as dishonest, accused them of theft and then led the crowd to the town hall. The mayors and councillors gave up their long-held positions; from the Commons a committee of 48 was elected to govern side by side with the council; Möller and the senior guild master of the shoemakers were appointed its leaders. The members of the council had to swear to observe the new ordinances which stipulated their rights and duties in detail. Soon after there was a clash with the clergy when the council demanded their participation in a war tax. The superintendent and prelates refused indignantly and hastily left Stralsund.[21]

In May 1523, the first follower of Luther preached in Stralsund to a vast crowd. The council issued a prohibition, but he continued to preach urged on by the people. The duke and the bishop ordered the 'lapsed monk' to be banished from the town, but several hundred guild members assembled and demanded he 'should stay or they wanted to risk their necks'. New prohibitions were equally disregarded. More 'lapsed monks' made their appearance; one of them preached 'in the presence of several thousands that it was Christian, commendable and equitable that the authorities, the regents of the towns, should account for their administration and actions to the burghers and their other subjects, as was their duty . . . He had been in countries and places where the subjects had deposed the high and mighty and held them to account; if they could justify themselves they were reinstated, but if not, others were elected and made regents . . .' When the superintendent returned to Stralsund in March 1524 the tension grew, as did the courage of the adherents of the new faith. A Catholic priest was pulled down from the pulpit by a pewterer and a weaver and their followers: 'a lapsed monk and seditious preacher mounted it to preach'.[22] When one of the mayors died in June 1524, Möller as the speaker of the Committee of 48 made a fiery speech against the council, the protector of the Papists, in front of the assembled Commons in the

[20] Barthold, op. cit., iv 2, pp. 137, 249; Wehrmann, op. cit., ii, pp. 7, 16, 19.
[21] 'Articuli exceptionales et defensionales borgermeister, rat, achtundevertich unde gantze gemeinte stat Stralesundt contra heren Hypolitum Steinwer et consorten', May 1529, *Baltische Studien*, xvii 2, pp. 104–5; Barthold, op. cit., iv 2, pp. 138–40.
[22] *Baltische Studien*, xvii 2, pp. 114–20, 122–3, 153; Barthold, op. cit., iv 2, pp. 153–6.

market place. The turbulent crowd installed him and another man, both not even members of the council, as new mayors in the town hall. The Commons elected eight new aldermen, the power of the Committee of 48 was fixed by new ordinances which the authorities had to sign. The last Catholic priests left Stralsund, and the rule of the patricians seemed to have come to an end.[23]

In April 1525 there was an outbreak of iconoclasm, supported by the journeymen, or as the council put it, 'mobile, fickle people'. It had summoned the poor and beggars to St. Nicolas' church to separate the natives from the 'foreigners' and to expel the latter from the town. The assembled crowd began to break the images in the church, while others resisted and the guilds tried to defend their altars; worried burghers hurried to save saints, paintings and holy vessels. The iconoclasts, about 1500 in number, then stormed from church to church, 'hacked and knocked to pieces and carted away whatever images they found. In the monasteries . . . they destroyed everything without any difference . . . and occupied the chapels and made bonfires from the cut up images and ate and drank all the monks' stores, and they chased from the town the monks and priests who feared for their lives in this turmoil . . .' Now the council took drastic measures and ordered everybody to carry to the market what he or she had taken from the churches, and whoever was innocent to exonerate himself by an oath. Hundreds of armed burghers stood guard during the night and several iconoclasts were arrested. The journeymen who had taken a leading part were frightened and left the town. The burghers who had carried images into their houses gave them up and apologized that they were not responsible. The council acquiesced as the use of force would have called forth violent resistance, and the remnants of Catholicism were eliminated.[24]

The council was seriously worried by this revolutionary outbreak. It was still led by Möller, but it seems that – raised by ducal favour and frightened by iconoclasm – he changed sides about this time. In any case, the council 'thought that it was bad for the town to remain in this state and to be on bad terms with their prince, and hoped that, if they were reconciled with their prince,[25] they could get help from him against the unruly and riotous Commons; thus they sent to the prince at Wolgast and negotiated with him and bargained hard that the princes must first confirm their old privileges, then they would swear an oath of allegiance. But the princes disagreed and demanded the oath first . . . and then they would confirm those privileges about which agreement

[23] Kantzow, op. cit., ii, p. 125; Barthold, op. cit., iv 2, pp. 167–72; Wehrmann, op. cit. ii, p. 20.
[24] *Baltische Studien*, xvii 2, pp. 127–30, 147–8; Kanztow, op. cit., ii, pp. 117–19; Barthold, op. cit., iv 2, pp. 183–7; Wehrmann, op. cit., ii, p. 20; J.G.L. Kosegarten's introduction to the documents in *Baltische Studen*, xvii 2, pp. 91–3.
[25] After the death of Duke Bogislav in 1523 Stralsund again refused to pay the toll at Wolgast and to render the oath of allegiance until the issue was settled.

would be reached, after the oath had been taken.' The delegates from Stralsund then 'gave way that the oath should come first, followed by the confirmation of the privileges . . . And at Petri and Pauli of this year 1525 the princes with 400 armed horsemen rode into Stralsund and took the oath of allegiance and confirmed the town's privileges . . . Then the princes settled all kind of wrongs and trouble in the town and departed again.'[26] It is uncertain when the rule of the patricians was restored in Stralsund, whether in 1525 with the conflict between Möller and the Committee of 48, or with his banishment from the town in 1526 and the return of his rival Smiterlow. In any case, the rule of the Commons, as so often in the town's history, only lasted a short time.

Religious unrest also occurred in other Pomeranian towns. In Stettin a Lutheran preached early in 1524 'in the cemetery where, apart from some guild masters, a big crowd from all guilds and trades assembled, some of them in full armour with halberds so as to protect the preacher from the Papists. Thereafter they surrounded the preacher and led him to St. Nicolas' church where he preached before the mass in front of such a vast concourse that a turbulence developed. The armed burghers surrounded the pulpit until the sermon was finished . . . At that time there was such unrest in Stettin that one almost thought they would strangle each other . . .' For eight weeks the Commons met every day in turbulent gatherings, and the council was only saved with the help of the merchants and skippers. The ducal officials held an investigation and forbade any further meetings of the Commons, but had to permit the appointment of a Committee of 48 to participate in the town government and the preaching of evangelical sermons. During the following years the disturbances continued. As the dukes were unable to enforce the prohibitions of the gatherings of the Commons, they transferred their court to Wolgast in 1532. But at the Diet of 1534 Stettin made its submission, swore fealty and paid a fine, whereupon the ducal court was re-established there.[27]

In Kolberg in eastern Pomerania internal strife and bloody clashes occurred between different patrician families as well as between the patricians and the burghers and their Committee of 48.[28] In 1525 the guilds of Greifswald rose against the council, demanded an account of the urban revenues, and accused the council of embezzlement and the sale of urban property. The dukes intervened, ordered accounts to be rendered and regulated the urban administration and the budget as well

[26] Kantzow, op. cit., ii, pp. 127–8, and *Chronik von Pommern in niederdeutscher Mundart*, ed. by W. Böhmer, Stettin, 1835, p. 166.

[27] H. Schwallenberg, 'Historia Pomeraniae pragmatica', *Baltische Studien*, iii 1, pp. 170–1; Kantzow, *Chronik von Pommern in niederdeutscher Mundart*, pp. 198, 219–20; Barthold, op. cit., iv 2, pp. 173–4, 205–6, 236–7, 266, 273–4; Wehrmann, op. cit., ii, pp. 21–2.

[28] Kantzow, *Pomerania*, ii, pp. 179–84; F. Wokenius, *Beytrag zur Pommerischen Historie . . .*, Leipzig, 1732, p. 80; Barthold, op. cit., iv 2, pp. 175–7.

as matters of police and justice; a Committee of twelve was elected to take part in the administration but dissolved again in 1534 as unsuitable for the purpose.[29] In addition, there developed radical movements directed against the princes and all authority. 'Enthusiasts came into the country who denigrated all official authority with their preaching, among whom Doctor Amandus was the most notable, who first in Stolp, then in other towns, and finally in Stettin preached publicly to throw rags at the princes and drive them out of the country, led the people to iconoclasm and all kinds of trouble and had many followers . . .'[30] Late in 1524 Amandus preached at Stolp. Then 'the burghers deposed the council, appointed new councillors, broke the images and altars in the churches except the main altar, and did much to annoy the clergy, so that they and the old council complained strongly to the prince. Therefore Duke George went there and ordered all burghers to assemble at the town hall and intended to take the leaders of the game by their necks and punish them. But there was a young man among the new, Hans Wulff by name; he accepted responsibility for the Commons and spoke so well and ably that Duke George was induced to forego any severity and to assess their misdeeds in the form of a fine, and thus they had to give many guilders and promise to restore the altars and to leave the old council in power . . .' The Catholic services were restored; by punishing a small town the duke had proved his zeal.[31]

Amandus fled to Stettin and continued to preach against the princes, so 'that he almost replaced Magistrum Paulum vom Rode in the pulpit and the people considered him and other pious preachers mere hypocrites and said of them that they did not dare to touch the princes and other authorities. And there would have occurred a terrible revolt, as it happened in the following year with the peasants' war in Upper Germany, if Magister Paulus vom Rode and other pious preachers had not stood fast . . .' Amandus was taken and imprisoned but 'strangely enough' he seems to have escaped and to have left Pomerania.[32] In the countryside too, social unrest became noticeable. 'The nobility thought that they were overburdened and had many grievances. The towns followed suit, and when the peasants became aware of this, all obedience and good will vanished and they plotted daily how to find cause and time to attack prince, nobility and towns and to get rid of their servitude . . .'[33] But, apart from this general remark by Kantzow, we have no detailed reports about peasant unrest in Pomerania.

---

[29] *Ibid.*, iv 2, pp. 193, 255; Wehrmann, op. cit., ii, p. 22.
[30] Kantzow, *Pomerania*, ii, p. 123.
[31] *Ibid.*, pp. 126–7; Barthold, op. cit., iv 2, pp. 194–6; Wehrmann, op. cit., ii, pp. 23–4.
[32] Kantzow, *Pomerania*, ii, pp. 123–4, and *Chronik von Pommern in niederdeutscher Mundart*, pp. 160, 165; Barthold, op. cit., iv 2, pp. 196–7.
[33] Kantzow, *Chronik von Pommern in niederdeutscher Mundart*, pp. 154–5, 173–4.

At the Hanseatic Diet of 1534 the mayor of Stralsund, Klaus Smiterlow, reappointed in 1526, opposed the democratic leader of Lübeck, Jürgen Wullenweber, and counselled against yet another war with Denmark. From Lübeck the Committee of 48 was informed of the attitude of their mayor; the people rose against 'Klaus the Peacemaker', assembled under arms, with the gates closed, and demanded that the council must account for its policy. They threatened to throw Smiterlow out of the window, and in the turmoil the 48 collected the votes for and against a war tax. The large majority voted in favour; Smiterlow was arrested and confined to his house. A few days later two new mayors and seven councillors were elected and the armaments strongly helped forward by a tax on the wealthy. 'All the towns here and in neighbouring lands became haughty . . . and this feud meant that, if the towns had continued thus, as was their intention, no prince or nobleman could have survived anywhere . . .'[34] When Duke Philip and his officials tried to intervene on behalf of the arrested mayor, the town rejected the intercession. In February 1535 the Committee of 48 forced the council to revive the ordinances of 1522 which circumscribed its rights and to agree to further limitations of its power. But the Hanseatic League was defeated in the war with Denmark, betrayed by their own patricians. In August, Wullenweber's rule was terminated in Lübeck and that of the patricians restored.[35] The natural consequence of the defeat was the overthrow of the popular party in Stralsund. In the spring of 1536 a determined persecution began of 'the knaves of 1522 and 1534'. In September ten suspects, among them the guildmasters of the shoemakers, the clothiers and the tailors, the leaders of the Committee of 48, were arrested; a master of the shoemakers was executed because the ordinances of 1535 were found in his possession. The persecution continued while any member of the Commmittee of 48 was still alive, all reforms were abrogated, and Smiterlow reappointed as mayor.[36]

After the suppression of the popular movements in Greifswald, Stettin and other towns, the strong movement in Stralsund was also forced to capitulate: a defeat that proved permanent. The guilds and Commons were not strong enough to prevail against the merchant aristocracies, in spite of numerous revolts. With the restoration of the rule of the patricians in Lübeck and Stralsund in 1535, the power of the towns at the Baltic coast and of their League declined decisively. The dukes of Pomerania were able to use the internal conflicts in the leading towns to increase their own power and to weaken that of the towns. But the class which benefited most from these and other social and economic changes was the nobility which became the dominating force, not only in Pomerania but in the whole of north-east Germany.

[34] *Ibid.*, pp. 207–11; Barthold, op. cit., iv 2, pp. 252–4.
[35] *Ibid.*, iv 2, pp. 260–2, 289–94.
[35] *Ibid.*, iv 2, pp. 294–7.

4

THE PEASANTS WAR OF 1525 IN EAST PRUSSIA

The social conflicts which erupted all over Germany at the time of the Reformation and led to outbreaks of popular unrest also affected the extreme northeast of the German lands, the Prussian state of the Teutonic Order. As early as September 1524 the Secretary Gattenhofer wrote to the Grand Master who was staying in the Empire: 'The mutiny in the country is so great that nothing would be more desirable than your return; for a big, disloyal peasant is hiding behind the fence, who will have to be ensnared at the right time by the right governor.'[1]

In April 1525, after the introduction of the Reformation, Prussia was transformed into a temporal principality which the last Grand Master, Albrecht of Hohenzollern, took as a fief from the hands of the king of Poland, and became the first duke of Prussia. After the secularization the commanders and other officials of the Order continued to administer its estates as before, only now as landlords in a secular capacity. They thus lost to some extent their official, separate status, derived their livelihood from agriculture and became the equals of the local noblemen: a more uniform landed nobility came into being with the same interests vis-à-vis the duke, the towns and the peasants. Through the dissolution of the Order the influence of the nobility grew and the duke became more and more dependent on it. In his absence the duchy was administered by a governor, von Polentz, originally the bishop of Samland and now a Protestant bishop, who owned large estates, was closely connected with the nobility by ties of friendship and

[1] Literature on the unrest of 1525: (N. Richau), 'Historie von dem Aufruhr der samländischen Bauren', *Erleutertes Preussen*, ii, Königsberg, 1725, pp. 328ff., 531ff.; L. von Baczko, *Geschichte Preussens*, iv, Königsberg, 1795, pp. 198ff., 450ff.; M. Töppen, 'Ein Blick in die ältere preussische Geschichte, mit Bezug auf die ständische Entwicklung', *Allgemeine Zeitschrift für Geschichte*, v, 1846, pp. 45ff., vi, 1846, pp. 485ff.; J. Voigt, 'Geschichte des Bauernaufruhrs in Preussen', *Neue Preussische Provinzialblätter*, iii, 1847, pp. 1ff., 310ff.; A. Seraphim, 'Soziale Bewegungen in Altpreussen im Jahre 1525', *Altpreussische Monatsschrift*, lviii, 1921; W. Stolze, 'Die Erhebung der samländischen Bauern im September 1525, ihre Gründe, ihr Ziel und ihre Bedeutung', *Jahresbericht 1928/29 des Königsberger Universitätsbundes*; E. Wilke, 'Die Uraschen der preussischen Bauern- und Bürgerunruhen 1525', *Altpreussische Forschungen*, vii, 1930, pp. 33ff., 181ff.; E. Weise, *Der Bauernaufstand in Preussen*, Elbing, 1935; H. Zins, 'Aspects of the Peasant Rising in East Prussia in 1525', *Slavonic and East European Review*, xxxviii, 1959, pp. 178ff.; H. Wunder, 'Der samländische Bauernaufstand von 1525', in A. Wohlfeil (ed.), *Der Bauernkrieg 1524–26 – Bauernkrieg und Reformation*, Munich, 1975, pp. 143ff. and 'The Mentality of Rebellious Peasants – the Samland Peasant Rebellion of 1525', in B. Scribner and G. Benecke (eds.), *The German Peasant War 1525 – New Viewpoints*, London, 1979, pp. 144ff.

family and was hated by the peasants. The discontent in the country grew, especially in the town of Königsberg where the Commons agitated against the ruling mayors and aldermen; from the town the movement spread into the countryside. A ducal mandate of July 1525, which had to be read in the churches on five consecutive Sundays and thereafter once every month, warned at five different places against rioting, revolt, unrest, mutiny and rebellious behaviour of any kind; the people were ordered to hand over all unusual weapons, such as long knives, pikes, halberds or muskets, to their local official, Junker or urban magistrate. Finally, a general Diet was summoned to meet on 24 August 'because we have noticed that all sorts of resistance is rendered by our subjects in town and country, and especially by the common peasantry'.

When the Diet was postponed the general unrest which had long smouldered erupted openly. Around midnight on 2 September 1525 a large number of peasants assembled in the village of Kaymen in northeastern Samland, summoned by the local miller who had secretly worked for a considerable time among the peasants of the neighbourhood. The local peasants were particularly enraged about the demands of the ducal *Amtmann* (the local official), Andreas von Rippe, a relative of the duke: he imposed labour services on them during the harvest, even from vacant holdings, made them bring in damp corn, then take it back to the fields, spread and dry it, and finally cart it back once more. The assembled peasants were addressed by the miller:[2] 'Dear brethren, neighbours and friends! This hasty gathering only takes place by the will of Almighty God who has taken to heart your grievous oppression, the afflictions which you have had to suffer so long from the nobility against all justice: now God will have pity on you and liberate you from them; this does not happen without the knowledge and permission of the Prince, for he has sincere compassion with you, and such freedom cannot be gained by any other means but as we have started now . . . What is the nobleman to us? Who has given them to us as our masters? for the only thing they can do is to harass the poor peasant. Now we possess the right means to free ourselves, and in particular because we have God, His Holy Gospel and the Prince's favour and good will on our side, for the time of our salvation has come . . . Therefore, whoever loves freedom, more than property, take heart and courage and follow me; we will gain fame with God's help, as will be told of us by our descendants, wives and children to our glory and honour in eternity.'

The German peasants agreed with the miller, but the Prussian peasants[3] had to be convinced of the duke's approval by being shown a

[2] Nearly all quotations are taken from Richau's chronicle, who was a contemporary observer and participant.

[3] In Samland Prussian was still spoken and Prussians were the majority of the people.

tax demand with the princely seal: they were accustomed to obey such missives. Early the next morning the crowd occupied the castle of Kaymen, Andreas von Rippe was fetched from his bed and forced to surrender to the peasants and to accompany them. The peasants were jubilant: now he would have to work for them and they would be his Junkers; they would teach his wife to dig, to bind hops, to dress flax and to carry manure. 'But the gloves must come off the hands, and all this we'll teach you free of charge; now you will have to spin for us as your labour service as we had to do it for you so long.' No harm was done to either of them. In the village they formed a ring as the lansquenets did, and in it the local priest had to preach 'the true word of God' as an 'evangelical preacher'.

The band grew quickly and first marched to Labiau near the coast with the intention to continue towards Königsberg. On 3 September the peasants contacted the Commons of the capital by sending two messengers to them: they should 'give advice what to do or not to do with the Junker'. In a letter of the following day the peasants expressly stated that they 'did not intend to take anything from anyone, neither to rob nor to steal, neither to kill nor to murder'. They further wrote to one burgher in each of the three towns of Königsberg,[4] who were their confidants, what some of the peasants had discussed with them had taken place; they would now like to hear from them what they could expect from them and from the whole Commons; the game had started and must be played to a finish. Those noblemen whom they still found at home they took along, either on a carriage or on foot, as their prisoners, but the majority escaped. The peasants broke into the noble larders and cellars, consumed whatever they found and took what weapons they could lay their hands on. When they reached Labiau they demanded from the *Amtmann* that the noblemen who had taken refuge in the castle should be handed over to them. But he urged them not to lay their hands on the duke's property and people; if they had a case against the nobility they should conduct it elsewhere. To avoid violence he supplied them with bread and beer. This they accepted and marched on to Tapiau. Wherever they found the noblemen gone they let them know that they must surrender, or their houses would be burnt down.

In northern Samland, in the district of Schaaken, a second band was formed under the leadership of a local innkeeper, Hans Gericke. It marched westwards to get hold of the *Amtmann* von Polentz, the bishop's brother, who was hated as 'a tyrant over the peasants', but he escaped. Everywhere the stores of the noble houses were consumed, noblemen taken prisoner, the windows, stoves, furniture and crockery of hated lords broken, the featherbeds torn up, money, cans, kettles and other goods taken away, and cattle slaughtered. The noblemen fled to

---

[4] Königsberg then consisted of three independent towns, the original Altstadt, the Kneiphof and the Löbenicht, each with its own mayor and aldermen.

Königsberg or to Fischhausen – which may have been the goal of the second band. The noblemen who sought refuge in Königsberg were received by the populace with shouts of 'Don't let them in, drive them out again, for they have long enough plagued the poor peasants; now they will be paid back.' Yet the assembled Commons assured their mayors they had no connection whatever with the peasants; if anyone should have such links he should answer for it himself. Even the three confidants of the peasants delivered their letters to their mayor and denied any knowledge of the affair.

The whole movement was directed solely against the nobility; towards the duke the peasants' attitude remained loyal and respectful. There are even reports that they believed to render him a service if they destroyed the nobility. The first demands of the peasants, written by the parson of Legitten who, a halberd in his hand, marched with the peasants, stated: 'We wish and demand only God and our most gracious master, Duke of Prussia, as our lord, and no other authority. As God has created us all equal, redeemed us and promised us one Kingdom, we do not want any nobles as lords, but desire to be all equal brothers and sisters in Christo.' To the duke the peasants promised to give the old dues, two marks from each Hufe; otherwise they wanted to be rid of labour services, money dues and other burdens: the 'rivers and woods, fish and game, the birds in the air' should be the common property of all and should not be forbidden.

On 7 September the two bands united at Zinkenhof and held common council after military custom. On the same day there arrived a delegation of the aldermen and Commons of the three towns of Königsberg, which had been sent at the suggestion of the ducal councillors. The peasants continued their march to Altkaymen where peasants from the whole area congregated. There another common council was held; Hans Gericke was elected their captain and an elected committee was to negotiate with the Königsberg delegation. Altogether about seven to eight thousand peasants had assembled. They were first addressed by Nicolaus Richau, mayor of the Alstadt Königsberg (the author of the principal chronicle of these events), who emphasized that the peasants stood completely alone, without any support from the duke or from Königsberg. Then Gericke spoke to the delegation: 'God through His Holy Ghost has moved us in our hearts to undertake this, so as to redeem the poor from their oppression and heavy labour services; we also know from the Holy Scriptures: thou shall have but one God and Lord, to whom thou shall render honour and obedience; therefore we must destroy the nests so that the crows cannot breed any young ones. For us the prince is enough of a master, and we do not consider the nobility an authority, for they never keep any promise, and they prohibit the birds in the air and the fish in the water, which God has created free for everybody.' But they would gladly follow the towns of Königsberg and give up their enterprise if the noblemen would only have patience until the duke returned; he should then see to it that everybody got his right and should protect them against violence and oppression, so that the poor peasant would not be burdened more heavily than he was in old times. Those from Königsberg replied they could not give orders to the nobility but would be pleased to take the suggestion to the ducal councillors; these would have to negotiate with the nobility which they hoped would not reject it and would accept equitable directions. This was accepted by the peasants who were discouraged by the refusal of the Königsberg delegates. When the masses which had collected in the course of the morning 'heard that the whole affair did not seem to prosper they melted away'.

It was then agreed to meet the representatives of the nobility the next day on a nearby hill and to settle how matters should be arranged until the duke returned; until then, the peasants would let rest their grievances; the noblemen of Samland meanwhile should not demand labour services and other burdens but keep the peace; they should not make any demands on the peasants, nor undertake anything against them on account of 'this rebellion or the damages they had suffered'. If the nobles promised to do so by word of mouth, the peasants would return home, otherwise they would 'devastate and burn the houses and estates of all the Samland noblemen'. With this reply the delegates returned to Königsberg. The ducal councillors and the aldermen of Königsberg – worried by signs of unrest in the town – urged the assembled nobility to accept these conditions. On 8 September the ducal councillors, representatives of the aldermen and Commons of Königsberg and about three thousand peasants assembled as arranged. Inside a ring they negotiated with the delegates of the nobility. Gericke accused the Junkers of oppressing the peasant: in future they wanted to be exempt from labour services and only the subjects of the duke of Prussia, for God had ordained, one God, one lord, and everybody to work with his own hands; the noblemen must do the same. Everything else should await the duke's return, to whom they would submit their grievances. This was accepted by the noblemen, but the peasants declared that they had never kept their word. Therefore the noblemen vowed to give letter and seal that they would not seek vengeance, 'neither by word nor deed', until the prince came back. Gericke released all the prisoners, the peasants returned what they had taken from the Junkers and began to sing 'Now we beg the Holy Ghost' – the same song which the bands of Thomas Müntzer had intoned four months earlier before their disastrous defeat in the battle of Frankenhausen.

The movement did not remain limited to Samland but spread to Natangen to the south of Königsberg. Near Friedland a clergyman removed the seals from the ducal missive which warned against rioting and revolt and put them on letters written by himself as a proof that the rising was taking place with the duke's approval. Day and night he traversed the country and called on the peasants 'to extirpate the nobility, the weed Zizania'; the time of redemption had come. But the messenger sent by the miller of Kaymen to Natangen with the news of the revolt was taken prisoner. The local Junkers feared the worst and fled in the early days of the Samland rising to the castle of Preussisch-Eylau and to the towns of Barten and Bartenstein. The latter town only received the fugitives if they accepted eight articles. They had to promise that while staying in the town they would refrain from any loud or overbearing behaviour, would in future not punish the burghers so harshly for taking wood or for other misdemeanours, and would not insist on a guarantee of protection by the town.

On 7 September the ducal councillors heard 'that in Natangen too the peasants were banding together'. Near Friedland and Schippenbeil strong crowds assembled and marched in a northwesterly direction, perhaps towards Königsberg. The father of Andreas von Rippe was taken prisoner by them. On the 8th the miller of Pöhlen issued a declaration: 'As you well know we have suffered severe oppression by the godless noblemen, . . . therefore we intend to erect a godly government to the joy of our children and grand-children. Thus we call upon you to stand by each other, to return Prussia to our most gracious master and to extirpate all the weeds . . .' On the 9th a rumour reached Königsberg 'that the peasants of Natangen were searching for noblemen and looting'. Immediately the ducal councillors and delegates of Königsberg were sent there.[5] When they told the peasants that the Samland revolt had been settled they 'dispersed and abstained from any violence'. Here too it was agreed to await the duke's return; but the noblemen distrusted the agreement, remained in the castle of Eylau and from there sallied forth to capture the ringleaders. In Samland also many complaints were raised that the noblemen did not observe the truce, uttered ominous threats and at night-time rode fully armed about the country. Already before his return to Prussia Duke Albrecht ordered eight peasant leaders to be arrested; when they were brought into Königsberg the crowd adopted a threatening attitude, but the peasants kept quiet.

In other parts of Prussia no large scale rioting occurred. In the area of Tilsit and Ragnit in the far northeast of the country, a band was formed and the ducal official in charge of Gerdauen feared their approach. In the northern district of Memel an uprising was expected, and links even existed with Courland further north. Another official advised to occupy the crossings over the Deime river, but these fears seem to have been

---

[5] According to Weise, op. cit., p. 42, the delegation included the parson of Legitten and the miller of Kaymen who were believed to be best suited to calm the peasants.

exaggerated, as were those of the bishop of Warmia which was adjoining Prussia in the west.

At the beginning of October Duke Albrecht returned to Prussia. Delegates of the peasants brought him a message: 'if he were a pious prince he should come to the mountain of Quednau; there they would give him his dues and taxes and what belonged to him'. The noblemen congregated at the court, gave exaggerated accounts of the events of the past weeks and attributed all the blame to those of Königsberg to whom the peasants had written and whose advice they had followed. The duke at first did not enter the town and asked the nobility, the bishops and the king of Poland for armed support. But his fears were allayed by a delegation from Königsberg; again Richau spoke very ably and the town promised to support him with a contingent of a thousand armed men; for the urban authorities knew that a victory over the peasants would at the same time settle the unrest inside the town. The other towns of the duchy were more reluctant in promising help. Only after these armaments Albrecht entered Königsberg and ordered the peasants to appear on 30 October with their weapons and captains on a nearby field where he would himself be present. There about three to four thousand peasants assembled. Albrecht with his army marched to meet them and asked them whether they wanted to give battle or put down their weapons and deliver those to him whose names would be read out. As their captain Gericke had not yet arrived the peasants did not know what to do, threw down their weapons and asked for mercy. 87 peasants whose names had been supplied by the nobility were called out and put into chains. Three were executed on the spot, the others and Gericke who had meanwhile arrived were taken to the castle of Königsberg and thrown into prison. During the following days eleven more peasants were executed in Königsberg and two in their villages. On 7 November Albrecht marched to Natangen and ordered further executions, among them those of three innkeepers. Strict mandates were issued and heavy punishments imposed in the country, by the duke and by the nobility.

What is remarkable about the revolt in Prussia is in the first place the close connection with simultaneous unrest in Königsberg, the influence which emanated from there,[6] and the (very limited) backing which the peasants received from inside the town. Even Richau, whose chronicle naturally aims at minimizing the participation of burghers of his town, names a fair number who were allies of the peasants, among them one shoemaker, one furrier and one coppersmith. The quick collapse of the rising was at least partly due to the weakness and isolation of the urban Commons – Könisberg was the only Prussian town in which they had any economic and political importance – and to the determined resistance

---

[6] This has been stressed very often, already by C. F. Pauli, *Allgemeine Preussische Staats-Geschichte*, iv, Halle, 1763, p. 430, and Baczko, op. cit., iv, pp. 201–3; more recently especially by Elisabeth Wilke, loc. cit.

of the urban patricians which the lower orders were unable to overcome.

Noticeable too is the clearly political character of the movement which was directed solely against the nobility, as shown by all the preserved speeches and documents. The religious ideas current at the time served the peasant leaders to express their programme in an understandable form. They demanded not just the rescinding of certain dues and services but the extirpation of the noble 'weeds', the destruction of the nests so that the Junkers would not have any offspring: only the duke should rule, and no other master.

Even more important is another fact. The small Prussian Freemen strongly participated in the rising; the share of the German preasants cannot be ascertained, but without any doubt German peasants took part and were among the leaders. But the Samland, the main centre of the movement, was largely inhabited by Prussian peasants. Richau mentions peasant leaders who came to the town hall in riding boots with spurs, wealthy village mayors and innkeepers among the rebels; many among them 'had served at court, expert riders'. Another chronicle speaks of 'the Freemen, innkeepers, and Prussians from all the villages' as participants. The ducal Secretary Gattenhofer reported on 9 September that 'nearly all the notable Freemen of Samland' were involved. Furthermore, Samland had not suffered at all during the devastating war of 1519–21, while the Oberland which had suffered very badly remained quiet.[7] Thus not the Prussian serfs, whose position was undoubtedly the worst, and not the peasants in the badly devastated areas revolted, but above all men who were economically and socially better situated, on whom new burdens were imposed but recently. Better-to-do, proud peasant groups were opposing the rise of the nobility.

This is a further proof that the better situation of the peasantry in the German lands to the east of the Elbe was not the cause that no risings occurred in the east-German principalities other than Prussia, as has so often been alleged.[8] In the year 1525 the quick rise of the nobility and the decline of the peasantry must have been noticeable throughout the east-German territories. Yet urban social movements, which could have been a catalyst for those of the peasants or which could have supported them, were absent in eastern Germany with its weakly developed towns and urban industries, or they were quickly suppressed; and their absence seems to have been decisive.

---

[7] Stolze, op. cit., p. 4; Weise, op. cit., p. 39; G. Franz, *Der deutsche Bauernkrieg*, Munich and Berlin, 1933, p. 460.

[8] For example by F. Engels, 'Zur Geschichte der preussischen Bauern', introduction to W. Wolff, *Die schlesische Milliarde*, in his *Gesammelte Schriften*, p. 65; F. Grossmann, *Über die gutsherrlich-bäuerlichen Rechtsverhältnisse in der Mark Brandenburg vom 16. bis 18. Jahrhundert*, Leipzig, 1890, pp. 17–18; K. Lamprecht, *Deutsche Geschichte*, 3rd edition, Freiburg, 1904, v, p. 515; Franz, op. cit., p. 473.

In December 1525, after the suppression of the revolt, the Diet which had been postponed in August finally assembled, after many reminders by the aldermen of Königsberg. As promised the complaints of the peasants were to be heard, adjudged and decided there. Delegates from some villages were invited and their grievances listened to, 'until the peasants of the von Kreutz and other peasants of the nearby nobility appeared who denounced many serious misdeeds'. Thereupon the noblemen induced the duke, stressing their common interest as landlords, to exclude the urban deputies from the Diet, for if 'the burghers who favour the peasants should sit in judgement over the noblemen, His Princely Grace and the nobility would be deprived of all their men and their rights'. Now the nobility and the duke were among themselves and it was ordained 'that every authority should settle with its subjects, whether they had Culmic law,[9] or were Prussians or Lithuanians, in the most friendly and benevolent way, after everybody's fashion and custom, as their labour services were uneven'. The new agreements in the majority of cases fixed the arbitrary increases of dues and services, as the peasants feared for their lives and could not offer any resistance.

The Prussian ordinances of 1526 reflected the defeat of the peasants, the growing power of the nobility and its close alliance with the duke. Their common interests prevailed, no longer hindered by any opposition: 'If a peasant of whatever condition he may be, or a peasant son moves from any lordship to another, he is not to be received by any lord or Junker without a written proof of his leave' from his former master. The ancient right of the German peasant to leave freely if he provided a successor to take over the holding was no longer mentioned, nor was there any provision under what conditions the permit to leave was to be granted. Apparently it was left to the lord to decide on what terms he would allow the peasant and his sons (this was even more of an innovation) to leave. The ordinances also stipulated that the peasant children had to serve their master before accepting any other service; they had first to report to their lord and to serve him if he paid the due and proper wages. The peasant too required a permit for any work outside the estate. The old right of the peasant to permanent possession of his holding was abrogated in one important case: if he continually neglected it, in spite of warnings by his lord, the latter could allocate it to another peasant; 'continuous neglect' was not defined and nothing was said what would happen to the dispossessed peasant, whether he could leave freely or not. The ordinances more or less treated the Prussian Freemen as hardly any better than the German peasants and they hardly mentioned the Prussian serfs. With the deterioration of the status of the peasants the differences between the various social groups began to disappear. As Richau put it in the final words of his chronicle, 'after-

[9] i.e., the German peasants.

wards the peasants were burdened so much, through a breach of their old and vested rights, by His Princely Grace as well as by the nobility, that they could neither forget nor get over it; and their revolt became for them a heavy burden all their lives.'

5

WAS THERE AN ECONOMIC DECLINE IN GERMANY BEFORE THE THIRTY YEARS' WAR?

It has often been asserted, and indeed it is the predominant opinion among historians, that the economic decline of Germany in the seventeenth century was not in the first instance caused by the Thirty Years' War: that it had begun already in the second half of the sixteenth century and was merely aggravated and accelerated by the war and its consequences.[2] Germany's failure to recover from the war thus appears not so much due to the war damage, but to a long-term decline merely emphasized by the war. In the view of some historians the Thirty Years' War consequently loses its importance as a catastrophe in German history and becomes no more important than the religious wars in France, or the revolt of the Netherlands, which lasted equally long or longer but did not cause a long-lasting economic and social decline.[3] It has even been alleged that the very term Thirty Years' War was not used by contemporaries, but that they distinguished between the Bohemian War, the Danish War, the Swedish War, etc., and did not treat the war as one whole, which was only done later for ulterior reasons.[4]

With regard to the economic decline of Germany in the later sixteenth century, historians have, above all, pointed to the decline of trade and industry and to that of the towns of northern as well as southern Germany. The decline of the northern towns has been attributed to the decline of the Hanseatic League, the rise of national

---

[1] I wish to express my thanks to the Central Research Fund of the University of London which enabled me to go to Munich, in the spring of 1954 and again in the summer of 1955, to work in the Bavarian archives.

[2] Thus R. Hoeniger, 'Der dreissigjährige Krieg und die deutsche Kultur', *Preussische Jahrbücher*, cxxxviii (1909), 443–7; F. Kaphahn, 'Der Zusammenbruch der deutschen Kreditwirtschaft im XVII. Jahrhundert und der Dreissigjährige Krieg', *Deutsche Geschichtsblätter*, xiii (1912), 153; R. Kötzschke, *Grundzüge der deutschen Wirtschaftsgeschichte* (2nd edn., 1921), p. 193; G. Wolf, in B. Gebhardt, *Handbuch der deutschen Geschichte* (7th edn., 1930), i. 733; C. V. Wedgwood, *The Thirty Years War* (1938), pp. 47, 510–11, 519; S. H. Steinberg, 'The Thirty Years' War', *History*, xxxii (1947), 98; O. Brunner, in P. Rassow, *Deutsche Geschichte im Ueberblick* (1953), p. 315.

[3] Thus Hoeniger, *loc. cit.* pp. 447–8; Steinberg, *loc. cit.*, passim.

[4] Steinberg, *loc. cit.* p. 92. In the State Archives, Munich, however, I have found a letter of the Elector Ferdinand Maria to the *Commissarien, Verordneten und Rechenaufnehmer der Landschaft* of 18 March 1659 in which the term 'Thirty Years' War' was used as if it were the usual way of referring to the campaigns which had only come to an end ten years before: 'Unser fürstenthumb der obern Pfaltz (welches gleichwol under vorgewestem dreissig Jerigen Krieg, vom anfang biss zum endt, ohne underlass mit freundt und feindtsvölckhern hart belegt, durch Mordt, Prandt und Raub aufs hechst ruinirt, mit Anlagen, durchzigen, exactionen und andern Kriegs pressurn vasst ganz aussgemörglet und mehr alss andre Landt beschwerdet worden) ...' ('Altbayerische Landschaft', no. 458, fo. 237).

states in northern Europe, the growing competition of the Dutch and English, the separation of the Netherlands from the empire and its consequences.[1] But nobody seems to have emphasized the rise of the landed nobility and their direct trading with foreign merchants, which killed many of the smaller towns, and few historians seem to have realized that the decline of the Hanse and the growing foreign competition were by no means new features of the sixteenth century. The decline of the south German towns has been attributed to the decline of their trade with Italy and the east, to that of the Rhine trade owing to the wars on the lower Rhine and the Dutch revolt but above all to the bankruptcies of the Spanish and French Crowns which seriously affected the south German banking houses and eventually led to their collapse.[2] The wealth of the burghers, it has been said, largely consisted of paper debts and titles which could not be realized, and the towns' indebtedness grew very considerably before 1618.[3] Most of the Free Imperial Cities were small and found it difficult to hold their own against the territorial princes and their measures in favour of their own territorial towns.

On the other hand, the decline of the towns was by no means universal. There were areas, such as Silesia and Lusatia, where urban industries flourished until the outbreak of the war; in some towns, especially in Augsburg and Nuremberg, taxable property increased in spite of many bankruptcies.[4] Frankfurt and Hamburg showed 'signs of stable and progressive prosperity'.[5] As Germany was not an economic whole, much more differentiation between the various areas and towns would seem essential. Even if it could be established that the majority of the German towns declined already before 1618, this would not necessarily entail a general decline, for economic activity might have shifted from the towns to the countryside. Indeed this was the case in north-eastern Germany where the sixteenth century was a period of peace and prosperity, of growing corn exports and quickly rising corn prices.[6] In the Black

[1] K. Lamprecht, *Deutsche Geschichte* (3rd edn., v, 1904), pp. 496–500; G. von Below, 'Die Frage des Rückgangs der wirtschaftlichen Verhältnisse Deutschlands vor dem Dreissigjährigen Krieg', *Vierteljahrschrift für Social- und Wirtschaftsgeschichte*, vii (1909), 164; Kötzschke, *op. cit.* p. 192; Wedgwood, *op. cit.* p. 47; Steinberg, *loc. cit.* p. 97.

[2] E. Gothein, 'Die oberrheinischen Lande vor und nach dem dreissigjährigen Kriege', *Zeitschrift für die Geschichte des Oberrheins*, xl (1886), 16–17; Lamprecht, *op. cit.* v. 492–4; von Below, *loc. cit.* pp. 164–5; Hoeniger, *loc. cit.* pp. 442–4; Kaphahn, *loc. cit.* p. 150; Kötzschke, *op. cit.* p. 192; Wedgwood, *op. cit.* p. 47; Steinberg, *loc. cit.* p. 97; R. Ehrenberg, *Das Zeitalter der Fugger* (1896), ii. 242.

[3] Hoeniger, *loc. cit.* pp. 444–5; Kaphahn, *loc. cit.* p. 153; Kötzschke, *op. cit.* p. 193.

[4] These points have been emphasized by Th. Mayer, 'Die deutsche Volkswirtschaft vor dem Dreissigjährigen Kriege', *Mitteilungen des Oesterreichischen Instituts für Geschichtsforschung*, xli (1926), 218–19; see also the literature quoted by him.

[5] Wedgwood, *op. cit.* p. 47, maintaining that these two were the only German towns showing such signs.

[6] See F. L. Carsten, *The Origins of Prussia* (1954), pp. 149, 163, 167–8.

Forest area the position of the peasants somewhat improved and cattle farming flourished before the outbreak of the war.[1] Moreover, there is little reliable evidence of the alleged general decline, and some historians have largely relied on the reports and complaints of contemporaries.

In Bavaria, for example, the Estates specifically and repeatedly pointed to the economic decline of the country, usually as a countermove to new tax demands by the dukes. Thus in January 1568 they stated that towns and markets were getting impoverished and losing their inhabitants and trades to neighbouring Imperial Cities because so many Protestants were expelled from the duchy.[2] In April 1570 they again complained that trade and industry were declining, that many burghers were emigrating, and that many noblemen had to sell their estates and castles for little money.[3] In December 1579 they declared that Estates and subjects were suffering badly on account of the rising prices, that all trades were languishing, that all taxes were yielding less than they had done, that the duty on drink, although recently doubled, was hardly producing more than before the increase.[4] Four years later the Estates complained that all trade and industry were moving abroad; and early in 1584 the nobility lamented that all money was drawn out of the duchy.[5] In January 1588 the Estates repeated that nearly all trades and industries in towns and markets were declining, so that nobody was willing to advance any money.[6] In November 1593 they again stated that all trades in towns and markets had deteriorated to such an extent that the common burghers, in spite of all their efforts, were hardly able to subsist.[7] In November 1583 the ducal councillors themselves declared that the trades and industries of Germany were badly affected by the high prices and even more so by the long-drawn-out wars and sufferings in the Low Countries and in France, so that tolls and customs brought in barely half of what they had yielded in their ancestors' time; in the following month they repeated that the decline was due to the endless wars in the countries which were the main fount of all trade, and that it was a general feature throughout Germany.[8] Although these complaints may have been more or less justified, it has to be borne in

---

[1] E. Gothein, *Deutschland vor dem Dreissigjährigen Krieg, Pforzheimer Volksschriften*, ed. K. Brunner, no. 2 (1908), pp. 9–10. Miss Wedgwood, *op. cit.* p. 47, on the other hand, asserts that 'the decline of agriculture was even graver than that of the cities'.
[2] *Der Landtag im Herzogthum Baiern gehalten zu München im Jahre 1568* (1807), p. 56.
[3] State Archives, Munich, 'Altbayerische Landschaft', no. 385; no. 443b, fo. 26.
[4] *Ibid.* nos. 390 and 391; no. 445, fo. 36.
[5] *Ibid.* no. 393; no. 394, pp. 56–7, 444; no. 395, fos. 37, 303; no. 446, fos. 31, 187.
[6] *Ibid.* no. 396, fo. 39; nos. 397–8; no. 399, fo. 35; no. 447, fo. 43; no. 447a.
[7] *Ibid.* no. 400, fos. 23–4; no. 401, fo. 20; nos. 402–5; no. 406, p. 34; no. 448, fo. 17; no. 448a.
[8] *Ibid.* no. 393; no. 394, pp. 16, 90–1; no. 395, fos. 9–10, 59–60; no. 446, fos. 9–10, 46–7.

mind that they were also moves in a game of chess and cannot be taken at their face value.

As more reliable evidence hardly seems to exist, it seems important that I have been able to find in the Bavarian archives complete returns of the duties levied by the Estates on alcoholic drinks in Upper Bavaria from 1576 to 1602, with some scattered years before (1543–5, 1548–9) and after (1606–8) these dates. Unfortunately, it has not been possible to find similar data for Lower Bavaria, the northern part of the duchy towards the Danube. Careful search in several archives has only produced figures for five scattered years (1543–4, 1544–5, 1548–9, 1577, and 1606), but in each instance these show that the figures for Lower Bavaria were only a fraction—usually about one-quarter—of those for Upper Bavaria. Thus the figures which have been preserved are those of the more important part of the duchy, including Munich, the capital. To the best of my knowledge there is no similar set of figures for any other part of sixteenth-century Germany: few German principalities levied duties on consumption, and taxes on property and houses were much more common.

Duties levied on alcoholic drinks would indicate clearly whether the prosperity of the country was growing or declining: in the latter case the consumption, and thus the yield of the duties, would have shrunk, especially as prices were rising. Unfortunately, the figures are difficult to interpret because the duties were increased several times during this period. For example, on imported wine 1*s*. was levied from each *Eimer* (containing 60 *Mass*) from 1543, when the duty was first introduced. This was increased to 2*s*. in 1565, to 4*s*. in 1572, and to 5*s*. in 1606; while the duty levied on Bavarian wine was at first 10 pfennigs, from 1565 20 pfennigs, and from 1594 30 pfennigs or 1*s*. Imported and exported beer was taxed from 1543, other beer only from 1572 at the rate of 1*s*. per *Eimer*; but beer brewed by members of the Estates remained free until 1577 when it became liable to the same levy. From 1595 the duty levied on beer brewed by non-members of the Estates was doubled, while that brewed by members of the Estates remained the same as before.[1]

The tax returns unfortunately do not distinguish between these different varieties of wine and beer, but only contain four categories: tolls levied at thirteen frontier posts on imported wine and mead and exported wine and beer; duties levied at the four wine markets

---

[1] There is a table giving these changes in the State Archives, Munich, 'Altbayerische Landschaft', no. 1993. But it contains some errors, for example, Bavarian wine was not only taxed after 1577 at 4 *Mass* per *Eimer*, but 10 pfennigs was levied from each *Eimer* since 1543 (*Der Landtag im Herzogthum Baiern auf den ersten November zu Ingolstadt im Jahre 1542* (1807), p. 97; State Archives, Landshut, Rep. 16, Fasz. 5, Fasz. 8, no. 84, Fasz. 15, nos. 199–200). This duty was doubled in 1565: State Archives, Munich, 'Altbayerische Landschaft', no. 380; no. 381, fo. 51; no. 443, fo. 47.

of Munich, Ingolstadt, Landsberg, and Aichach; duties levied from 1572 on beer, spirits and mead in the districts of Munich, Ingolstadt, and Burghausen; and lastly the new four-*Mass* duty (i.e. 1/15 from each *Eimer*) levied on all drinks in town and country since 1577, which was increased to 6 *Mass* in 1606. I have therefore given the absolute figures of the tax returns in Table I, arranged in these four

TABLE I[1]

UPPER BAVARIA

Year	Frontier toll mainly on imported wine			Levy at 4 urban wine markets			Levy on beer, spirits and mead in the country			Levy of 4 Mass in 60(6 Mass from 1606) on all drink			Total		
	fl.	*s.*	*pf.*	*fl.*	*s.*	*pf.*	*fl.*	*s.*	*pf.*	*fl.*	*s.*	*pf.*	*fl.*	*s.*	*pf.*
1543-4	27,518	2	24												
1544-5	27,002	3	8												
1548-9	39,641	4	5½												
1576				22,488	5	12	4,536	3	13						
1577	92,564	6	16½	21,533	0	12	5,365	2	8						
1578	96,902	2	28	19,803	3	21	6,557	5	0	35,422	4	22	158,686	2	11
1579	95,847	5	4½	21,187	0	22	7,537	1	7	43,803	5	9½	168,375	5	13
1580	77,427	4	24	17,520	2	1	8,207	5	9½	37,862	4	26½	141,018	3	1
1581	87,253	2	4	19,685	2	3	5,730	6	25½	39,197	6	18	151,867	3	20½
1582	116,786	4	7½	21,616	5	15	7,318	3	27½	41,171	5	23	186,893	5	13
1583	96,461	4	24	23,042	3	14	6,740	3	3½	41,668	3	3½	167,913	0	15
1584	114,360	2	25½	24,977	5	2	6,646	6	6½	43,909	1	25½	189,894	1	29½
1585	127,005	4	9	25,758	3	15	6,517	3	10	43,829	6	21	203,111	3	25
1586	109,569	6	15	22,907	5	24	6,303	2	10	44,966	5	27½	183,747	6	16½
1587	118,978	3	19½	22,437	1	3	5,729	1	15½	46,703	2	5½	193,848	1	13½
1588	89,506	5	9	20,875	3	17½	6,288	2	23	41,828	2	25	158,499	0	14½
1589	73,503	6	7	16,265	5	5	8,874	4	13½	36,900	5	24½	135,545	0	20
1590	67,566	1	7	14,369	0	0	8,916	5	13	38,828	2	22	129,680	2	12
1591	82,778	0	9	15,468	4	6	7,656	2	11	41,138	4	3	147,041	3	29
1592	70,289	4	25½	16,470	4	3½	5,999	5	0	45,453	5	9	138,213	5	8
1593	64,488	5	8½	17,770	2	17½	11,287	6	14	50,582	5	16	144,129	5	26
1594	66,738	6	3	19,447	6	16	9,996	6	19½	39,162	6	12	135,346	4	20½
1595	74,615	6	29	23,407	0	12½	16,983	0	13½	39,314	2	16	154,320	3	11
1596	78,768	3	2½	24,180	2	1.6	21,271	0	25½	42,151	5	28	166,371	5	12
1597	85,778	5	6½	26,272	5	20	22,050	4	13½	41,347	5	16½	175,449	6	26½
1598	76,899	1	5	21,473	1	6	20,063	0	16	43,484	1	5	161,919	4	2
1599	104,853	3	21½	13,590	1	4	19,245	6	17	45,435	4	16	183,125	1	28½
1600	119,345	4	25	12,413	4	1	18,205	3	17	47,341	5	23½	197,306	4	6½
1601	80,413	4	25½	10,912	2	14	19,315	6	5	52,263	4	12	162,905	3	26½
1602	92,281	0	7	14,951	4	7	19,505	6	29	48,093	2	22	174,832	0	5
1606	140,472	1	19	36,549	0	26½	38,609	2	29	90,556	2	20	306,187	1	4½
1608	143,852	6	7	34,011	5	0	33,591	5	28½	89,485	5	4½	300,942	1	10

[1] Table I gives the absolute figures of the tax returns for Upper Bavaria. In Bavaria the guilder was divided into 7s., and the shilling into thirty pfennigs. State Archives, Munich, 'Staatsverwaltung', no. 1788, and State Archives, Landshut, Rep. 16, Fasz. 8, no. 84, contain the figures for 1543-5; State Archives, Landshut, Rep. 16, Fasz. 8, no. 84, also those for 1548-9; State Archives, Munich, 'Altbayerische Landschaft', no. 1548, contains the figures from 1576 to 1582; *ibid.* no. 1973 those from 1582 to 1585; *ibid.* no. 1549 those from 1584 to 1588; *ibid.* no. 1550 those from 1584 to 1590; *ibid.* no. 1552 those from 1588 to 1598; *ibid.* no. 1554 those from 1589 to 1593; *ibid.* no. 1555 those from 1591 to 1592; *ibid.* no. 1558 those from 1594 to 1597; *ibid.* no. 1561 those from 1598 to 1601; *ibid.* no. 1563 those from 1599 to 1602; *ibid.* no. 1566 those from 1606 to 1608. Unfortunately, the first five pages are missing in no. 1548 so that the figures for the year 1576 are incomplete. The figures I have quoted are those of the receipts before the deduction of expenditure, and the additions throughout are mine.

categories (the additions are in each case mine). In Table II I have tried to take account of the changes in the rates of taxation by reducing all figures to the level of the years 1572 to 1594, by quadrupling those for the years 1543–9, and by deducting what I consider adequate percentages in those columns where increases were effected after 1594. But it is impossible to estimate accurately what proportion of beer was brewed by members of the Estates and what by non-members: in this instance I have deducted after 1594 one-third from the figures given in Table I, which I consider more than adequate (see column 3); but there naturally remains an element of uncertainty.

TABLE II[1]

Year	Frontier toll mainly on imported wine	Levy at 4 urban wine markets	Levy on beer, spirits, mead in the country	Levy of 4 Mass in 60 (6 Mass from 1606) on all drink	Total
	fl.	fl.	fl.	fl.	fl.
1543–4	110,074				
1544–5	108,010				
1548–9	158,566				
1576		22,489	4,536		
1577	92,565	21,533	5,365		
1578	96,902	19,804	6,558	35,423	158,687
1579	95,848	21,187	7,537	43,804	168,376
1580	77,428	17,520	8,208	37,863	141,019
1581	87,253	19,685	5,731	39,198	151,867
1582	116,787	21,617	7,319	41,172	186,895
1583	96,462	23,042	6,740	41,668	167,912
1584	114,360	24,978	6,647	43,909	189,894
1585	127,006	25,759	6,517	43,830	203,112
1586	109,570	22,908	6,303	44,967	183,748
1587	118,979	22,437	5,729	46,703	193,848
1588	89,507	20,876	6,288	41,828	158,499
1589	73,504	16,266	8,875	36,901	135,546
1590	67,566	14,369	8,917	38,828	129,680
1591	82,778	15,469	7,656	41,139	147,042
1592	70,290	16,471	6,000	45,454	138,215
1593	64,489	17,770	11,288	50,583	144,130
1594	66,739	19,448	9,997	39,163	135,347
1595	74,616	15,605	11,322	39,314	140,857
1596	78,768	16,120	14,181	42,152	151,221
1597	85,779	17,515	14,700	41,348	159,342
1598	76,899	14,315	13,375	43,484	148,073
1599	104,854	9,060	12,830	45,436	172,180
1600	119,346	8,276	12,137	47,342	187,101
1601	80,414	7,275	12,877	52,264	152,830
1602	92,281	9,967	13,004	48,093	163,345
1606	112,378	24,366	20,592	60,371	217,707
1608	115,082	22,675	17,916	59,657	215,330

[1] Table II gives the same figures as Table I adjusted to the level of taxation in force between 1576 and 1594. The figures for the years 1543–9 are quadrupled to account for the higher frontier toll after 1572. The figures for the years 1595–1602 are the same in columns 1 and 4 where no increase took place; those in columns 2 and 3 are reduced by one-third to allow for the higher rate of taxation. In addition to that the figures for the years 1606 and 1608 are reduced by one-fifth in columns 1 and 3 and by one-third in column 4 to allow for the new increases which came into force in 1606. The figures are in guilders only.

Even after these deductions there remains the surprising fact that the figures do not show any decline of wine and beer consumption; this was particularly high about 1585; then it fell, but rose again after 1595; in 1600 it reached almost the previous record figure, and in 1606 and 1608 it was considerably higher than ever before. No figures seem to have been preserved for the years after

1608. Only for Lower Bavaria are there returns for the war years, from 1621–2 to 1648–9, and these show a steady decline after 1630–1 when the war reached Bavaria, although this was less marked than might have been expected (see Table III). In Upper

TABLE III[1]

LOWER BAVARIA

Year	*Frontier toll, mainly on imported wine*			*Levy on beer, spirits, mead in the country*			*Wine Market of Landshut*			*New levy in Landshut (from 1620)*			*Total*		
	fl.	*s.*	*pf.*	*fl.*	*s.*	*pf.*	*fl.*	*s.*	*pf.*	*fl.*	*s.*	*pf.*	*fl.*	*s.*	*pf.*
1543–4	7,611	3	4½												
1544–5	7,505	2	9½												
1548–9	9,648	4	14												
1577	18,175	5	26½	12,611	0	17	4,290	0	0				35,076	6	13½
1588							3,145	2	18						
1589							2,567	6	0						
1590							2,957	5	21						
1591							2,939	5	18						
1592							2,755	4	12						
1593							2,834	4	0						
1594							3,736	1	12						
1606	6,713	0	1½	40,743	2	3	3,315	0	15				50,771	2	19½
1621–2	3,164	1	25½	63,753	4	5	9,522	4	6½	4,094	4	27	80,535	1	4
1622–3	4,710	4	18	32,634	5	7	3,847	3	23½	4,435	3	22½	45,628	2	11
1623–4	15,929	5	20	64,612	2	18	9,118	4	15	3,000	2	20½	92,661	1	13½
1624–5	15,693	0	23	63,355	3	4½	8,270	1	26	1,849	4	27	89,168	3	20½
1625–6	20,763	5	12	65,665	0	29	8,194	2	29½	1,953	6	0	96,577	1	10½
1626–7	10,077	6	5	44,108	1	10½	7,402	2	6½	1,557	0	28	63,145	3	20
1627–8	11,081	5	7	67,169	0	29½	6,523	1	12	637	6	2	85,411	6	20½
1628–9	8,878	6	17	50,375	2	25	6,365	6	2	567	1	22½	66,187	3	6½
1629–30	12,683	4	15½	56,562	1	4½	6,339	1	1½	1,050	1	20	76,635	1	11½
1630–1	19,958	4	29	64,815	3	24	7,547	4	11½	2,207	3	8	94,529	2	12½
1631–2	15,429	6	1	26,325	0	0	2,828	6	26½	1,074	2	3	45,658	1	0½
1632–3	24,515	5	20½	49,128	2	11	2,542	0	21	371	4	6	76,557	5	28½
1633–4	13,532	2	10	9,613	6	7½	4,444	4	1½	250	0	0	27,840	5	19
1634–5	10,319	2	2½	38,479	1	17	6,663	2	24	432	3	20	53,894	3	3½
1635–6	8,526	2	26	50,385	6	20½	6,535	6	7½	980	4	20	66,428	6	14
1636–7	11,920	3	9½	51,172	4	13½	6,564	5	26½	877	5	11	70,535	5	0½
1637–8	12,286	4	17	51,818	2	26½	6,394	0	16	872	5	11	71,371	6	10½
1638–9	12,179	6	27½	54,858	6	20½	7,657	5	18½	1,264	1	26	75,961	0	2½
1639–40	12,642	6	17½	54,277	1	19	7,890	5	28½	1,791	1	26	76,602	2	1
1640–1	14,617	3	23	45,217	1	23½	7,383	6	12	1,623	5	11	68,842	3	9½
1641–2	7,462	4	13	54,326	0	11½	9,008	3	25	1,350	5	4	72,147	6	23½
1642–3	7,981	3	18½	46,119	5	26	8,448	5	25	1,419	0	26	63,969	2	5½
1643–4	8,411	2	3	51,349	5	25	9,171	6	7	1,621	0	3½	70,554	0	8½
1644–5	10,225	2	16	49,886	3	17	8,653	4	8	1,165	1	26	69,930	5	7
1645–6	5,345	2	3½	49,039	3	18½	8,635	3	23	1,306	1	19	64,326	4	4
1646–7	3,292	6	29	42,161	3	5½	9,835	1	26½	788	5	26	56,078	3	27
1647–8	5,549	0	19½	24,320	1	28½	6,296	4	8	1,343	1	0	37,509	0	26
1648–9	5,594	0	8½	24,797	5	7	3,030	1	7	250	6	19	33,672	6	11½

[1] Table III gives the absolute figures of the returns for Lower Bavaria. State Archives, Landshut, Rep. 16, Fasz. 8, no. 84, contains the figures for the years 1543–5 and 1548–9; the former are also to be found in State Archives, Munich, 'Staatsverwaltung', no. 1788; the figures for 1577 are in State Archives, Landshut, Rep. 16, Fasz. 8, no. 84; those for 1588 to 1594 in *ibid.* Rep. 16, Fasz. 6; those for 1606 in *ibid.* Rep. 16, Fasz. 19, no. 224; those for the years 1621 to 1649 in *ibid.* Rep. 16, Fasz. 21, no. 226. These seem to be the only figures available for Lower Bavaria, partly because many accounts were pulped in the later nineteenth century as of no historical interest. The rate of taxation remained the same between 1620 and 1649.

Bavaria, which was the heart of the duchy and had important commercial connexions with Austria, the Tyrol, and Italy, the period before 1608 seems to have been a time of slowly growing prosperity. This does not justify the assertion that the same was the case elsewhere in Germany; but neither does the opposite assertion seem justified unless it is based on more detailed investigation and research.

6

THE STATES GENERAL AND THE ESTATES OF CLEVES ABOUT THE MIDDLE OF THE SEVENTEENTH CENTURY

The towns of the duchy of Cleves on the lower Rhine, especially Wesel, Emmerich and Rees on the right bank, of old maintained close commercial relations with the neighbouring Netherlands. They acted as middlemen for the important transit trade from Germany into the Netherlands and for Netherlands exports into the Rhenish and Westphalian lands. As the Netherlands and Cleves also had close political and cultural ties, the States General got quickly involved in the succession war which began after the dying out of the ducal house of Jülich and Cleves in the year 1609. In 1610 they were asked for support by the Elector of Brandenburg and the Count Palatine of Neuburg against the Emperor Rudolf II, and in 1614 by Brandenburg against Palatinate-Neuburg and Spain.[1] Dutch troops occupied Emmerich, Rees and other towns in Cleves and the States General guaranteed the Treaty of Xanten, by which the territories of Jülich, Cleves, Berg, Mark and Ravensberg were provisionally divided between Brandenburg and Palatinate-Neuburg, Cleves and Mark were allocated to Brandenburg, and the old privileges of the Estates of the divided territories were confirmed and extended.[2]

Through the garrisons of the Dutch in Wesel (taken by them from the Spaniards in 1629), Rees, Emmerich, Gennep and Orsoy large sums of money were brought into the country and the commercial relations with the Netherlands became considerably closer. When traffic on the Meuse was paralyzed by the Thirty Years War the towns of Cleves became the principal entrepots for Dutch exports into the neighbouring Spanish Netherlands.[3] It was therefore quite natural that the Estates of Cleves, and in particular the towns, should look to the States General and their garrisons as their protectors in the conflicts with the young Elector Frederick William of Brandenburg; many members of the

---

[1] 'Kort Begrip Waerom Haer Ho. Mo. recht hebben de Cleefsche Steden beset te houden', pamphlet in the Koninklijke Bibliotheek in The Hague; L. van Aitzema, *Saken van Staet en Oorlogh in, ende omtrent de Vereenigde Nederlanden*, iii, The Hague, 1669, pp. 182–4.

[2] The Treaty of Xanten and the declaration of guarantee by the States General are printed by Aitzema, op. cit., i, The Hague, 1657, pp. 106–8.

[3] A. von Haeften, *Urkunden und Actenstücke zur Geschichte des Kurfürsten Friedrich Wilhelm von Brandenburg*, v, Berlin, 1869, p. 94 (quoted as U & A v).

Estates would have preferred to join the Dutch altogether,[4] rather than belonging to the distant House of Brandenburg, the possessions of which stretched all over northern Germany.

These conflicts usually concerned the taxes requested by the Elector for the maintenance of the Brandenburg forces and the recruitment of new troops he considered necessary for his ambitious foreign policy plans. But the duchy of Cleves had suffered badly from the devastation of the Thirty Years War and the depradations of the for ever changing armies of occupation;[5] and the arrival of more peaceful times, so the people hoped, would bring them an alleviation of their burdens. They were the more disappointed when 'in the year 1644 there started the recruiting of foot soldiers in the principality of Cleves . . . and in March 1645, instead of marching them away, another five cavalry companies recruited in the Brandenburg Mark and in Prussia were quartered in the small towns of Calcar, Duisburg, Dinslaken and Sevenaer'. These armaments for a new war against Palatinate-Neuburg took place without the consent of the Estates and were bound to arouse their opposition because they 'were free and exempt from all contributions and taxes . . . on the strength of their privileges . . . unless they had freely consented to them at an ordinary Diet'; they also claimed the privilege 'that their prince was not entitled to recruit or engage any soldiery for the country's defence . . . without the prior consent of the Estates'. But in spite of their repeated complaints the Elector refused to discharge the troops and declared that 'if the Estates did not furnish the means for their maintenance, he must permit the occurence of disorder and military executions', meaning the forcible levying of the taxes by the soldiery. Thereupon the Estates complained several times to the States General,[6] until these requested Frederick William in 1646 'to remove and do away with the troops recruited in the land of Cleves or brought there from outside . . .'[7]

When this request went unheard the States General in October 1646 ordered the commandants of their garrisons in Cleves 'until further order not to permit any military execution to take place . . . within the range of the cannon of the town (or place) entrusted to them and even less to condone any such attempt'. The Dutch commandants of Wesel,

[4] That plans were being hatched in the Netherlands to annex Cleves Frederick William told his ambassador in Münster on 25 September 1647: B. Erdmannsdörfer (ed.), *Urkunden und Actenstücke . . .*, iv, Berlin, 1867, p. 71.

[5] The sums levied by the Dutch troops in Cleves in the years 1616–41 were reckoned to amount to 1,403, 703 thalers by the Cleves official L. Blaspeil, not counting the 150,000 thalers forcibly levied by the soldiers of Count Wilhelm von Nassau: U & A v, p. 137.

[6] For these see Aitzema, op. cit., iii, pp. 106, 143–4.

[7] All quotations from the letter of the States General to the Elector, of 12 September 1646, printed in 'Refutatie In name ende van wegen de Land-Stenden uyt Ridderschap ende Steden des Hertogdoms Cleve . . .', The Hague, 1647, pp. 10–13, copy in the Koninklijke Bibliotheek in the Hague.

Emmerich and Rees were informed that 'the Estates of the nobility and towns of the principality of Cleves had repeatedly complained on account of the military exactions, . . . therefore we have not been able to abstain from writing to Your Honour that you should stop and prevent these executions by all suitable means'.[8] Already in August the Dutch officer in charge at Wesel, Martin von Juchen, had resisted the tax executions of Brandenburg officers near Wesel, demanded from the Brandenburg officer commanding at Calcar the return of impounded cattle under threat of using force, and ordered his soldiers to put up posters which in the name of the Estates of Cleves urged the inhabitants to refuse the payment of taxes which had not been granted by them.[9]

These measures achieved that in the wealthier parts of Cleves the forcible levying of taxes by the military became impossible. They irritated the Elector so much that he asked the assembled States General through his councillor von der Borch to rescind the orders to their commandants and argued that the reports sent by the Estates were untrue, emanated from a minority which was disloyal to the House of Brandenburg and consisted of partisans of the Count Palatine of Neuburg.[10] In their reply the Estates were able to declare that their grievances were raised 'not by a minority . . . but in truth by all the Estates of nobility and towns . . . which have been forced by necessity to preserve their liberty'; they added that the submission of the Elector that the recruitment 'was not at all meant to diminish their privileges is . . . frivolous, impertinent and puerile'.[11] Early in 1647 the Estates of Jülich, Cleves, Berg, Mark and Ravensberg renewed their 'hereditary union' going back to the year 1496, to support each other with advice and help and to resist jointly any attempt to infringe their privileges and liberties, whether it came from their prince or any other person.[12]

Through their garrisons on the right bank of the Rhine the States General were able to prevent the forcible levying of taxes; but as they had only a few garrisons on the left bank, the military executions continued there unabated. A few months later the Estates again complained to the States General about the grinding down of the exhausted country by recruiting, forcible levying of taxes and military executions.[13] In May 1647 the representative of the Estates in The Hague, Lieuwe van Aitzema, submitted to the States General a detailed complaint about the misdeeds of the electoral forces which had

[8] On 4 and 20 October 1646: U & A v, pp. 299, 303.
[9] On 26, 28 and 30 August 1646: *ibid.*, p. 287.
[10] 'Refutatie In name ende van wegen de Land-Stenden . . .', p. 3.
[11] The Estates to the States General, 9 January 1647: *ibid.*, pp. 5, 7.
[12] 'Erf-Vereeninge der Landt Stenden uyt Ridderschap ende Steden der Hertogdommen Gulick, Cleve, Berge, ende der Graefschappen Marck ende Ravensperg', 15 February 1647. Printed copy in the Koninklijke Bibliotheek, as the other pamphlets quoted.
[13] On 2 April 1647: U & A v, p. 332.

allegedly started a great fire in the town of Calcar: 'On 30 April some horsemen of Captain von Kleist billeted in the town said to each other: what a pity that this town should be burnt down. Thereafter on the first of this month of May . . . a fast terrible fire started in the town of Calcar simultaneously at three different places and in barns which had no hearths; so that on account of the strong wind blowing it was impossible to quench the fire which within an hour consumed more than three hundred houses and barns . . . The rumour has spread throughout the country that this fire was caused by the soldiers. Only a few days ago it happened in the town of Cleves that some soldiers . . . remarked that one should do the same as they had done in Calcar; the horsemen billeted in the town of Sevenaer expressly informed some burghers they would suffer the same fate as Calcar . . .' Other horsemen had plundered peasant farms and wounded many without suffering any punishment. At the end the Estates once more begged the States General to see to it that the Brandenburg forces were removed and the people 'were restored to their free status and old liberties from the state of suppression and intolerable slavery'.[14]

This pamphlet the Elector answered by the publication of a counter-pamphlet in which an anonymous 'Cleves Patriot' expressed his regrets about the ever growing conflict between Frederick William and the Estates, which allegedly emanated only from 'a few oppositional and restless heads which . . . are seeking their own advantage under the cover of maintaining their privileges and liberties and . . . want to fish in troubled waters, to the detriment of the Elector and the whole country'. In opposition to the parliamentarian leanings of the Estates the pamphlet declared that 'the glory of a loyal subject consists in obedience rather than in examining and interpreting the intentions of its master'. And, to deter the States General from taking the side of the Estates, these were pictured as revolutionaries: 'A short while ago some of the principle troublemakers have remarked . . . that they would do to His Electoral Highness what the English Parliament had done to their king . . . And in a public lodging house in The Hague . . . some members of the Cleves Estates have been given the title of Parliamentarians without any contradiction . . .'[15] In reply the Estates published another pamphlet which sharply repudiated the various accusations, especially that their complaints only came from a few, and not from the whole corpus of the Estates.[16] In fact, Frederick William during these years was unable to impose his will on the Estates: in the

[14] 'Aen Hare Hoogh Mogh. de Heeren Staten Generael Der Vereenighde Nederlanden', 20 May 1647.

[15] 'Cleefsche Patriot. Verthoonende de intentie van de Missive, gesonden aen hare Ho. Mogende Heeren Staten Generael der Vereenighde Nederlanden, van wegens de Cleefsche Landtstenden', Wesel, 1647, pp. 3, 7, 23.

[16] 'Ontdeckinge van den valschen Cleefschen Patriot, Of Korte weder-legginghe van seker fameus Geschrift . . .', The Hague, 1647.

Recess of 1649 they succeeded in preserving their old rights and privileges and even in gaining some new ones, not least because of the support they received from the States General.

A few years later, however, the attitude of the States General towards the Estates of Cleves changed. The conflict between them and the Elector was renewed in the course of a new clash between Brandenburg and Palatinate-Neuburg in 1651. The Estates again complained to the States General and to the Emperor Ferdinand III, and in November 1652 they decided to send a deputation to Ratisbon to submit their grievances to the Emperor.[17] When the deputies returned from Ratisbon in 1654 Frederick William ordered Colonel Jacob von Spaen to arrest them. Not even the governor of Cleves, Prince Johann Moritz von Nassau, was informed of this plan because he was favouring a compromise with the Estates. As Spaen did not possess the military means to carry out the order, he asked the Dutch commandant of Rheinberg, Count Georg Friedrich von Nassau, to give him twenty horsemen for the transport of valuable jewels and documents; and one of the deputies sent to Ratisbon, von Wilich, was arrested with the help of the Dutch soldiers.[18] But the States General ony expressed their 'serious misgivings' to Frederick William about this illegal procedure.[19]

In 1655 the town of Wesel complained several times to the States General about the forcible levying of taxes and military exactions which had been threatened, and asked to be maintained in its old rights and privileges; orders to that effect should be given to the Dutch commandant of Wesel. Soon after the latter reported that the threatened executions were being carried out and that the mayor of Wesel had asked him for protection, but he replied he could not protect them against their master without an express order from the States General.[20] These in their turn informed the Brandenburg Minister after the receipt of the letters from Wesel that they 'would not resolve anything before they had heard him and were informed of the rights and wrongs of the affair'.[21] Since 1646 their whole attitude had changed. In The Hague Aitzema in vain tried to reinforce the complaints of Wesel by numerous petitions and representations to the States General; but he had to note resignedly that 'previously the States used to protect the Estates in their privileges, according to the act of guarantee of the Treaty of Xanten, but now on the contrary the States are supporting the Elector and themselves are helping to suppress the Estates', and that 'the times have completely changed'.[22]

[17] U & A v, pp. 544–5, 552, 622–5.
[18] *Ibid.*, pp. 733–4, 745.
[19] *Ibid.*, p. 745.
[20] *Ibid.*, pp. 807–8, 811 (June 1655).
[21] U & A iv, p. 138.
[22] U & A v, pp. 808, 810, 813 (with quotation from Aitzema's journal); Aitzema, *Saeken van Staet en Oorlogh*, iii, p. 1204.

The Estates of Cleves and Mark also addressed the States General on behalf of Wesel and with their own grievances: within six to seven months large scale recruiting and billeting of troops had taken place in the country; more than 300,000 thalers had been levied so that they were totally exhausted; now new demands were raised and more troops quartered without their consent; the States General should see to it 'that we are maintained in our privileges gained by so many sacrifices . . . and are not aggravated with impositions, recruiting and invasions of the military without our consent, even less oppressed by military executions as has happened recently, and the two principalities brought to total ruin'.[23] Even the governor, Prince Johann Moritz, thought that the country was burdened too heavily and wrote to the Brandenburg Minister in The Hague he should remember 'that within eight months the two principalities have raised 300,000 thalers, not counting the damages caused by the soldiers', and the Elector should be informed of the conditions.[24]

After the outbreak of the Northern War (1655–60) the Estates of Cleves tried to induce the States General to supply 'Sauvegards' to prevent the quartering of foreign troops, for it was 'vital to maintain our neutrality and to protect us in it'. To achieve this the Estates sent a deputation to The Hague which several times approached the States General and described to them 'the sorry state of the country'. On 10 October 1656 the States General acceded to the petition but only in so far as ordering their commandants in Cleves to protect the country against all billeting of foreign forces as far as the cannon of their garrisons would reach.[25] That was all the deputation was able to achieve. In spite of calls for help by the Estates of Cleves to the States General and the States of Holland and Friesland against 'the arbitrary severe contributions not granted by them', as they had supported them in the years 1646 and 1647, and in spite of the intervention of the States of Holland and Friesland, the States General could not be moved to any action on behalf of those of Cleves. Equally unsuccessful was a memorandum of the town of Wesel handed over by Aitzema, which asked for protection not only against foreign troops, but also against those of Brandenburg, and yet another plea by the town for help against the forcible levying of taxes and the deeds of violence committed by the electoral forces.[26] Triumphantly the Brandenburg Minister in The Hague, Weiman, wrote: 'In the affairs of Cleves nothing is being done here any longer however much those of Wesel have pressed for it.'[27]

[23] U & A v, pp. 817–18 (19 August 1655).
[24] Letter of 25 August 1655 to Weiman in The Hague: *ibid.*, p. 820.
[25] *Ibid.*, pp. 858–9, 863–4, 867–8 (September–October 1656).
[26] *Ibid.*, pp. 865, 871, 874–5 (October–December 1656).
[27] Letter to von Schwerin, 19 December 1656: *ibid.*, p. 874.

The change of attitude in The Hague had several causes, political as well as economic. In 1655 – at the beginning of the Northern War – the Netherlands were on the verge of concluding an alliance with Frederick William about which the Brandenburg envoys had negotiated for a considerable time.[28] The closer the relations between the two states became the less the States General were interested in protecting the Estates of Cleves. In his turn Aitzema tried time and again to include a guarantee of the Estates' privileges in the alliance or to prevent its conclusion altogether. As he noted, the Estates of Cleves had submitted 'a sharp memorandum which at least would show how little they are satisfied with the electoral government, and to influence those of Holland against the alliance and to alienate them from it . . .' The States of Holland were opposed to the Brandenburg alliance because they rightly feared that then the Dutch garrisons would have to be withdrawn from Cleves, to the detriment of their trade, hence they made all kinds of difficulties.[29]

Apart from this, the anti-Orangist party which dominated the States of Holland feared that Frederick William – who through his marriage with Louisa Henrietta of Orange as well as personal and political links was closely allied with the House of Orange – was pursuing aims in internal Dutch politics with his proposal of an alliance: 'From England they write that Your Electoral Highness intend by the alliance to strengthen the princely House of Orange in this state, and thereafter to support and restore the Royal House of Stuart', the Brandenburg resident in Amsterdam wrote to his master. Or as Aitzema expressed it, Holland should keep friendship with countries which were opposed to Brandenburg, for it was well known that Brandenburg stood at the head of those who tried to bring the young Prince of Orange back to the helm; hence Holland should keep in good correspondence with Sweden, England and Spain, for they were not interested in the cause of the Prince, 'but the Elector and his following are trying day and night to submit everything here to the Prince'.[30] This was the reason why it had taken to long to negotiate the alliance.[31]

Finally, however, the economic interests of the large towns, above all of Amsterdam, prevailed against the political interests of the anti-Orangist party to which Amsterdam usually belonged. The principal aim now was to prevent a Swedish occupation of the Prussian ports on the Baltic coast which were of vital importance to Dutch trade. The Brandenburg Minister reported: 'those of Amsterdam are very active in the cause . . . They have resolved in the Senate that it was necessary to

[28] U & A iv, pp. 62–140.
[29] Aitzema's journal, 11, 12, 21 June and 23 July 1655: U & A v, pp. 811–13, and *Saken van Staet en Oorlogh*, iii, p. 1205; U & A iv, pp. 90–2, 95, 103.
[30] Matthias Dögen to the Elector, 14 October 1652: U & A iv, p. 93; Aitzema's journal, 23 July 1655: U & A v, pp. 813–14.
[31] U & A iv, pp. 21–2.

reach agreement with Your Electoral Highness and their deputies in The Hague are earnestly to press for it.' And three months later: 'Amsterdam is moving strongly; Rotterdam and Leiden are seconding it energetically.'[32] Aitzema's wrath was directed above all against Amsterdam: 'The alliance is solely the work of Amsterdam, Amsterdam wishes to keep the domination of trade to itself alone, for it fears that, if Sweden were to make itself the master of Prussia, trade would be opened freely to others and Holland would suffer.'[33]

Meanwhile the interests of the Netherlands in Cleves had become less important than they had been in 1646. After the Peace of Westphalia it was no longer necessary to transport Dutch goods via the towns of Cleves into the Spanish Netherlands, and Dutch capital was slowly withdrawn from the duchy. Thus the interest in concluding an alliance with the rising power of Brandenburg became stronger than that in the protection of the Estates of Cleves, and the alliance was signed on 27 July 1655. Although in June the States of Holland, Zeeland and Utrecht had still been in favour of including in it a guarantee of the Treaty of Xanten, it was not done.[34] As Aitzema reports, the Brandenburg Minister was 'so clearly against this that he said several times: I would rather have my nose cut off, rather explode, than permit this.'[35] The only thing Brandenburg was unable to achieve for the time being was the withdrawal of the Dutch garrisons from Cleves.

During the following years the connections between the Netherlands and Cleves became looser and looser, to the detriment of the Cleves towns. In 1664 they complained that their wealth was declining rapidly, their burghers no longer lived from trade and industry but only from agriculture, the few merchants left were emigrating to the Netherlands, and the number of the impoverished was growing fast.[36] During the wars against France the Dutch garrisons had to be finally withdrawn, and the links with the Netherlands became even more tenuous, while the towns' decline continued apace. In 1675 a memorandum of the Estates described how much the withdrawal of the garrisons had hit the country, 'where hardly any trade is left, where few men pass through and only few people and cattle are left, where the majority have neither bread nor beer but poverty and penury are ruling, where the consumption which existed at the time of the strong Dutch garrisons has vanished, as has the supply of money which then flowed into the country.'[37] Even if the picture is overdrawn it provides a vivid

[32] Weiman's reports, 16 March and 8 June 1655: *ibid.*, pp. 117, 127.
[33] Aitzema's journal, 30 July 1655: U & A v, p. 814. See also U & V iv, pp. 22–4.
[34] Aitzema, op. cit., iii, pp. 1200–4; Weiman's report of 22 June 1655; U & A iv, p. 133.
[35] U & A v, p. 997.
[36] *Ibid.*, p. 948; O. Hötzsch, *Stände und Verwaltung von Cleve und Mark in der Zeit von 1666 bis 1697*, Leipzig, 1908, p. 336.
[37] Hötzsch, op. cit., p. 553.

description of the plight of Cleves after many years of war and forced levying of taxes. The duchy had to remain part of the nascent Hohenzollern state whose interests and social structure were so different from its own.

7

THE EMPIRE AFTER THE THIRTY YEARS WAR

WHEN the Peace of Westphalia was signed on 24 October 1648 and the warring parties finally laid down their arms, a settlement was reached which, in its essential features, was to last until the dissolution of the Holy Roman Empire in 1806. For a century and longer civil war had been endemic in Germany, and there were to be many minor upheavals in the future; but until 1740, when Frederick II of Prussia chose to invade Silesia and to break the peace of the Empire, that peace was not disturbed by any major internal war. Yet, while the conditions of the Empire were settled by the peace of 1648, the same did not apply to the conditions of Europe. Wars continued in the west and in the east, against France and against the Turks; and Louis XIV found it easy to find allies among the German princes and to use them against the Empire which he was fighting. Internally, however, an equilibrium was reached between the Emperor and the princes, between Protestants and Catholics, between the centrifugal forces and those aiming at more centralisation. A compromise solution was found which, by its very durability, proved that it was not unsatisfactory.

In practice the Empire now consisted of Germany and the Habsburg hereditary lands: its frontiers had contracted; but Switzerland and the Netherlands had long ceased to be parts of the Empire, and the official recognition of this fact was an advantage, and not a loss. It was much more important that parts of Alsace were ceded to France, and western Pomerania with Stettin, Wismar and the duchies of Bremen and Verden to Sweden. This meant not only a loss of territory, but provided both powers with endless opportunities of making further claims and of fishing in troubled waters, of which France in particular was not slow to avail herself. Sweden not only gained those scattered territories and thus controlled the mouths of the Oder, Elbe and Weser, but she also received a war indemnity of 5,000,000 guilders which had to be raised by the impoverished principalities of the Empire. It was not until June 1650 that the Swedish army was disbanded and left the non-Swedish territories; it took another three years before it evacuated eastern Pomerania (which had fallen to Brandenburg), and only on condition that Sweden would receive half the revenue from the harbour tolls and customs. In 1652 the Swedish army opened hostilities against the Free City of Bremen which had not been ceded to Sweden—in contrast with the duchy of Bremen—and therefore declined to render homage to her. The burghers resisted with determination, and the Emperor as well as neighbouring princes tried to mediate. In 1654 a compromise was reached which left it open whether Bremen was a Free Imperial City, but obliged the burghers to render a conditional oath of allegiance to Sweden. After the death of King Charles X, however, they again refused to render homage to Charles XI as his subjects and instead sent deputies to attend the Imperial Diet. Thereupon the Swedish army in 1666 laid siege to Bremen; but the burghers' resistance and the intervention of Denmark, the United Provinces and several German princes forced the Swedish government to make peace and to recognise Bremen as a Free City. Until 1700, however, it was not permitted to send deputies to the Imperial Diet.

That the stipulations of the peace treaty facilitated the interference of foreign powers was shown even more clearly in the Rhineland. At the end of 1654 the archbishops of Cologne, Trier and Mainz, the bishop of Münster and the count palatine of Neuburg, who was also the duke of Jülich and Berg, concluded a Rhenish Alliance which was to protect its members against attacks and to become a mediating factor in European politics. Its importance was increased by the fact that the elder son and elected successor of the Emperor Ferdinand III had died in the same year, while his younger son, Leopold, was but fourteen years old. His youth provided Cardinal Mazarin with an argument for supporting the candidature of a non-Habsburg prince, either the Elector of Bavaria or the Count Palatine of Neuburg. When Ferdinand III died in April 1657 no successor had been elected, and the interregnum, which lasted for fifteen months, was filled with intrigues, threats and promises on the side of France. In July 1658, however, the young Leopold was unanimously elected Emperor by the Electors, having promised that he would render no support whatever to Spain in the war with France which was still continuing. Four weeks later many German princes—the archbishops of Cologne, Mainz and Trier, the bishop of Münster, the count palatine of Neuburg, the landgrave of Hesse-Cassel, the dukes of Brunswick and Lüneburg, and the king of Sweden as duke of Bremen and Verden—signed the Rhenish Alliance, which was joined on the following day by France. The army of the league was to number 10,000 men, 2400 of whom were to be French. The aims of the league were the maintenance of the peace treaty, of the liberties of the Estates of the Empire, and of a balance between France and the Habsburgs. But the German members were much too weak to pursue an independent policy or to form a third force, and in reality the league became an instrument of French foreign policy. It was renewed several times and joined by other German princes, among them the Elector of Brandenburg; but it was dissolved in 1668. By that time it had become clear that the German liberties were not threatened by the Emperor Leopold, but by Louis XIV. As the Crowns of France and Sweden were recognised as guarantors of the peace, and as Sweden acquired two seats in the Imperial Diet, both powers continued to play a very important part in the internal affairs of the Empire: until the reign of Louis XIV reached its end and the Swedish Empire collapsed in the Great War of the North.

During the Thirty Years War the Habsburgs had made strenuous efforts to increase the powers of the Emperor, to create a centralised monarchy, to subdue the Protestant princes, and to advance the cause of the Counter-Reformation—and they had come very close to success. The Peace of Westphalia buried these endeavours, but it also buried the opposite tendency: the attempts of the Calvinist princes to transform the Empire into an aristocratic republic, to carry the banner of Protestantism into the very heart of the Habsburg lands and to lay low the power of the Habsburgs. The Peace of Westphalia was a compromise. The unity of the Empire was preserved; the Imperial Crown remained in the Habsburg family as long as the House of Austria continued in the male line; its power was strengthened through the defeat of the Bohemians and the introduction of the Counter-Reformation in its hereditary lands; even in the Empire the power of the Emperor was by no means negligible. He continued to influence the decisions of the Imperial Diet, to defend the frontiers of the Empire against foreign attack, to act as arbiter in cases of internal conflict between the princes and within the principalities. His hereditary lands—soon to be expanded towards the south-east—made him a prince much more powerful than any of the Electors. Ferdinand III and Leopold I were far from showing political resignation and continued to focus their attention upon the Empire. The siege of Vienna by the Turks[1] led to a revival of Christian and Imperial solidarity, transcending the frontiers of the Empire. This feeling remained alive during the successful campaigns against the Turks, and the Emperor remained its living symbol. The people hoped that, after the end of the wars, he would restore the good old laws of the Empire and revive the authority of the Emperor. Nor was this entirely a pious hope: the century after 1648 saw a distinct revival of his authority, especially so under Leopold's successors, Joseph I and Charles VI. The rise of the Habsburgs in the power politics of Europe had clear repercussions within the Empire.

Yet the Empire after 1648 was incapable of acting as a unit and had no will of its own. The Estates of the Empire followed their own particular interests; they watched each other with jealous eyes and attempted to strengthen their own power, internally as well as externally, and to decrease that of the Emperor. It is true that the French policy of granting full sovereignty to the German princes had not prevailed at Westphalia: they had been accorded only a *jus territorii et superioritatis* by the terms of the peace. It seems doubtful, however, whether this made a great difference in practice. If the princes were granted the right of concluding

[1] See *New Cambridge Modern History*, vol. v, edited by F.L. Carsten (Cambridge, 1961), ch. xxi, pp. 515-17.

alliances amongst themselves and with foreign powers, this was a right which they had long exercised. If they were forbidden to conclude such alliances against the Emperor and the Empire, this prohibition could be interpreted in different ways. It is not surprising that the political writers of the time found it difficult to define what the Empire really was. Hippolythus a Lapide denied that the Emperor was a sovereign and held that the Empire was an aristocracy of the princes; while Samuel Pufendorf, in his *De Statu Imperii Germanici* (1667), aimed at a reconciliation of the different factors wielding influence in the Empire and declared that it was an '*irregulare aliquod corpus et monstro simile*'. It certainly was irregular, although perhaps not a monster but a marvel. So was the fact that, in spite of all tensions and rivalries, the internal frontiers fixed by the Peace of Westphalia remained substantially the same for more than half a century—only France continued to encroach upon Imperial territory in the west.

Even more stable proved the frontiers drawn between the warring creeds. Protestantism was eliminated from the Habsburg lands, Bohemia, and the Upper Palatinate, but the secularised abbeys and bishoprics were not restored. After 1648 very few German princes exercised their right of driving out those of their subjects who adhered to a religion different from that of the ruler. In their depopulated lands subjects were valuable, and the more enlightened princes tried to attract immigrants even if they belonged to different religious persuasions; the persecuted Protestant sects and the Jews found a home in Brandenburg and elsewhere. Many princes were not strong enough, or not fanatical enough, to enforce their religion upon their territories. Thus the Calvinist Electors of Brandenburg and the landgraves of Hesse-Cassel ruled over Lutheran principalities and did not attempt to make Calvinism the State religion.[1] When later in the century the Electors Palatine and the Electors of Saxony became Roman Catholics,[2] Protestantism remained the dominant religion of their principalities. The Counter-Reformation did not advance any further. Religious passions had cooled and self-interest dictated the adoption of a more tolerant course. Thus, to a very large extent, the religious map of modern Germany is that of 1648.

Many problems remained unsolved, or it took many years before a solution emerged. The restoration of law and order was a difficult task. The mercenary armies were paid off although there was extremely little money. But what should be done with the mercenaries, and how could they be fitted into civil life? There were as yet no standing armies into which they might be absorbed. During the disorders resulting from the war many people had taken to brigandage and crime, or had learned to live by their wits; bands of former soldiers roamed the country. Certain

[1] *Ibid.*, ch. vi, pp. 126-7.
[2] See below, pp. 113, 115.

Estates of the Empire co-operated to suppress lawlessness and disorder. The continuing war between France and Spain and that between Sweden and Poland which broke out in 1655 absorbed some mercenaries who had not learnt any other trade; so did later the wars of Louis XIV. Even greater difficulties stood in the way of economic recovery. It was not only the fact, which has been emphasised so often, that the mouths of all the great rivers flowing through the Empire were controlled by foreign powers. It was not only that trade had dwindled or sought alternative routes to avoid the disturbed areas. It was, above all, the egotism and mutual jealousy of the princes and towns which, under the influence of the ideas of 'mercantilism', imposed more and more barriers upon trade and enterprise, erected innumerable customs stations at the frontiers of each principality and along the course of all the rivers, levied new impositions and taxes which drove away trade and delayed the recuperation by decades. If France recovered surprisingly quickly from long periods of war and civil war, this was partly due to the enlightened policy of a centralised government. The political disunity of Germany had grave consequences in the economic field.

A *Political Discourse on the real Causes of the Rise and Decline of Towns, Countries and States*, published in 1668 by Johann Joachim Becher, pointed to the wealth which the United Provinces derived from the sea: they would never have amassed their riches if they feared the sea as much as the German nation did. 'The result is that in Germany there is hardly any trade and enterprise, all commerce is ruined, no money is to be found either among the great or among the small people.' In the same year the officials employed to levy the wine-duty at Öttingen in Bavaria attributed the steep decline in the yield of the duty to the fact that 'in previous good years the sweet wines had been sent not only into the country, but frequently also into Austria, Bohemia and to Prague, even to Cracow in Poland, but at present times sales had nearly ceased on account of the manifold wars and widespread deaths which had caused the country's ruin and scarcity of money', and the same applied to the sale of Austrian wines.[1] At Munich, Augsburg, Speyer, Frankfurt and Leipzig the price of rye in the 1660's was between 13 and 34 per cent, and the price of oats between 15 and 29 per cent below the pre-war level. The depopulation of the towns, which lasted for a long time after the end of the war, led to a sharp decline of the consumption of corn, to a shrinking of the corn trade and to a severe fall in the price of land. In Berlin the price of rye and wheat remained depressed throughout the second half of the seventeenth century.

There can be no doubt that wide areas of Germany not only suffered severely from the war and its aftermath, but also lost a large part of their

---

[1] State Archives Munich, 'Altbayerische Landschaft', no. 1993: report to the deputies of the Estates supervising the levy of the wine-duty of 20 November 1668.

population. While the towns could protect themselves more easily against hostile forces, they suffered all the more severely from outbreaks of plague. Austria, the Tyrol, Salzburg and Switzerland were hardly touched by the war and their population grew. Large parts of north-west Germany—Slesvig, Holstein, Lower Saxony, Oldenburg, Westphalia and parts of the Rhineland—did not suffer much depopulation. Even in Silesia and Bohemia it probably amounted to only 20 per cent. But other parts fared much worse. In the various districts of Brandenburg between 15 and 60 per cent of the farms were deserted in 1652, on an average perhaps about 50 per cent. Berlin lost only 25 per cent of its population, but Potsdam and Spandau over 40, and the town of Brandenburg over 60 per cent. In six small towns of the Old Mark (to the west of the Elbe) 2444 hearths were counted in 1567: a century later there were 1021. In its most important town, Stendal, 2980 children were born during the first decade of the seventeenth century: during the seventh decade the number was 969; and Stendal was a town which had been neither conquered nor looted. But it has to be remembered that the decline of the Brandenburg towns had started in the sixteenth century. At the other end of Germany, in Württemberg, over 41,000 destroyed houses and barns were counted in 1652, and about one-third of the arable land was deserted, a total of 309,957 *Morgen* (about 241,000 acres). Fifty-one local districts reported that they had had 58,865 burghers before the war, but that only 19,071 remained; the other twenty-four districts merely reported that they had lost 18,546 burghers. The town of Nagold lost only 8 per cent of its population, but Urach 75 per cent. In Pforzheim in Baden so many houses were still deserted in 1667 that the margrave was forced to intervene. The population of Munich fell from 18,000 or more to 9000. Among the south-western territories the Palatinate and Württemberg suffered most; among those in the north-east, Mecklenburg and Pomerania. Many inhabitants migrated to the safer north-west where Hamburg and Bremen grew in importance, exporting corn overseas and receiving English and Dutch goods; the destruction of Magdeburg contributed to the rise of Hamburg, its rival. Ulm and Nuremberg, while declining in population, to some extent profited from the influx of Austrian Protestants and of the capital which they brought with them. In Augsburg, however, 143 people had paid between 50 and 100 guilders each in taxes in 1617, but in 1661 there were only 36; while the number of those paying more than 100 guilders fell from 100 to 20, although taxation was enforced more strictly. Thus no generalisation is possible, but the picture is grim enough.

The depopulation of the countryside had divergent effects in the different parts of Germany. In Bavaria the nobility, whose income consisted of peasant dues and rents, became impoverished and dependent upon money-lenders. Even the estates of the wealthier families were burdened with heavy debts. Those of the less well-to-do often came into the hands of the monasteries, of speculators, of officers or officials who invested their capital in real estate. At the diet of 1669 the nobility strongly complained about the buying-up of noble estates: if any came on the market the religious foundations offered the best price; their ready cash was pushing aside the nobility. Only a minority were still able to live according to their custom and to send their children abroad 'to learn the noble exercises'. On account of the prevailing low corn prices demesne farming held no attraction for the landlords; a tendency in that direction did not really develop and was later reversed. The Bavarian peasants, on the other hand, benefited from this situation. Because of the scarcity of tenants the landlords were forced to grant them better conditions. As the prelates put it in 1669, if they did not want their farms to become completely deserted, they had to accept whatever they were offered; if they wanted to put new tenants on their deserted lands, they had to improve their legal position, to allow them freedom from dues for many years, and to be content with what the peasants were willing to pay.

Exactly the opposite occurred in Brandenburg, Pomerania and Mecklenburg, where demesne farming had become prominent and the position of the peasants had deteriorated since the fifteenth century. The depopulation forced the nobles to take much more deserted peasant land under their own ploughs because they were unable to find new tenants. The peasants were burdened with much heavier labour services because their number had shrunk and the demesnes had grown. Their children were forced to serve as menials or labourers on the estate. The peasants with their entire families were not only tied to the soil—that had already happened in the sixteenth century—but many became personally unfree: even their bodies belonged to their masters (*Leibeigenschaft*). They equally controlled their peasants' private lives; their consent was required for marriages; many peasants were sold or exchanged like chattels. During the following decades many more peasants were evicted or bought out. In Brandenburg the size of the noble demesnes grew by about 30 per cent during the second half of the seventeenth century. In Lower Saxony, on the other hand, a strong and independent peasantry came into being at that time, because this area had lost only a small part of its population and benefited by immigration from the devastated districts. A purposeful government policy supported this tendency, while in north-eastern Germany the governments only too easily gave way to the demands of the nobility, which aimed at a complete subjugation of the peasantry and a further extension of its demesnes. It was only along the coast of the Baltic—in Mecklenburg, Pomerania, Brandenburg, the duchy of Prussia, Poland and Livonia—where there were easy facilities for export, that the *Gutsherrschaft* (large noble estates producing corn for the market with the help of the labour services of serfs) was established in the course of the seventeenth century. Even in Saxony and Magdeburg, which were equally 'colonial' in character and possessed easy facilities for sending corn down the Elbe, this was not the case. There peasant farming remained the preponderant form of agriculture, and serfdom never assumed the rigours which it acquired in the territories along the Baltic coast. There the local nobility did not become all-powerful, but its influence was balanced by that of the towns, especially of Leipzig whose fairs acquired European importance. Bohemia and Moravia, on the other hand, resembled the territories of the north-east, from which they were separated by Saxony and Silesia. The Bohemian nobility also possessed large estates, demesnes, sheep-farms, breweries and fish-ponds, which were farmed with labour services; the peasants were serfs and many had to serve as often as they were bidden by their masters, while in the Austrian lands their services were more limited, usually to twelve days in the year.[1]

Wherever demesne farming was less prominent and the noble estates small and scattered—as in western and southern Germany—serfdom had in practice disappeared and the labour services often been commuted into quit-rents. There the depopulation of the Thirty Years War could not lead to a revival of the manorial system, but the peasants' position continued to improve. These enormous differences in the social development can be illustrated by the figures of population density. About 1700 Brandenburg had only about 30 inhabitants per English square mile, the duchy of Prussia only 28, and Pomerania only 19; but Bavaria had about 73, Hanover 63, Magdeburg 78, Saxony 93, and Württemberg 105 inhabitants per English square mile, the latter figures approximating to those of the Netherlands and France and surpassing those of England and Wales. Clearly the condition of the peasantry was worst where the population was smallest. Not that the Thirty Years War had caused this uneven distribution of the population; it merely enhanced a tendency which had existed for centuries.

In north-eastern Germany there was no improvement in the condition of the peasantry in the century following upon the Thirty Years War. In the New Mark of Brandenburg, in the early eighteenth century, labour services of three days a week were considered a light burden: usually, they amounted to four, and often to six days a week, from sunrise to sunset, which left the peasants far too little time for their own farms. About two-thirds of the total arable land belonged to the nobility and another quarter to the royal domains. In the Brandenburg districts of Beeskow and Storkow 429 peasants were counted in 1746, while there had been 814

---

[1] Wolf Helmhard von Hohberg, *Georgica Curiosa. Das ist: Umständlicher Bericht und klarer Unterricht von dem Adelichen Land- und Feld-Leben...* (Nuremberg, 1682), I, 46, 53, 150. It is interesting that this Austrian nobleman considered the serfdom of the Bohemian peasants and their unlimited labour services as something that 'is not customary in the German lands', thus not taking into account the conditions in north-eastern Germany. For further details, see *N.C.M.H.*, v, ch. xx, pp. 480-1.

before the Thirty Years War; but the number of cottagers had increased from 172 to 828. In eastern Pomerania there were 6514 peasants under the nobility at the end of the sixteenth century, but only 3419 about 1670 and 3584 in 1718. Many peasants escaped across the Polish frontier to seek better conditions. In 1684 a clergyman painted the following picture of the local peasantry:

The peasants are indeed human beings, but somewhat more churlish and uncouth than the others....In his movements, he would only seldom think of his hat and take it off,...but if he does so he turns it round like a potter's wheel, or spits into his hands and polishes it....When they eat they do not use a fork, but they dip their five fingers into the pot....If soldiers steal they do it out of extreme need; but most peasants who help themselves do it out of malice....It is also well known that those who keep on good terms with the vicar are maltreated by the other peasants, for they give them all kinds of bad names, call them traitors, lickspittles, toadies, talebearers....The peasants have that in common with the stockfish: these are best when beaten well and soft. The dear peasants too are only well-behaved when fully burdened with work; then they remain well under control and timid....[1]

And in 1710 a high Prussian official, von Luben, reported to his king:

Because in some places there is strict personal serfdom [*Leibeigenschaft*] and those of the nobility do not want to abolish it but want to retain the great power over their subjects, they plague them with heavy Egyptian services, with manifold corn and other carrying duties, harsh punishments and other dues to such an extent that they remain poverty-stricken; one cannot squeeze the contribution and other taxes out of them, or they run away; if they do so they are fetched back and things go worse with them; the people are punished and treated cruelly....They cannot obtain justice at the governments and regional and local courts because the nobles sit in them, and these have an interest on account of their own estates and peasants and do not want to prejudge their own cases....The rents, services, dues, billeting and contribution have been increased so often that the people can hardly maintain themselves; therefore the serfs have long been poor and get poorer still and remain so, and finally there is nothing left but to run away....[2]

Yet the pictures drawn of east-German noblemen were hardly more flattering. In a satirical story from Silesia there occurs this description of a young noble by his own mother:

The rogue knows already that he is a Junker; therefore he does not want to learn anything, but rather rides about with his stable-boy....But in the end I will have to buy a spelling-book for him....If only it did not cost anything and the learned chaps need not have so many books....I have always heard that in other countries there are not such proper noblemen as we have them....[3]

---

[1] *Des Neunhäutigen und Haimbüchenen schlimmen Baurenstands und Wandels Entdeckte Ubel-Sitten und Lasterprob*, von Veroandro aus Wahrburg (1684).
[2] *Friedrich Wilhelm I. in seiner Tätigkeit für die Landescultur Preussens*, Publicationen aus den K. Preussischen Staatsarchiven, II (Leipzig, 1878), pp. 213, 216–17: relation of 14 October 1710.
[3] Paul Winckler, *Der Edelmann*, in Verlegung Christoph Riegels (Nuremberg, 1697).

Another critic of the nobility wrote:

> If one visited another the beer mug immediately appeared on the table; it went round without distinction, whether the guest was thirsty or not.... If they arrived in the afternoon the drinking started right away, with medium-sized mugs which held almost a jug; then the host drank to the guests, emptying either the whole mug, or half a mug, and the guest had to respond. Thus they got drunk before the evening, and in the early morning some drank ordinary spirits, others warm beer with eggs and ginger....[1]

Other observers too commented on the excessive drinking habits. From Hamburg it was reported about 1650 that 'nowadays people first send for spirits before they go to church' on a Sunday.[2] And from Ratisbon the English envoy, Sir George Etherege, wrote in 1686:

> the Gentlemen of this Country go upon a quite different Scheme of Pleasure... and they take more care to enlarge their Cellars than their patrimonial Estates. In short, Drinking is the Hereditary Sin of this Country, and that Heroe of a Deputy here, that can demolish (at one Sitting) the rest of his Brother Envoys, is mentioned with as much Applause as the Duke of Lorain for his noble Exploits against the Turks and may claim a Statue erected at the public Expence in any Town in Germany.... They are such unmerciful Plyers of the Bottle, so wholy given up to what our Scots call Goodfellowship, that 'tis as great a Constraint upon my Nature to sit out a Night's Entertainment with them, as it would be to hear half a score long-winded Presbyterian Divines Cant successively one after another....[3]

A wide gulf separated the nobility from the commoners, and this distinction was equally upheld by the urban patrician families. At Augsburg, Nuremberg, Frankfurt and Ulm the noble families were strictly secluded from the burghers. At Nuremberg they considered it dishonourable to engage in commerce. At Frankfurt the Society of Old Limpurg demanded from new members proof of eight noble ancestors and abstention from all commerce. Apart from these old noble families there were many recently ennobled ones: officers, officials and merchants, whose families engaged in ostentatious display. They drove round in gilded carriages, their wives would wear lace only from Paris or Venice, their houses were luxuriously furnished. Those whose patents of nobility dated from an earlier time looked down upon the newcomers. An eighteenth-century writer, Johann Michael von Loen, critically compared the attitude of the German nobles with those of England, where 'even the sons of the greatest peers were not ashamed to become advocates, so that later they could become magistrates and be elected to parliament', and those of Spain, where 'young noblemen from the oldest families took doctorates...'. He also remarked upon the decline of the German nobility, which went hand in hand with more splendour and greater

---

[1] A. Tholuk, *Vorgeschichte des Rationalismus*, II, 2 (Berlin, 1862), 197–8.
[2] *Ibid.* II, 1 (1861), 121.
[3] *The Letterbook of Sir George Etherege*, ed. Sybil Rosenfeld (London, 1928), pp. 413–14.

expenditure, so that many noblemen had to enter military services. 'For this there is now the best opportunity because the *miles perpetuus et mercenarius* has been introduced in all European States....'[1] The economic difficulties which undoubtedly faced the nobility in the period after the Thirty Years War indeed explain the willingness with which that of Brandenburg and Pomerania entered the Hohenzollern army and became professional officers. The same was the case in some other German principalities. In Bavaria, however, the impoverished nobility showed a clear preference for civil employment and eagerly sought State and court offices and sinecures. As there were about 500 or 600 courts in Germany, not counting those of the Imperial Knights, there were indeed many openings for impecunious noblemen.

If, in many parts of Germany, the nobility was a declining class and had to seek offices and preferments, the towns were not in a much better position. With the exception of Hamburg and Frankfurt, which grew considerably in importance, the Free Imperial Cities were mere shadows of the past. After the loss of the Alsatian cities to France their number was fifty-one, the large majority situated in the south-west of Germany. Most of them were very small and unable to hold their own in the struggle with the principalities which surrounded them. But even the more important Imperial Cities—Augsburg, Nuremberg, Ulm, Ratisbon in the south and Cologne, Aachen, Bremen, Lübeck in the north—found it difficult to adapt themselves to changed conditions. The south-German towns were hard hit by the decline of the trade with Italy and the bankruptcies of the great banking houses of the Fuggers and the Welsers. The north-German towns suffered from overwhelming Dutch, and to a lesser extent English, competition. Foreign merchants exported German raw materials and produce and imported colonial and foreign goods. The Hanseatic towns had long declined under the double impact of foreign and noble competition. They no longer sent their own ships across the seas, but were satisfied if they could act as intermediaries between foreign visitors and the hinterland. Bremen and Cologne had to fight hard to preserve their status of Free Imperial Cities. The power of the princes and the rise of the principalities made any progressive development of the Free Imperial Cities impossible: hemmed in on all sides they survived, undiminished in number, until the *Reichsdeputationshauptschluss* of 1803, but the days of their power and splendour were past. Even the economic recovery of the eighteenth century did not lead to their revival.

The decline of the Free Imperial Cities did not result in a progressive development of the towns situated within the principalities and fostered by their princes. Their trade and industry had suffered severely. In Munich, for example, the number of cloth-makers fell from 148 in 1618 to 56 in 1649, that of cloth- and linen-weavers from 161 to 82, that of hat-

[1] Johann Michael von Loen, *Der Adel* (Ulm, 1752), pp. 271, 290.

makers from 23 to 9, that of tailors from 118 to 64. After the end of the Thirty Years War the Electors of Bavaria made strenuous efforts to revive the Bavarian cloth industry, but with little success, and the number of cloth-makers declined further. The heavy taxes and monopolies imposed by the princes only too often hampered the recovery of trade and enterprise. The import of many foreign goods was prohibited, as was the export of raw materials, such as wool or hides, before there were any domestic industries which could absorb these materials or supply the internal demand. Even if certain articles could be produced locally, the foreign goods were often cheaper and better. Thus many of the prohibitions and monopolies had to be rescinded, only to be reimposed later, with the same disastrous results. In Brandenburg the export of raw wool was prohibited no less than ten times during the reign of the Great Elector, but—as the nobility was exempt from this prohibition—it proved ineffective. The repeated prohibitions of the import of iron and metal goods were equally disregarded, even by the State officials. The trade down the Elbe was so burdened with tolls that even corn, 'the soul of commerce', was shipped along different routes and transport over land became cheaper. The Elbe tolls at Lenzen were farmed out for some years, with very bad results for trade; but matters did not improve when they were again managed by State officials. The Great Elector considered these heavy tolls entirely justified; three conferences summoned to discuss the Elbe tolls produced no result because, against the advice of his privy councillors, he refused to make any concessions. The commandants of Frankfurt-on-Oder and Spandau levied their own duties on passing carriages and ships, and others did the same with travellers, in spite of official prohibitions. The number of ships putting into Königsberg declined steeply on account of new duties and tolls imposed by the government.

Equally bad was the effect of the new excises, the favourite instruments of seventeenth-century governments. In Saxony an excise was introduced in 1640 and not rescinded after the end of the war. Therefore many goods by-passed Saxony and were transported along alternative routes. Silk and other costly goods from Italy went north through Thuringia, linen from Bohemia and Silesia went through Brandenburg (before the excise was introduced there). It was in vain that the Estates of Saxony complained that the excise caused the ruin of the country, especially of the cloth and linen industries, and favoured Saxony's neighbours. It was equally in vain that the Hanseatic and the south- and west-German towns repeatedly declared that under these conditions their trade with Leipzig could not revive. There was much passive resistance, but the excise remained; only on home-produced goods was it rescinded temporarily, but reintroduced in 1681. By that time the excise had also been introduced in Brandenburg, with even more negative effects. For there it was not introduced for the country as a whole, but only for the towns, so that each small town was surrounded by artificial customs barriers and the excise had to be levied at the town gates. Thus urban trade and enterprise were burdened with the new tax, while those carried on outside the town walls remained free and the tax-exemption of the nobility was preserved. It also meant that the towns had to carry a disproportionate share of the taxes: it is not surprising that their recovery was so slow. And this was the system which was gradually extended from Brandenburg to the other Hohenzollern territories. Other principalities were more fortunate. Following the Brandenburg example, in 1700 an excise was also introduced in the duchies of Jülich and Berg on the lower Rhine; but there the Estates and the towns got it rescinded after a few years, for urban enterprise was declining and trade was migrating into neighbouring territories.

The towns within the principalities also suffered from the efforts of their rulers to extend their sway over the towns. Since 1648 Archbishop John Philip of Mainz tried to enforce his prerogative over the town of Erfurt in Thuringia which vigorously resisted all his threats and even the ban of the Empire. In 1664 he decided to use force and, supported by France and the Rhenish Alliance, laid siege to Erfurt. A month later the town surrendered, rendered homage to John Philip and accepted a princely garrison. Two years later the Great Elector forced Magdeburg to do the same. In a similar fashion the city of Münster was subjugated by Bishop Christopher Bernard von Galen and the town of Brunswick by the dukes of Brunswick-Lüneburg. The opposition of Königsberg, the capital of the duchy of Prussia, and of the towns of the duchy of Cleves, which resisted the imposition of arbitrary taxes and the depredations of the military, was broken by military force. The introduction of the urban excise in the early eighteenth century spelled the ruin of their old prosperity. Within twelve years the most important town of Cleves, Wesel, lost over a quarter of its inhabitants and all the towns of Cleves over 11 per cent of theirs.

It is true that the rise of Hamburg continued during this period, that the fairs of Leipzig became a focal point of exchange between east and west and south; that the Silesian linen industry continued to prosper; but these exceptional cases merely emphasise the general stagnation. The continuing decline of many German towns, often caused by government action, provided great opportunities for foreign merchants and financiers. Already before the Thirty Years War Dutch merchants had penetrated up the Rhine and from the Baltic ports into the hinterland. After the war their influence increased and at certain places became predominant. The Dutch with their capital resources and trading connections, with their many ships and cheaper freight rates, were at an enormous advantage compared with the small merchants of petty German towns. The Thirty Years War and the collapse of the great banking houses had ruined all credit and consumed most of the capital. Timidity and narrow-mindedness were the characteristics of the day. For his naval and colonial enterprises the Great Elector had to use Dutch experts and sailors, Dutch companies and financiers, because no such resources were available in Brandenburg and Prussia. For the same reason he welcomed Jewish merchants, especially if they also represented Dutch interests. Thus Moses Jacobson de Jonge in 1664 received an important privilege which entitled him to take up residence at Memel—at a time when the Jews were still excluded from the duchy of Prussia. He soon established a flourishing trade with Poland, Lithuania and Livonia, almost monopolised the highly important trade in salt and successfully competed with the local merchants; in 1694–6 he paid 80 per cent more in customs duties than all the merchants of Memel together. No wonder that they as well as the Estates of Prussia violently complained about the newcomer. In Cleves the Gomperz family played an important part in financial matters, advancing sums to the government and to the Estates, anticipating the yield of taxes, and meeting the arrears of French contributions. In 1700 Ruben Elias Gomperz was appointed chief tax-collector for the principalities of Cleves and Mark, and under Frederick William I members of the same family were again employed on official business. Because there were so many courts and so many impecunious princes, because their splendour and their ambitions were continuously growing, because they had to have standing armies which had to be supplied with food and equipment, hundreds of court Jews had to try to meet the ever-increasing demands of the princes.

Thus the Thirty Years War exercised a profound influence on the course of German history, especially in the social and economic field. In popular opinion it became the cause of all evils; even the deserted villages of the later Middle Ages were attributed to destruction by the Swedes or to some other calamity of the great war. Naturally, the popular literature of the time, as well as of modern times, tended to over-emphasise the horrors and the hopelessness of the situation. If this picture is too one-sided and biased, so are the attempts of some modern historians to 'debunk' the Thirty Years War and to attribute much of the bleakness to later propaganda. It has also been alleged that contemporaries did not think of the war as one war, but divided it into a number of separate wars. But it can be proved that one name—'the great German war', or 'the Thirty Years War'—was used soon after the fighting had come to an end. It is true, of course, that the political disunity of Germany was not caused, but merely exacerbated, by the Thirty Years War, and that some of the negative features described above were due to political disunity. But it also remains true that the social and economic decline was at best local before the outbreak of the war and was made much more general by the war. It is equally true that the rise of the western European countries began long before the outbreak of the war; but it seems at least possible that

Germany might have been able to participate in that rise if the war had not intervened. In the sixteenth century Germany was still a flourishing country; it took her a century or longer to reach once more the level of development she had attained before the outbreak of the Thirty Years War.

If the economic and social development of Germany during the second half of the seventeenth century presented a picture of almost unmitigated gloom, the same is not entirely true of the constitutional field. The institutions of the Empire—in spite of all its decline and disintegration—continued to work better than might have been expected. A certain stability was reached which was to persist into the eighteenth century; and no serious efforts were made to upset the balance of forces which had come into being. Perhaps it was the continuous threat from France which brought about some cohesion between divergent forces, or the pressure from the Turks; but the latter were far less dangerous than they had been in the fifteenth and sixteenth centuries, and the siege of Vienna was only a passing episode. Louis XIV always had his partisans and clients in Germany: in that respect French power was an element of disruption, and not of cohesion. Only certain parts of the Empire were threatened by foreign foes. Yet it was not only the States of the Rhineland which combined against France—on the contrary, there Louis XIV found many more or less willing 'allies'—and not only those of the south-east which fought against the Turks. If one remembers that the Empire had about 360 different Estates—not counting the 1500 Free Imperial Knights—it seems a miracle that some unity was preserved in spite of so much disunity.

Not all the 360 Estates were represented in the Imperial Diet, which met at Ratisbon and debated upon matters such as the coinage, sumptuary laws, measures against vagabonds and beggars and, above all, military affairs and taxes to be levied for defence or other purposes. For, with the sole exception of a levy for the maintenance of the Imperial High Court, there were no permanent Imperial taxes, but only the 'Roman months' voted by the Diet.[1] Another weakness of the Imperial Diet was that it possessed no executive authority if some of the Estates declined to carry out decisions taken by the Diet. In that case, there was only the possibility of a trial before the Imperial High Court which was notorious for its delays and for creating complications. The Diet consisted of three houses or 'colleges'. The first was that of the Electors: in 1648 their number was increased to eight, but the Elector of Bohemia (the Habsburg Emperor) did not exercise his electoral dignity. There were thus four Catholic Electors—Bavaria and the archbishops of Cologne, Mainz and Trier—

[1] Originally levied to finance Imperial expeditions to Rome, the 'Roman months' since the sixteenth century were grants made by the Diet for the Imperial army, which were repartitioned among the Estates of the Empire according to a fixed quota.

and three Protestant ones—Lutheran Saxony and two Calvinists, Brandenburg and the Palatinate. In the Palatinate, however, a Catholic line of Electors succeeded in 1685, and twelve years later the Elector of Saxony also became a Roman Catholic. This was balanced only to some extent by the creation of a ninth Electorate for Hanover—granted in 1692 by the Emperor acting on his own authority, without any consultation with the Electors or other princes, who had no alternative but to acquiesce. Thus at the end of the century there were only two Protestant Electors, against six Catholics (excluding Bohemia). The Elector of Mainz was the leader of the *corpus catholicorum*, and the Elector of Saxony of the *corpus evangelicorum*; but in religious controversies neither side could outvote the other.

The second house was that of the princes, separated into ecclesiastical and temporal 'benches'. There were thirty-seven ecclesiastical and sixty-three temporal votes, six of which were composite: the Swabian and the Rhenish prelates and four groups of Imperial Counts each exercising one vote. In this house also the Catholics had a majority, but not a large one. The third house was formed by the fifty-one Free Imperial Cities, thirteen of which counted as Catholic, thirty-four as Protestant, and four as 'mixed'. Their influence, however, was very restricted because the Diet of 1653 granted them a *votum decisivum* only *after* an agreement had been reached between the two upper houses, so that they could no longer influence the outcome in case of a disagreement between the houses. As the English envoy, Sir George Etherege, wrote in 1685, 'the deputies of the towns serve only for form's sake, and have never any business transmitted to them till the other two Colleges have agreed...'.[1] In that case the deputies of the cities had practically no alternative but to consent, for it was an accepted principle that none of the houses could be outvoted by the others. As far as Imperial taxation was concerned, it became equally accepted since 1653 that a vote of credit required unanimity, for—as a decision of the Lower Saxon Circle put it in 1652—it would be 'entirely contrary to natural freedom...if someone by his vote could decree what someone else should give'.[2] The Emperor Ferdinand III had to give up his plan of making majority decisions in questions of taxation binding on the minority: the Estates' liberties triumphed once more and the opposition of the princes, led by Brandenburg, prevailed.

In 1654 the princes gained another point: paragraph 180 of the *Recess* drawn up at the conclusion of the Diet stipulated that the subjects of each Imperial Estate were obliged to make grants in aid to their prince or lord with respect to the manning and maintenance of the essential fortresses, places and garrisons. If this was a blow aimed at the local Estates, which in most principalities still exercised the power of the purse, a further step

---

[1] *The Letterbook of Sir George Etherege*, p. 61.
[2] Karl Lamprecht, *Deutsche Geschichte* (Freiburg, 1904), VI, 377.

in that direction was made after the death of Ferdinand III in 1657. Before the young Leopold was elected Emperor he had to make far-reaching concessions. The Electors of Brandenburg and Cologne, involved in complicated struggles with their own Estates, demanded that these should maintain the fortresses with their own resources and have no right to dispose of local taxes without the consent of the prince in question. Brandenburg in addition requested that the Estates should be forbidden to meet without a summons by the ruler or to make a complaint about him to the courts of the Empire; while the Palatinate, Saxony and Trier were satisfied with the preservation of the *status quo*. Saxony in particular opposed the prohibition of appeals to the Imperial courts, from which it would not have benefited: at that time only the possessions of the houses of Saxony and Bavaria, of the Electors Palatine and of Mainz had received a *privilegium de non appellando* which exempted them from the jurisdiction of the Imperial courts; but of the Hohenzollern territories such an exemption had been granted only to the Brandenburg Mark, not to their other possessions. Yet, if Leopold wanted to be elected Emperor, he had to accept the Electors' conditions. Hence it was stipulated that the local Estates were not entitled to refuse contributions to the 'necessary' fortresses and garrisons, to meet without a summons, or to dispose independently of local taxes. If in such cases they sent complaints to the Imperial courts, these should not be heard, nor should complaints against paragraph 180 of the *Recess* of 1654. If the Estates possessed privileges contrary to these stipulations they should be revoked, and equally alliances or unions between the Estates of several principalities. Only thereafter was Leopold elected Emperor by a unanimous vote. Henceforth the princes possessed a legal title which they could always employ against their Estates. Contrary to this prohibition, however, the Imperial courts, especially the Aulic Council, continued to entertain complaints of local Estates against their rulers: a factor which was to be of great importance.[1]

The dangers threatening from the Turks and domestic circumstances induced the Emperor to summon another Diet. It was opened early in 1663 and, after deliberations stretching over more than twelve months, consented to support the Emperor against the Infidel with an army of about 30,000 men. But only one-third of that number finally appeared in the field, and they participated only in the last stages of the campaign. The discussion of other subjects was even more prolonged—so much so that no *Recess* was ever concluded: the Diet became permanent, consisting of envoys of the princes, whose instructions they had to seek on each issue. It thus became a congress of diplomats wrangling over questions of rank and procedure, as described in letters of Sir George Etherege from Ratisbon in 1687-8: 'The business of the Diet for the most part is only fit

[1] See below, pp. 116-17.

to entertain those insects in politics which crawl under the trees in St James's Park....' And four months later: 'The cabals and intrigues for and against the Count de Windisgratz's pretensions have been the only business of the Diet this long while....' After another five months nothing had changed: 'Those who are unacquainted with the proceedings of this assembly would wonder that, where so many ministers are met and maintained at so great a charge by their masters, so little business is done, and the little that is so slowly....' The lot of the English envoy, who disliked the drinking bouts of the Germans and found their ladies 'so intolerably reserv'd and virtuous...that 'tis next to an impossibility to carry on an Intrigue with them...', was not an enviable lot.[1] What heights of folly the system could reach may be illustrated by the behaviour of the representative of the Elector of Mainz in 1701. When leaving his coach at the quarters of the Imperial representative he demanded to be led to him through a secret staircase because he had found in the files that this had been the previous practice. When he was informed that this was impossible for the simple reason that the secret staircase no longer existed, but had disappeared during building operations, he insisted nevertheless and declared that under these circumstances he did not dare to seek an audience, but would write to his master for instructions.

When the War of Devolution broke out in 1667[2] the Imperial Diet was confronted with the question whether the Spanish Netherlands, which formed the 'Burgundian Circle' of the Empire, should be protected. The French ambassador used all the means at his disposal to prevent such a decision, while the Imperial representative, the archbishop of Salzburg, tried to counteract his influence. Meanwhile Louis XIV conquered town after town, but the Imperial Diet remained silent. In September the Electors pronounced in favour of mediation, ignoring the question whether the Spanish Netherlands formed a part of the Empire. Among the princes the Salzburg resolution which affirmed the latter point obtained only thirty votes, while forty-one were in favour of mediation and thirteen without any instructions. During the following weeks both sides continued their efforts: as the influence of the French ambassador was gaining ground, the archbishop of Salzburg did not persist and the matter was quietly dropped. It was only in 1674, after new acts of aggression, that the Imperial Diet finally declared war on France. But even then only part of the Estates furnished the contingents to the Imperial army which this decision obliged them to provide, and the Franconian and Swabian Circles as well as Bavaria protested against the billeting of the Emperor's forces within their frontiers. After the Peace of Nymegen (1679) no fewer than six of the Electorates—Bavaria, Brandenburg, Cologne,

---

[1] The quotations are from *The Letterbook of Sir George Etherege*, pp. 210, 270, 328, 416.

[2] See *New Cambridge Modern History*, v, ch. ix, pp. 210-12.

Mainz, Trier and Saxony—belonged to the French party, seeking to achieve their aims through an alliance with Louis XIV or compelled by their geographical position to remain on good terms with him. After 1680, however, the new Electors of Bavaria and Saxony adopted a more friendly policy towards Vienna and left the leadership of the French party to the Great Elector of Brandenburg.

It was during these years, when the power of Louis XIV stood at its height, that real progress was made by the Imperial Diet with the creation of an army to defend the Empire. An Imperial law of May 1681 fixed the figure of the *simplum* of the army at 40,000—12,000 horse and 28,000 foot-soldiers. The total was then distributed among the ten Circles of the Empire, the Austrian Circle having to contribute about 20 per cent, and the Burgundian, Lower and Upper Saxon, Swabian and Westphalian Circles about 10 per cent each. Within each Circle, the various Estates had to furnish their military contingents, the details of distribution being left to the Estates of the Circle in question. This meant that in the Swabian Circle, which had by far the largest number of Estates, contingents had to be provided by ninety-one different Estates, including thirty-one Free Imperial Cities. At the same time an Imperial War Chest was set up. The Emperor in person could command the Imperial army or nominate an Imperial Field-Marshal, while the Imperial Diet appointed a number of generals. The fortresses which Louis XIV had built on the right bank of the Rhine—Philippsburg and, after 1697, Kehl—were maintained and garrisoned as Imperial fortresses after their restoration by France. The *simplum* of 1681 could be increased in case of need, and was indeed augmented immediately by 50 per cent to 60,000. By a law of November 1702 it was increased to 120,000, 80,000 of which were to be kept in permanent readiness (*duplum*). Difficulties were, however, raised by those Imperial Estates which already possessed a standing army of their own, for example Brandenburg, because they did not want to furnish their contingents to the armies of different Circles. In practice, therefore, the whole organisation only functioned in the western Circles of the Empire which were directly threatened by Louis XIV. In 1697 the Bavarian, Franconian, Swabian, Westphalian and two Rhenish Circles concluded an Association which undertook—on the basis of the law of 1681—to raise an army of 60,000 men, reduced to 40,000 in peace-time, and regulated its organisation in detail. It was this army which for many years defended the Rhine frontier against France and garrisoned the Imperial fortresses on the Rhine. It thus proved that there was no need for each principality to acquire a standing army of its own, that the Empire was capable of defending its own frontiers, and that the institution of the Circles could be of great practical importance. Some of the Circles successfully dealt with matters of trade, customs, coinage, building of roads, law and police, health and welfare. In the south-west they took steps to bring about greater uniformity in legal and economic affairs—steps which were essential for the progress of the most divided region of the Empire.

The other institution of the Empire which showed signs of real life in the later seventeenth and eighteenth centuries was the Aulic Council at Vienna. For the subjects and Estates of the princes the Imperial courts were the remaining link with the Empire because to them they could complain or appeal, even against their prince, unless he had been granted a *privilegium de non appellando*, and that applied only to four or five princes, such as those of Bavaria and Saxony. The Aulic Council (*Reichshofrat*) was steadily gaining in importance because it dealt with cases more quickly and efficiently than the Imperial High Court, was freer in its rules of procedure and had better means of enforcing its decisions. Thus its jurisdiction was preferred by many parties. It was competent to deal with questions of fiefs and privileges and was the last court of appeal within the Empire. It depended entirely on the Emperor, who nominated its president, its vice-president, and its eighteen councillors, six of whom had to be Protestants. In 1654 he issued on his own authority regulations for the procedure of the Aulic Council which excluded the Imperial Estates from all participation and influence. The jurisdiction of the Aulic Council was instrumental in protecting the subjects of several German princes against the worst excesses of princely despotism and prevented the dukes of Mecklenburg, Württemberg, and Jülich and Berg from making themselves absolute. Its field of competence, however, was progressively curtailed in the eighteenth century by the grant of *privilegia de non appellando* to several princely houses, even outside the Electoral group.

The other Imperial court, the *Reichskammergericht* (Imperial High Court), was steadily declining in importance. Until 1688 it was situated at Speyer, and after the second devastation of the Palatinate it was transferred to Wetzlar. It was the last court of appeal for the subjects of the princes, but a court of first instance for those who were not the subjects of any prince, for example Free Imperial Knights, and in cases of denial of justice. It stood much less under the influence of the Emperor, who nominated its president, and much more under that of the Imperial Estates. Twenty-four of the judges were to be nominated by the Electors, twenty-four by the Circles, and only two by the Emperor. Because of lack of funds, however, the number of judges never exceeded eighteen and was often much smaller. The Imperial High Court was notorious for its dilatory procedure: cases dragged on for decades, and sometimes for centuries, without ever reaching a conclusion. The devastation of the Palatinate and internal strife further contributed to its decline and to the rise of the Aulic Council, which was favoured by the Emperor. An Imperial Deputation was appointed to speed up the appeals pending, but did not start its work until 1767. Apart from the two Imperial courts, there was an Imperial Chancery, under a Vice-Chancellor, which served the Emperor as a secretariate for purposes of the government of the Empire—as distinct from that of his hereditary territories, which were administered by organs such as the Imperial Privy Council, the Privy Conference, and the Court Chancery.[1]

If the Empire had almost lost the character of a State, the weight of political life had shifted into the principalities. The major princes, adopting the principles of absolute government, tried to gain more power at the cost of weaker neighbours and of their own subjects. Their policy of consolidation and of becoming 'more considerable' was bound to lead to conflicts with those institutions which acted as a brake on such endeavours, especially their own Estates. In most principalities these possessed far-reaching privileges, above all the power of the purse which made the ruler dependent on their voting of taxes, whether it was for his growing court expenditure, for his military forces, or for the waging of war. Furthermore, in many principalities the local Estates had acquired a strong influence in the field of administration: by taking over more and more debts of the prince they had gradually built up their own organs of administration, with their own officials and permanent committees, side by side with, or superseding the machinery of the State. In some principalities they had acquired the privilege of periodical meetings, or could meet without a summons by the ruler. Such privileges were extremely irksome to princes who wanted to be independent of any fetters and aimed at the building up of their own administration. This tendency clearly emerged before the election of Leopold I to the Imperial throne, but many princes were not satisfied with the concessions gained. They wanted to extend the rights obtained through the *Recess* of 1654 to all their military enterprises and to see the Estates' power of the purse abolished. In 1670 the Imperial Diet passed a proposal to this effect, but the Emperor refused to give his assent. Therefore the princes with particularly strong inclinations towards absolute government—Bavaria, Brandenburg, Cologne, Palatinate-Neuburg, etc.—in June 1671 concluded an alliance to help each other if their Estates resisted them by force of arms, or if they refused to pay what was necessary for defence purposes or the conservation of fortresses, or what the Empire and the Circles had agreed upon. Against their own Estates the German princes found it easy to co-operate: thus the Great Elector of Brandenburg and the Count Palatine Philip William, the duke of Jülich and Berg, jointly tried to achieve the repeal of the hereditary unions which bound the Estates of Jülich, Cleves, Berg and Mark together.

It was the example of Louis XIV and of his unlimited power which inspired many German princes. If they could not hope to rival the splendour of the French king, if their armies remained woefully inferior to his, they at least had to build a little Versailles on the banks of the Neckar or

[1] For these Habsburg organs of government see *N.C.M.H.*, v, ch. xx, pp. 477, 485.

the Spree. John George II of Saxony built an opera-house and maintained an orchestra with one conductor-in-chief, two assistant conductors, four Italian composers, and forty-six singers. In Württemberg in 1684 a French opera with a ballet was enacted by the court under the title *Le rendez-vous des plaisirs*. A visit to Versailles became almost obligatory for the sons of the German princes, and their example was soon followed by the higher nobility. In 1671 the president of the Württemberg privy council, full of pride, described to the deputies of the Estates the grand tour of the Württemberg princes in France. After their arrival in Paris the two princes

> were immediately visited in their lodgings by the highest grandees and frequently entertained magnificently in their palaces; until finally Marshal de Turenne conducted them in his carriage to an audience in the royal Louvre where they were received in the most friendly fashion by His Majesty; before they were admitted to his presence they were informed that the King would not wear his hat during the audience, but would talk with them bareheaded; and thus it was done in his private closet where he entertained them for a full half hour discoursing with them most graciously, which otherwise was quite unusual....[1]

The sun of Versailles lent lustre even to very minor stars. French fashions and French modes of government penetrated across the Rhine, and French money was an extremely powerful influence at many a princely court. In Berlin, after 1679, the French ambassador, Count Rébenac, wielded enormous influence and distributed his largesse among the servants of the Great Elector, exactly as the French ambassador to the court of St James's did among the supporters and opponents of Charles II.

Among the German principalities the four lay Electorates continued to be the most important ones. Yet during this period the Palatinate lost the leading position which it had occupied for so long. When the Elector Charles Louis in 1649 returned to his devastated lands he used the methods of absolute government; he tried to revive trade, to direct the economy, to improve education, and to settle the religious strife. He also founded a standing army—which in wartime grew to over 8000 men—and a military administration with a war council. For their maintenance permanent taxes on wine, fruit and meat were introduced. The Elector was strongly opposed to all privileges and to any curtailment of the power of the State. Under his strict rule the country began to recover from the ravages of the Thirty Years War, but in 1673 the taxable capital and property were estimated at only about one-quarter of the figure of 1618; in the different local districts it varied from one-sixth to three-fifths of the pre-war figures. Yet the worst was still to come. In 1685 the Simmern branch of the Electors Palatine died out and was succeeded by the Neuburg branch which also ruled in the duchies of Jülich and Berg. Already

[1] State Archives Stuttgart, *Tomus Actorum*, vol. LXXI, fo. 270: report of 13 February 1671.

The Empire after the Thirty Years War

in 1674 the Palatinate had been terribly devastated by the French; now Louis XIV claimed it in the name of his brother who was married to Elisabeth Charlotte, the sister of the last Elector of the Simmern line. The result of the ensuing war was a second devastation, even more thorough and deliberate than the first. Among the many towns and villages destroyed was the capital, Heidelberg, with its ancient university and beautiful palace. From these repeated blows the Palatinate was unable to recover. In addition, the new Elector, John William, was a Catholic and soon began to oppress the Calvinists, many of whom sought refuge abroad. Thus the Palatinate lost its leading position among the German principalities and became one among many minor States; even in the eighteenth century it was unable to resume its former place.

The other Wittelsbach Electorate, Bavaria, emerged from the Thirty Years War considerably strengthened, in spite of the ill-effects of the war. Maximilian I was the acknowledged leader of the Catholic League, gained the Electoral dignity and conquered the Upper Palatinate, where he suppressed the Estates and introduced the Counter-Reformation. In Bavaria also he followed the principles of absolute government. As he wrote shortly before his death in the 'Information' which he left to his wife: in almost every country there was a clash of interests between the prince and the Estates, for they always tried to increase their privileges and liberties and to escape the burdens and taxes to which the prince was entitled by right, or at least to whittle them down by all kinds of means; therefore, it was not advisable to hold diets without a highly important cause, because the Estates only used them to raise their grievances and new pretensions.[1] In spite of the Estates' demands, no diet was summoned after the end of the war, but they were successful in achieving the disbanding of the army, with the exception of only a few garrisons. Maximilian's successor, Ferdinand Maria (1651–79), continued his father's methods of government. Its heart and soul was the privy council; the other central authorities, for financial, military and religious affairs, were made subordinate to it and became its executive organs. For the supervision of the local authorities and matters of 'police', agriculture, trade and industry, the Church and the schools, the *Rentmeister* were used as the long arm of the government, their manifold functions corresponding to those of the *intendants* in France. The Elector administered the country as though it were his private estate and ruled his subjects as if he were their guardian. Through the introduction of new taxes and the judicious use of monopolies the electoral revenues grew considerably and were partly used to encourage music and the arts. A standing army of a few thousand men came into being, but only during the wars against Louis XIV did it reach a

---

[1] Christian Ruepprecht, 'Die Information des Kurfürsten Maximilian I. von Bayern für seine Gemahlin vom 13. März 1651', *Oberbayerisches Archiv für vaterländische Geschichte*, LIX (1895–6), p. 317.

more substantial size. After many years and repeated petitions of the Estates' committee Ferdinand Maria consented to summon a diet. It met in 1669, after an interval of fifty-seven years: the last in the history of the *ancien régime*. The Estates granted 372,000 guilders a year for nine years and took over most of the Electoral debts. They further empowered their twenty deputies to grant another 200,000 guilders in case of need and, if this was insufficient, to summon the Estates; but some days later the Elector changed this clause by a decree which empowered the deputies to decide with him what was necessary and to co-opt new members in case of any vacancy. Thus the Estates' deputies continued to meet several times each year, to grant the taxes required by the government, to raise grievances, and to supervise the financial administration of the Estates and the work of their officials. Ferdinand Maria's successor, Max Emanuel (1679–1726), paid even less regard to the privileges of the Estates: he considered them a useless institution and an obstacle to his ambitious foreign policy. During the War of the Spanish Succession he sided with Louis XIV, was put under the ban of the Empire and, after Blenheim, driven out of the country.[1] After his restoration in 1714 he continued his absolutist policy; but he did not dispense with the remaining rights of the deputies of the Estates.

Even more than Catholic Bavaria, it was the two Protestant Electorates in the east of Germany, Brandenburg and Saxony, which came to the fore in the period after the Thirty Years War. More will be said about Brandenburg in another chapter,[2] but at this time Saxony was still the much more developed, wealthy and populous of the two. As a result of the war it had acquired Lusatia and the secularised bishoprics of Meissen, Merseburg and Naumburg. Soon a much greater prize, Poland, was to loom large in the policy of the Electors. But it was a gain of very doubtful value, for vast sums of money had to be spent in Poland, partly on bribes to the electors; and the kingdom absorbed the energies of the House of Wettin which thus could not concentrate on the development of their own State—the policy to which the Hohenzollerns adhered so faithfully. Poland and the wars in which the Electors found themselves involved because of Poland—especially that against Sweden in the early eighteenth century, during which Saxony was occupied by the Swedish army[3]— contributed to the decline of Saxony. From the point of view of Brandenburg it was extremely lucky that the ambition of the Great Elector and his eldest son to become king of Poland was not fulfilled. In contrast with Brandenburg and with Bavaria, the Estates of Saxony did not lose their powers: on the contrary, the enormous debts of the Electors forced them to make new concessions to the Estates. In 1661 their deputies were granted the right of free assembly on their own initiative to discuss

---

[1] *N.C.M.H.*, vi, ch. xiii.   [2] *N.C.M.H.*, v, ch. xxiii, pp. 543 ff.
[3] *N.C.M.H.*, vi, ch. xx.

important affairs; if the Elector attempted to change the established religion, Lutheranism, the Estates' votes of credit were to be null and void. The religious issue stiffened their resistance to absolute monarchy; for in 1697 Frederick Augustus I, to secure the Polish Crown, became a Roman Catholic and thus lost his rights of supreme headship over the Saxon Church which were transferred to the privy council. He had to sell or pawn many lands and prerogatives; but he made his capital, Dresden, a centre of the arts and founded the Meissen porcelain manufactory, the first in Germany, soon to become famous. A standing army of about 10,000 men came into being in the later seventeenth century. During the wars against the Turks, in which it took a prominent part, it was increased to nearly 20,000: less only than that of Brandenburg. Yet the growth of the *miles perpetuus* did not destroy the power of the Estates, and diets continued to be summoned at fairly regular intervals. Their influence only declined when, early in the eighteenth century, the general excise was introduced on the pattern of Brandenburg. The need of money and more money, the religious opposition, and the Electors' preoccupation with Poland prevented them from following the Hohenzollerns' example more closely; the standing army remained comparatively small, and Saxony remained a constitutional monarchy—in contrast with the kingdom of Prussia.

The development of Hanover, which in 1692 became the youngest Electorate, was considerably delayed by conflicts among ducal brothers, so common in German princely families, and the resulting divisions of their territory. New partitions were effected in 1641 and in 1665; but in 1683 Ernest Augustus of Hanover introduced primogeniture for his possessions, and in 1705 his son, the Elector George Louis, succeeded in reuniting the ducal territories, nine years before he mounted the British throne. In the later seventeenth century dukes John Frederick and Ernest Augustus of Hanover built up a strong army which enabled them to participate actively in the wars against Louis XIV and the Turks and the rebellious Hungarians. The elevation of Ernest Augustus to the Electoral dignity by the Emperor Leopold was a reward for services rendered. The former also supported the expedition of William of Orange to England. The administration of the Electorate was carried on, under the Elector's control, by the privy council, with four colleges responsible for finance, law, war, and the Church respectively. The court was under the influence of the philosopher Leibniz.[1] The ruling group, however, consisted of the nobility, and this prevented the establishment of a completely absolute government. This tendency was strongly reinforced in the eighteenth century, because the Electors were so often absent abroad and the government was in the hands of regents drawn from the native nobility. All important posts were reserved to a few families, social dis-

[1] For Leibniz, see *N.C.M.H.*, v, ch. iv, pp. 82-5; ch. v, pp. 114-17; ch. vi, pp. 145-6.

tinctions were rigidly upheld, and the Estates dominated by the nobility in practice ruled the country. Even the historical divisions remained a reality; the Estates were divided into seven different corporations for the several duchies and counties which made up the Electorate. Exactly as the preoccupation of the Electors of Saxony with Poland prevented them from playing a leading part in Germany, so the preoccupation of the Electors of Hanover with Britain prevented them from concentrating on the development and unification of their German possessions.

In the duchy of Holstein, to the north of Hanover, on the other hand, the Estates lost all their influence in the later seventeenth century. There the joint rulers—the dukes of Holstein and the kings of Denmark—used to the full the rights granted by the Imperial *Recess* of 1654,[1] which were backed by a decision of the Lower Saxon Circle. The rulers maintained that they alone were entitled to decide upon the maintenance of fortresses and garrisons, while the Estates declined to grant them the necessary means. After the accession of Duke Christian Albrecht in 1659, however, a tax for military purposes was demanded regularly every spring: if the Estates did not consent to it, it was nevertheless levied by the government. When the Estates referred to their privileges the government declared that these constituted only a private law, while the decisions of the Empire and the Circle were fundamental and public laws. When the Estates insisted that their grievances be redressed first, the rulers refused and proceeded with the compulsory levies. In 1675 the last diet was summoned: after renewed disputes it was adjourned, never to meet again, and the Estates lost all their influence. Very similar was the development in the margraviate of Baden-Durlach, in the south-west of Germany, which had suffered severely from the Thirty Years War and was to suffer even more during the wars of Louis XIV. There also the diet met for the last time in 1668: without any opposition it transferred the power of the purse and the administration of the debts to Margrave Frederick VI. The constitution was not abrogated, but the diet was no longer summoned because its usefulness had disappeared. The country was ruled by the methods of patriarchal absolutism which eliminated all conflicts and promoted economic recovery. A memorandum drawn up in 1771 pointed out correctly that the very name of the Estates had long been forgotten.

In some other principalities, however, exactly as in Saxony, the Estates during and after the Thirty Years War succeeded in retaining and even extending their powers. In the duchy of Mecklenburg, to the east of Holstein, the dukes also claimed the right of levying taxes for military purposes without a grant by the Estates. In 1659–63 these complained to the Emperor Leopold and the Aulic Council where their privileges were confirmed. Encouraged by this support from the highest authorities of the Empire they refused in 1671 to pay the aid granted by the Imperial

[1] See above, p. 106.

Diet to the United Provinces, whereupon the dukes levied it by force. When the Estates renewed their complaint to the Aulic Council it was rejected; yet the conflict went on. In 1698 the Aulic Council decided that, if the issue was a tax for the Empire, the Estates were obliged to pay. Three years later it was agreed that for such purposes 120,000 thalers were to be levied annually, one-third of which was to be given by the nobility, the towns, and the ducal domains respectively; and this was confirmed by the Emperor, but rejected by a part of the nobility. New conflicts broke out during the War of the North in which Duke Charles Leopold participated on the side of Peter the Great and Russian troops occupied the duchy.[1] The Estates refused to grant the large sums demanded and Rostock, the only important town of the duchy, again appealed to the Aulic Council; but in 1715 the town had to surrender and to accept the ducal conditions. In the same year the Emperor Charles VI, after petitions of the Mecklenburg Estates and the Elector George Louis of Hanover, decreed an 'Imperial Execution' against Charles Leopold and entrusted its execution to the princes of Hanover and Brunswick. Their troops occupied the duchy after the departure of the Russian troops and virtually deposed Charles Leopold. By a decision of the Aulic Council the government was in 1728 entrusted to his brother, and the constitution was restored with the help of the Estates. In the middle of the eighteenth century the conflict was renewed; but the Estates, backed by the Aulic Council, were again victorious over the duke and their privileges remained in force.

If the Mecklenburg Estates were dominated by the nobility, the opposite was true of the duchy of Württemberg in the south-west: there the Estates consisted only of the deputies of about sixty towns and fourteen secularised monasteries and were unicameral—a very exceptional development, due to the fact that the noblemen had become Free Imperial Knights. In Württemberg also the main issue between the dukes and the Estates was the question of the standing army. The Estates strenuously refused to grant the means for its maintenance in peace-time and achieved its reduction to a few hundred men as soon as the wars came to an end. When Duke Frederick Charles in the 1690's transformed the militia into a regular army the Estates declared that this was unconstitutional and complained to the Aulic Council, but without much success. The conflicts continued in the eighteenth century during which the Estates at first steadily lost ground, but finally succeeded in re-establishing their influence, thanks to support from the Aulic Council and the kings of Prussia and Britain. In Württemberg also, the fact that, from 1733 onwards, the Estates were fighting against Roman Catholic dukes strengthened their resistance to despotic government.

Thus constitutional developments varied enormously in the different

[1] For these events, see *N.C.M.H.*, vi, ch. xx.

parts of Germany, with repercussions which have lasted into the twentieth century. But the events in the Palatinate and Baden, in the south-west, and in Mecklenburg, in the north-east, show that it was by no means the south-west which remained more constitutional and 'liberal' and the north-east which became more autocratic. The divergent developments cannot be explained by factors of geography, nor by differences of social structure; for the Estates of Mecklenburg—like those of Poland and of Hungary—were dominated by the nobility, and those of Württemberg by the burghers of small towns. Only in Saxony did there exist a balance between the nobility and the towns, among which Leipzig was by far the most important. In Brandenburg and Prussia, on the other hand, where the nobility was as predominant as in Mecklenburg, absolute government triumphed, and a standing army was established which was far larger than in any other German principality. This was due, above all, to the determined policy of the Hohenzollerns: their single-mindedness helped them to overtake the Wittelsbachs and the Wettiners during the century following upon the Thirty Years War. The personal factor was of vital importance in this respect. Outside Prussia, the standing armies remained small, and the Estates with their ancient liberties and constitutional rights disappeared only in a few of the other principalities. Wherever their influence was preserved, and wherever that of the army did not permeate the whole State, a tradition remained alive which was to facilitate the establishment of modern self-government and representative institutions.

THE CAUSES OF THE DECLINE OF THE GERMAN ESTATES

For most of the German principalities — with the significant exception of Württemberg (¹) — we do not possess any satisfactory history of the Estates: the study of their history has been neglected, yet its outlines are fairly clear. After a period of growth beginning in the later Middle Ages they reached the highest point of their power in the 16th, or even in the earlier 17th century — considerably later than the French States General and Provincial Estates or the Spanish Cortes; but upon that period there followed a period of rapid decline, particularly so in the later 17th century, and in certain principalities the Estates disappeared as an institution (²). In many other principalities, however, they survived, although with restricted powers, to the end of the *ancien régime,* and in the 18th century there occurred a distinct revival of their influence, above all in Württemberg and Mecklenburg. In the majority of German principalities the fate of the Estates was very different from that which befell them in the absolute monarchies of western Europe, but equally different from their rôle in Britain and the United Provinces where they gained decisive influence and became part of the machinery of government. Within Germany, there was a world of difference between the absolute military monarchy of the Hohenzollerns, in which the Estates had virtually disappeared, and the principalities which were governed constitutionally, such as Saxony, Hanover or Württemberg. Yet even within the Hohenzollern monarchy the Estates of Cleves and Mark continued to function and to provide a practical alternative to absolute government, as the Freiherr vom Stein had occasion to observe as late as the end of the

(¹) Walter GRUBE, *Der Stuttgarter Landtag, 1457-1957,* Stuttgart, 1957.

(²) In the Rhine Palatinate, where the Estates had never properly developed as an institution, they disappeared completely with the events of the Thirty Years War and the restoration of the Elector Charles Louis at the end of the war. In the Upper Palatinate, Maximilian of Bavaria abolished the Estates during the war after the conquest of the territory because they had allegedly forfeited their privileges by participating in the Bohemian venture of their prince, Frederick V of the Palatinate. The Estates of the margraviate of Baden-Durlach and of the duchy of Holstein were abolished during the third quarter of the 17th century. In most of the Hohenzollern territories they practically disappeared soon afterwards.

18th century; and in Bavaria — another absolute monarchy — the Estates' committees continued to meet regularly and to exercise the functions of the Diet, which was no longer summoned, especially in the field of taxation and financial administration.

Most of the German Estates in the 16th century possessed far-reaching privileges and wielded the power of the purse; they had their own officials and standing committees which could meet without a summons from the ruler; they took an active part in legislation, which was often due to their own initiative, to the *gravamina* which they raised during the sessions of the Diet; they frequently acted as arbiters in cases of conflict between members of the ruling house; they participated through their own deputies in treaties and alliances concluded by their princes; they exercised the regency on behalf of rulers who were minors or incapable, and their consent was often required before the beginning of a war or other foreign venture. Above all, when the Estates took over their princes' debts in the course of the 16th century, they acquired a decisive voice in the financial administration of the principality, collecting the taxes through their own deputies and officials, paying from the revenue the interest on the debts, and in general allocating supply in the interests of the principality. They thus entered the field of general administration and, after the Reformation, they even acquired a voice in religious affairs: many a prince had to promise that he would not alter the established religion of the principality without the Estates' consent; and the revenues from the secularized monasteries were partly used for pious and educational purposes at the insistence of the Estates, for otherwise they might have been entirely squandered. In Catholic Bavaria the Estates did achieve that the chalice was, for a time, granted to the laity; and in Lutheran Prussia the Estates completely dominated the Church and all appointments in the religious as well as the secular sphere. Although it has often been asserted that the power of the princes grew as a result of the introduction of the Lutheran Reformation [3], there

---

[3] Otto HINTZE, *Typologie der ständischen Verfassungen des Abendlandes*, in *Staat und Verfassung*, ed. Fritz HARTUNG, Leipzig, 1941, p. 128, in general sees in the transfer of spiritual powers to the temporal rulers since the Council of Basle and the Reformation one of the principal causes of the development of absolutism, under the Tudors, in Denmark and Sweden, and especially in France, Germany, Southern Italy and Spain. The example of the Tudors alone shows how doubtful this generalization is.

is no evidence that this applied to the relationship between prince and Estates. Like Henry VIII of England, most German princes were forced by lack of money to sell or pawn many of the monastic lands, mainly to members of the nobility — a factor which strengthened the local Estates. Even where a large proportion of the monastic lands remained state domains they were administered — as in the duchy of Prussia — by members of the local nobility for their own benefit; or their revenues were used to pay the interest on the prince's debt and to support schools and universities, functions which were supervized by members of the Estates.

In Bavaria, on the other hand, and later in the Habsburg territories, it was the introduction of the Counter-Reformation which strengthened the power of the prince and weakened the Estates — for the simple reason that in all these lands (with the exception of the county of Tyrol) the leaders of the opposition among the Estates were Protestants. The triumph of the Counter-Reformation before and during the Thirty Years War meant that the political and the religious aspirations of these leaders were defeated simultaneously. The religious privileges which had been granted previously were withdrawn; the Protestant leaders were tried, imprisoned and forced into exile; the nobility, a declining class, was disunited and offered but feeble resistance; the ruin caused by the Thirty Years War completed the work begun by Albert V of Bavaria and Ferdinand of Styria. Although the Estates survived as an institution and retained a certain influence, their power of resistance was broken and their political ambitions were extinguished when the disastrous war reached its end. They had become subservient to the prince, and he saw no reason why he should abolish them altogether, as they performed useful services as collectors of taxes, in billeting and recruiting, and in the sphere of local government.

In the Lutheran principalities also the Thirty Years War decisively influenced the relationship between the prince and the Estates, not only in the sense that their power of resistance was broken through devastation and depopulation. Many principalities were occupied by hostile armies, Swedish, French or Imperialist, which levied contributions without any regard for the Estates' privileges; and this example was followed by Maximilian of Bavaria no less than by Count Schwartzenberg, the ambitious minister of the Elector of Brandenburg. In Brandenburg the Estates never recovered from this period of military rule, soon to be followed by a much harsher and more permanent military régime. Yet in other principalities — Saxony, Württemberg, Hesse — the princes after the end of the war needed the support of their Estates to promote the recovery of their devastated lands. And in the duchies on the lower Rhine — Jülich, Cleves, Berg and Mark — the Estates' position was strengthened through the long-drawn-out conflicts over the succession to this rich inheritance and the competition of the European powers for influence in this vital area, which strengthened the ties between the United Provinces and the Estates of Cleves. If there had been a long period of peace and recuperation after the peace of Westphalia, the Estates might have been able to retain and to consolidate their influence.

This, however, was not to be. Only six years after the end of the great struggle, the War of the North between Poland and Sweden offered to the Great Elector of Brandenburg his chance to gain the sovereignty over the duchy of Prussia and to establish a régime based on military force in those of his territories which were not directly touched by the war. His growing forces allowed him to disregard the Estates' privileges in Brandenburg as well as in Cleves and Mark — a policy he continued to apply after the end of the war in the duchy of Prussia. The foundation of the Brandenburg standing army ensured that in future taxes could be levied by the military if the Estates hesitated to make grants. The establishment of a military bureaucracy enabled the Great Elector to dispense with the services of the local officials, drawn from and supervised by the Estates, in the collection and administration of the taxes. The introduction of a permanent tax — the urban excise — made the summoning of the Diets unnecessary and deprived the Estates of their *raison d'être*. The adoption of different systems of taxation in the countryside and the towns divided the corporation of the Estates and made out of their once united edifice a heap of rubble, as the Estates of Prussia pointed out to the Elector [4]. By skilfully playing off one Estate against the other and using their antagonistic

---

[4] «alss nach dem übel gesinnete den einen leib der dreyen Stände dieses landes zergliedert, einen Krepel daraus gemacht, die Städte undt freyheiten von dem lande undt die woll-priviligirte Cöllmer undt freyen von dem Adel, wieder Königl. Churfürstl. undt fürstliche Assecurationes mit himmelschreyender Unbilligkeit getrennet...»: Declaration of the Prussian nobility of 5 Juli 1683: *Ostpreussische Folianten*, vol. 718, f° 1210 (also in vols. 717, 719, 722), in the KÖNIGSBERG STATE ARCHIVES, now at Göttingen.

interests he successfully destroyed their political power. The creation of the officer corps soon reconciled most of the nobility to the establishment of absolute government. The example of the powerful Prussian state and the imposing Prussian army strongly influenced other German princes, the Electors of Saxony no less than the landgraves of Hesse and the dukes of Württemberg, especially in the 18th century.

Yet in the later 17th century — which saw a far more rapid decline of the Estates' power than the 18th century — it was not so much Brandenburg but France which exercised a decisive influence on German affairs. The wars of Louis XIV forced the German states along the Rhine to take defensive measures. Many German princes used the opportunity to create their own standing armies (which proved of little avail against the might of France) and in doing so encountered the determined opposition of the Estates: they correctly emphasized the plight of the country after the terrible devastations of the Thirty Years War, their inability to pay heavy taxes, and the uselessness of these armaments. In the long-drawn-out struggles which ensued many German princes were successful in establishing small standing armies and in fatally weakening their own Estates. Eventually most Estates had to accept the principle of a standing army and of more or less fixed contributions for its maintenance: their power of the purse in practice ceased to exist.

Louis XIV not only influenced constitutional developments inside Germany through his wars of aggression, but equally through his example, which set a pattern for so many European countries. He was the most powerful king of Europe, unfettered by any representative institutions or privileged corporations: nobody dared to oppose his will. It became the ambition of many a German prince to make himself more «considerable», inside and outside his principality. If there were any privileges of the Estates which stood in his way, these were out of tune with the times and must be revoked; it was the duty of subjects to obey, and not to argue. Time and again German princes pointed this out to their intimidated Estates. As early as 1657 an official of the Great Elector informed the Estates of Cleves that subjects must not grumble, but rather pray when their prince was fighting [5]. Such admonitions did not stop them from grum-

---

[5] «Unterthanen müssten dagegen nicht murren, sondern viel eher beten, wenn der Fürst fechtete...»: *Urkunden und Actenstücke zur Geschichte des*

bling, but there was virtually no resistance to the imposition of arbitrary taxes and their collection by military force: the spirit of the Sea-Beggars and of the Roundheads was not abroad in Germany. This was partly due, I think, to the general economic decline caused by the Thirty Years War and the subsequent wars, and partly to the Estates' ingrained attitude of obedience to the prince according to the doctrine of the Divine Right of Kings and the teachings of Luther; this had prevented the Lutheran noblemen of Bavaria from rendering resistance to Duke Albert V in the 16th century, and it deeply influenced their successors in the 17th century.

Against the violation of their privileges the Estates of many principalities complained to the Emperor and the Imperial courts, especially to the Aulic Council, or — in Prussia at the time of the Great Elector — to the crown of Poland, but with little effect. The enfeeblement of the Empire and the Emperor's need of princely support against France and against the Turks meant that these complaints were hardly ever entertained; if a suit developed the decision usually went against the Estates. The Great Elector with impunity could arrest the deputies of the Estates of Cleves on their return from Ratisbon where they had submitted their complaints to the Emperor. The decisions of the Imperial Diet of 1654 and the capitulation granted before his election in 1658 by the Emperor Leopold I expressly forbade all complaints by the Estates to the Imperial institutions against the maintenance of their rulers' garrisons and fortresses and prohibited any assemblies of the Estates without a summons. When the danger from France had subsided, however, such complaints were not only heard again by the Aulic Council; but, what is even more important, its decisions went in favour of the Estates, at least in the two memorable cases of Mecklenburg and Württemberg. In the 18th century the institutions of the Empire once more upheld the case of the Estates, with highly significant results. Even in the 18th century the Empire was by no means dead.

The main issue between the princes and the Estates undoubtedly was finance. The power of the Estates lasted as long as they possessed

Kurfürsten Friedrich Wilhelm von Brandenburg, vol. V, Berlin, 1869, p. 891: letter of 14 March 1657. References to out-of-date privileges were much more frequent in the 18th century, claims which were hardly ever disputed by the Estates.

The Causes of the Decline of the German Estates 125

the power of the purse and controlled taxation and financial administration. Wherever the prince did not need the financial aid of the Estates, for example in the Rhine Palatinate, they remained weak or even insignificant. Wherever the prince succeeded in obtaining a substantial revenue of his own, be that from former monastic lands or, as in Bavaria, from decimations of the clergy, his hand was strengthened against the Estates. Wherever a permanent tax was introduced, which was no longer dependent on a vote of credit by the Estates, their privileges disappeared. The best-known example of this kind was the introduction of the urban excise by the Great Elector, an example which was imitated by the Electors of Saxony and other princes. It is noteworthy, however, that in Bavaria, Württemberg and elsewhere an excise on consumption was also introduced; but it was only granted for limited periods at a time and it continued to be administered by the Estates: hence their privileges survived, at least to a certain extent.

There are thus strong parallels between the history of the German Estates and that of the English Parliament. While in the 16th century many German Estates were stronger and exercised a greater political influence on the principality in question than did the English Parliament, in the course of the 17th century this relationship was reversed. In England, Puritanism became a militant creed, the heart and soul of the Parliamentarian opposition. No parallel for this can be found anywhere in Germany, although there Lutheranism at times — for example in Hesse, Saxony and Württemberg — strengthened the hand of the Estates against a Calvinist or a Catholic prince [6]. Antagonized by a new, inexperienced and inapt dynasty the English Parliament developed from strength to strength, while the German Estates declined rapidly. As I have tried to show, this was partly due to the Thirty Years War and to other calamities over which they had no control, partly to the influences emanating from France. Further causes of their decline were their own divisions and lack of tactical skill, the absence of able leaders, the Estates' unwillingness or inability to resist princely encroachments, and

[6] The best-known example is the resistance of the Estates of Hesse-Cassel during the Thirty Years War to the forward Protestant policy of the Landgrave Maurice which led to his abdication. The opposition of the Estates of Saxony and of Württemberg to the absolutist policy of their rulers was strengthened by the fact that their Catholicism (from 1697 and 1733 onwards respectively) aroused much animosity in these strongly Lutheran principalities.

their readiness to make large grants, even for purposes of which they strongly disapproved, such as the creation of the *miles perpetuus*. Yet it remains true that the German Estates fulfilled very important functions, that they had the interests of their principalities at heart, and that they represented the whole country. Wherever their liberties were destroyed, liberty suffered the same fate. Although liberties and liberty did not mean the same thing, they were nevertheless closely connected. The Estates indeed belong to the main stream of German history, as they do in the majority of European countries. They deserve a much more honoured place than has been accorded to them by the historians ([7]).

([7]) The detailled evidence for the arguments advanced in this paper will be found in the author's *Princes and Parliaments in Germany*, Oxford, 1959.

9

THE COURT JEWS: PRELUDE TO EMANCIPATION

THE 17th and 18th centuries are the period of the court Jews in German history. It was only during this comparatively short period that individual Jews — not the Jews as such — played a vital part in the financial and business affairs of all the more important German rulers; it was only in Germany and Austria that they achieved such pre-eminence at that time: neither in the more advanced countries of western Europe, nor in the more backward countries of eastern Europe, where the large majority of the Jews lived.

A number of questions arise from this limitation of the influence of the court Jews in time as well as in area. Why were there no court Jews of any importance before the Thirty Years' War? Why did they disappear as a distinctive group with the early 19th century? Why did they not play a similar part in other countries? What were their main characteristics and distinctive features, distinguishing them from the non-Jewish financiers and businessmen of their own time and from the Jewish traders and men of affairs of other periods? What is the general importance of this period for Jewish and for German history?

In this essay an attempt will be made to answer these questions as far as our knowledge allows. Such answers have been facilitated by the publication in recent years of detailed works on the subject of the court Jews; a more general one, by Selma Stern-Taeubler, summarises her earlier and detailed work in Germany on this subject: *'The Court Jew, A Contribution to the History of the Period of Absolutism in Central Europe,* Philadelphia, 1950. A much more detailed one, by a younger German historian, Heinrich Schnee, publicises the results of his research in many North-German archives: *Die Hoffinanz und der moderne Staat, Geschichte und System der Hoffaktoren an deutschen Fürstenhöfen im Zeitalter des Absolutismus,* 3 volumes, Berlin, 1953—5. The research of both authors has shed much new light on a question of general interest. The material which they have assembled during many years deserves to be made accessible to a wider public, which might easily be deterred by the form in which it is presented and by the mass of often repetitive detail.

Both authors, as shown by the sub-titles of their books, consider the court Jews to be a feature of the period of princely despotism which began in the 16th century and came to an end with the French Revolution and Napoleon. Yet princely despotism was a general European phenomenon; absolute rule was more pronounced in France and Spain, in Russia and the Ottoman Empire, than in Germany or Austria, where the Estates of the many principalities in question for a long time prevented the setting-up of strong governments and where the princes prevented the Emperor from ever acquiring absolute power. The court Jews, however, were a feature of these territories only, and they did not assume any importance before the middle of the 17th century.

By that time the governments of France and England were much stronger than those of Germany and Austria; France and England were advanced countries with a prosperous middle class, a well-developed machinery of taxation and a native bureaucracy which raised the money required by the government from the king's subjects. There were native bankers and merchants who would be willing to lend money to the government if they received adequate security. In England the Jews were only readmitted about the middle of the 17th century, by which time the native middle classes were strong and wielded considerable political influence through Parliament. Although the French bourgeoisie possessed no comparable institution, it dominated the administration of the kingdom, and the great tax-farmers advanced large sums to the Crown for which they recouped themselves at the cost of the people. In neither country was there any need of Jewish financiers and merchants, and the Jews did not play an important part in the economic life of the country.

The latter was also true of Spain, from which the Jews had been expelled in the late 15th century; in the 17th century Spain was in a state of decline, among the causes of which were the expulsion of the Jews and the Moors and the victimisation of their descendants, even if they had been baptised. The kings of Spain were heavily indebted to Spanish and foreign bankers, but the Inquisition did not permit the Jews to operate in Spain. In the Dutch Republic, on the other hand, Jewish bankers and merchants played an important part, side by side with those of Dutch stock. The religious toleration and civil equality prevailing in Holland, among other factors, enabled the Dutch Republic to become the most advanced country economically and the most important money market of Europe.

The rising prices of the 16th century and the growing expenditure of the rulers at a time when their revenues remained stationary forced many princes to resort to borrowing, partly from their own subjects, partly from foreign bankers and moneylenders. Germany and Austria were no exception to this rule: not only the Habsburg Emperor, but the large majority of the territorial princes became heavily indebted, however wealthy they originally had been. Not even the introduction of the Reformation and the confiscation of church property proved a solution of their financial problems, any more than those of Henry VIII were solved by the dissolution of the monasteries.

The German princes of the 16th century, however, did not borrow from the Jews: Germany was still a very wealthy country with flourishing towns connected by the main arteries of European trade. The Habsburgs and the other princes were able to borrow large sums from the great German banking houses, such as the Fuggers and the Welsers, and equally from their own subjects. The pronounced impecuniousness of the rulers and their constant need for money were the main cause of the rise of the Estates. In most territories the Estates took over their ruler's debts, but only against weighty concessions in the political and economic fields. In many cases the Estates themselves took over the financial administration of the principality, the levying and collecting of taxes, the control of revenue and expenditure, and thus securely established their political power. The large sums of money they granted year after year to pay off their ruler's debts are proof of the wealth available in the country.

All this changed with the outbreak of the Thirty Years' War and the collapse of the great banking houses, partly as a result of the war, partly as a result of the bankruptcies of the Spanish kings, to whom the Fuggers and the Welsers had advanced many millions. The frightful debasement of the coinage at the time of the *Kipper und Wipper* ruined all credit and caused a general cessation of trade.[1] Whatever wealth there still was, whatever was produced or hidden away, whatever escaped the depredations of the ill-disciplined soldiery, was consumed by the long drawn-out war. Heavy contributions had to be paid to occupying armies, many towns were sacked or pillaged; Germany became a battlefield of the armies of Europe. Even after the end of the struggle heavy war indemnities had to be paid to France and Sweden. Nor was there any chance of an economic recovery.

Only a few years after the end of the Thirty Years' War, the first great War of the North broke out, followed by the wars of Louis XIV, during which large parts of Germany were systematically devastated by the French. Even in the areas not affected by these wars the burdens imposed upon the impoverished inhabitants increased steeply, for it became every ruler's ambition to have a standing army, a *miles perpetuus,* in place of the mercenary forces hired only in case of war. It became equally every ruler's ambition to imitate the great king at Versailles, to construct at least a little Versailles on the banks of the Isar, the Spree or the Elbe, to vie with his rivals in luxury and splendour, in dazzling festivals and ostentatious buildings. The princes needed money and more money, but there were no longer any native bankers to whom they could turn, nor were their subjects able to lend them millions as in the preceding century.

This situation proved the great opportunity for those Jews who provided the armies with food and fodder, bought the soldiers' booty at advantageous

[1] In Württemberg, for example, the debased guilder was no longer accepted by the neighbouring districts and the bad coins flooded back into the Duchy. Eventually, in 1623, a decree was promulgated putting the value of the debased guilder at one-sixth of its original value (10 instead of 60 kreuzers), and that of the debased shilling at one-third (2 instead of 6 pfennigs). Through this decree the Estates of the Duchy alone suffered a loss of 248,551 guilders: Christian Friedrich Sattler, *Geschichte des Herzogthums Würtenberg unter der Regierung der Herzogen,* Ulm, 1773, Vol. VI, pp. 194, 200; State Archives, Stuttgart, A. 34—5, *Büschel* 40, no. 27; *Büschel* 41, no. 4c.

prices and traded in the wake of the armies. Because there were so many princes and because they all needed loans so badly, this was the opportunity not only for a few Jews attached to one court, but for dozens and even hundreds, working for many different princes, to supply them with what they needed, or rather more often what they did not need. Because there were so many small states, all trying to foster their own trade and industry and to hinder that of their neighbours, because there were so many customs frontiers and staple rights, because there was no unity and no economic policy, the economic recovery of Germany and of the native middle classes was delayed to a very considerable degree.

Thus the court Jews filled a real gap and many princes simply could not manage without them. Already during the great war many princes and generals, such as the Habsburgs and their generalissimo Wallenstein, had protected the Jewish ghettos against looting and requisitioning because they needed the money of the Jews for the conduct of the war. Especially in the trade with precious metals the Jews now predominated. The enormous destruction of capital increased rather than decreased this dependence on the Jews after the end of the war. Many of the court Jews of the later 17th and 18th centuries were the descendants of people who had made their fortunes during the Thirty Years' War.[2] In this respect, as in so many others, the great war exercised a profound influence upon the course of German history.

It was, above all, the financial needs of the rulers which induced them to use the services of the court Jews. Whether it was the court which had to be supplied with money, or the army which had to be maintained; whether the outbreak of a war led to increased expenditure, or economic experiments were to be carried out in peace-time; whether jewels had to be procured, debts to be settled or loans to be raised, it was to the Jews that the princes turned in their predicament when all other means had failed. When Augustus the Strong of Saxony required millions of thalers to further his election to the Polish throne, it was to the Jew Behrend Lehmann that he addressed his demands, apart from his own Estates. When the same prince was in a state of the greatest distress owing to the outbreak of the War of the North in the early 18th century and his army had to be provided with food, shoes, horses and other necessities, it was Lehmann and his brothers-in-law who supplied his needs. When Archbishop Joseph Clemens of Cologne found the subsidies of Louis XIV insufficient to satisfy his political ambitions and his lust for glory and luxury, he turned to Meyer zum Goldstein and Joseph Cassel to furnish his requirements of clothes, silk, velvet, jewels, food, fodder, etc. Many more Jews were employed by the Archbishop after his return to Cologne in 1715, when the war of the Spanish Succession ended.

Above all it was the Habsburg Emperors — whose treasury was always

[2]Schnee, *op. cit.*, I, 79; II, 223; III, 173, 178—9.

empty and who often could not pay the troops engaged in the long drawn-out wars against the Turks — who had to rely on the aid of Jewish bankers and financiers. Samuel Oppenheimer in Vienna paid the subsidies the Emperor had promised to other German states, provisioned and paid the army and bore a large part of the cost of the war. Margrave Louis of Baden, commander of the Imperial troops, confessed that without Oppenheimer the war could not have been carried on and everything would have ended in defeat. Upon Oppenheimer's death in 1703 Samson Wertheimer had to undertake the financing of military operations in the Low Countries, Germany and Italy, during the War of the Spanish Succession, the payment of generals, officials and ambassadors, and of the princes of the Empire who received Imperial subsidies. Wertheimer placed his entire credit at the disposal of the Emperor's brother Charles, the claimant to the Spanish throne, on whose behalf the allies fought against Louis XIV. When the peace conference finally met at Utrecht, Wertheimer had to pay the expenses of the Imperial ambassador as well as the costs of the conference, which Charles, now himself the Emperor, was unable to provide, exactly as Oppenheimer had paid the expenses of the peace conferences of Ryswick and Carlowitz at the end of the 17th century.[3]

The Habsburgs were strict Catholics, but they preferred to employ Jewish financiers because they could supply their needs more cheaply and, above all, because they were prepared to wait longer for their payment. The Emperor did not possess the administrative machinery to pay and supply the army, so that the court Jews were indispensable. The Emperor Leopold, for reasons of conscience, would have preferred to use non-Jewish entrepreneurs, but the attempt failed because they could not compete with the Jewish ones. It was only in the 19th century that the army administration became sufficiently developed to supply itself the requirements of the forces with the result that the Jewish suppliers and financiers were no longer needed. Yet as late as 1806, when the Duchy of Brunswick was occupied by the army of Napoleon, it was a Jewish banker, Israel Jacobson, who had to raise the lion's share of the war contribution of 5,625,000 francs that was imposed upon the Duchy. As late as 1812—17 the firm of Berend & Co. lent nearly 2,500,000 thalers to the Prussian state, more than any other Berlin bankers did during these years when the financial fortunes of Prussia were at a very low ebb on account of the war against Napoleon. Jewish banking houses continued to be among the leading firms of the Prussian capital. When the Dresdner Bank was established in 1865, Jewish bankers were most prominent among the founders.[4] Since the 17th century the machinery of the Prussian state was much more highly developed than that of the Habsburgs, yet in times of war and financial difficulty it had to use Jewish firms and entrepreneurs. This was especially true during the

[3]Schnee, *op. cit.*, II, 172, 180; III, 14—16; Stern, *op. cit.*, pp. 86—7, 92—3.
[4]Schnee, *op. cit.*, I, 212—4; II, 255; III, 198; Stern, *op. cit.*, pp. 29, 93.

Seven Years' War, when Frederick the Great employed several Jews to carry through the debasement of the coinage, above all in conquered Saxony, without which the King would not have been able to hold out against his many enemies. The result was that the neighbouring states imitated his example and Germany was flooded with heavily debased coins, to the detriment of all trade and enterprise. The Jews were particularly suitable for such purposes because they dominated the trade in precious metals and, through their family and other connections, could buy up the good coins and distribute the new bad ones. Whenever a ruler wanted to debase the coinage he would make use of the Jews, who then earned the opprobrium of the people, the victims of these practices, in place of the prince on whose orders they acted.

Jewish financiers and entrepreneurs, however, were not only active in supplying the armies, in financing wars, in arranging loans and settling debts; they were also prominent in the fields of trade and industry. Many court Jews supplied jewels to the princes for whom they worked. In 1720 Moses Levin Gomperz, of the famous family from Cleves, was entrusted by Frederick William I of Prussia with the sale of hundreds of jewels, estimated at 220,000 thalers, in Amsterdam, but was only able to sell about one-third of them. In 1732 Jacob Gomperz, a member of the same family, undertook to procure for the King well-grown giant grenadiers at the price of 300 thalers for one of six feet, 400 thalers for one of 73 inches, 500 for one of 74 inches, 1000 thalers for one of 75 inches, and as many as 2000 thalers for a recruit of 76 inches.

In Mecklenburg at the end of the 17th century two court Jews were even granted a monopoly of the trade in jewels and silver, against the protest of the local goldsmiths. They also acquired a monopoly of the tobacco trade and held it for many years, until in 1708 the government and the Estates achieved the abolition of all monopolies. Later the government declared that monopolies were contrary to the constitution of the Duchy and detrimental to commerce.

A well-known example of a successful merchant is Moses Jacobson de Jonge, who in 1664 was permitted to take his permanent residence at Memel, at a time when the Jews were still excluded from the Duchy of Prussia. He soon established a flourishing trade with Poland, Lithuania and Livonia, almost monopolised the highly important salt trade, limiting the quantities he imported from Holland so that the price remained high. He bought up so many goods that he could load whole ships and deprived local merchants of their livelihood: matters which caused frequent complaints. During the years 1694–96 he paid 80 per cent more in customs duties than all the other merchants of Memel put together, so that the electoral revenue increased considerably and the King of Poland attempted to attract the successful merchant to his country. No wonder the ever-repeated complaints of the town of Memel, which were taken up by the

Estates, about de Jonge and his practices met with no success. The Great Elector, as well as his son, the first King of Prussia, energetically took the side of de Jonge. At the end of the century four Christian merchants were severely punished for attacking him, and the urban authorities of Memel were severely reprimanded, while de Jonge's privileges were renewed by the Elector in spite of all local protests.[5]

The majority of the court Jews engaged in trade, especially in that in jewels and precious metals. In Prussia, however, where the development of the native middle classes was much retarded by the backwardness of the country and the military interests of the Hohenzollerns, Jews were instrumental in fostering the growth of industry. Under Frederick William I Levi Ulff founded a ribbon factory at Charlottenburg which supplied the army. David Hirsch founded in Berlin an important cloth factory and later, at Potsdam, a factory for the manufacture of velvet and plush. His workmen were recruited in Holland, France and Switzerland at royal expense. In 1731 he was granted a monopoly for velvet, and two years later one for plush, privileges against which the Berlin merchants objected in vain. In 1736 the import of all foreign velvets was forbidden, so that Hirsch now possessed a complete monopoly. His heirs added a silk factory.

In 1752 Bernhard Isaak was granted a concession for a silk factory in Berlin and a few years later for another one at Potsdam, in which Moses Mendelssohn was employed as a bookkeeper and overseer. Other silk manufacturers were Moses Ries, Isaak Benjamin Wulff, David Friedländer, Israel Markus and Levi Moses Levi, so that Jewish entrepreneurs predominated in this branch of industry so much fostered by Frederick the Great. Since 1745 Veitel Ephraim was engaged at Potsdam in the manufacture of Brussels lace; he employed 200 orphan girls, who were trained by him, and he possessed a monopoly for this manufacture. In 1762 he and his sons took over the manufacture of gold and silver braid and galloon, which was also carried on in the Potsdam orphanage; for this they received a monopoly which the family possessed until 1820. In 1752 Benjamin Elias Wulff founded a cotton and calico factory in the Tiergarten, for which he received royal support. At Breslau Jewish financiers founded cotton and cloth factories, at a time when the Christian merchants could not be persuaded to invest in industry.

In no other German state were there so many and so important Jewish industrialists as in Prussia. It was the considered policy of Frederick the Great to induce his wealthy court Jews to invest part of their profits in industrial enterprises. In Brunswick, Hanover and Mecklenburg we find Jewish tobacco manufacturers, appointed and privileged by the rulers of

---

[5]Schnee, *op. cit.*, I, 82, 89, 106—7; II, 296—7; *Urkunden und Actenstücke zur Geschichte des Kurfürsten Friedrich Wilhelm von Brandenburg*, XVI, Berlin, 1899, pp. 636, 659, 662, 778—9, 809, 816, 989; State Archives, Königsberg, *Ostpreussische Folianten*, Vol. 698, fos. 261, 823—4; Vol. 702, pp. 323, 1372; Vol. 712, nos. 4—5; Vol. 713, pp. 281—2; Vol. 718, fos. 1268, 1328; Vol. 723, nos. 32, 42.

those principalities; but the Jewish pre-eminence in the textile industries was a Prussian phenomenon. Frederick the Great favoured the court Jews by all the means at his disposal because they helped him to achieve the aims of his mercantilist policy.[6]

Through their manifold activities the court Jews were brought into intimate contact with the internal government of many German principalities and became advisors in matters of financial administration and taxation. In 1700 Ruben Elias Gomperz was appointed chief tax collector for the Duchies of Cleves and Mark, against which the local government as well as the Estates protested strongly, but these protests were overruled by the Elector Frederick III. Many Jews were employed on diplomatic missions and as diplomatic representatives. Thus Behrend Lehmann played an important part as the political agent of Augustus the Strong of Saxony, especially in connection with his election to the Polish throne; for these services he was appointed the king's resident in the Lower Saxon Circle and maintained a grand establishment at Halberstadt.

In Anhalt Moses Benjamin Wulff actively participated in the diplomatic negotiations through which the wife of Leopold of Anhalt-Dessau was elevated to the princely Estate; later he was entrusted with diplomatic missions in Vienna in connection with the investiture of Leopold by the Emperor with the whole of Anhalt and with the introduction of primogeniture in the principality, for which the assent of the Emperor was required. In Brunswick Alexander David was not only the banker and jeweller, but also the political agent of the dukes. In Mecklenburg the Hinrichsens fulfilled similar functions as late as the 19th century.[7] At some of these smaller courts Jewish influence was especially pronounced, for there the ruler had fewer resources and often found it difficult to overcome the opposition of his Estates, who in certain instances controlled the government; thus the Jews were a welcome counter-weight against the local influences which the ruler wanted to curtail.

The most famous example of the court Jew who wielded political influence, if only for a brief period, was Süss Oppenheimer, better known as Jud Süss, who acted as the confidential advisor to Duke Charles Alexander of Württemberg. Charles Alexander was a convert to Roman Catholicism; he succeeded his Lutheran predecessor in October 1733 and died in March 1737. In a strictly Lutheran Duchy, in which the Estates for centuries had wielded considerable influence, he aimed at making himself absolute, at increasing the small standing army to 12,000 men, at introducing much heavier taxation and at gaining a better, if not a dominant, status for Roman Catholics. In his endeavours he was helped by newly-appointed Catholic officers and officials, by the Prince-Bishop of Würzburg and

---

[6]Schnee, *op. cit.*, I, 116—7, 148—9, 182—5, 189—90; II, 82, 88—9, 296; III, 180, 187; Stern, *op. cit.*, pp. 152—6.
[7]Schnee, *op. cit.*, I, 86; II, 91—4, 173, 180, 188, 264—5, 304—8.

Bamberg, a protagonist of princely power and Catholicism, and by Süss Oppenheimer, who was made a Privy Finance Councillor and Cabinet Treasurer. He was entrusted with procuring the financial means for this policy, with the mint and with matters of wardship and taxation, and thus naturally came into open conflict with the Estates who controlled the financial administration.

According to the Estates' declaration 'against the evil councillors' of the late Duke, drawn up a few weeks after his death, Süss had advised the Duke to arrest the Estates' leaders. With respect to the old treaties which guaranteed the Estates' privileges, they accused him of holding the opinion that it was to be borne in mind at what times they had been concluded: what had been good years ago was no longer suitable at present and, if the Duke found that laws and customs stood in his way, he was the only one who could alter them. In Süss' opinion, the subjects had no right to share in the government or to question their ruler's actions; if they offered resistance, force should be used. The Catholic general who was put in command of the army curtly informed the Estates' deputies that subjects had no right to put conditions to their prince, who had the right to issue orders; a clever prince knew himself what was good for his subjects and did not need any Estates; when the French *Parlement* had not obeyed the king he had assembled 10,000 men to make his will felt, and the same fate, he threatened, could befall the Estates.[8]

These plans were in accordance with the general tendencies of the age: representative government and the liberties of the Estates were considered out-of-date, and people admired the police state which the Hohenzollerns had established in Prussia. Yet these plans failed because of Charles Alexander's premature death and the accession of a minor duke: an opportunity which the Estates used to take vengeance on their late master's tools. Süss Oppenheimer was immediately arrested because of the pernicious advice he had rendered, together with several other officials and officers. After a lengthy trial he was publicly hanged in Stuttgart in February 1738 because 'he had sown distrust against the ministers, councillors and Estates, had infringed all basic treaties and rent asunder all laws and constitutions.' He became a victim of the policy he had advocated, while the other culprits escaped with more lenient punishments. The despised Jew was the object of general hatred and was considered guilty of 'countless crimes such as had not been committed by any Jew in Christian countries'.[9] In reality, however, he had been merely the spokesman of the tendency towards princely despotism.

We may have sympathy with him; but we can also sympathise with the political aspirations of his enemies. They succeeded in preserving their

[8]State Archives, Stuttgart, *Tomi Actorum Provincialium Wurtembergicorum*, Vol. 142, fos. 621—4; Vol. 144, fos. 289—92; Vol. 145, fos. 180—95; Vol. 148, fos. 553, 557—9, 569; Stern, *op. cit.*, pp. 130—1; Schnee, *op. cit.*, III, 189.
[9]State Archives, Stuttgart, *Tomi Actorum,* Vol. 145, fo. 128; Vol. 146, fos. 19—20.

liberties and privileges and thereby ensured that the Württemberg constitution was preserved and that the tradition of representative government did not die out, in contrast with the development in many other German principalities. In my opinion, it is not justified to say that these absolute rulers and their 'restless activity ... served to stimulate the political and economic energies of the populations', and that 'Württemberg was in a condition of stagnation', as Selma Stern does. The Württemberg burghers and peasants were very active in the political as well as the economic field, and Württemberg was more highly developed than Prussia. In Prussia it was not only the general, unpropitious conditions of the country, but also the dead-weight of the over-large army and the policy of her rulers which prevented a progressive development, especially in the political field, while the prevalence of serfdom militated against economic progress. Nor am I able to agree with her that Charles Alexander's 'own desires were identical with the interests of the country and his personal ambition served as an invigorating force in the State of Württemberg', that he 'considered it his chief task to bring order into the economy, pay off the country's debts, restore its credit and adjust expenditures and revenues'.[10] If Charles Alexander's plans had been carried through, Württemberg would have been burdened with the maintenance of a large army and a magnificent court and this would have frustrated its economic development. The country's debts resulted from the ambitions of previous rulers; Charles Alexander's ambitions would have added to them and would have involved the country in many wars with its neighbours, as Selma Stern herself admits. Surely, in this case, the Estates served the interest of their country much better than an over-ambitious Duke whose policy was opposed by the whole country. Surely, it is not the task of the historian to extol the example of Prussia and of her kings, however much their contemporaries might have been impressed by her might and her success.

In other principalities also the Estates were bitterly opposed to the admittance of the Jews and to the privileges granted to the court Jews. Partly they saw in the Jews the representatives of an absolutist policy, but primarily they feared for their economic interests. The many monopolies which were entrusted to the Jews were particularly obnoxious to the towns which everywhere formed one of the Estates. The dues and customs paid by the Jews went directly to the prince and were not liable to the financial control which the Estates exercised in many principalities; they thus weakened them, while the ruler's financial position became stronger. Equally, in many principalities the officials themselves were members of the Estates and thus less reliable from the ruler's point of view than complete strangers. The Estates in their turn were not only opposed to the Jews, but to all newcomers, especially when these belonged to a religion different from their own. In the complaints of the Estates of Brandenburg and

[10]Stern, *op. cit.*, pp. 118—9.

Prussia the Jews were put side by side with Arians, Baptists, Mennonists, Quakers, Socinians, Weigelians, Zwinglians, 'and other heretics'.[11] All these were equally obnoxious to the strictly Lutheran inhabitants of the Hohenzollern provinces; while their ruler, who was a Calvinist and for that reason opposed to Lutheran orthodoxy, welcomed all immigrants with open arms because his territories were so backward and so thinly populated. Thus the Jews became a focal point in the struggle between the ruler and the Estates. Wherever these were defeated the court Jews reaped the benefit and served the absolute state which protected them.

As swift as was the rise of many court Jews, as swift could be their decline. It is true that certain families, such as the Gomperz in Cleves or the Hinrichsens in Mecklenburg, retained their influence for generations. Frequently, however, the court Jews became the scapegoats of a policy which they merely executed. Often it was the death of a ruler and the accession of his successor which caused the fall of the favourites of the previous reign: a contingency against which some court Jews tried to insure themselves by keeping in the good books of the heir to the throne. Everywhere not only the Estates, but even more so the people, the tradesmen and artisans were bitterly hostile to the Jews, from whose competition they suffered. Their hatred was directed not against the prince, who was surrounded by the trappings of divine right and so high that he could not be reached by their criticisms, but against his 'evil councillors' who levied taxes in his name and carried out his policy. Among these councillors the Jews were particularly vulnerable because they had no recognised status, because they were strong only if protected by the prince: the moment this protection was withdrawn they fell and could be attacked with impunity. They presented a tempting target through their great wealth and outward splendour, especially at times of war or economic crisis. It was for these reasons that so many court Jews fell, rather than 'because they were the bearers of a new and revolutionary political and economic conception which was bitterly attacked by the old legitimist powers', as Selma Stern thinks.[12] The ideas of absolute government and economic mercantilism had existed long before the 18th century; since the 16th century Germany had been the home of great banking houses; the 'feudal and patrimonial forces of the Middle Ages' had long withered away; no revolution was as yet threatening the established order. The anti-Semitism of the masses could easily be unleashed for less deep-seated reasons, for they were suffering under the exactions of vexatious and arbitrary governments.

The wealth and luxury displayed by many court Jews indeed made them an easy target of popular wrath. Many maintained great houses and loved ostentatious, grand displays, as so many princes and nobles did. The town

---

[11] *Urkunden und Actenstücke zur Geschichte des Kurfürsten Friedrich Wilhelm von Brandenburg*, X, pp. 233—4; XV, pp. 399, 522, 526; XVI, pp. 31—2, 365, 435, 437, 491, 494, 530, 535, 538, 558, 564, 610—11, 767, 815, 887.

[12] Stern, *op. cit.*, pp. 13, 266—7.

council of Mannheim complained bitterly that the court Jews occupied the most beautiful houses in the best streets and used magnificent carriages. Behrend Lehmann at Halberstadt drove about in a carriage with six horses, two liveried servants standing in front and one behind. Diego Texeira was seen driving through Hamburg in such a magnificent carriage that bystanders mistook him for a prince.

The town council of Mannheim in 1717 forbade the Jews to wear clothes embroidered with gold or silver. In 1719 the Senate of Hamburg issued a decree against the luxurious dresses worn by the Jews and forbade them to appear at the exchange with walking-sticks, swords or pistols. In the same year Moses Levin Gomperz was granted the privilege to carry a sword by Frederick William I. His grandfather's house in Cleves was described by a Jewish visitor as the 'house of a king, in all manners furnished like the palace of a ruler'. Süss Oppenheimer possessed houses in Frankfurt and Stuttgart which he furnished with costly furniture and paintings by Rubens, Teniers, Jordaens, van der Velde and other Dutch painters, with precious china, rare engravings, gold vessels and beautifully bound books. The court Jews wore short coloured coats in the French or Spanish style and wigs like noblemen, their wives multicoloured heavy gowns of silk and velvet, with puffed wide sleeves and long trains, and beautiful jewels. As early as 1644 a pamphlet published in Hamburg accused them of wearing gold and silver, pearls and diamonds. Süss Oppenheimer, dressed in a coat of red silk, conversed gracefully with the Duchess and the court ladies; like his master he maintained an official mistress. Many princes, noblemen and ambassadors were entertained by the court Jews in a princely style; the weddings of their children were attended by illustrious guests, such as the Crown Prince of Prussia, the later Frederick I, Prince John Maurice of Nassau, the Crown Prince of Saxony; Queen Christina of Sweden stayed at Diego Texeira's house in Hamburg.[13]

Some court Jews not only acquired grand town houses, but extensive landed property. Thus Behrend Lehmann possessed the castle of Seeburg with thirteen villages, a noble estate at Blankenburg and many large estates in western Poland around Lissa. Israel Jacobson, early in the 19th century, owned six estates in Mecklenburg, nine more near Magdeburg and in central Germany, a country seat at Steglitz outside Berlin and other landed property. The court Jews were not only assimilated in their way of life, their manners and their clothes to the ways of the ruling-classes, but equally in their ideas and their *esprit*. There was a gulf between them and the mass of ordinary Jews who lived in ghettos, wore their distinctive dress and were sharply distinguished by their religious and other habits from the people amongst whom they lived. Naturally the court Jews early tried to gain permission to dwell outside the ghettos in the new quarters of the towns, and this wish was frequently granted. In matters of religion Süss Oppen-

[13]Schnee, *op. cit.*, I, 80, 88; II, 188; III, 211; Stern, *op. cit.*, pp. 104—10, 227—36.

heimer and some other court Jews were sceptical; he did not attend the synagogue nor keep the Jewish dietary laws. He once confessed that he was a voluntary member of all religious creeds; he had absorbed the spirit of the early enlightenment wholeheartedly. Yet he did all his business with other Jews and gave the contracts for military and court supplies only to them; and he obtained permission for the Jews to settle in Württemberg, thus arousing the enmity of the population.[14]

The emancipated court Jews often quarrelled or bickered with the ghetto Jews. These conflicts became particularly acrimonious when a court Jew was appointed by the prince as head of the Jewish communities of the principality in question. Thus the Great Elector made Berend Levi 'commander in chief' or *shtadlan* in all Brandenburg territories to the west of the Elbe. As an official of the new state he acted entirely in the interest of the ruler. The result was that the Jews of Cleves and Mark, and soon also those of other provinces, revolted against his 'tyrannical rule' and his 'lack of modesty'. They were joined by the Estates of Cleves and Mark, by the town of Wesel and by the governor, Prince John Maurice of Nassau, while Levi was upheld by the central government in Berlin. The combined opposition, however, achieved that after two years he was dismissed as the leader of the Jews of Cleves and Mark and only retained his position with regard to Halberstadt, Minden and Ravensberg.

Leading among the opposition in Cleves had been the Gomperz family; but in 1717 Moses Levin Gomperz was appointed Chief Elder of the Jews of Berlin and all the Prussian territories; and two years later he was granted the right to carry a sword 'like other servants' of the King. During the preceding reign the Berlin Jewish community was dominated by Esther Liebmann, who succeeded her husband as court jeweller and banker; she was feared and hated by her co-religionists and ruled them with an iron hand through her son who was appointed Chief Elder. Under Frederick the Great the Berlin Jews complained that their Chief Elder, the court Jew Veitel Ephraim, forced them to submit to his laws, and that he held meetings in his own house so that he could exclude those he disliked. These Chief Elders received salaries and behaved like royal officials, acting not in the interests of their co-religionists, but in those of the government whose instruments they were.[15]

Although the court Jews were very assimilated in their way of life and their mode of thinking, although they were far removed from the world of the ghetto, they remained Jews. They studied the Thora and the Talmud, they possessed Hebrew libraries, had the works of Jewish scholars and religious books printed at their own expense, invited learned rabbis to stay with them and had poor Jewish students attached to their households. Wherever they settled with their large families and establishments they

---

[14]Schnee, *op. cit.,* II, 150—1, 199, 249—50; III, 220; Stern, *op. cit.,* pp. 227, 238—40.
[15]Schnee, *op. cit.,* I, 66—7, 88, 97—100; III, 221; Stern, *op. cit.,* pp. 181—6.

tried to gain permission for other Jews to follow them, and they often interceded with the authorities on behalf of their co-religionists; for many princes made a sharp distinction between the court Jews, whom they needed, and the others, to whom they were reluctant to grant permits of residence and to extend the facilities enjoyed by the court Jews. Many of the latter founded synagogues or Jewish schools, or left considerable sums for such foundations. Thus Michael David at Hanover gave a synagogue to the Jewish community and founded an institute to further Jewish learning. His son founded a school for Jewish boys which existed till the early 20th century. At Hanover Isaak Jacob Gans set aside a capital of 30,000 thalers, the interest of which was to support poor Jews, to educate two Jewish boys, to pay a Jewish scholar and to provide lights for the synagogue. Alexander David gave a synagogue to the Jewish communities of Brunswick and of Wolfenbüttel. Behrend Lehmann built a house at Halberstadt for three Jewish scholars, with a library and a synagogue, and used his connections to further the admittance of Jews at Halle and Dresden. Salomon Oppenheim at Cologne and Joseph Jacob van Geldern at Düsseldorf built synagogues for the Jewish communities of their town. If they prospered the court Jews felt that this was due to God's grace, and they were willing to render Him their thanks and their homage in this visible and lasting form.[16]

Yet in many instances the descendants of the court Jews, especially in the 19th century, left the religion of their fathers. They were baptised, intermarried with Christian families, often of great wealth or rank, and in many cases themselves acquired patents of nobility. They quickly merged with the German people; they not only infused new wealth into many an impoverished noble family, but their sons quickly rose to important positions in state and society. The sons and grandsons of Baer Moses Levy Isaak became Prussian officers. One of them in 1866 commanded the Prussian forces which defeated the Hanoverians and forced them to capitulate, and became a lieutenant-general. A grand-daughter of Veitel Ephraim, court and mint Jew of Frederick the Great, married in 1797 Prince Henry XIV of Reuss, a member of a ruling dynasty and a Field-Marshal in the Imperial army.

Many sons of court Jews bought noble estates and became squires; their sons studied at Bonn, Heidelberg or Göttingen and joined the feudal students' corporations of Borussia or Saxonia; if possible they served with the guards' cavalry, the most exclusive regiment of the Prussian army. Only a few of them were active in commerce or industry where little social prestige could be gained; for in Germany there was no close interlinking between the world of the city and that of the broad acres which has always been characteristic of English society. Thus the Junker class received new blood and new strength, but this did not contribute towards merging its members

---

[16]Schnee, *op. cit.*, II, 14, 73, 75, 82, 99, 178, 188, 270; III, 53, 64, 116, 191—2; Stern, *op. cit.*, pp. 210—26.

The Court Jews

with those of other classes; its power and its exclusiveness were maintained until the end of the Hohenzollern monarchy. In Austria also, from the end of the 18th century onwards, the great Jewish families were ennobled and became barons; while their wives, daughters of Berlin court Jews, demonstratively showed their Prussian sentiments and became hysterical if anybody made anti-Prussian remarks, showing how quickly and to what extent the Prussian Jews took over the national prejudices and the ideology of the leading social group, whose equals they wanted to become and whose ranks they wanted to enter.[17]

How can we explain the amazing rise of so many court Jews within such a short time? It was not only the weakness or decline of the native middle class that gave them their opportunity after the Thirty Years' War which had destroyed so much capital and so many goods. It was also the fact that they possessed special qualifications which made them eminently suitable for their task, such as great experience in trade and money matters. They had no ties with the Estates or any other native group, but were entirely at the disposal of the prince, his tools which could be made and unmade. They had close links with their co-religionists all over Europe and thus received from them important commercial and political news; they could use them as agents and middlemen and could buy from them and sell to them. They thus possessed a whole network of agents and suppliers, living in the most important trading centres, in Holland with its banking facilities, in Frankfurt and Leipzig with their fairs. As the mediaeval merchants had done, they often sent out their sons and nephews to represent them in other towns or countries and used them as their aids in the family business. They possessed more capital than their rivals and, above all, better credit facilities; they could afford to wait longer for payment and thus secure valuable orders with no immediate prospect of payment, which their rivals had to decline.

Most of the great families of court Jews intermarried and were related to each other; they were 'one large family', especially those of Berlin, Breslau, Dresden, Leipzig, Brunswick, Hanover, Dessau, and concluded matrimonial alliances with those of Vienna and southern Germany.[18] It seems much more doubtful, however, whether their success was also due 'to their spiritual attitude and piety based on their study of the Talmud and Thora', whether there was 'an internal connection between the Jewish religion and moral teaching, between the Old Testament puritanical spirit and the economic activities of the court Jews', as asserted by Dr. Schnee, following the ideas of Max Weber and Werner Sombart. This much, however, is probably true that the Jews, like the Calvinists, were especially hardworking and determined to be successful, especially eager to escape from the

---

[17]Schnee, *op. cit.*, I, 54, 133—4, 161, 175—6, 244; II, 152, 202, 252, 255; III, 53, 155, 217—8, with many examples of ennoblements etc.
[18]Stern, *op. cit.*, pp. 18, 27—8, 43; Schnee, *op. cit.*, III, 180—1, 221.

poverty of the ghetto. On the other hand, it seems to be quite erroneous to attempt to explain the outstanding successes of Süss Oppenheimer and Michael von Derenburg by their alleged 'mixed' racial origin, based on the popular legend of their time, as Dr. Schnee does.[19] As there are many more rational explanations, such theories are of little value.

In general it seems a pity that Dr. Schnee's careful and detailed researches in many archives are marred by an anti-Jewish bias which is especially apparent in his first volume. This is perhaps not surprising in view of the fact that he published the first results of his work in notorious Nazi journals during the last war;[20] but it seems that the eight years between the end of the war and the publication of his new book did not substantially modify his views. For example, he makes two quite uncalled-for remarks against Heinrich Heine, asserting that his real name was Chajim Bückeburg and calling a somewhat shady financier 'the true ancestor' of Heine; but there is no evidence whatever for the first assertion in the section on the Heine family in the third volume.[21]

It is also contradictory to maintain of one court Jew that he 'naturally made substantial profits', while stating on the same page that he went bankrupt; or to assert of the same man that he 'was financially in a very favourable position' because he received one hundred thalers a year plus certain allowances for food and fodder, while we find in the later volumes that the great court Jews received, in addition to such allowances, salaries of 300 to 400, and that salaries of 150 or 200 thalers were 'not particularly high'.[22] The Jews who were employed by Frederick the Great to debase the coinage are criticised because they lacked 'all noble motives, all interest in the state'; and several Jewish banking-houses because they declined to lend money to the Prussian government after the defeat of Jena and Auerstädt:[23] as though the bankers and financiers of other creeds had made profits out of the nobility of their hearts. It seems equally superfluous to express surprise that a court Jew bought jewels at an auction for 54,000 thalers and subsequently sold them singly for 57,000, a profit of less than six per cent; or that at other auctions the Jews reached an agreement not to bid against each other and in consequence the prices remained low, a practice known to dealers at auctions all over the world.[24]

A greater knowledge of business affairs would have shown Dr. Schnee that there is nothing particularly 'Jewish' in such practices, and it would have been better if such petty criticisms had been suppressed. It seems even more unnecessary to say that Moses Levin Gomperz 'had apparently gone

---

[19]Schnee, *op. cit.*, III, 192, 200, 253.
[20]See *Weltkampf — Die Judenfrage in Geschichte und Gegenwart*, 1944, pp. 91 ff. and *Deutsches Archiv für Landes- und Volksforschung*, VIII, 1944, pp. 367 ff.
[21]Schnee, *op. cit.*, I, 68, 75; III, 112—22.
[22]*Ibid.*, I, 50; II, 35; III, 54, 207—8.
[23]*Ibid.*, I, 92, 130, 213.
[24]*Ibid.*, III, 17, 35—6.

off his head' because he 'dared' to appear in front of Frederick William I in a kind of uniform imitating that of the giant grenadiers, especially in view of the fact that the king expected his servants to wear uniform.[25] Gomperz probably hoped that his action would please the king: that this was not the case and that the king used his stick on the unfortunate Jew is much more indicative of the lack of mental balance of Frederick William I than of Gomperz.

If Dr. Schnee's comments are sometimes uncalled for, it must also be recognised that his research has brought to light many new facts and interesting details. I would agree with his general conclusion that the court Jews were only one of the many aids and supports of the modern state; even in the financial field their contribution should not be overestimated.[26] The main financial contribution to the creation of the Prussian or the Bavarian state came from taxation, i.e. from the non-privileged classes. It was the burghers and the peasants who were taxed extremely heavily so that their rulers would be able to follow a policy of expansion and aggrandisement. It was the peasants' sons who served in the armies which conquered new provinces. It was the state officials who administered the revenues and domains, collected the taxes and acted as the long arm of the ruler reaching into every corner of his territories. Nobody would deny that the court Jews fulfilled important and useful functions; but their work has to be estimated in comparison with the contributions of other groups and other organs of the absolute state. Their role came to an end with the general economic progress of Germany in the 19th century and the development of a more efficient state machinery, and equally with the general emancipation of the Jews during the same period, which their own earlier emancipation had helped so much to bring about.

[25] *Ibid.*, I, 88.
[26] *Ibid.*, III, 255—6.

10

PRUSSIAN DESPOTISM AT ITS HEIGHT

The foundations of the Hohenzollern despotism were laid in the second half of the seventeenth century by Frederick William, the 'Great Elector' of Brandenburg. He eliminated the Estates as a political factor in the government of his territories, although they continued to meet and to exercise certain functions, without being able to resist the growth of absolute government. He created the standing army and the bureaucracy which became the unifying framework of the Hohenzollern state. He introduced the urban excise which became the cornerstone of the system: it was administered by the new bureaucracy, provided the major part of the army's financial needs, deprived the Estates of the power of the purse, and the towns of the remnants of self-government. He began to inculcate in the native nobility of Brandenburg and Pomerania the custom of serving the state, be it in the army or in the government and administration.[1] He laid the foundations which enabled his successors to make eighteenth-century Prussia a major European power.

Under the Great Elector, however, the machinery of government which made this policy possible was not fully developed, and the deployment of despotism was still hampered by local resistance and insufficient revenue. It was only under the stringent government of Frederick William I (1713–40) that despotism reached its highest point. Perhaps no other German ruler has influenced the development of his state so deeply as the 'soldier-king', the 'drill-sergeant of Potsdam'. Not only did the system which he perfected continue almost unchanged until the early nineteenth century, and would have persisted longer had it not been destroyed by Napoleon on the battlefield of Jena; but if anyone can be dubbed the father of Prussian militarism, it is this king who never started a major war and hardly ever used his magnificent army.

Frederick William (and his son after him) ruled himself, in a more direct sense than Louis XIV had done. His ministers were merely his subordinate tools; he was his own finance

---

[1] For all details see: 'The Great Elector and the Foundation of the Hohenzollern Despotism', *English Historical Review*, lxv (1950), 175–202; and *The Origins of Prussia*, (1954), pp. 179–201, 253–277.

minister and commander-in-chief,[2] and thus in charge of the two most important functions of his state, both closely connected, as military expenditure consumed over seventy per cent of the total revenue.[3] The officials, ministers and generals reported in writing to the king, who made the decisions himself, helped not by any qualified advisers but only by subaltern secretaries.[4] The authorities simply had to execute the royal decrees, which reached them either as marginal comments of the king scribbled on to their reports, or as decisions dictated by him to a secretary.[5] There was no council and no discussion, and hardly any possibility of changing the royal ruling once it had been made. As early as 1716 the Hanoverian resident in Berlin reported that the king did not trust his ministers and often rebuffed them in such a form that they did not dare to propose even the most obvious things; that all affairs were reported in writing to the king, who was seldom in Berlin; that he wrote his decisions with his own hand, according to his whims and without any consultations, which led to many incongruities.[6]

Every year Frederick William visited his provinces to inspect them personally, to review his troops, to receive complaints, and to administer rewards and punishments.[7] He regulated even small matters down to minute details. When in 1723 the general directory was founded as the highest financial and internal authority of the whole state, he decreed that only one lackey was to serve at their dinners, that four silver plates and one glass were to be put in front of each diner, and that a large basket was to be kept ready to receive the dirty plates, so that the room would not be congested with footmen.[8] In 1729 the general directory reported to the king that the *Oberrechenkammer* (auditing department) petitioned for the allocation

[2] O. Hintze, in *A.B.*, vi (1), 60; G. Schmoller, *Preussische Verfassungs-, Verwaltungs- und Finanzgeschichte* (1921), p. 127. (For abbreviations used, see n. 148.)
[3] Hintze, *Geist und Epochen der preussischen Geschichte* (1943), p. 25; Schmoller, *op. cit.*, p. 112; H. Prutz, *Preussische Geschichte* (1900), ii, 361.
[4] Hintze, in *A.B.*, vi (1), 62; Schmoller, *op. cit.*, p. 128.
[5] Prutz, *op. cit.*, ii, 350–1.
[6] The Hanoverian resident Heusch to count Bernstorff on 11 February 1716: *A.B.*, ii, 224–5.
[7] L. von Ranke, *Zwölf Bücher Preussischer Geschichte* (ed. 1929), ii, 315; Schmoller, 'Die innere Verwaltung des preussischen Staates unter Friedrich Wilhelm I', *Preussische Jahrbücher*, xxv (1870), 591.
[8] Cabinet decree of 20 January 1723: *A.B.*, iii, 669.

of three to four more stacks of firewood, as the six stacks they received were quite insufficient: every year they had to have an advance, especially during the prevailing severe winter. The king, however, decided that six stacks had to do: they should stoke the fires gently.[9] The members of the royal family fared not much better. In 1729 the queen, 'bathed in Tears', told the British ambassador that she had had 'to send by a trusty Servant a Boxfull of Fowles and other Eatables' to the crown prince because he 'often rises (from table) without getting one Bit. . . .'[10] At the end of the reign the roles were reversed: Frederick, liberally supplied with money by George II, sent his mother 'privately every Day, both at Noon and Night, a great many Dishes from his Kitchen, the sick Governor having retrenched so much in his Table of late, that his family wants common Necessaries. . . .'[11]

The over-centralization entailed an enormous amount of work for the king and killed any initiative among his officials.[12] The system revolved around his person and could function only as long as he was able and willing to shoulder the burden. This in part explains Frederick William's fury at his son's musical and literary interests, which he considered a mere waste of time. In the instruction for his successor he emphasised that the ruler must see to all his affairs himself; rulers were chosen to work and not to lounge about or to dally with women; but unfortunately most princes let their ministers decide and 'occupied themselves with mistresses and carnal lusts', with 'comedies, operas, ballets, masques, balls, guzzling and boozing': these should be suppressed by his successor.[13]

The king considered himself first and foremost an officer. Not only had all aspects of civil government to be subordinated to his military interests;[14] but he actually preferred generals as heads of civil departments and used them for many administrative tasks.[15]

[9] Report of the general directory of 26 February 1729: *A.B.*, iv (2), 440.
[10] Col. du Bourgay to Lord Townshend, on 19/30 July 1729: S.P., xxiv.
[11] Guy Dickens to Lord Harrington, on 12 April 1740: S.P., xlvii.
[12] Hintze, 'Die Entstehung der modernen Staatsministerien', *Staat und Verfassung* (1941), p. 290.
[13] Royal instruction of January–February 1722: *A.B.*, iii, 442, 445.
[14] Hintze, in *A.B.*, vi (1), 60.
[15] Schmoller, 'Der preussische Beamtenstand unter Friedrich Wilhelm I', *Preussische Jahrbücher*, xxvi (1870), 153; W. L. Dorn, 'The Prussian Bureaucracy in the Eighteenth Century', *Political Science Quarterly*, xlvii (1932), 267–8.

According to the British resident, he paid more regard 'to the advices and oppinions of military men even of the lowest rank than to those of a first Minister. . . .'[16] In Prussia it was not the civil service which controlled the army, but the army which more and more influenced the aims and methods of the administration. The reasons for this royal partiality are obvious. Military officers were accustomed to obey orders and not to argue, and arguments to Frederick William smacked of insubordination and opposition. When some old and experienced officials petitioned not to be transferred from Königsberg to the wilds of Tilsit, the irate king considered them rebels and mutineers and ordered 'the *canailles* with their powdered wigs' to be sent to a fortress for forced labour; he threatened them with proceedings under martial law and the punishments of the military code; 'when I give an order to an officer I am obeyed, but the cursed inkshitters want to have preference and to disobey me; I will put them to fire and sword and will deal with them as a tyrant; this has to be heeded by the general directory. . . .'[17] On a later occasion the king, to clinch an argument, simply declared: 'the scoundrels must not argue.'[18] And the East Prussian government was informed that he did not expect 'any useless arguing' whether appeals in criminal cases were necessary.[19]

His preference for former officers in civil appointments could induce the king to neglect all qualifications of training and experience. When the president of a provincial consistory died, he conferred the vacancy upon a captain of horse and exempted him from the required examination; the East Prussian government pointed out his lack of qualifications, but was overruled.[20] The regimental commanders had to notify the provincial chambers of the names of non-commissioned officers who were no longer fit for active service; they had to be given suitable posts according to the order of notification.[21] The

[16] James Scott to Charles de la Faye, on 6 July 1723: S.P., xvii.
[17] Royal decisions of 3 and 5 November 1714: *A.B.*, ii, 130–2.
[18] Marginal order of the king to a report of the Magdeburg government of 1 February 1718: *A.B.*, iii, 10.
[19] Royal decree of 9 August 1718: *A.B.*, iii, 68.
[20] Royal orders of 19 May, 31 July and 3 November 1738 and 21 January 1739, with rejoinder of the Prussian government of 24 September 1738: *A.B.*, v (2), 454–5.
[21] Royal orders of 17 December 1729, 2 March 1736 and 19 March 1738: *A.B.*, iv (2), 511; v (2), 7–8.

post of controller of the East Prussian chest was conferred by the king upon a former valet;[22] he thus sent an unsuitable applicant to a province which he disliked.

His love for the army, in particular for his giant grenadiers, even made Frederick William abandon one of the most vital principles of the Prussian civil service: that offices were not for sale. A special fund, the *Rekrutenkasse*, was instituted to finance the recruiting of these mercenaries. All newly appointed or promoted officials had to contribute, usually one year's salary, and sometimes more. When the post of secretary to the Cleves chamber fell vacant the appointee had to pay 120 *Taler*, from a salary of 100 p.a.[23] For two subordinate posts under the same chamber the king fixed the price at 550 *Taler*, which were duly paid by a former sergeant-major.[24] The system easily led to the sale of the post to the highest bidder regardless of qualifications. An appointment to the Samland consistory was conferred upon the applicant who offered 1000 *Taler*, none of the others bidding more than 800.[25] A *Landrat's* post in Pomerania was given to the applicant offering 300, while his competitor only proffered 200 *Taler*.[26] For the appointment of archivist at Cleves one candidate bid 1200 *Taler*, and his rival, considered the more suitable, 1000; the king decided in favour of the former and he received his patent, whereupon the other also offered 1200; the decision was then revoked and the latter candidate was appointed, but against payment of 1600 *Taler*.[27] All these appointments concerned comparatively minor posts. Yet even the highest officials had to pay fees to the *Rekrutenkasse*, even for purely honorary titles. When a minister protested against such 'pretensions', the king ordered him to produce instead a man of six foot four inches.[28] There is no indication, however, that the most important posts were

---

[22] Royal orders of 16 and 20 December 1717: *A.B.*, ii, 594–5.
[23] Marginal decree of the king of 24 June 1727: *A.B.*, iv (1), 520.
[24] Reports of the general directory of 1 and 13 April 1728 and 22 March 1729, with marginal notes of the king: *A.B.*, iv (2), 290–1.
[25] Report of 28 October, with marginal decision of the king, and appointment of 13 November 1725: *A.B.*, iv (1), 765.
[26] Appointment of 30. August 1738: *A.B.*, v (2), 604, note 2.
[27] Report of the Cleves government of 9 March 1739, with marginal decision of the king, patent of 11 March, and order to the Cleves government of 16 April 1739: *A.B.*, v (2), 496.
[28] Report of the general directory of 6 October 1732, with marginal order of the king: *A.B.*, v (1), 317.

granted to the highest bidder: to that extent appointments were not influenced by financial considerations.[29]

Financial considerations also dictated the punishment of negligent officials. When a deficit of 7728 *Taler* was discovered in the customs accounts of Königsberg (3228 of which had already been refunded), Frederick William refused to let the trial of the responsible official proceed and decreed that either he should pay, or if unable to do so he should be tried and hanged. The criminal court, however, found him not guilty and set him free.[30] Other officials were less fortunate. When it was discovered that the *Kriegsrat* von Schlubhut had used 2800 *Taler* of public funds and had lent another 1065 to lower officials (a practice forbidden two years before), criminal proceedings were taken against him. Although he was unable to refund the money the *advocatus fisci* suggested a mild punishment; but the king decreed the death penalty, and the accused was hanged 'and afterwards put in Irons and fixed to a Gibet . . . and without the least form of a Trial before any Court of Justice. . . .'[31] Shortly afterwards the Berlin criminal court passed sentence on the *Landrentmeister* Hesse who was accused of the embezzlement of 37,207 *Taler*. It found that Hesse had merely acted negligently and had not kept his books properly, and sentenced him to six years' forced labour; but the king ordered him to be hanged in chains. The general directory pointed out that, according to Prussian law, in cases of negligence only forced labour or corporal punishment could be inflicted and that it was not customary to impose the death penalty without a proper legal verdict. The royal comment only was: 'must hang', and Hesse was duly executed.[32]

In other cases also the king reversed judicial decisions and sentenced the accused by his own plenary powers. The most famous was that of the friend of the crown prince, lieutenant von Katte, who was tried for desertion after Frederick's attempted flight in 1730. The court-martial condemned von

[29] Hintze, 'Der Commissarius und seine Bedeutung in der allgemeinen Verwaltungsgeschichte', *Staat und Verfassung* (1941), p. 240.

[30] Royal decreees of 2 January and 24 March 1725, with marginal decision of the king: *A.B.*, iv (1), 648–9.

[31] Royal orders of 26 May and 13 August 1731: *A.B.*, v (1), 261–2. Guy Dickens to Lord Harrington, on 4 September 1731: S.P., xxxi.

[32] Reports of the general directory of 28 October and 12 November 1732, with marginal decisions of the king: *A.B.*, v (1), 452–5. Guy Dickens to Lord Harrington, on 15 November 1732: S.P., xxxiii.

Katte to imprisonment for life because the desertion had not been accomplished, and refused to change its verdict 'tho' His Prussian Majesty sent it back to them twice, to make it Death. . . .'[33] The king, however, had him executed, in spite of all endeavours to obtain a reprieve, and Frederick had to witness the execution.[34] Death was the only punishment fit for desertion: not only peasants trying to escape abroad,[35] but even the abetters of deserters were to be hanged as soon as they were convicted.[36] Death by hanging 'without mercy' was also to be the punishment of advocates who, well knowing the royal predilection for his grenadiers, used a soldier to present a legal petition to the king.[37] This edict seemed so obnoxious to the contemporaries that it was omitted in the official collection of decrees.[38] When, however, many 'of the tall granadiers quarter'd at Potsdam combined together to desert', it was decided 'to take no other notice of the mutineers . . . than by sending some of the Ringleaders to Spandau. , . .'[39] On a similar occasion one was 'hanged for Example Sake, and all the rest to be pardoned. . . .'[40]

The king might also interfere with the administration of justice in favour of one of these soldiers. He summoned the judges who had sentenced one of them to be hanged for the theft of 6000 *Taler*; as they attempted to justify the verdict, he used his stick on their heads to such an effect that one judge lost several teeth and the others were driven down the staircase with bleeding heads. Nothing more was heard about the punishment of the thief.[41] Frederick William used to thrash members of his own family as well as officials who dared to oppose his will.[42] One morning at 6 a.m. he observed the arrival of passen-

---

[33] Guy Dickens to Lord Harrington, on 4 November 1730: S.P., xxix.
[34] The same to the same, on 7 November 1730: S.P., xxix. Prutz, *op. cit.*, ii, 399.
[35] Prutz, *op. cit.*, ii, 348.
[36] Royal decree of 20 December 1722: *A.B.*, iii, 601.
[37] Royal order of 15 and edict of 16 November 1739: *A.B.*, v (2), 864–5.
[38] Schmoller, in *Preussische Jahrbücher*, xxvi (1870), 2.
[39] Col. du Bourgay to Lord Townshend, on 22 August/2 September and 5/16 September 1724: S.P., xviii.
[40] The same to the same, on 6/17 January 1730: S.P., xxvi.
[41] A. Kamp, 'Friedrich Wilhelm I und das preussische Beamtentum' *Forschungen zur Brandenburgischen und Preussischen Geschichte*, xxx (1918), 39.
[42] Col. du Bourgay to Lord Townshend, on 29 November/10 December 1729: S.P., xxv; and on 19/30 January 1730: S.P., xxvi; Guy Dickens to Lord Harrington, on 18 July and 5 September 1730: S.P., xxix; Schmoller, in *Preussische Jahrbücher*, xxv (1870), 591.

gers at the coaching-house of the Potsdam postmaster, who was still asleep. When they eventually succeeded in arousing him and he opened the door still grumbling, the king gave him a severe beating and dismissed him on the spot.[43]

Other officials were dismissed because they had petitioned not to be transferred,[44] or because they submitted estimates which the king considered exorbitant: in this case it was of no avail that the man had served the royal house for thirty-six years and that his superiors interceded for him. He was not even given an opportunity to justify his accounts verbally, as the king believed this to be impossible.[45] The presence of another official at his former office was considered necessary by the ministers for purposes of information, but Frederick William refused permission as he considered him a rogue and ordered his dismissal.[46]

In general the king believed that only by threatening them with dire consequences could his officials be made to work. The members of the *collegium sanitatis* were informed that they would be branded if the plague spread in the country.[47] When von Viereck was appointed president of the Brandenburg provincial chamber he was enjoined not to gamble so much and not to remain as slow and lazy as in the past, otherwise he would be the enemy of his prince.[48] One is left to wonder why a man with such a bad record was promoted to this key post. Another appointee was told that the fortress was not far away if he did not want to accept.[49] The officials of the East Prussian provincial chamber were repeatedly threatened with the gallows and the fate of von Schlubhut if they did not mend their ways, did not execute the royal commands without arguing, or if anything was found wanting on the royal domains under their charge.[50] The instruction for the general directory

---

[43] The Saxon ambassador to field-marshal count Flemming, on 1 April 1713: *A.B.*, i, 381–2.

[44] Report of 9 October 1714, with marginal decision of the king: *A.B.*, ii, 65.

[45] Report of the general directory of 7 June 1725 and request for free transport for the dismissed official of 11 March 1726, with marginal decisions of the king: *A.B.*, iv (1), 727–8, 747.

[46] Representations of the ministers to the king of 23 December 1726 and 2 January 1727, with marginal decisions of the king: *A.B.*, iv (2), 193.

[47] Royal decree of 28 December 1713: *A.B.*, i, 643.

[48] Royal order of 15 January 1723: *A.B.*, iii, 664–5.

[49] Royal decree of 20 December 1717: *A.B.*, ii, 595.

[50] Royal orders of 18 March 1732, 7 and 18 July 1734: *A.B.*, v (1), 384, 676.

stipulated that those who did not follow it in every detail, but continued in the old vein, would be punished ruthlessly and in 'good Russian' fashion.[51] On another occasion the king wrote to his ministers 'that their heads would pay for their Councill.'[52] Or he fulminated against his officials: 'they must dance to my tune, or the devil take me; I will have them hanged and roasted as the Czar does, and treat them as rebels.'[53] In Prussia punishments were somewhat less arbitrary than in Russia, and the royal despotism was checked to some extent by legal provisions and the law courts, so that the example of Peter the Great could not be followed entirely. 'Still', as Frederick William put it, 'We are master and king and can do as We please.'[54] The system which he applied to his family he also applied to the state; it was paternal government in the strictest sense of the term and he functioned as a God of revenge. He also saw to it that the same methods were applied by his officials to their families. A high official, the *Generalfiscal* Wagener, received, through the minister of justice, the royal order to box the ears of his wife in the presence of eight officers so that she would learn to treat them more politely.[55]

Frederick William at least had no illusions about the attitude of his subjects towards himself. When he was dying there was a severe famine, and the general directory was pressing him to relieve the distress; but he replied: 'the *canaille* wants me to die; let them kick the bucket along with me.'[56] Ten years before, after the execution of von Katte, the British minister had reported: 'the hatred as well as abhorrence of the present doings is so general, that I verily believe a body of fifteen thousand men would march from Cleves to Köningsberg without meeting any opposition. The Margrave Albert calls the King publickly a Tyrant, and a Nero. . . .'[57] Yet throughout the reign there was no sign of active opposition in any of the Prussian provinces. The peasant serfs were far too downtrodden to rebel, and their immediate grievances were not against the government but against their landlords. An urban

[51] Royal instruction of 20 December 1722: *A.B.*, iii, 649.
[52] Charles Whitworth to James Stanhope, on 6/17 September 1719: S.P., ix.
[53] Royal notes of 3 November 1714: *A.B.*, ii, 130.
[54] Instruction for the general directory of 20 December 1722: *A.B.*, iii, 649.
[55] Royal order of 15 April 1733: *A.B.*, v (1), 517, note 1.
[56] Count von Manteuffel to count Brühl, on 30 May 1740: *A.B.*, v (2), 952.
[57] Guy Dickens to George Tilson, on 28 November 1730: S.P., xxix.

middle class in the western sense did not exist; and the leading group, the *Junkers*, were loyal towards the state, which protected their interests and maintained the army in which they served.

As an autocratic ruler Frederick William was strongly opposed to the holding of diets and to the privileges of the Estates. As these had never been abrogated, the Estates of the various provinces, when assembling to render homage to the new ruler, petitioned for a confirmation of their privileges, especially of the *Recesse* in which they had been embodied. The king most easily dealt with the *gravamina* of the Brandenburg Estates, whose power had been completely crushed by his grandfather. He simply refused to confirm the *Recesse* until he knew whether they were still applicable, and whether they might not be improved upon.[58] In East Prussia the Estates were persuaded to forego the formal confirmation of their rights and to be satisfied with a *declaratio de non praejudicando*; their *gravamina* could not be dealt with 'because of the short time' that the king was present there. They also took the oath of allegiance without attaining their aims.[59] Opposition in East Prussia, however, remained stronger than in Brandenburg; it later caused the famous royal outburst that he would 'stabilize the sovereignty and make the crown as strong as a *rocher de bronce* and leave the *Junkers* the wind from the Diet.'[60]

Victory was less complete in the western provinces, in Cleves and Mark. There also the Estates demanded the confirmation of the old *Recesse* by which their power had been preserved to some extent under the Great Elector.[61] Strangely enough, their demand was conceded on 20 April, 1713, and only thereafter, on 29 June in Cleves and on 20 July in Mark, did the Estates take the oath of allegiance.[62] Obviously the authorities had tried to follow the same course as in Brandenburg and East Prussia and had failed. A few months later, however, a decree forbade the Estates to meet before they had notified the government of the agenda and the costs of the diet, thus

[58] Royal resolution of 22 April 1713: *A.B.*, i, 379.
[59] Diet and oath of allegiance, 31 August/11 September 1714: *A.B.*, ii, 34–41.
[60] Royal order of 24 April 1716: *A.B.*, ii, 352.
[61] See: 'The Resistance of Cleves and Mark to the Despotic Policy of the Great Elector', *English Historical Review*, lxvi (1951), 219-41; and *The Origins of Prussia*, pp. 229-52.   [62] *A.B.*, i, 409.

curtailing the privileges just confirmed by the king. The Estates replied that they could not report the agenda before the meeting had begun; whereupon the king ordered such 'costly meetings, for which they did not know the cause in advance,' to cease altogether.[63] He did not prevail, however: the diets continued to meet regularly, and the Estates formally retained the power of the purse; but it became very precarious, their contribution being fixed at 180,000 *Taler* p.a.[64] In some smaller Prussian territories in western Germany, *e.g.* Minden and Guelderland, diets were also held regularly once or twice a year; but their influence was a mere shadow of what it had been in the past.[65] In the other provinces the diets disappeared, and small committees of the Estates took their place, which met irregularly and did not have any representative character.[66] We do not know why Frederick William abolished the diets in most provinces but left them in being in others. Perhaps he considered his western territories too far away and too unimportant to interfere more seriously with their customary form of government. He certainly found it much easier to suppress those diets whose political power had already disappeared in the seventeenth century than those which still had strong roots and some powers.

Frederick William strongly disliked the territories which showed any signs of independence and opposition, in particular East Prussia and Cleves. He thus refused to sanction the promotion of an official because he 'is a real Prussian'; 'is a Prussian, thus I am not for him.'[67] Or he wrote on an application: 'if he is a stupid ass they shall make him a councillor in the Cleves government: for that he is good enough.'[68] The king equally strongly differentiated between the nobility of his various provinces. He often praised the *Junkers* of those districts where his orders were obeyed and where service in the army or bureaucracy had become customary, and vented his wrath on the nobility of those parts where this was not the case. Thus he wrote in the instruction for his successor: the 'Pomeran-

[63] Royal decree of 22 March, reply of the Estates of 23 April and royal order of 3 May 1714: *A.B.*, i, 603–6.
[64] Hintze, in *A.B.*, vi (1), 9, 473, 476.
[65] Hintze, *ibid.*, 447, 473, 489–90.
[66] Hintze, *ibid.*, 8–9, 416–20, 432, 451.
[67] Marginal notes of the king of 17 February 1725: *A.B.*, iv (1), 669, 673.
[68] Marginal decisions of the king of December 1723: *A.B.*, iv (1), 392–3.

ian vassals are as loyal as gold although they argue at times. . . . The vassals of the Middle and Ucker Marks are the most faithful of all and they will obey your order willingly and gladly whatever it may be . . .'; those of the Old Mark, however, 'are bad and disobedient men who never do anything readily . . . and the vassals from Magdeburg are almost worse than those from the Old Mark . . .'; in Cleves and Mark 'the vassals are as stupid as oxen but malicious as the devil, . . . the nation is false and very fond of intrigues, and they drink like beasts, that is all they know. . . .'[69] In view of the later history of the *Junker* families of East Prussia and the Old Mark, the royal scorn for them is noteworthy. In the Old Mark it was directed above all against the von Alvensleben, von Bismarck, von dem Knesebeck, and von der Schulenburg,[70] all of whom were to produce so many loyal servants of the Hohenzollern house.

It is interesting to note that the king found the *Junkers* of the districts with the poorest soil the most willing to obey and to serve him. To the present day the Middle Mark and eastern Pomerania (the west was still Swedish) are well known for their barrenness; while East Prussia, Magdeburg and the Old Mark, not to speak of the western territories, are on the whole more favoured by nature. The greater willingness to serve the state may at least partly be explained by the poverty of many *Junker* families and their inability to provide for their younger sons.[71] When their cherished privileges were concerned, especially their freedom from taxation, these noblemen were as determined as their brethren elsewhere to resist any royal attempts to make them pay the land-tax.[72] Only in East Prussia was Frederick William successful in making them pay the *Generalhufenschoss* as the peasants did; but the East Prussian *Junkers* had never been exempt from taxation owing to the strong government of the Teutonic Knights.[73] The well-known investigation, so strongly opposed by the local nobility, was

[69] Royal instruction of January–February 1722: *A.B.*, iii, 451–3.
[70] Royal instruction of January–February 1722 and decree of 27 February 1722: *A.B.*, iii, 452, 473.
[71] Hintze, 'Der österreichische und der preussische Beamtenstaat im 17. und 18. Jahrhundert', *Staat und Verfassung* (1941), p. 341, holds a similar view.
[72] Hintze, in *A.B.*, vi (1), 11–12, and 'Die Hohenzollern und der Adel', *Geist und Epochen der preussischen Geschichte* (1943), p. 48.
[73] Report of the East Prussian government of 30 March 1713: *A.B.*, i, 334; Hintze, in *A.B.*, vi (1), 12.

not aimed at the introduction of new taxes or at the establishment of new principles: it merely tried to abolish abuses and to discover 'hidden' land which had escaped taxation.[74] In general the noblemen and their demesnes remained exempt wherever this principle had been established, *i.e.* in the large majority of the Prussian provinces, and in common with most continental countries.

Frederick William certainly disliked the nobility of some of his territories and attempted to curtail their privileges in so far as they ran counter to his own interests, to crush any opposition, and to eliminate the influence of the Estates and their diets. This, however, did not imply that his government was directed against the nobility as such, or that he had pro-bourgeois leanings and was a foe of the noblemen, as has been asserted repeatedly.[75] This opinion is contradicted by his own utterances as well as by his practice. With regard to the East Prussian *Junkers* and their protests he declared that he wanted to conserve his vassals and to support them against their will.[76] He instructed his successor to employ the noblemen in the army and to educate their sons in cadets' colleges, and to treat the nobility of all his provinces obligingly and graciously.[77] Accordingly he refused to let young noblemen enter foreign services and had them conveyed every year to the cadets' colleges, if necessary by force.[78]

Most of the well-known generals of this period came from native *Junker* families; some were foreign noblemen or princes, such as prince Leopold of Dessau or the duke of Holstein-Beck. And these generals played an equally important part in the civil administration.[79] Most of the officers also were native noblemen. As early as 1724 it was asserted that, with few exceptions, all Pomeranian noblemen had served or were serving

---

[74] Hintze, in *A.B.*, vi (1), 12; Schmoller, 'Die Verwaltung Ostpreussens unter Friedrich Wilhelm I', *Historische Zeitschrift*, xxx (1873), 53–6.

[75] E.g. by Schmoller, in *Preussische Jahrbücher*, xxvi (1870), 159, and in *A.B.*, i, 130–1, 139–40; Hintze, in *A.B.*, vi (1), 283, and 'Die Hohenzollern und der Adel', *Geist und Epochen der preussischen Geschichte*, pp. 49, 53; Kamp, *loc. cit.*, p. 33; Dorn, *loc. cit.*, pp. 262, 265; R. H. Dorwart, *The Administrative Reforms of Frederick William I*, (1953), p. 194.

[76] Marginal note of the king of 13 March 1721: *A.B.*, iii, 287.

[77] Royal instruction of January–February 1722: *A.B.*, iii, 450–1.

[78] Marginal order of the king of 22 January 1726: *A.B.*, iv (2), 6; Schmoller, in *Historische Zeitschrift*, xxx (1873), 61.

[79] Schmoller, in *Preussische Jahrbücher*, xxvi (1870), 153.

as officers.[80] It was their duty to serve their king, and the army had preference over the civil service. As the king put it when deciding upon the appointment of young von Schlabrendorff to a provincial chamber: 'only if he is five foot four inches; for if he is taller he must become a soldier.'[81] Throughout the eighteenth century and beyond, the army was to have priority. Of 1300 Brandenburg and Pomeranian noblemen serving in 1767, 960 were officers and only 340 were officials, while only 400 of those listed rendered no services at all.[82]

In the civil service there was naturally a higher proportion of commoners than there was among the officers. It cannot be maintained, however, that Frederick William aimed at a balance of nobles and commoners within his bureaucracy,[83] or that he preferred, as the Tudors and Louis XIV had done, officials of non-noble origin.[84] It has been asserted that 'for every two nobles appointed to the provincial chambers the king added two officials of bourgeois origin';[85] but there was no general policy to this effect. Only once, in 1723, the general directory enquired whether four young men, two nobles and two commoners should be appointed as *extraordinarii* to each provincial chamber, and a corresponding decree was issued.[86] These, however, were merely training posts not carrying any salary, and the initiative did not come from the king. A few months earlier a similar instruction for the Brandenburg chamber had been promulgated without any clause as to the origin of the trainees.[87] From this isolated and unimportant case no general conclusions can be drawn. Indeed there is documentary evidence that the alleged policy was not pursued and that Frederick William was as partial towards noble officials as his grandfather had been.

In 1719 Samuel von Cocceji, a high legal official and a scion of an ennobled burgher family from Bremen,[88] submitted that it would be useful to appoint a commoner to the East Prussian

[80] *Ibid.*, 538; Ranke, *op. cit.*, ii, 302.
[81] Royal order of 17 October 1739: *A.B.*, v (2), 467.
[82] Dorn, *loc. cit.*, p. 263, n. 106.
[83] This is the opinion of Dorn, *loc. cit.*, p. 262; Dorwart, *op. cit.*, p. 194.
[84] This opinion is held by Schmoller, in *A.B.*, i, 139–40, and in *Preussische Jahrbücher*, xxvi (1870), 162–3; and by Hintze, in *A.B.*, vi (1), 283.
[85] Thus Dorn, *loc. cit.*, p. 262; Dorwart, *op. cit.*, p. 194.
[86] Report of the general directory of 5 April 1723: *A.B.*, iv (1), 163.
[87] Instruction of 26 January 1723: *A.B.*, iii, 684.
[88] Hintze, in *A.B.*, vi (1), 108.

tribunal (which was an ancient *Junker* domain) and that it might be advisable to have there bourgeois and noble judges in equal numbers. His suggestion was then watered down: a commoner should be appointed as soon as there was a vacancy after a nobleman's death; but the king decided against any change.[89] In 1725 two vacancies actually occurred, one deceased judge being a commoner. The East Prussian government accordingly suggested another commoner to take his place, yet the king decided to appoint a nobleman. The minister replied that the vacant post was not a noble one and that, according to Prussian law, it should be given to a commoner, especially as the deceased had been one of the most learned men in Prussia. Frederick William, however, refused to change his decision. The East Prussian government was informed, apparently behind the king's back, that the nobleman appointed was to have the place of the other deceased judge (who had been a nobleman); but the king had already appointed another nobleman to this post, so that finally both vacancies went to native *Junkers*.[90] By 1734 there were seven vacancies in the same court. Cocceji submitted a list of suitable candidates to the king and suggested the appointment of three noblemen and four commoners as the president and vice-president were noblemen. Frederick William, however, selected four noblemen and three commoners, thus giving the former a two-to-one majority; eventually four of each group were appointed.[91] In 1737 the proportion was seven to four in favour of the nobility, again owing to the royal nomination of two noble judges.[92] These instances refer to East Prussian *Junkers*, whom their ruler otherwise disliked so strongly.

There are similar examples from other provinces. In the New Mark the old custom, confirmed by the Great Elector in 1653, was that the government should consist of noblemen and commoners in equal numbers, not counting the head of the

[89] Letter of Cocceji of 1 January and proposal of 4 January 1719, with marginal decision of the king: *A.B.*, iii, 115, 123.

[90] Report of Katsch of 13 November 1725, with marginal decision of the king, report to the East Prussian government of 14 November 1725, and declaration of 7 January 1726: *A.B.*, iv (1), 788–9.

[91] Report of Cocceji with the royal decision of 13 February 1734: *A.B.*, v (1), 608–9.

[92] Royal order of 3 January and nominations of 13 and 15 January 1737: *A.B.*, v (2), 189–90, 340–4.

government. The actual relation in 1730 was ten to two in favour of the nobility, who also got practically all the salaries. The New Mark towns repeatedly petitioned the king to appoint at least two more commoners, but without success. Their wish was fulfilled only in 1732.[93] By 1740, however, the number of commoners had again been reduced to three, and all leading posts were in noble hands.[94] In fact the number of *Junker* officials was increasing; but the king's intention was to employ them outside their native province.[95] This he emphasised frequently in the instructions for his successor and for the general directory; he even forbade the latter to suggest any natives of the province for appointments to the provincial chambers.[96] Even this policy was carried out only very imperfectly; for at the end of the reign, of the eight presidents of provincial chambers, those in charge of the three most important (von Grumbkow in Pomerania, von Lesgewang in East Prussia, and von der Osten in Brandenburg) were natives of the province in question, and every president of a provincial government was a nobleman and a native of the province which he administered.[97]

Noblemen equally predominated in the highest ranks of the central administration. At the end of the reign, of the three ministers employed in foreign affairs, two were Pomeranian *Junkers* and one was an ennobled commoner, and the proportion had been the same in 1713 and in 1728.[98] Of the three ministers in charge of legal matters, one was a Brandenburg *Junker*, the second an ennobled commoner, and the third was the chancellor Cocceji, whose father had already been ennobled: he had married the daughter of a Prussian general and had acquired noble estates in Pomerania with the native noble privileges, his sons were Prussian officers, and his daughters had married native noblemen.[99] The general directory was headed by four ministers: two were Brandenburg *Junkers* (one recently immigrated from Mecklenburg), one was an ennobled commoner, and the fourth came from a Brandenburg

---

[93] Petition of the New Mark towns of 21 February 1730: *A.B.*, v (1), 27–9.
[94] Hintze, in *A.B.*, vi (1), 369–70.
[95] Schmoller, in *Historische Zeitschrift*, xxx (1873), 60.
[96] Royal instruction for his successor of January–February 1722 and for the general directory of 20 December 1722: *A.B.*, iii, 452–3, 578.
[97] The names are listed by Hintze, in *A.B.*, vi (1), 293–472.
[98] Hintze, in *A.B.*, vi (1), 72–3; cf. *ibid.*, i, 313; iv (2), 389.
[99] Hintze, in *A.B.*, vi (1), 108, 119, 121, 123–4.

family of officials which had been ennobled in the late seventeenth century: he possessed noble estates in Brandenburg and had married into an old *Junker* family.[100] The ecclesiastical department, finally, was in charge of two ministers, one a Brandenburg *Junker*, and the other an ennobled commoner.[101] Out of a total of twelve ministers, six were *Junkers*, four ennobled commoners, and two were of bourgeois origin but had acquired noble estates, had married into *Junker* families, and were considered their equals by the native nobility. East Prussia was the only province not represented by a single minister, another proof of the royal bias against its inhabitants.

In the less important posts of the central departments in Berlin as well as of the provincial chambers, on the other hand, commoners usually outnumbered the noblemen. This was almost inevitable because of the priority given to the army, and because commoners usually had to do the bulk of the work.[102] It is not proof of any deliberate royal policy. If there had been such a policy commoners would have been promoted to the highest ranks in preference to *Junkers*. Under Frederick the Great, who strongly preferred noblemen to commoners, they were still represented in nearly equal numbers in the most important provincial chambers, in spite of this royal policy.[103] A deliberately anti-noble policy would have been incompatible with the royal predilection for officers in civil appointments, as most of them were native noblemen. Another proof that he did not follow such a policy is an utterance of Frederick William himself. About fourteen months before his death he declared that in future he would prefer to employ low-born men or *Kläffer* (curs) because they stood less on the point of honour, because he could treat them as he pleased, and because they had to execute his wishes without arguing; while noblemen and gentlemen would not obey his orders blindly and always made representations.[104] Thus the king himself did not think that he had preferred commoners to noblemen, and there is no indication that his policy changed in the last year of his life. This opinion of later historians probably arose through a com-

[100] Hintze, *ibid.*, 158–9, 162.   [101] Hintze, *ibid.*, 137–8.
[102] Hintze, *ibid.*, 203.   [103] Dorn, *loc. cit.*, p. 265.
[104] Report of count von Manteuffel to count Brühl of 18 April 1739: *A.B.*, v (2), 763.

parison between Frederick William and his son, whose partiality towards the *Junkers* was so much more marked; but that does not justify the supposition that his father had the opposite bias.

In general it seems that Frederick William continued the policy initiated by the Great Elector of appointing by preference native noblemen, in the army as well as in the civil service, but not exclusively so, and of showing less bias against able commoners than Frederick the Great was to show. This policy took account of the realities of Brandenburg-Prussia where the *Junkers* were the ruling class: they depended on employment by the state, while the ruler could not dispense with their support without destroying the basis of his state. In spite of his plenary powers, the king was powerless to carry any measure that was contrary to the *Junkers'* interests, above all to alleviate the lot of the serfs. Thus *Leibeigenschaft* (strict personal serfdom) on the royal domains was abolished in eastern Pomerania in 1706, as being contrary to the royal interests and detrimental to agriculture, commerce and industry.[105] The local authorities, however, objected and continued their opposition under Frederick William, who again decreed, in 1718 and 1719, that personal serfdom was to disappear, and fulminated against the 'paltry arguing' of his officials.[106] Then 'the matter seems again to have been forgotten', until the case of a serf who had moved to Danzig and wanted to buy his freedom brought it anew to the king's attention: he resolved, in 1727, that personal serfdom was to go.[107] The general directory again mustered all the arguments in favour of retention, and the Pomeranian chamber reported that the earlier decrees had not met with any success, and that everything had remained on the old footing.[108] In spite of renewed orders to proceed with the reform it successfully maintained its passive resistance.[109]

Towards the end of his reign Frederick William attempted to forbid the eviction of serfs by their masters, which 'desolated

---

[105] Report of the governor of eastern Pomerania of 18 July 1706: *A.B.*, i, 39–41; G. F. Knapp, *Die Bauernbefreiung und der Ursprung der Landarbeiter in den älteren Theilen Preussens* (ed. 1927), ii, 16.

[106] Royal decisions of 23 May, 25 October 1718 and 19 January 1719 and patent of 22 March 1719: Knapp, *op. cit.*, ii, 17–19.

[107] Knapp, *op. cit.*, ii, 24.

[108] Reports of the general directory of 30 October 1727 and of the Pomeranian chamber of 6 March 1728: Knapp, *op. cit.*, ii, 24–5.

[109] Knapp, *op. cit.*, ii, 26.

the farms and depopulated the country.' The East Prussian government objected that this decree did not fit the actual conditions of their province and that it infringed the rights of the *Junkers* who owned the peasant farms.[110] A long correspondence ensued between the central authorities and the provincial government which continued into the next reign, but without any result. There was no change.[111] In 1749 a new effort was made to prevent the expansion of noble demesnes at the cost of peasant land. One expert feared from the outset that this edict also would remain '*res publica platonica*, nice on paper, but impracticable to put into practice.'[112] His fears were only too justified: the local officials stressed the difficulties of making the required investigations; and nothing further was done about it until the various decrees were rediscovered fifty-six years later, to the great surprise of the authorities.[113] Thus the Prussian bureaucracy, largely staffed with native noblemen, was able to thwart the orders of their strongest rulers when the interests of their class were at stake.

The *Junkers* remained the preponderant class, economically through their management of estates farmed with labour services, politically through their positions in the army and the civil service. Prussian despotism could not exist in a vacuum. It had to rely on the existing social forces, among which the *Junkers* were by far the strongest; or it would have to foster the rise of new forces, of the urban middle classes, to make them the counterweight against the *Junkers*. The Great Elector had deliberately chosen the former course, and the kings of the eighteenth century followed in his footsteps. Their choice was probably influenced by the strength of the nobility and the weakness of the middle classes in their eastern provinces, on which their interests were concentrated. They never attempted to shift the centre of gravity towards the west, or to let the conditions prevailing there influence those in the east.

* * * * *

In France, in the seventeenth and eighteenth centuries,

[110] Royal orders of 12 and 14 March 1739, memorandum of the *Landrechts-Kommission* of 12 April, and report of the East Prussian government of 4 May 1740: Knapp, *op. cit.*, ii, 33–4.   [111] Knapp, *op. cit.*, ii, 35–7.
[112] Royal edict of 12 and expert opinion of 16 August 1749: Knapp, *op. cit.*, ii, 51–3.
[113] Report of the East Prussian chamber to the general directory of 9 January 1806: Knapp, *op. cit.*, ii, 97–8.

the old nobility did not fulfil any useful function in society and played no active part in the economic life of the country. There was almost a noble monopoly of higher posts in the army and in the ecclesiastical hierarchy;[114] but the noblemen did not take a leading part in the administration as they did in Prussia. The nobility to the east of the Elbe had become farmers on a large scale, producing for the market and profiting from the rising corn prices; as a rule they lived on their estates; they had thus been able to preserve and to increase their economic strength. In France this transition had not taken place, as the nobles had let out their land at fixed rents—although still retaining seigneurial rights which they could revive and reinforce—and as generally they did not undertake demesne farming.[115] The gradual decline in the value of money made life more and more difficult for them and forced many to sell their estates, while it enriched the *Junkers*.

The decline of the old French nobility was matched by the rise of the bourgeoisie. Its members were growing wealthy and were investing part of their wealth in land, exactly as did their English counterparts. In the north, for example, sixteen to seventeen per cent of the land was in bourgeois hands.[116] People of bourgeois origin were acquiring noble estates and were becoming *seigneurs*, side by side with the old nobility:[117] a position to which German burghers could not aspire. In a country in which most offices were for sale the French bourgeoisie invested its growing wealth in offices. In the seventeenth and eighteenth centuries the administration of France was conducted by ministers and officials who came from the bourgeoisie or the *noblesse de robe*.[118] The highest officials amassed large fortunes and acquired vast landed properties; their children married into the oldest nobility, the sister of Louvois and three daughters of Colbert all marrying dukes.[119]

[114] H. Sée, *La France économique et sociale au xviii⁹ siècle* (1925), pp. 57, 74, 76.

[115] E. Lavisse, *Histoire de France*, vii (1), 378–9; J. Boulenger, *The Seventeenth Century* (1920), p. 106; G. Pagès, *Naissance du Grand Siècle* (1948), pp. 157–8.   [116] Sée, *op. cit.*, p. 13.

[117] Pagès, *op. cit.*, pp. 67, 159, and *La Monarchie d'Ancien Régime en France* (1946), p. 10; H. Hauser, *La Prépondérance Espagnole* (1933), p. 451; Sée, *op. cit.*, pp. 94–5, 97–8, 163.

[118] P. Sagnac, *La Formation de la Société Française Moderne*, ii (1946), p. 75; C. Seignobos, *A History of the French People* (1938), pp. 253, 263.

[119] Sagnac, *op. cit.*, i (1945), 102, 107–10.

The monarchy had to lean on the official class and could not rule against it; at the time of its greatest strength it even leant on, and gave support to, the men of the third Estate against the *seigneurs*.[120]

Although theoretically the monarchy retained all judicial authority, it did not in fact, as it did in Prussia, set itself up as an arbitrary power above the law and the courts, and did not disregard their verdicts (the *lettres de cachet* were not used for this purpose). Nor were the generals and officers of the army allowed to dominate the civil administration and the municipalities. In Prussia, on the other hand, the garrison commanders imposed their will upon the towns, treated the urban authorities with scant respect, and were feared by them even more than were the royal officials set over them.[121] In Prussia also some high officials married into old noble families and acquired noble estates and privileges. These instances, however, were so few that the newcomers could be absorbed and assimilated by the native nobility within a short time. There was no social group comparable with the French bourgeoisie, the *noblesse de robe*, or the official class which ruled France. These groups gave to French despotism a character quite different from its Prussian counterpart, in spite of all obvious similarities and all Hohenzollern endeavours to emulate the Bourbon example. In Prussia the rise of the urban middle classes was hampered and delayed by the workings of the bureaucratic machine and by the dominant role of the army. As early as 1723 the British resident reported: 'the number of useless mouths is dayly augmented, and . . . those who might be of real use to the country by arts and manufactures, are discouraged, and overloaded by excises and taxes of all sorts. . . .'[122] In France the bourgeoisie grew in strength and independence until it was able to throw off the autocratic authority which had once protected it and to stand on its own feet. Yet the methods of the Prussian bureaucracy were more advanced: the higher offices were not for sale, there was little corruption, and the taxes were not farmed as they were in France.

[120] Sagnac, *op. cit.*, i, 62, ii, 130; Pagès, *Naissance du Grand Siècle*, pp. 68, 163.
[121] Hintze, in *A.B.*, vi (1), 22–3.
[122] James Scott to George Tilson, on 27 March 1723: S.P., xvii.

If French despotism differed very considerably from Prussian despotism, there are some striking similarities between the latter and Russian despotism as it was reshaped by Peter the Great. Peter was strongly influenced by Prussian examples in military matters, and by the character of the Prussian king,[123] while the latter was equally impressed by the personality and the unlimited powers of the Czar. In 1719 Frederick William wrote of Peter: 'he is my only true friend, I cannot abandon him. . . .'[124] When Peter died the British ambassador reported: 'the King of Prussia's grief on the Czar's death was greater than could be well represented. . . .'[125] Both rulers were frugal in their habits, opposed to pomp and ceremonies, worked hard, controlled personally every detail, were suspicious, harsh and cruel, eager to punish alleged misdeeds on the spot and without an investigation. Both were ready to sacrifice everything to their work; if Peter had his son executed because he would reverse his father's reforms and destroy his work, Frederick William was only with great difficulty persuaded not to do the same for the same reasons.

Although the conditions of the two countries were in many ways quite different, there were important similarities in the internal policy of the two rulers. It is true that Peter the Great's policy was much more revolutionary than Frederick William's, who on the whole followed more traditional lines: in Prussia the whole problem of westernization and everything it entailed did not arise. Yet in both countries the internal policy was dictated by military necessities, by the requirements of the army, and by the need for higher revenues for military purposes: Peter's reform policy is understandable only from this angle.[126] If in Prussia over seventy per cent of the revenue was spent on the army, in Russia the proportion was still higher, reaching nearly eighty per cent in 1710, and seventy-five in 1724;[127] but 1710 was a war year, and this expenditure covered the navy as well as the army. The military spirit accordingly permeated the administration of both countries. In Russia

---

[123] V. O. Klyuchevsky, *A History of Russia* (1926), iv, 30.

[124] Charles Whitworth to James Stanhope, on 6/17 September 1719: S.P., ix.

[125] Col. du Bourgay to Lord Townshend, on 13/24 March 1725: S.P., xviii.

[126] Klyuchevsky, *op. cit.*, iv, 58, 60, 152.

[127] Klyuchevsky, *op. cit.*, iv, 67, 144–5; V. Gitermann, *Geschichte Russlands*, ii (1945), 135; K. Waliszewski, *Peter the Great*, ii, 184.

also, military officers were used for civil tasks, sent into the provinces with powers of control and punishment, or instructed to deal with negligent officials. Meetings of the senate were attended by officers of the guards, and a French diplomat saw with surprise *'les sénateurs se lever de leurs sièges devant un lieutenant et le traiter d'une façon obséquieuse.'*[128]

Peter the Great found already established an obligation of the members of the *dvorianstvo* (lower nobility) to serve the state personally and indefinitely. He reinforced this obligation, which eminently suited his purposes, made exemptions more difficult and extended the period of service. The sons of the nobility, including the most aristocratic families, were registered and reviewed periodically by the Czar himself. They were then allocated to various regiments, naval establishments or training schools. Defaulters had to suffer very heavy penalties, and recalcitrants were fetched if necessary by military force.[129] The navy and army had priority: only one third of each family's members were allowed to become officials; on the whole the civil service was left with those unfit or too old for military service, with those who had evaded their military duties, and with officers during periods of leave.[130] Indeed it seems that the *dvoriané* were as little anxious to join the forces as were their Prussian counterparts, so that force had to be used on a large scale, quite in contrast to the turbulent and bellicose spirit of the French nobility.[131] If the *dvoriané* had been allowed to choose they would have opted 'almost exclusively for obtaining posts in the civil departments.'[132] Once enrolled, the young nobleman was sent to serve in a distant province so as to forget the ties linking him with his native district.[133] Both rulers preferred to employ their noblemen outside their native provinces and wanted to create a nobility animated by a national spirit and considering it a duty to serve the state.' As Peter's reforms were made or initiated before the accession of Frederick William, it seems likely that the latter was influenced by them.

[128] P. Milioukov, *Histoire de Russie*, i (1932), 392.
[129] Klyuchevsky, *op. cit.*, iv, 74–6, 154–5; Gitermann, *op. cit.*, ii, 125; Milioukov, *op. cit.*, i, 388–9; K. Stählin, *Geschichte Russlands*, ii (1930), 140.
[130] Klyuchevsky, *op. cit.*, iv, 79–80; Stählin, *op. cit.*, ii, 140.
[131] Lavisse, *op. cit.*, vii (1), 382; Sagnac, *op. cit.*, i, 26, 103.
[132] Klyuchevsky, *op. cit.*, iv, 80.
[133] Klyuchevsky, *op. cit.*, iv, 83, 155.

We know that in 1737 Vockerodt, erstwhile secretary to the Prussian legation in St. Petersburg, drew up a lengthy report which described Peter's reforms and emphasised his unchallenged authority and his subjugation of the nobility.[134]

Peter the Great created his service nobility from several different components. As the *dvoriané* above all had to serve in the forces, members of other classes, some of very low origin, had to be appointed to civil posts. From a certain rank upwards they all received patents of nobility. Peter's aim was to create an upper class whose members served the state and owned landed estates; the *dvoriané* were to constitute its core, to which newcomers would become assimilated[135]—in other words, to create a more homogeneous hereditary nobility. Significantly this class was called by the borrowed Polish name of *shliachetstvo*, and its sons were called *Junkers*.[136] The *dvorianstvo* continued to provide the bulk of the civil servants,[137] and even the old *Boyar* aristocracy which had lost its independent power continued to hold high posts in the administration. In 1714, of the twelve members of the senate, more than half (three members of the Dolgoruky family, the prince Romodanovski and the counts Golofkin, Pushkin and Tolstoy[138]) came from its ranks; and in 1725 their number had risen to two thirds; among these were the princes Dolgoruky and Golitsyn and the counts Apraxin, Golofkin, Pushkin and Tolstoy.[139] These old families were even more strongly represented among the provincial governors and other high authorities; six out of eight provincial governors in 1710 came from the old nobility.[140] In short, there was no anti-noble bias in the administration of Peter or in that of Frederick William.

Both rulers were equally powerless to act against the private interests of the nobility. In 1721 Peter instructed the senate to stop the buying and selling of serfs and, if that was impossible,

[134] Vockerodt's report (edit. E. Hermann, 1872), pp. 27, 29.
[135] Klyuchevsky, *op. cit.*, iv, 82, 90, 243; Milioukov, *op. cit.*, i, 387, 390–1; Waliszewski, *op. cit.*, ii, 165–6.
[136] Klyuchevsky, *op. cit.*, iv, 202; Milioukov, *op. cit.*, i, 389; Stählin, *op. cit.*, ii, 140; Waliszewski, *op. cit.*, ii, 165.
[137] Klyuchevsky, *op. cit.*, iv, 202.
[138] C. F. Weber, *Das Veränderte Russland* (1721), p. 23.
[139] Weber, *Des veränderten Russlands Zweyter Theil* (1739), p. 203.
[140] See the lists for 1710 given by the Austrian ambassador Pleyer, in *Zeitgenössische Berichte zur Geschichte Russlands* (edit. E. Hermann, 1872), pp. 134–40.

at least to prevent the break-up of families and households. Contrary to his habit, this *ukaz* was not put forward as a peremptory order, but merely as a proposal. Apparently Peter himself had doubts whether he could prevail against the opposition of the lower nobility, who were strongly interested in the serf trade.[141] Serf auctions continued throughout the eighteenth century, and Catherine the Great still found it impossible to suppress them. In Prussia the monarchy was at least strong enough to forbid the sale of serfs without the land on which they dwelt. In 1744 a Königsberg newspaper advertised for sale a cook, his wife and their three daughters, 'all accustomed to serve'; but the authorities reprimanded the editor, as well as the owner of the serfs, and declared this trade to be unchristian and detestable.[142] Even there, however, legal opinion considered such sales justified, and in 1773 a decree once more had to interdict them.[143]

If the urban middle classes were weak in Prussia, they were almost non-existent in Russia. In the whole country there were only about 300 towns.[144] On the average there were about 500 male taxpayers (including boys) in each of them; the total urban male population was only 170,000, or three per cent of all inhabitants of Russia, in 1724.[145] At that time the urban population in Brandenburg, the central Hohenzollern province, amounted to 38 to 40 per cent of the total.[146] They lived in about forty towns, with an average of about 3,600 inhabitants per town; yet the corresponding figure for Russia was only over 1,000 inhabitants per town.[147] Peter the Great thus had no middle classes which he could have used as a balance against the nobility, while the Hohenzollerns at least had some freedom of choice. In both countries the nobility remained

[141] Klyuchevsky, *op. cit.*, iv, 104.

[142] E. Weise, *Der Bauernaufstand in Preussen* (1935), pp. 66–7.

[143] W. von Brünneck, 'Die Leibeigenschaft in Ostpreussen', *Zeitschrift der Savigny-Stiftung für Rechtsgeschichte*, viii (1887), 56–7, quoting von Sahme, *Gründliche Einleitung zur Preussischen Rechts-Gelahrtheit*, Königsberg (1741), p. 28.

[144] 341 according to Klyuchevsky, *op. cit.*, iv, 159; 271 according to Weber, *op. cit.*, i, 48.

[145] Klyuchevsky, *op. cit.*, iv, 144.

[146] See the figures for 1725 and 1728 in O. Behre, *Geschichte der Statistik in Brandenburg-Preussen* (1905), p. 172.

[147] Twice the number of male taxpayers, plus a comparatively small number of people exempted from taxation.

the ruling class, and serfdom the condition of the majority of the population, until the nineteenth century.

The social structures of Russia and of Prussia, in spite of many divergencies in detail, were similar in their broad outlines, and so were the types of their despotic governments in the eighteenth century. Perhaps, owing to the absence of strong middle classes and the prevalence of serfdom, autocracy was the only alternative to the gradual dissolution of the state which took place in Poland, whose social structure was similar to that of its two neighbours. Perhaps the only way of overcoming the resistance of the landed nobility to strong government was to hand over to them important positions in the state, and to associate them with the new bureaucracy. The latter, with all its power, preserved the established social order, the powers of the landlords over their serfs, and the strict separation of the social classes. In Russia as well as in Prussia, the development of the middle classes was retarded, and not furthered, by the characteristics of the despotism of the eighteenth century.[148]

---

[148] The two main sources used for the compilation of this paper are: the *Acta Borussica, Die Behördenorganisation und die allgemeine Staatsverwaltung Preussens im 18. Jahrhundert*, i–vi, Berlin, 1894–1912 (quoted as *A.B.*), and the State Papers, Foreign, Prussia, vols. viii–xlvii, in the Public Record Office (quoted as S.P.). I am most grateful to Professor Alfred Cobban for advice and comments on eighteenth-century France, to the late Dr. B. H. Sumner and to Prince Nicholas Galitzine for advice and comments on Peter the Great. I should like to point out that the comparisons with France and with Russia are not based on a study of the sources.

11

BRITISH DIPLOMACY AND THE GIANT GRENADIERS OF FREDERICK WILLIAM I

Frederick William I, who ruled from 1713 to 1740, was the real creator of the Prussian state and of the Prussian army, which was to make his country one of the major European powers. During his reign, everything was subordinated to the interests of the army, and the king himself spent far more time reviewing his troops and dealing with military affairs than with the administration of his kingdom. As the British ambassador to the court of Berlin, Sir Charles (later Lord) Whitworth, put it in June 1722:[1] 'I have initiated Mr. Scott (his successor) with the Ministers here, but the King has been too much taken up with his reviews to give audiences'; and James Scott reported a few days later: 'I have not yet had the honour to wait on his Prussian Majesty who hath been taken up all this week in reviewing the regiments which are quartered in and about Berlin.' In addition, Frederick William, year after year, travelled through his far-flung territories, inspecting the troops quartered in every province, each review usually taking several days of his time.

Among the strange passions of this royal sergeant-major was his well-known bias in favour of tall soldiers whom he collected in his Potsdam Lifeguards: although he was extremely parsimonious in every other respect, no expense was too great and no means were too despicable if he could add to the number of his giants. About their treatment Whitworth reported in March 1720: 'The men are very well used, and have large pay in proportion to their bulk.' They certainly received much milder punishment for desertion and for mutiny than was the lot of any other soldiers, or even of civilians caught trying to escape from Prussia or aiding deserters. Many European rulers, among them the Emperor Charles VI and Peter the Great, sought to win the good graces or the friendship of Frederick William by trading on this passion and by offering him some particularly tall specimen for incorporation in his Lifeguards. These tall recruits also played a considerable part in the

---

[1] The dispatches of the British ministers to Berlin, from which extracts are quoted below, are to be found in the State Papers, Foreign (Prussia), in the Public Record Office, in particular in vols. xii (1720), xiii (1721), xvi (1722), xxix (1730), xxxi (1731), xli (1736), xliii (1737), and xliv (1738). The original spelling has been kept.

British diplomacy of the time, and the efforts of the Prussian recruiting sergeants to procure men of the desired size extended to the British Isles. The dispatches of the British ministers from Berlin bear witness to the importance attached to this question and to the extent to which it influenced relations between London and Berlin.

When relations between George I and Frederick William became rather strained early in 1720, it was the Queen of Prussia, George's daughter Sophia Dorothea, who suggested that a judicious present of tall men would influence her husband's attitude towards his father-in-law. At the beginning of March 1720, Whitworth reported to Lord Stanhope: 'Your Lordship will have often heard of the King of Prussia's extream passion for men of an extraordinary seize: it passes all imagination, and the news of any acquisition of this nature has a very visible effect on his countenance and temper: I here inclose the measure of the tallest man in his great Grenadeers, which was given me by the Queen's orders, and if it be possible to find any men near that seize, I am sure it would be the most valuable present his Majesty could make and much more esteemed here than so many first-rate men of war.' In London the measure was found to be seven feet high.

The British government were not slow to adopt this suggestion: fifteen tall Irishmen were duly found and sent to Berlin. The desired effect, however, to give the credit for the present to Sophia Dorothea, was not achieved, as Frederick William had already been notified of their arrival by his own resident in London. Thus Whitworth reported in February 1721: 'the King of Prussia has been taken up these three or four days in ranging your fifteen great Irishmen in his battaillon at Potsdam: they have been extremely liked, tho' they are not of a size with some of the monsters there . . . The Queen complained to me last night that she had a letter from His Majesty about a fortnight ago with a list of these men, their age and sizes, but when she thought to have come the first with this agreable news to the King, she found he had already a list in his pocket, and so was disappointed of the pleasure and merit: I suppose Wallenrodt had got a copy and was officious to make his court with it, but I hope when the next recruit comes, better care will be taken to let the good Queen have the satisfaction of giving the first advice.'

In the following year, however, 'an ugly dispute' arose between London and Berlin because, as Whitworth wrote from Berlin in January 1722, 'some of the Prussian officers have seized one of His Majesty's subjects at Althona near Hamburgh, and brought him hither by force: they have kept him here close prisoner above five weeks, in order to force him to take service in General Löbens regiment, which he still refuses. As he is a man of substance, has a wife and family and two houses, and was at Althona with a considerable barge of hops for sale, the Regency of Hannover have desired me by two or three letters to solicit his discharge, which I did, and the King assured me last week that he was set at liberty: but the officers taking advantage of his unaccountable passion for great wellmade men, keep him still and pretend at least a sum of money for his release: I renew'd therefore my solicitations yesterday, but am afraid to no great purpose, since no answer has been returned me. I have done all I can to stiffle or make up the accidents of this nature which formerly happen'd, but the present injustice was too great for me to dissemble . . . Some stop must be put to these insolencies of the Prussian officers, and tis better the King here should be displeased with me once, than to have perpetual occasion of such complaints which cannot but create ill blood.' The officers maintained their demand for a ransom of fifty thaler under the pretext of expenses incurred by them: a claim which moved Whitworth to the exclamation '*Il n'y a que les pirates d'Afrique qui rançonnent les Chrétiens de cette manière.*' At the beginning of February, at last, he could report that 'business about the recruits is . . . settled to satisfaction,' that is without the payment of the ransom, as he was 'convinced that such a complaisance would only have encouraged the officers in the like violences for the future.'

Nevertheless, such practices continued, growing worse as the reign advanced, for it was not the officers who were chiefly to blame but the king himself. As he told the Imperial ambassador who had made representations about Prussian recruiting methods: 'he had given the necessary orders for putting an effectual stop to those practices in other Princes Dominions . . . But, as he expected that his officers should allways be compleat and have good men, he could not act with the same rigour against them if the case should happen in his own Dominions: therefore, if his neighbours subjects, or any other Princes, would not be exposed to those accidents, their only way was to keep out of his country, and that he should be glad they would, for he did not know what they had to do in it.' (Guy Dickens to Lord Harrington from Berlin in December 1731.) And in March 1738 the same minister reported that the Prussian officers were openly criticizing the system: 'they all wish, great and small, that their Master would engage in a War, tho' it should prove unfortunate, it being, as they think, the only Remedy to cure him of his Passion for tall Men, so fatal to them, that . . . they are not sure of their Bread unless they shew at every Review a great number of tall Recruits.' The contingency of a war, however, was extremely unlikely, as Guy Dickens himself had realized in July 1737: 'it is a great doubt here with many whether this Court could be persuaded to run the hazard of discomposing the front rank of any of their battaillons for the sake of Juliers and Bergue, were the Maritime Powers even disposed to join with them in vigorous measures for putting them in possession of those Dutchies.' The reign of Frederick William, in spite of all his martial inclinations, was one of the most peaceful in the whole history of Prussia: for his foreign policy was influenced by his fear of losing any of his tall soldiers.

The recruiting activities of the Prussians were by then extended to England itself. The valet of Baron Borcke, the Prussian envoy extraordinary in London, one Cregar, and an Irishman, formerly a trooper in a British regiment of horse, Hugh Montgomery, were trying to entice tall Englishmen to serve in the Prussian army. As these activities were forbidden, they had to do so by underhand means. Montgomery became acquainted with the son of a yeoman 'of Great Barford, in the County of Bedford ... William Willis, aged about 23 years, a hopeful and industrous young man,' but unfortunately '6 feet and 4 inches high without shoes,' and promised to procure him employment in the service of an Irish Lord. He showed Willis 'several letters, which he pretended was sent him from the said Lord, or by his order, wherein he was desired to procure a servant, a good looking young man for the said pretended Lord, who should be 6 feet and 4 inches high without shoes ... the Lord keeping two servants of that stature as his porters.' Under this pretence Montgomery in March 1735 enticed young Willis to come with him to London; 'he then told him that the Irish Lord was in Holland' where he induced Willis to go, 'from which place he was conducted under several pretences into the King of Prussia's territories, and then had a guard set over him and was conveyed to Potsdam;' in all of this Cregar helped actively. Willis was not the only Englishman who had fallen a victim to this stratagem: one John Evans had been lured to Potsdam by similar devices; and both accused not only Cregar, but also the Prussian envoy, Baron Borcke, of complicity.

At Potsdam Evans and Willis, 'refusing to take the oath of fidelity to the King of Prussia, were (amongst other inhumanitys) beaten in such a violent manner that they were forced to keep their beds for several days after.' Willis, however, persisted and accused Cregar of 'decoying him away, for which he was taken out of the ranks and received a most severe bastinado, under which he fell; notwithstanding that, he was upheld from the ground to receive the full compliment of blows allotted him for his punishment, and afterwards sent prisoner to his quarters.' Nothing was known in England about the whole affair until Evans' wife, 'under pretence of fetching her children from England ... was permitted to come over.' She brought a letter from Willis addressed to his father, which was the first news the latter received from his son since his disappearance. Willis' father then took steps against Montgomery, who was put 'in Bedford goal, for seducing His Majesty's subjects into fforeign service.' Later he 'was tried and convicted last assizes at Bedford for enticing the said Willis ... for which offence the court fin'd him five pounds – to continue in goal three months longer – to find sureties for his good behaviour for three years.' He thus escaped surprisingly lightly.

Willis' father also addressed a 'humble petition' to Lord Harrington, the Secretary of State for the Northern Department, to have his son freed. George II 'ordered that the facts should be enquired into and verifyed in an authentick manner,' and the petition (followed by the evidence) was forwarded to Berlin in July 1737 for further action. Guy Dickens was not surprised, but replied to Lord Harrington from Berlin the same month: 'most of the facts set forth in the said petition have been known to me for some time: Cregar, Baron Borcke's servant mentioned therein, is his Valet de Chamber, and because of the hand which he had had in these, and I doubt not several other practices of the like nature, his master did not think proper to take him over to England, the last journey he made thither.' From the outset Guy Dickens was rather sceptical as to whether his endeavours on behalf of Evans and Willis would meet with any success, and events proved him right.

Early in August he reported to Lord Harrington that he had communicated the petition to the Prussian ministers: but 'they appeal'd to me, saying, that having been here as many years as I had, I could not but be sensible of the great trouble and vexation which this sort of affairs gave them, by the humour of the King their Master, who was deaf to all their representations when they tended to deprive him of any of his tall recruits.' Frederick William's chief minister, Field-Marshal von Grumbkow, was much more outspoken; he told Guy Dickens: 'as to the two men I desired to have discharged, he knew no other way for us to get them, than to come and fetch them with an army of an hundred thousand men; that nobody was more to be pitied than the Prussian officers, who were obliged to pay their court by such practices, but – it was their Master's humour, and they had no other way to favour and preferment: and the Feldt-Marshall Gromkow was obliged to play the pyrate as well as others, insomuch that was the Emperor's first kettle-drummer a man fit for his purpose, he would steal him away, if he was within his reach; that we in England or else where might hang as many of their recruiters as we could ketch: we were even in the right to do so, but all that would never put it out of his Master's head, *qu'ils avoient icy une hypothèque sur tous les grands hommes de l'Europe.*'

After this unpropitious start the unfortunate British minister laboured for the remainder of the year on behalf of Evans and Willis, but without success. Later in August he reported a new incident: 'this humour or Passion for Tall Men, like some Rivers and Torrents, grows the more violent from any opposition it meets. Not many weeks ago, a discharged cook of Baron Demeradt's, the Imperial Resident, was taken up, tho for his greater security that Minister had not only given him a passport, but lent him one of his servants and his own horses to conduct him as far as Saxony.' When Baron Demeradt made representations, the Prussian ministers merely expressed the hope that such a 'trifle' would not make any difference between the two countries. By the end of the year Guy Dickens had given up hope: 'I shall speak no more to you about our Potzdam Grenadiers: for I do not see any the least probability of getting them out of jeopardy. They laugh at me when I mention the thing, and ask me, half in jest, and half in earnest, how I can urge such a matter seriously and think it is possible they can part with a man, who has six feet four inches, and that I should be thought less unreasonable if I demanded a province or two.' This was the last time that the fate of these two unfortunate Englishmen was mentioned in the dispatches from Berlin. Relations between London and Berlin, and between George II and his brother-in-law Frederick William continued to be difficult; and it was obviously impossible to achieve any redress, as the giant grenadiers remained one of the chief preoccupations of their royal master.

Guy Dickens' comments on the happenings in Berlin not unnaturally became more and more scathing. At the end of 1730 he had reported: 'of all places, this is now become the most barren, for surely the conversation of men out of their senses half the day is not a fit subject for a dispatch to a Secretary of State.' In September 1736 he became more explicit and thus commented on Frederick William: 'this Prince may bluster in his own Dominions, teaze and chicane his neighbours in small matters as about recruits and other things that are not likely to have serious consequences, but will hardly be ever persuaded to make any attempts, which may be attended with danger and expence. The least opposition he sees – two or three bold declarations from powers who have at heart the peace of Europe will always stop him short, and make him renounce the thoughts of aggrandizing himself by the ways of arms.' And in the following month he added: 'as things are managed here at present, I see few powers who would not rather have this Court for an Enemy than a Friend. As an Enemy, experience has shewn they are not to be feared, and as a Friend, They will be always false, useless, troublesome and burthensome.'

This analysis was shrewd enough as far as Frederick William was concerned. Guy Dickens obviously could not take into account the fact that the reign would only last another four years, and that then a young ruler would come to the throne, who was to be far more ambitious, and far more eager to risk the army bequeathed to him in battle for the sake of acquiring new provinces. The giant grenadiers, on the other hand, did not survive into the new reign, but were dissolved on the accession of Frederick II; characteristically, the money thus saved was used to enlarge the army by ten thousand men. A military realist had ascended the throne, and the costly trimmings had to disappear; war was to consume the financial resources of Prussia.

12

BRITAIN AND PRUSSIA

In the course of several centuries the British attitude towards Prussia naturally changed, but there were also certain constant factors which played a prominent part in the 18th as well as in the 19th century, and even in the 20th century still exercised some influence. There existed above all a strong admiration for Prussia as a military power, but at the same time a vivid criticism of the forms which Prussian militarism took: admiration for the military genius of Frederick the Great and later military leaders who in three long wars extending over more than half a century were Britain's allies and decisively contributed to the rise of the British Empire. At the same time the peculiar traits of Prussian absolute government evoked much criticism, already in the 18th century, and more so at the time of the Constitutional Conflict in Prussia, especially of Bismarck's unconstitutional regime and his methods which were so clearly contrary to British forms of government. Yet this did not mean that Prussia was considered an enemy, perhaps in a future war, but rather that it was hoped Prussia would slowly, in spite of all opposition, approximate to the British model of constitutional monarchy, and many sympathized with those forces which inside Prussia worked in the same direction. A real enmity to Prussia only developed from the end of the 19th century, principally on account of the building of the German battle fleet, and that had very little to do with Prussia.

'Prussian militarism' influenced the relationship between the two countries from the outset, in the reign of King Frederick William I (1713–40). Conflict arose on account of his passion for 'giant grenadiers' which included British citizens. It thus became the difficult and disagreeable task of the British Minister in Berlin, Captain Guy Dickens, to obtain the release of such unfortunate victims of the royal passion who were lured to Potsdam by very dubious methods, but he was usually unsuccessful. In 1737 Dickens reported to London: 'This humour or Passion for Tall Men, like some Rivers and Torrents, grows the more violent from any opposition it meets.' In the following year he wrote all the Prussian officers wished 'that their Master would engage in a War, tho' it should prove unfortunate, it being, as they think, the only Remedy to cure him of his Passion for tall Men, so fatal to them, that . . . they are not sure of their Bread unless they shew at every Review a great number of tall Recruits.'[1] When it was established that the Prussian Minister in London, von Borcke, was implicated in the kidnapping of such giants the British

---

[1] Dickens to Lord Harrington, 20 August 1737, 8 March 1738: Public Record Office (PRO), State Papers Foreign 90, vol. 43.

government insisted on his recall and carried its point in spite of strong Prussian opposition.[2]

The strong criticsm of the British Minister in Berlin was also aroused by the royal treatment of the crown prince after his attempt to flee to England and by the death sentence imposed by the king on Lieutenant von Katte, Frederick's friend. In 1730 Captain Dickens reported: 'The Horror, and Indignation conceived here by people of all Ranks on account of the arbitrary Sentence pronounced by the King himself upon that young Man, as also on account of the Cruelty in ordering it to be executed before the Eyes of the Prince [Frederick], is not to be expressed'; he did not dare to repeat, even in a coded letter, all the remarks he heard every day; the king's uncle, Margrave Albrecht, 'calls the King publicky a Tyrant, and a Nero'. Two years later Dickens wrote of new expressions of 'consternation of Persons of all Ranks' when Frederick William ordered an official, who had been legally sentenced to three years imprisonment for embezzlement, to be hanged and this was carried out.[3] Clearly, many of the royal subjects shared Dickens' detestation of their master's methods of government. On the other hand, the growing importance of Prussia was recognized in England. In a book on Germany published in 1738 it was noted that Prussia had become powerful and wealthy through religious toleration; the admission of the Huguenots encouraged trade and manufactures and brought a growth of state revenue – the most important precondition of the growth of the army; the king was transforming the whole country into a single garrison by forcing parents to enter their young children in the recruitng lists and thus to cede their rights to the state.[4] For a country which since the days of Oliver Cromwell rejected all military coercion the Prussia of Frederick William I had little attraction. As Dickens thought, even 'as a Friend, They will always be false, useless, troublesome & burthensome',[5] and the relations between London and Berlin remained more than cool.

This changed quickly under Frederick William's successor although Britain and Prussia fought on opposite sides in the Silesian wars. On the British side it was recognized that with Frederick's victories Prussia had gained the rank of a great European power. In November 1751 Horace Walpole wrote: 'It is plain that the King of Prussia at present holds in his hands the balance of Europe. We may be sorry for it, but we cannot help it; so it is, and so it is likely to be.' Prussia alone formed a stronger bastion for the protection of 'Europe's freedom' than any coalition. In

[2] M. Schlenke, *England und das friderizianische Preussen 1740–63*, Munich, 1963, p. 89.
[3] Dickens to Lord Harrington, 7 November 1730 and 15 November 1732, to George Tilson, 28 November 1730: PRO, State Papers Foreign 90, vols. 29, 33.
[4] *The Pressent State of Germany*, London, 1738, i, pp. 115, 120, 122.
[5] Dickens to Horace Walpole, 6 October 1736: PRO, State Papers Foreign 90, vol. 41.

March 1752 *The Gentleman's Magazine* added: 'Prussia, from her connection with the Empire, has by a stroke in politics hardly to be paralleled, risen to command the balance of power in Europe, so long the boast of the maritime powers.'[6] These statements come from the years before the 'diplomatic revolution' and the alliance between Britain and Prussia which inaugurated the Seven Years War. They show how realistically London saw the situation – in preparation for a dramatic change in foreign policy.

This took place early in 1756 by the Treaty of Westminster by which Britain and Prussia for the first time became allies: to defend together 'the Protestant cause' in Europe and America. The Prime Minister, William Pitt, was convinced that the common religion would forge stronger ties between the new allies than had ever existed between Britain and Austria, and in the publications of the war years the religious emphasis remained prevalent. Frederick was seen as the 'rock' on which all 'Papist machinations' would be wrecked, as the defender of the 'Liberties of Europe'. Especially his victory over the French and contingents of the Imperial army at Rossbach in November 1757 caused storms of enthusiasm in Britain. In the House of Commons the son of Lord Chancellor Hardwicke expressed the general satisfaction that the speech from the throne asked for generous financial support of Prussia; Frederick, he declared, showed the same traits as the greatest princes of Europe, the generosity and military gifts of Gustavus Adolphus and the genius of the Great Elector.[7] The *Scotts Magazine* put Frederick in verse even above Julius Caesar:

> You came, saw, you overcame: Caesar, 't was bravely done;
> But Frederick twice has done the same, and double laurels won.

The victory of Rossbach and Frederick's birthday on 24 January were enthusiastically celebrated in the whole country, not only by the upper classes. Frederick's portrait appeared on innumberable beer mugs, plates and coffee pots. Until the First World War numerous pubs were called 'The King of Prussia'. The Prussian example was also copied in military matters. In London 'The Loyal Prussians' met once a week on a parade ground 'to learn the Prussian exercise'. In Scotland the gentlemen enrolled their tenants in the militia 'who have learned the Prussian exercise and went through their evolutions and firings with an exaction which have surprised even such of the military as were present.'[8] Frederick was 'the great support of the Protestant Religion on

---

[6] Horace Walpole, November 1751, and *The Gentleman's Magazine*, March 1752, quoted by Schlenke, op. cit., pp. 203–4, 218.

[7] Schlenke, op. cit., pp. 232, 234, 236–7.

[8] *Ibid.*, pp. 238, 247–8, 278–80, with quotations from the *Scotts Magazine* of December 1757, the *London Chronicle* of 3–5 January 1758, and the *Edinburgh Evening Courant* of 31 January 1758.

the Continent of Europe', another Gustavus Adolphus.

More than eighty years after Rossbach Macaulay wrote in the *Edinburgh Review*: 'Never since the dissolution of the empire of Charlemagne had the Teutonic race won such a field against the French. The tidings called for a general burst of delight and pride from the whole of the great family which spoke the various dialects of the ancient language of Arminius. The fame of Frederic began to supply, in some degree, the place of common government and of a common capital. It became a rallying point for all true Germans, a subject of mutual congratulation to the Bavarian and the Westphalian, to the citizen of Frankfort and the citizen of Nuremberg . . . Yet even the enthusiasm of Germany in favour of Frederic hardly equalled the enthusiasm of England. The birthday of our ally was celebrated with as much enthusiasm as that of our own sovereign; and at night the streets of London were in a blaze with illuminations. Portraits of the Hero of Rossbach, with his cocked hat and long pigtail, were in every house . . . This enthusiasm was strong among religious people, and especially among the Methodists who knew that the French and the Austrians were Papists and supposed Frederic to be the Joshua or Gideon of the Reformed Faith.' Interestingly enough Macaulay added that at this time there first appeared 'that patriotic spirit' which 'still guards, and long will guard, against foreign ambition the old freedom of the Rhine'.[9] In his vision France, not Prussia, still threatened the liberties of Europe. For nearly a century this was one of the most important motives of Anglo-Prussian friendship. In Macaulay's interpretation romantic and national feelings combined with admiration for the 'racially related' Prussia; and the legendary Arminius appears as a common ancestor and protector of both nations.

In the spring of 1758 a senior British officer visited the camp of Frederick in Silesia and reported to his father, the Lord Chancellor Hardwicke, that the king enjoyed the complete confidence of his men, conversed freely with officers and other ranks and saw to it that they were not needlessly exposed to fatigue. The report compared the Prussian army to a machine which only the king could run: it 'is created, subsists and is put in motion solely by the genius of the Prince that presides over it.'[10] If these words also contained a certain criticism – what would happen to the army when Frederick no longer commanded it? – this emerged more clearly in the anonymous 'Observations and Reflections upon the Present Military State of Prussia, Austria and France' written some years later: 'The ranks are filled up perhaps more than a third part with strangers, deserters,

---

[9] T. B. Macaulay, Frederic the Great, *Historical Essays contributed to the Edinburgh Review*, Oxford, 1913, pp. 698–9.

[10] Major-General Yorke's report of 31 July 1758, quoted by Schlenke, op. cit., pp. 289–92.

prisoners and enemies – of various countries, languages and religions. They cannot therefore be actuated by any of the great moving principles which usually cause extraordinary superiority in Armies; they have neither national spirit, nor attachment to their prince, nor enthusiasm, nor hopes of Fortune, nor even prospect of a comfortable old age to inspire them. In an Army thus composed it is wisdom and sound policy to sink and degrade all intellectual faculties, and to reduce the men as nearly as possible to mere machinery, and indeed as nature has formed the bulk of the King of Prussia's native subjects that task is not very difficult.' The maxim of the Prussian system was 'not to reason, but to obey'. Already in 1748 a British traveller had noticed the high Prussian taxes and the system of forcible recruiting which made the country the most unhappy in Europe; it did not benefit from having a 'good king', for his armaments did not permit him to fulfil his real task, to promote the welfare of his subjects.[11] Thus admiration for Frederick the Great, who helped Britain to acquire a colonial Empire, mixed with criticism of the Prussian form of government and the unlimited power of the king who suppressed all initiative even among his own ministers.

Admiration and criticism also extended to the other features of the Prussian monarchy. Thus Oliver Goldsmith considered the Prussian Academy of Sciences 'one of the finest literary institutions that any age or nation has produced', where 'true learning has found an asylum'; but he also thought that it was an 'artificial' creation, dependent solely on the royal favour, so that the king's death would cause it to wither away. Several British visitors greatly admired Berlin which had magnificent buildings, well built homes and broad streets meeting at right angles. In 1764 James Roswell even wrote: 'It is the finest city I have ever seen. It is situated on a beautiful plain, and like London has its river.'[12] In any case, during the reign of Frederick the Great, in spite of certain criticisms, the feelings in London for Prussia remained very friendly. In the last year of the reign a high-ranking British officer, Lord Cornwallis, visited Berlin to assure the king in the name of George III 'that the connexion formed between them by the German association gave him great satisfaction, especially as he hoped it might lead to a more intimate and close connexion between England and Prussia, which was a thing he most earnestly desired.' At the same time the Foreign Secretary, Lord Carmarthen, stated in the name of the members of the Cabinet that they 'would be glad, by endeavouring to render mutual good services to each other, to lay the foundation of a

---

[11] *Ibid*, pp. 270–1, 372–3, 294 note 118, quoting British accounts of 1748–49, 1762 and the late 1760s.

[12] *Ibid.*, pp. 327–8, 332–3, quoting leters of July 1758 and July 1764, and Oliver Goldsmith, *An Enquiry into the Present State of Polite Learning in Europe*, London, 1759, p. 61.

firm and lasting alliance'. Cornwallis added verbally that 'these strong professions of friendship' were 'a convincing proof how sincerely they preferred a Prussian alliance to that of any other power'.[13] That was in the year 1785, and only a few years later there followed the alliance against revolutionary France which – with certain interruptions – was to last for more than twenty years. Exactly as in the Seven Years War France was the common enemy, and the fight continued until the defeat of Napoleon in the battle of Waterloo where the Duke of Wellington was saved from his difficulties by the timely arrival of the Prussians under Blücher.

In fact the British interest in Prussia in the years 1813–14 was above all a military one, and the reports sent by Lieutenant-General Charles Stewart to Lord Castlereagh, the Foreign Secretary, contained almost exclusively military news. This included fulsome praise of 'the glorious career of the Silesian Army' commanded by Blücher: 'it has been fighting daily since the opening of the Campaign, and daily covered itself with Laurels, and now stands preeminent in the advance next to the foe, with its venerable and gallant Leader anxiously awaiting new opportunities to augment his heroic reputation.'[14] This was written a week before the battle of Leipzig, but without mentioning Gneisenau who as chief of staff was principally responsible for the successes of the army. Early in February 1814 Stewart reported from France: 'If Marshal Blücher was not long immortalized, this Day would have crowned him in the Annals of Fame, for . . . the Marshal steadily pursued the combination upon which the Result of the day depended: This Foresight, Judgement and Decision is done Justice by all the allied Army.'[15] Apart from the military news the British representative also reported the desiderata of the Prussian king and his government, their wishes for the same subsidies as were paid to Russia, and for the conferment of the Order of the Garter which had been promised to Alexander I; this 'has caused a considerable anxiety on the part of the Prussian Government . . . I understand the King himself has very strong feelings upon the Subject'. Stewart praised the conduct of Frederick William III which was acclaimed 'by the whole of the Allied Powers'. He added: 'if the Efforts of the Monarch were backed by an able and efficient Government, I believe He would yield to none in the importance of his Alliance to Great Britain, and in Ability to forward her Objects'.[16] Clearly he was not convinced that Prussia possessed an

---

[13] Report by the British Minister in Berlin, 10 September 1785: PRO, Foreign Office 244, file 1. The 'German Association' referred to in the report was the so-called League of Princes directed against Austria. Cornwallis was soon after appointed Governor-General of India.

[14] Stewart to Castlereagh, Rothenburg, 11 October 1813: PRO, Foreign Office 244, file 5.

[15] Same to same, Chateau de Brienne, 2 February 1814: *ibid.*, file 6.

[16] Same to same, Töplitz, 4 September 1813: *ibid.*, file 5.

able and efficient government, but this was almost his only remark about the internal conditions in Prussia.

Stewart also observed the first signs of an awakening German nationalism. In August 1813 he mentioned that the Hussar regiments of the Kingdom of Westphalia 'have come over from the Enemy and are most eager to be ranged in Battle against them to take their Revenge for the Misery they have entailed upon their Country.'[17] When the Allied forces marched into Leipzig on 19 October Stewart felt unequal to the task of describing 'the Acclamations and Rejoicings of the People': 'Handkerchiefs waving from the Windows, Hands clamorous in Applause, and lastly, but most forcibly Tears rolling from the Eyes, marked the delightful Aera of the liberation of the World from the Tyranny of the Despot to be at hand: The moment was too excitingly delicious to an Englishman to describe.'[18] In Prussia, however, national enthusiasm was soon replaced by disappointment with insufficient territorial aggrandisement, although the kingdom not only received the lands lost in 1807, but almost the whole of Rhineland and Westphalia and half of the kingdom of Saxony. In February 1815 the British Minister reported from Berlin that 'the Majority of the Nation would have been satisfied with nothing less than the whole of the Country [Saxony], and even the more moderate among them, who consider Prussia as sufficiently indemnified with respect to *Territory*, find fault with the extended line they now have to defend, and still more with their not having gained Anspach and Bareuth' (Bayreuth), which had been given to Bavaria. Prince Blücher was 'the head of the Malcontents; the first day the news reached us he expressed his Sentiments in the most publick and undisguised language, and even went so far as to write a letter to the King in which he stated that he owed it to His Country, and to the blood which she had so copiously and, as it now seemed so uselessly shed, to demand his dismission.' Only the 'earnest Entreaty' of the War Minister, General Boyen, had induced Blücher to suppress the letter. The national discontent was combined with 'a great jealousy of England' who was accused 'of having sacrificed the interest of this Country to her own separate Views.'[19]

Britain was above all interested in restoring the European balance of power; she was willing to establish Prussian power on the Rhine as a protection against France and to recognize Prussia as the leading power in north Germany, but not in the whole of Central Europe. There too a balance was to be restored, which existed in fact until 1866: only that Prussia held all the trumps by gaining the Rhenish and Westphalian lands. The battle of Waterloo on 18 June 1815 reinforced the military

---

[17] Same to same, Zehista (Silesia), 27 August 1813: *ibid.*, file 5.
[18] Same to same, Leipzig, 19 October 1813: *ibid.*, file 5.
[19] George Jackson to Edward Cooke, Berlin, 26 February 1815: *ibid.*, file 6. He added that Frederick William III 'by no means joins in this ungrateful clamour'.

bonds between Britain and Prussia and caused new British enthusiasm for Prussia. This found its practical expression in a public subscription for the families of the wounded and fallen soldiers, and the British Minister in Berlin was authorized to contribute the considerable sum of 200,000 Prussian thaler 'in the name of the people of the British Empire'. The memory of Waterloo lived in Britain for a long time, in the arts as well as in popular opinion. In 1858 it found symbolical expression in the painting of Daniel Maclisle which showed the meeting of Wellington and Blücher at the farm of Belle Alliance after the battle of Waterloo and found its place in the gallery of the new British Parliament.[20]

During these fifty years it remained an important aim of British foreign policy to preserve Prussia as a great European power representing the Protestant interest. An Austrian solution of the German question would have left Britain as the only bulwark of Protestantism and the European liberties, so that British policy favoured Prussia, but it was hoped at the same time that a Prussian solution of the German problem would also be a liberal one. Especially Queen Victoria and her consort dreamt of a liberal Prussia which would unite Germany in the form of a liberal, parliamentarian and Protestant Empire. In July 1849 Palmerston wrote to the British Minister in Berlin: 'It appears therefore to Her Majesty's Government that if Germany is to be organized upon a principle of intimate union, such an orientation can be effected only under the Leadership of Prussia, and it is most desirable for the working out of such a scheme, that Prussia should disarm the jealousies and allay the fears of the small sovereignties by respecting their Political Existence, and by not expecting from them any sacrifice which would be incompatible therewith . . . Prussia, retaining her position as a European Power, would be the head of a German Confederation combining in its organization many of the advantages of Unity without destroying those moral springs of action which derive their strength and elasticity from feelings of local nationality.' Palmerston even desired a German Confederation under Prussian leadership to conclude an alliance with Austria 'for all purposes of common defence' – an anticipation of the later solution of the German question.[21]

The rejection of the Imperial crown by Frederick William IV and the defeat of the revolutionary movement of 1849 buried not only the hopes of the German Liberals, but also the British hopes that the German question could be solved in a constitutional way. The

---

[20] Minutes of the Joint Committee of the Waterloo Subscriptions, London, 17 October 1815, *ibid.*; Günter Hollenberg, *Englisches Interesse am Kaiserreich – Die Attraktivität Preussen-Deutschlands für konservative und liberale Kreise in Grossbritannien,*, Wiesbaden, 1974, p. 15.

[21] Palmerston to Earl of Westmorland, 13 July 1849, quoted by V. Valentin, *Bismarcks Reichsgründung im Urteil englischer Diplomaten*, Amsterdam, 1938, pp. 501–3.

discrepancy of the political systems in the two countries led to friction. The Prussian government was indignant that German political refugees could pursue their activities in London without intervention by the police. The Prussian Prime Minister reproached the British Minister that the English police only dealt with criminals but left political wrongdoers alone. The Minister replied that his government could only act according to the law; fortunately, the police were only responsible for public security, and only people who infringed English law could be expelled from the country.[22]

In spite of the bitter experience of 1849 Queen Victoria steadfastly adhered to Prince Albert's 'great maxim of Prussia becoming Germany and a great German Empire' – hopes which were apparently reinforced by the marriage of her eldest daughter Victoria or Vicky to the Prussian Crown Prince Frederick William in 1858. The beautiful and intelligent princess was to function as a kind of mediator between the two countries. As Lord Clarendon wrote after his visit to Berlin to attend the coronation of William I in October 1861: 'All my political sympathies are for Prussia, the greatest Protestant Power in Germany. The marriage of the Crown-Prince with the highly gifted daughter of our Queen has only knitted still closer the old ties between the two countries.' But he added warningly: 'I am beginning to think that Constitutional Government in Prussia is impossible. Certainly neither the King nor his Ministers have any notion of the volcano seething underneath their feet.' The new king, whom Clarendon had advised to introduce a parliamentary regime, 'has no idea of the duties of a Constitutional Sovereign'.[23] For William was deeply convinced that he owed his crown solely to God; he had also played a decisive part in the suppression of the revolutionary movement of 1849.

The warning uttered by Lord Clarendon was confirmed by the outbreak of the Prussian constitutional conflict in which the British sympathies were clearly with the Liberal majority of the Prussian Diet and the Prussian crown prince was seen as a symbol of resistance to an arbitrary regime. Full of indignation Vicky wrote to her mother in June 1863: 'The way in which the Government behave, and the way in which they have treated Fritz [her husband], rouse my every feeling of independence. Thank God I was born in England, where people are not slaves, and too good to allow themselves to be treated as such.'[24] Soon after a prominent and influential British diplomat, Sir Robert Morier,

[22] Lord Bloomfield to Palmerston, Berlin, 14 August 1851, quoted by Valentin, op. cit. pp. 81–3.
[23] Queen Victoria to Crown Princess, 11 August 1866: R. Fulford (ed.), *Your Dear Letter – Private Correspondence of Queen Victoria and the Crown Princess of Prussia 1865–71*, London, 1971, p. 89; W. E. Mosse, *The European Powers and the German Question 1848–71*, Cambridge, 1958, p. 105, quoting Clarendon's report of October 1861.
[24] Crown Princess to Victoria, 8 June 1863: F. Ponsonby (ed.), *Letters of the Empress Frederick*, London, 1928, p. 33.

reported from Berlin: 'Is the nation to have or not to have a voice in the imposition of the blood tax paid by itself? This, I repeat, is the real point at issue . . . The stand, therefore, made by the Chamber against that position of the budget, which represents the extra cost entailed by the reorganisation [of the army], is a stand made for the right of the nation to have a vote in the imposition of the taxes on bone, sinew, and blood furnished by its kind.' At the same time Morier provided a detailed analysis of the importance of the *Landwehr* (territorials) and its officer corps; its officers were distinct from those of the regular army: 'They have felt themselves not to be a separate caste with no sympathies with the nation at large, but on the contrary immediately bound up with it'; they had a strong *esprit de corps* and formed 'the constitutional bulwark of Prussia in her preconstitutional days'. The officers of the regular army, on the other hand, educated in cadet schools and animated by 'the narrowest spirit of caste' were looking 'upon the *Landwehr* with jealousy and an ill-merited contempt'; for a long time they had tried to deprive the *Landwehr* of its influence on the young. Morier was strongly opposed to Bismarck's anti-liberal policy, yet he was not anti-Prussian but an advocate of an Anglo-Prussian alliance. He and others thought above all of the time after Bismarck, when the victory of liberalism would be guaranteed by the new king and the rise of the middle classes. Morier also supported the German claims to Sleswig and Holstein and tried to induce his government to put diplomatic pressure on Denmark to grant self-government to the two duchies.[25]

A radical change in British public opinion occurred only in the course of the wars of 1864 and 1866. As early as May 1864 Queen Victoria regretted the strong anti-Prussian current in her country: 'I am grieved and distressed to say that the feeling against Prussia has become very *violent* in England, and quite ungovernable, as I heard from everyone. The people are carried away by imaginary fancies, and by the belief that Prussia wants to have the duchies for *herself.*' She knew these ideas to be wrong, but the people would not listen to reason.[26] But the people's feelings about Sleswig and Holstein were correct, and the queen was wrong. The crown princess too complained to her mother about the anti-Prussian mood in Britain: 'It is so dangerous and productive of such harm! . . . Prussia has gained unpopularity for itself since some time, on account of the King's illiberal government, but the feeling against us now in England is *most* unjust!'[27] Yet in British government circles the attitude towards Prussia remained friendly, and in favour of a consolidation of Germany under Prussia. In September 1865 Palmerston

[25] Letter of 3 August 1863: *Memoirs and Letters of the Right Hon. Sir Robert Morier from 1826 to 1876*, London, 1911, i, pp. 327–30; Hollenberg, op. cit., pp. 17–18.

[26] G. E. Buckle (ed.), *The Letters of Queen Victoria*, 2nd Series, London, 1926, i, pp. 206–7. Emphasis in the original.

[27] Letter of 26 May 1864: Ponsonby (ed.), op. cit., p. 54.

wrote: 'Germany ought to be strong in order to resist Russian aggression, and a strong Prussia is essential to German strength. Therefore, though I heartily condemn the whole proceedings of Austria and Prussia about the Duchies, I own that I would rather see them incorporated with Prussia than converted into an additional asteroid in the system of Europe.'[28] In a similar vein the British ambassador in Berlin, Lord Napier, reported that the creation of a German or Prussian fleet 'need not inspire us with any jealousy or apprehension', for England had fought three great wars in alliance with Prussia and never against it; a 'German fleet might be a useful counterpoise in the Baltic to the fleet of Russia . . . and England was in all time desirous that Germany should be united and strong.'[29]

Bismarck's policy, on the other hand, was sharply criticized. His measures during the constitutional conflict, which included a suppression of the liberal press and the right of free assembly, were considered despotic by the British ambassador, Sir Andrew Buchanan. In June 1863 the Prime Minister, Earl Russell, denied Bismarck's claim that in Prussia nothing stood between the throne and revolutionary democracy, for all reports confirmed that the middle classes were loyal to the monarchy and the king: if this was no longer so the change had to be attributed to Bismarck and his colleagues; Bismarck's attitude to the crown prince was 'most disrespectful . . . and most unjustifiable on the part of a minister of the King'.[30] Lord Clarendon, the Foreign Secretary, severely condemned the measures taken by Bismarck against Austria. When Count Bernstorff, the Prussian ambassador, read to him a long despatch of Bismarck about the vast military preparations of Austria on the Silesian frontier Clarendon simply stated 'that he did not believe these returns, as the information he had received was in direct contradiction to them.' He was convinced that there was no cause for war and hoped that King William would 'before he decides for war, become aware of the truth, notwithstanding all the unscrupulous contrivances resorted to to conceal it from him.'[31]

The Austro-Prussian war only lasted a few weeks and ended with further large annexations of German territory by Prussia. In July 1866 Sir Robert Morier sent an indignant report to London about the treatment of the Free City of Frankfurt by the Prussian army which he had witnessed: the billeting of the soldiers 'on the inhabitants has been carried out with a vindictive barbarity directed against individuals supposed to be Austrian in their sympathies . . . The first act of General von Falckenstein was to seize and throw into the common jail two of the leading Senators of the

[28] Palmerston to Lord Russell, 13 September 1865: Mosse, op. cit., p. 222.
[29] Napier to Lord Russell, 20 April 1865: Valentin, op. cit., p. 523.
[30] Russell to Buchanan, 17 June 1863: Valentin, op. cit., pp. 190–1; in general, see *ibid.,* p. 188.
[31] Clarendon to Victoria, 3 April 1866: Buckle, op. cit., i, p. 316.

city . . . All the editors of journals hostile to Prussia were committed to the cells of common vagabonds in the city lockup.' Falckenstein's successor, General von Manteuffel, demanded the payment of 25 million florins in silver within 24 hours, although Frankfurt had not participated in the war. When it was pointed out to him that it was impossible to raise such a sum in the time given, the general threatened 'that if not paid up the town would be given up to pillage'. In fact the demand was later moderated to 14 million florins. When the Prussian authorities tried to deny the threats uttered by Manteuffel the British ambassador refuted the dementi and declared that the general was responsible for his behaviour; it was a stain on the glory of Prussia to take such spiteful vengeance and only damaged its cause.[32]

At the outbreak of the Franco-Prussian war British public opinion and all persons of influence were entirely on the Prussian side; for was there not in Paris a second Napoleon who tried to follow in the footsteps of his uncle? The Prime Minister, Gladstone, sharply rebuked Napoleon's attitude in the Spanish succession question and wrote that, convinced of French superiority, he overstated his case. In general it was thought that the French had no right to dictate to the Germans. In July 1870 Queen Victoria wrote to her daughter in Berlin: 'We must be neutral *as long as* we can, but no one here conceals their opinion as to the extreme *iniquity* of the war, and the unjustifiable conduct of the French! Still *more, publicly*, we cannot say; but the feeling of the people and the country here is *all* with you, which it was not *before*. And need I say what I *feel?*' In September the queen repeated: 'In England I can assure you the feeling is far more German than French, and far the greater part of the press is in your favour. All reflecting people are . . .'[33] In the same month the crown princess wrote to her mother: 'It is a great satisfaction to me to see how Prussian *Wesen*, discipline, habits etc., is now appreciated and seen in its true light, its superiority acknowledged with pleasure and pride, instead of jealousy, fear, scorn, and hatred . . . We are worthy of England's sympathy and approbation and feel sure that it will not long be withdrawn from us.'[34] More cautiously George Goschen, President of the Poor Law Board, declared: 'On the whole I have cordially sympathised with the German victories and quite think the downfall of the military prestige of France will be of incalculable benefit. But I confess I see great danger ahead in the unbounded success not only of the German arms, but of Bismarck's unscrupulous, cynical and cruel policy.' Already in August 1870 Morier recognized that the result of the war would be 'the preponderance of Germany over Europe

---

[32] Morier to Lord Stanley, Frankfurt, 20 July 1866: Valentin, op. cit., pp. 527–8.
[33] Victoria to Crown Princess, 20 July and 13 September 1870: Ponsonby (ed.), op. cit., p. 77; Fulford (ed.), op. cit., p. 299. Emphasis in the original. In general see Valentin, op. cit., p. 426, and Ponsonby, op. cit., p. 74.
[34] Crown Princess to Victoria, 3 September 1870: Ponsonby (ed.), op. cit. p. 92.

for centuries'; he believed the Germans 'will henceforth rule the world.'[35]

Yet it was not the fear of German preponderance which caused a change in British opinion, but the course of the war, the severe measures taken in occupied France, the bombardment of Paris, and above all the planned annexation of Alsace and Lorraine. In August Morier wrote to a German friend: 'You will know without my telling you, how heart and soul I am with Germany at this great turning point, not of her history only but of that of mankind. What untold heights of civilisation may not the world attain to with a German Empire preponderant over the destinies of Europe – if only there is as much wisdom in the upper stories of the building as there has been valour and self-sacrifice in the lower . . . The taking [of] two large provinces, the inhabitants of which are more Gallic than the Gauls . . . is something I do not like as the *début* of a German Empire in the nineteenth century . . . A hostile occupation of this kind means more or less the continuance of armed peace and the impossibility of disarmament.' Early in 1871 the same diplomat observed, after a visit to the German camp at Metz, that he had witnessed an 'extraordinary difference' between the language and behaviour of the officers there and before the war; the 'unparalleled successes . . . which have attended the German arms, and the consequent absolute power which the German nation has acquired over Europe, will tend especially to modify the German national character, and that not necesarily for the better. Arrogance and overbearingness are the qualities likely to be developed in a Teutonic race under such conditions, not boasting and vaingloriousness.'[36] At the end of 1870 Queen Victoria wrote to her daughter: 'You say that the Germans are convinced that the French will try and begin a new war as soon as they can, and that therefore Alsace and Lorraine are necessary to rectify and fortify the frontier. Whereas here everyone says – that the only objection to the taking of Alsace and Lorraine is that there never will be a durable peace, if they are taken, as the French will . . . never rest until they get them back!'[37] So clearly the future was seen as early as 1870.

When the radical democrat Johann Jacoby was arrested in Königsberg because he had protested in a public meeting against the annexation of the two provinces and demanded that the population be consulted, Lord Granville, the Foreign Secretary, asked the British ambassador in Berlin, Lord Loftus, for a report. According to this, all parties agreed that the arrest was rash and injudicious and legally doubtful, in spite of the existence of a state of siege; in the Cabinet Gladstone suggested to

---

[35] Goschen to Granville, 30 September 1870: Mosse, op. cit., p. 331; Morier to Mallet, 9 August 1870: *Memoirs and Letters of the Right Hon. Sir Robert Morier*, ii, p. 165.
[36] Morier to Stockmar, 21 August 1870 and 27 January 1871: *ibid.*, pp. 165–6, 243.
[37] Victoria to Vicky, 10 December 1870: Fulford (ed.), op. cit., pp. 311–12.

aim at a consultation of the inhabitants, but Lord Granville opposed this as incompatible with a policy of strict neutrality.[38] In March 1871 Queen Victoria in a letter to her daughter lamented the growth of enmity between the two nations 'which I am bound to say began first in Prussia, and was most unjust and was fomented and encouraged by Bismarck'; this was 'a great sorrow and anxiety' to her, 'and I cannot separate myself or allow myself to be separated from my own people. For it is alas! the people, who from being very German up to three months ago are now very French! I tell you this with a heavy heart but it is the fact.' From Berlin the crown princess confirmed the strength of the anti-British feeling which was of recent date: 'now people are frantic at the anti-German feeling in England, which reveals itself more every day.'[39] The unexpectedly long duration of the war in France which became ever more bitter and the starvation of Paris during the siege reinforced the hostile mood. The original sympathy with Germany turned into rejection and sharp criticism, and the same hostility developed in Germany. In November 1872 the British ambassador, Odo Russell, reported rather worried from Berlin: 'The feeling against us in Germany in consequence of our supposed French proclivities is as unreasonable as it is distressing, and the growing hatred of France is to my mind as alarming as it is unfounded.'[40]

During the following years British criticism was much less directed at Prussia or Germany than at Bismarck's policy, his disregard of parliament and the constitution, his treatment of other, smaller nations. In 1875 Queen Victoria wrote to her daughter: 'But Bismarck is a terrible man, and he makes Germany greatly disliked; indeed *no one* will stand the overbearing insolent way in which he acts and treats other nations, Belgium for instance. You know the Prussians are not popular unfortunately, and *no one* will tolerate any Power wishing to dictate to all Europe. This country, with the greatest wish to go hand in hand with Germany, cannot and WILL *not stand it.*'[41] Odo Russell, the British ambassador in Berlin, wrote in 1881: 'When the old Emperor dies, – and I regret to say that he has lately shown the first symptoms of failing health – then Bismarck's irresponsible power ought to come to an end – that is, if the Crown Prince has the moral strength to compel his Chancellor to submit to the Constitution of the Empire and accept the accidents of a parliamentary system based on universal suffrage, which at present, Bismarck absolutely refuses to do.' But would the crown prince possess this 'moral strength'? Russell doubted it and

---

[38] Valentin, op. cit., pp. 437–8.

[39] Victoria to Vicky, 1 March 1871: Fulford (ed.), op. cit., p. 322; Vicky to Victoria, 10 February 1871: Ponsonby (ed.), op. cit., p. 122.

[40] Russell to Granville, 3 November 1872: P. Knaplund (ed.), *Letters from the Berlin Embassy 1871–1874, 1880–1885*, Washington, 1944. p. 73.

[41] Victoria to Vicky, 8 June 1875: Ponsonby (ed.), op. cit., p. 140. Emphasis in the original.

added only a few days later: 'The Crown Prince has liberal aspirations and disapproves of the arbitrary manner in which the Emperor and the Chancellor deal with the Constitution – but the Chancellor's powers of persuasion are so great, that he generally comes round to Prince Bismarck's views and policy after hearing him explain them.' Early in 1882 Russell reported briefly and decisively: 'While Bismarck lives, parliamentary Government cannot flourish in Germany.'[42] The hopes of the ambassador concentrated on the crown princess who was 'a convinced Constitutionalist', but he clearly had strong doubts as to what extent she would be able to influence her husband. In general, the liberal inclinations of the crown prince were attributed to the influence exercised by his wife. She was the 'English woman' intriguing against Germany, and Bismarck certainly was not innocent of this widely held opinion. Her own opinion of Bismarck was, as she wrote in 1887, that he 'has made Germany great, but neither loved, happy, nor has he developed her immense resources for good! Despotism is the essence of his being; it cannot be right or good in the long run!'[43] This letter was written only six months before the death of the old Emperor William I. But the short government of Frederick III did not bring the hoped for change in favour of more liberal forms of government.

During the years after the dismissal of Bismarck criticism of Germany in Britain became much stronger, especially on account of the irresponsible and often anti-British behaviour of the young William II and the building of a German high seas fleet. Neither of these, however, was connected with Prussia, but with the aim of the German Empire to become a world power. This Empire on the other hand was often regarded as an extended Prussia, for example by the well known historians J. A. R. Marriott and C. Grant Robertson: their book, *The Evolution of Prussia – The Making of an Empire*, was published soon after the outbreak of the First World War and remained for many years the general textbook on Prussian history. They thought that, instead of 'Deutschland, Deutschland über Alles' it would be more appropriate to sing 'Preussen, Preussen über Alles'; if a conflict of interest were to arise between Germany and Prussia, 'Prussia must prevail, for it is Prussia's strength that makes the Empire formidable and Prussian institutions and Prussian organization that are the secret of dynastic splendour and Imperial power.' Like Macaulay and Carlyle before them, the two Oxford historians were full of admiration for Frederick the Great and believed that, standing with the sentries in the centre of Berlin, they could hear 'the trumpets of Ziethen's and Seydlitz's hussars'. Frederick 'inherited a crown of the second rank and the blue and red uniform; he

---

[42] Reports by Russell, 19 and 26 November 1881 and 14 January 1882: Knaplund (ed.), op. cit., pp. 235–6, 248.
[43] Vicky to Victoria, 27 September 1887: Ponsonby (ed.)., op. cit., p. 247; and in general *ibid.*, pp. 470–1.

had been bred in the graceless and starving atmosphere of the barrack-yard, the parade ground, and the 'Tobacco Parliament' . . . The Europe of 1740 was as unconscious of what Frederick was, and of what genius could make of Prussia, as was the Europe that made epigrams on the Junker, 'a red reactionary and smelling of blood', who became Minister President in 1862 . . . It was Frederick the King, the incarnation of Prussia, who stamped himself on the imagination and became the model for the governing classes to come.'[44] The praise of Frederick from the year 1915 was almost as enthusiastic as that of Macaulay seventy years before – and this was in the midst of the war which was allegedly fought to destroy 'Prussian militarism'.

Thus British criticism of Prussia in the course of the 19th century became a criticism from the viewpoint of British liberalism and parliamentarianism which came from both political parties. Until 1871 British public opinion favoured the unification of Germany under Prussian leadership. Thereafter Bismarck's methods of government were much criticized, and even more so the impetuous and irresponsible policy of William II. Side by side with that, however, there was much enthusiasm for Prussia, its rise from very modest beginnings, the deeds of its great king and his army. In my opinion it would be a mistake to conclude from the totally different social and political systems in the two countries that their conflict was inevitable. For surely tsarist Russia differed even more strongly from Britain – and this led to frequent sharp attacks – and yet the two countries fought on the same side in the Great War. Between Britain and Prussia no conflicts existed which were bound to lead to a war. Whether the conflict between Britain and the German Empire was 'inevitable' is an entirely different question.

---

[44] J. A. R. Marriott and C. Grant Robertson, *The Evolution of Prussia – The Making of an Empire*, Oxford, 1915, pp. 13, 16, 22, 26.

13

FROM SCHARNHORST TO SCHLEICHER:

THE PRUSSIAN OFFICER CORPS IN POLITICS, 1806–1933

THE two generals whose names have been chosen as the title of this study, Scharnhorst and Schleicher, have little in common except the alliteration, the first the revolutionary soldier of the Napoleonic period who created the new Prussian army, the second the intriguer behind the scenes who made and unmade governments until in the end he dug his own grave. Yet these two names do mark the beginning and the end of an epoch: the period when the Prussian officer corps played a decisive, perhaps *the* decisive, part in the political development of Prussia, and since 1871, of Germany. For a century and longer the officer corps tried to preserve its traditional ideas and ideals, attempted to oppose and to destroy all forces which it considered inimical to its own aims, to form a State within the State, and at times to exercise a military dictatorship. No such tendencies existed before Napoleon destroyed the old Prussia on the battlefields of Jena and Auerstädt: the officer corps of Frederick William I and Frederick the Great owed allegiance to the King. The large majority of its members were drawn from the native nobility of Brandenburg, Pomerania, and Prussia; they preserved in a non-feudal epoch the attitude of the vassal towards his liegelord, still so clearly shown a century later in the ideas of Bismarck and Roon and many others, in the strong bonds of fealty which tied them to the person of their King.[1] Politics in eighteenth-century Prussia, however, were made by the King, and his subjects had to obey, even if they were of noble birth. As the Estates had ceased to meet, the noble officers did not have the means of expressing their disapproval, even should they have wished to do so. As the King maintained their privileges and granted them the leading positions in the State, they identified their own interests with those of the State and regarded themselves as its natural leaders. But they had no politics of their own. It is misleading if Professor Craig's recent book on *The Politics of the Prussian Army* starts with the year 1640.[2] For the first century and a half of its existence the rôle of the Prussian army was in no way different from that of the standing armies of France or the Habsburg Empire; it was a tool in the hands of the ruler, used to carry out his policy of aggrandizement, but played no part in politics.

Again, with the debacle of Schleicher's policy in 1933 the political rôle of the officer corps came to an abrupt end. The all-powerful new government indeed fulfilled the *military* wishes of the generals, but saw to it that they no longer exercised any influence on home or foreign affairs, that they became the tools of the government, used to carry out its dreams of world conquest, without being allowed a share in the shaping of these plans. Whoever was not satisfied with that rôle or raised criticisms against that policy had to go. And in the end the once famous Prussian officer corps was led to its final doom by the yes-men of the Führer who unquestioningly accepted and executed the decisions of his master mind. It is true that a few courageous individuals opposed his policy from the outset. But even their most outstanding leader, the Chief of the General Staff, General Ludwig Beck, who was to die on 20th July 1944, declared in 1938:

"mutiny and revolution are words which do not occur in the vocabulary of a German soldier;"

he resigned from the army, rather than leading a military *fronde*.[3] The truth of the matter is that the officer corps could only play a political part, could only attempt to impose its will upon the country under *weak* governments. Being confronted with a strong government, determined to model the state *and* the army according to its own ideology, and supported by a strong mass movement of a revolutionary character, the officer corps gave up its political ambitions and resigned itself to its military functions, so much so that later even these were constantly interfered with by Hitler's genius. Thus in 1933 the officer corps ceased to be a factor of importance in the political life of Germany.[4] Whether the new German officer corps of our own days will, or will not, play a political part, seems to depend less on its own tendencies than

The Prussian Officer Corps in Politics, 1806–1933   195

on the strength and determination of the government and of parliament.

The man who started the Prussian officer corps on its political career was not a Prussian, and not a nobleman. Gerhard Scharnhorst was a peasant's son from Hanover, began his military career in the Hanoverian army, and only entered the Prussian service at the age of forty-five, in 1801.[5] But he fought against the armies of the French Revolution in the Low Countries during the campaigns of 1793–5, and he soon recognized the causes of their military superiority.[6] A few months *before* the catastrophe of Jena and Auerstädt he submitted his military and political programme to his new master, Frederick William III of Prussia. There he pointed to the radicalism of the French Revolution and demanded similar measures in Prussia, an appeal to the nations of Europe, the proclamation of a *national* war, the extension of military service to *all* classes of the population, the arming of the *people*, principles which were completely alien to the Prussia of Frederick the Great.[7] Scharnhorst's great hour came with the collapse of the old Prussia and its re-organization after 1807. The complete reform of the Prussian army, which had been defeated so ignominiously by Napoleon, was a precondition of the survival of Prussia. But this military reform could not be achieved without far-reaching political changes, through which the citizens would begin to take an active share in politics and administration. It is part of Scharnhorst's greatness that he clearly saw this interlinking of the political and the military issues; indeed, his political ideas were far more radical than those of the civilian reformers, such as Stein and Hardenberg.[8] If the nation was to take up the cudgels against France, then class privileges must cease; the officer corps must be thrown open to all men of talent and education; the degrading corporal punishments must be abolished; the army must become the nursery of the nation; the people must stand behind the soldiers; its ideas must permeate the army; as the absolute monarchy was unable to wage this popular war, it must disappear, and "the government must conclude something like an alliance with the nation".[9] To Scharnhorst and his pupils the coming struggle against Napoleon was not only a war of liberation, but a war for liberty, for a free constitution, for a new Germany.[10]

Naturally, these radical ideas met with strong opposition on the side of many generals and noblemen, to whom Scharnhorst and his friends were Jacobins and revolutionaries.[11] Even General Ludwig von Yorck (who some years later concluded, against the wishes of his King, the famous convention of Tauroggen with the Russians and thus started the war of liberation) welcomed the dismissal of the Freiherr vom Stein by Frederick William III with these words:

"one nonsensical head has already been squashed, soon the remaining brood of vipers will dissolve themselves in their own poison. I hope that things will improve soon . . ."[12]

Under a weak and vacillating king, surrounded by the adherents of the old order, the military reformers were soon ousted. It had been Scharnhorst's plan to draw the new officers for the standing army from the formations of enthusiastic young middle-class volunteers who joined the colours in 1813.[13] This, as so many of his ideas, came to nought during the period of reaction which set in after 1815. Although it proved impossible in the nineteenth century to maintain the noble monopoly of posts in the officer corps, which had existed in the eighteenth century, the proportion of noble officers remained very large, especially in the higher ranks. In the Prussian officer corps of 1860 sixty-five per cent. of the officers were noblemen, and eighty-six per cent. of the generals and colonels; there were hardly any commoners among the officers of the Guards, the cavalry, and certain infantry regiments.[14] Among the commoners, many were the sons of professional officers and were, in their outlook and customs, thoroughly assimilated to the standards of the Prussian nobility. As late as 1895 the Chief of the General Staff, Count Waldersee, noted in his diary that the Guards, many cavalry, and some infantry regiments had only noble officers, a state of affairs which in his opinion was untenable.[15]

In 1860 Prince Frederick Charles of Prussia, the later field-marshal and victor over the Danes, wrote a memorandum in which he pointed out that

"the preponderance of the nobility in our officer corps, in the sense that it believes that the officers' posts are its due and the commoners are there merely on sufferance, did not always exist in the Prussian officer corps, not even in the cavalry. . . . Traits which recur in some of our regimental officer corps are noble pride, a feeling of superiority over other corps and other classes, excesses in all directions..."[16]

Prince Frederick Charles, with his intimate knowledge of the Prussian army, clearly recognized the decisive point: what mattered was not so much the preponderance of noble officers, but the spirit which permeated the whole corps and affected noblemen and commoners alike. The Prussian officers thought that the events of 1848 were leading to anarchy and tyranny, were brought about by the rousing of the rabble by professional agitators, mainly foreigners; such beasts and barbarians had to be subdued by the sword.[17] The result of the revolution was that the officer corps grouped itself even more closely and more consciously around the person of the King; it deeply resented the constitution the King had been forced to grant because it curtailed the royal prerogative.[18]

It was precisely this constitution, which gave to the Prussian Diet the right to grant and supervise expenditure, that led to the great conflict between king and army on the one hand and parliament on the other: the "army conflict" of the 1860's, which has been called "the central event in the domestic history of Germany during the last hundred years".[19] Many issues were involved in this conflict: there were the rights of the crown versus parliament; there was the question of army reform, through which the front-line strength of the Prussian army was to be increased and that army was to be made more suitable for offensive operations; there was the problem of two or three years' service with the line; there was that of the "reliability" of the defence forces (*Landwehr*), which Scharnhorst had created fifty years earlier; there was the question of the separate – and largely middle-class – officer corps of these defence forces, which was to be amalgamated with the regular officer corps; there was the strong sentimental attachment of the middle classes to the defence forces and their officer corps, going back to the war of liberation; there was the professional officer's criticism of the military weaknesses of the defence forces,

"which lacked the true, real, strong military spirit, ... this bellicose ardour, this fire, this warmth for the earnest execution of their bloody and painful duty in case of a war ...", and equally his desire to strengthen Prussia so that she would be able

"to make good and to assert her claim to power through the menacing weight and edge of her sword, always ready for battle...." [20]

As the proposed measures of army reform entailed an increase of annual expenditure by one-third, and also for political reasons, the Prussian Diet at first granted the required sums only provisionally, and later refused them altogether. This brought the latent conflict between army and parliament into the open. In April 1861 General Albrecht von Roon, the Minister for War, counselled the King to make his royal will felt and thus to

"break the chains of the eagle; the King by the grace of God remains, at the head of his people, the centre of gravity in the state, master of the country, unfettered by ministerial responsibility and parliamentary majorities..." [21]

In his opinion

"there is nothing worse for Prussia than its absorption into the doctrinaire swindle. Out of the mud-bath of a new revolution Prussia can emerge with new strength; in the sewer of doctrinaire liberalism she will rot without redemption..." [22]

Prince Frederick Charles wrote to the Minister for War during the crisis he should remain firm:

"no ministerial responsibility, for then the centre of gravity in the fatherland moves to the second chamber, instead of remaining with the King, no concessions in general in a truly revolutionary time.... In times of revolution... the satisfaction with concessions does not last a fortnight, ... for the progressives want to go on and on, to the logical conclusion of the Terror and the Republic. A barrier has to be built against every revolution. If we only met it in the streets in the form of riots, uprisings, etc., that would be extremely simple with powder and shot..." [23]

And this advice came from a general who, according to his biographer, "for reasons of principle was once and for all determined not to meddle with politics".[24] On this issue the Prince and von Roon spoke for the large majority of the officer corps.

Von Roon repeatedly urged the King to find a way out of the crisis through the appointment of Otto von Bismarck as Prime Minister of Prussia, to fight out the battle with the Diet, and in the end he prevailed over the hesitating King.[25]

Bismarck's subsequent victory over the Diet and the defeat of the liberals, which exercised such profound influence on the course of German history, reinforced the position and the prestige of the officer corps, which were even more enhanced by the Prussian victories in the wars of 1864-71. The officer corps remained outside the field of parliamentary control, and continued to function along its traditional lines of noble predominance and social exclusiveness. The separate officer corps of the defence forces was amalgamated with that of the regular army; the officer of the reserve became the faithful image of the regular officer, if not in origin, then in manners, political attitude, and social outlook. To enter this privileged corps became the ambition of the sons of the middle classes, who would aspire to at least the dignity of a commission in the reserve. The officer corps preserved and cultivated the attitude, the customs, the ideology of the Prussian landed nobility; it regarded itself as the bulwark of absolute monarchy against the forces of destruction.[26] As General von Roon put it at the end of his career:

"an efficient army ... is the only feasible protection against the red as well as against the black spectre. If they ruin the army the end has arrived; then fare-well to Prussian military glory and to German splendour!"[27]

This ideology, opposed to that of large sections of the population, showed itself above all in the attitude adopted towards parliament and the political parties. The ill-successes of the government in domestic affairs were blamed on religious and political agitators and on parliament, to which the officer corps showed a deep and lasting antipathy.[28] In 1878 Count Waldersee, the later Chief of the General Staff, noted in his diary:

"how deeply I despise the national-liberal parliamentary majority, which does not get beyond theoretical verbiage and is pulling back country and people further and further every year ..."[29]

and thus commented on the parliamentary debates of the law against the Socialists:

"it is very sad to have to watch such transactions; they prattle in ridiculous way; everybody wants to explain his own point of view; there is no question of a far-sighted conception. The Centre Party behaves with the utmost perfidy; I hope these gentlemen will have to pay for it one day..."[30]

General von Einem, Minister for War in the early years of the twentieth century, confessed in the 1930's:

"I have hated the Social Democrats all my life. Until the present day I have not been able to discover a single one of their ideas which was not in principle somehow detrimental to State and nation. I have waged the struggle against them with the purest conscience and from innermost conviction..."[31]

In his opinion it was the tragedy of the German people that no chancellor ever found the courage to employ against parliament the well-known "lieutenant and ten men" to disperse it by force of arms.[32] Count Waldersee, then the Chief of the General Staff, openly advocated the abolition of the general franchise, which he considered a calamity, and told the Emperor William II in 1896:

"Your Majesty is strong enough to undertake anything; it is only necessary to use force..."[33]

With regard to the Social Democrats he advised the Emperor a few weeks later:

"I think it is in the interest of the State not to leave it to the Social Democratic leaders to decide the moment of the great reckoning, but to accelerate this moment as best we can! The State with certainty is still able to crush any uprising..."[34]

He also expressed his longing for street battles, for in these the army would be victorious.[35] Count Waldersee at times considered the Social Democrats, and at times the Catholics, to be "the worst enemies",[36] thus showing his implacable hostility to the two largest parties in the country.

The views of the Chief of the General Staff on foreign policy were equally primitive and biased, and this was of great importance because he believed that he had a flair for foreign affairs and did not hesitate to intervene in this field.[37] In 1888 he considered war inevitable and assiduously propagated the idea of a preventive war against Russia, thus counteracting Bismarck's foreign policy.[38] In 1890 he lectured the Emperor:

"If Your Majesty wants to preserve peace, it is better to do so by firm measures; Slavs want to be treated with kicks; they kiss the boot which has kicked them . . ."[39]

The Chief of the General Staff also advocated the creation of a Greater Germany to the Adriatic Sea under a Hohenzollern Emperor, including not only the German parts of Austria, but

"naturally equally Bohemia which has to be re-Germanized."[40]

But the main villain of his ambitious dreams of expansion was Britain, which he classified as the natural enemy of Germany, determined to destroy her greatest commercial rival.[41] In 1890 he admitted he had

"no judgement with regard to our relations with England; I only know that hitherto we have been incredibly conciliatory and timid, and that the English in East Africa continuously act with impudence and complete lack of consideration . . ."[42]

A few months later he complained bitterly about

"the immeasurable impudence of the English in opposing our really very modest colonial claims . . ."[43]

and in 1896 about

"the hair-raising abuse and impertinence shown by the English press against the Emperor . . ."[44]

The astonishing fact, however, is that Count Waldersee vehemently disclaimed that he was a political general, a feature which in his opinion was characteristic of a decaying state.[45]

Under the masterful civilian government of Bismarck sharp clashes between the Chancellor and an officer corps so strongly interested in politics were almost inevitable, especially because no clear demarcation line could be drawn between military and non-military affairs. Even Helmuth von Moltke, the first great Chief of the General Staff, disliked any civilian interference in what he considered semi-military matters. In September 1861, after the failure of negotiations with Austria, he declared:

"If military-political affairs were only left to a few efficient and reliable officers, without diplomats, the officers would soon agree to everybody's satisfaction . . ."[46]

And a few years later, when he drew up the plan of campaign against Denmark, he wrote:

"Neither diplomatic negotiations nor political considerations should interrupt the further military progress"

after the beginning of mobilization; from that moment the political advisers should remain silent and should leave matters to the generals.[47] Bismarck, however, not only made it clear that it was not the business of the army leaders to express opinions on political questions, but did not hesitate to invade their professional sphere and to meet the officers on their own ground, a behaviour which outraged the General Staff.[48] There had been sharp clashes on this account during the wars of 1864 and 1866, but matters came to a head during the Franco-Prussian war. The Chancellor complained bitterly that the generals were withholding vital information; his diplomatic designs were openly opposed by Prince Frederick Charles and other leading generals; Bismarck was not told about planned operations, and in vain demanded that he must be informed about everything.[49] As a revenge he excluded the generals from the negotiations for the surrender of Paris and from the armistice talks, leaving them deeply dissatisfied with the terms of the capitulation which they thought much too lenient.[50] Thus Bismarck emerged victoriously from his feuds with the General Staff. With regard to the peace terms Moltke and the generals, backed up by public opinion in Germany, were successful in achieving the cession of Metz to Germany, which Bismarck did not want to press; while Belfort, which in Moltke's eyes had less military value, remained French.[51] At the end of his career Bismarck again acted sharply and decisively in defeating the plans of the General Staff for a preventive war against Russia and its attempts to interfere with his direction of foreign policy; even technical military questions he considered to come within his province, to the intense annoyance of the soldiers.[52]

Under Bismarck's weak and changing successors, however, the army leaders recovered the ground which they had lost. The young Emperor William II surrounded himself with officers of the Guards and listened to their opinions and advice, which he preferred to that of the competent ministers and diplomats.[53] It is a safe assumption that their political views were closely akin to those of Count Waldersee and other generals quoted above. This military entourage was influential enough to bring about the resignation or dismissal of civilian ministers. There was no Bismarck to stand up to them and to confine them to their proper sphere of influence. The position of the Chancellor was further weakened by the fact that the army stood directly under the command of the "supreme war lord", the Emperor, that his "power of command" was not liable to control by the Chancellor or any other authority.[54] Thus the army became

"a state within the state, claiming the right to define what was, or was not, to the national interest and to dispense with those who did not agree with the definition." [55]

If this state of affairs was already very noticeable in peace-time, it became much more pronounced in the course of the Great War when the moral authority of Hindenburg and Ludendorff assumed "legendary" proportions.[56] This allowed them not only to supersede the powers of the civil government, but even to invade the royal prerogative. Hindenburg and Ludendorff were able to wield such power because the officer corps, and the large majority of the Germans, saw in them, and in them alone, the only people able to save the country from utter ruin.[57] Because Hindenburg and Ludendorff knew they were indispensable, they forced the Emperor, by using the threat of resignation, to dismiss one Chancellor, two Secretaries of State for Foreign Affairs, and even the Chief of his own Civil Cabinet; in place of von Bethmann-Hollweg they then secured the appointment of a new Chancellor who met with their approval, although the Emperor had never met him. The Supreme Command also reserved to itself the right of conducting diplomatic and peace negotiations and of defining Germany's war aims; it demanded such far-reaching annexations that any hope of a negotiated peace was dashed to the ground.[58] The generals thus undermined the constitutional foundations of Bismarck's Reich, reduced the power of the Emperor to that of a shadow, and established a military dictatorship, which finally led the Second German Empire to its doom. In no other belligerent country of the Great War did the powers of the generals become so unlimited, were the civilian authorities pushed aside so forcefully and successfully, was the constitution disregarded so blatantly as in Germany between 1916 and 1918.

The result of the Great War was the end of the Hohenzollern monarchy, but not of the Prussian officer corps, in spite of the inaptitude of its political leadership during the war, and in spite of the fact that it had not in time revealed the seriousness of the military situation. The inexperienced leaders of the new republic thought they depended on the generals for protection against radical outbreaks at home and hostile neighbours abroad, especially on the eastern frontier. This led to the famous understanding between Friedrich Ebert, the leader of the new government, and the Supreme Command of the army, arrived at as early as November 1918. Yet this understanding did not make the army a loyal servant of the republic. From the outset the army leaders followed their own aims, at home as well as abroad. As early as December 1918, a few weeks after the collapse, General Hans von Seeckt, who fifteen months later was to become the head of the new army, emphasized during a discussion at a general staff meeting that Germany as quickly as possible must again be "able to conclude alliances". As one of those present at the meeting felt, it was the spirit of the army which was beginning to stir anew.[59] A few weeks later General von Seeckt wrote to his wife:

"With Herr Ebert and comrades I can *perhaps* co-operate, in spite of our diametrically opposed conceptions of the world and economic affairs, because I consider these people *relatively* honest, if ideologists and weaklings . . ." [60]

In the same spirit von Seeckt later prevented Ebert, who then was the President of the Republic, and thus according to the constitution the commander-in-chief of the army, from ever attending any exercises of that army, and issued an order that no guards of honour were to parade in front of the President.[61] Towards parliament General von Seeckt showed the Prussian officer's traditional antipathy: in 1923 he told the Chancellor that in his opinion it was the cancer of the time.[62] He was never present when the anniversary of the constitution was celebrated, because on these occasions "his duty unavoidably kept him away from Berlin", as his official biographer puts it.[63] Von Seeckt did not want the army to enter into any relations with the republican régime:

if they became negative, this would result in a military revolt by which nothing would be achieved; if they became positive, this would in his opinion be the end of the German military spirit.[64] On his retirement he gave this toast to the assembled officers of his former regiment:

"I drink to Prussia and to the Prussian army, I drink to the Prussian Guards, I drink to the Prussian infantry . . ."[65]

General von Seeckt's attitude towards military revolt emerged clearly when the Free Corps, which had fought in the Baltic States against the Red Army and equally at home against the Communists, in March 1920 resisted orders to disband and turned against the republican government. When the Minister for War, Gustav Noske, called the generals together to deliberate upon action against the mutineers, only one general pronounced in favour of strong military measures in defence of the legitimate government. He was opposed by von Seeckt who declared:

"Soldiers do not fire on soldiers. Do you intend, Herr Minister, to tolerate a battle in front of the Brandenburg Gate between troops who a short while ago fought shoulder to shoulder against the enemy? . . . If Reichswehr defeats Reichswehr, that is the end of all comradeship within the officer corps. If this happened, that would be the true catastrophe which has been avoided with such endless pains on 9th November 1918 . . ."[66]

Thus the officer corps refused to defend the republican government and the constitution it had sworn to defend. It was even more symptomatic that after the defeat of the mutineers by a general strike General von Lüttwitz indeed had to resign as commander because he was too deeply compromised, and that then the assembled officers elected as their new chief General von Seeckt, the man who had just refused to take action in defence of the existing order and had spent the critical days at his home.[67] In this strange way General von Seeckt became the Chief of the Army Command (*Chef der Heeresleitung*), a position which he used to limit the authority of the civilian Minister of Defence to administrative functions and to exclude him from all influence on questions of personnel.[68] General von Seeckt thus became "the king of the army", a substitute for "the royal shield" which the officer corps had lost on 9th November 1918.[69]

While Germany was shaken by political and economic convulsions culminating in the year 1923, General von Seeckt built up his own position into one of extraordinary strength. When President Ebert demanded to know where the army really stood, he replied coolly:

"The Reichswehr stands behind *me*." [70]

In September 1923 President Ebert was finally persuaded to entrust the army with the executive authority in Germany. General von Seeckt then attempted to act as a mediator in the quarrel between the Bavarian and the central governments and to work for the establishment of a non-party Directorate with dictatorial powers.[71] He used the army against the left-wing governments of Saxony and Thuringia, but declined Ebert's demand for similar measures against the right-wing government of Bavaria. He declared that the army was unable to defend the Reich against Right and Left while Gustav Stresemann was Chancellor because he was too much distrusted, that the Chancellor did not enjoy the confidence of the Reichswehr, that civil war would break out if there was no change of government; he thus forced Stresemann to resign.[72] The officer corps once more decided upon the fate of the cabinets, as it had done under the Second Empire.

On the other hand, General von Seeckt did not favour a policy of armed risings and was determined to oppose *coups d'état* attempted by the dissolved Free Corps and the extreme Right. As he put it at that time:

"The task of the Reichswehr is to preserve the unity of the Reich, and those who endanger this unity are my enemies, whatever their origin," [73]

a remark directed not only against the Left, but also against the Putschists and Separatists of the Right. Nor would he tolerate political dissensions within the army:

"Political fights within the Reichswehr are incompatible with the spirit of comradeship as well as with discipline, and can only be detrimental to the military training . . .",[74]

as he put it in 1920. The unity and coherence of the officer corps were to be preserved at all cost: they would break down if politics penetrated into the corps. Only if they were preserved could the army gain supreme importance in the State, become the real power behind the empty throne. In achieving these aims General von Seeckt was extraordinarily successful; his task was facilitated by the small size of the officer corps stipulated by the Treaty of Versailles, which made it possible to eliminate all undesirable elements, and by the professional character of the army laid down in the Treaty.

As to the foreign policy of the republic, there again General von Seeckt did not hesitate to go his own way, if need be against the government's official policy. He aimed above all at an understanding with Soviet Russia, which would enable Germany to regain her lost Polish provinces and to circumvent the military clauses of the Treaty of Versailles. In the autumn of 1922 he submitted a memorandum to the Chancellor in which he pointed out:

"The existence of Poland is intolerable, incompatible with Germany's conditions of life. It must disappear, and it will disappear through its own weakness and through Russia – with our help. For Russia Poland is even more intolerable than for us . . . Russia and Germany within the frontiers of 1914 should form the basis of an understanding between the two . . . We want two things: first a strengthening of Russia in the economic and political fields, and thus indirectly a strengthening of ourselves, through our strengthening of a potential ally; we further want, at first cautiously and tentatively, to strengthen our own position directly by helping to build in Russia an armaments industry which would serve us in case of need. With regard to all these measures the participation and even the official notification of the German government have to be entirely excluded . . ." [75]

General von Seeckt continued this pro-Russian line in foreign policy during the years that Stresemann tried to bring about better relations with France and to get Germany into the League of Nations.[76] Her entry into the League was strongly resisted by von Seeckt, as was the whole policy leading to the Treaty of Locarno and the rapprochement with France, bound to disturb his good understanding with the Russians.[77] In July 1925 General von Seeckt wrote:

"The ugly point around which the question revolves is, of course, Herr Stresemann . . . On the face of it it is undesirable to bring about a government crisis just now – one does not change the jockey during a race – but the question is whether it is not more important to get at last rid of this man, and thus to prepare the way for a different foreign policy..."

and a few months later:

"I can only predict evil things emanating from Locarno. Relatively the best would be a failure of the conference; bad would be an understanding which could bring us only disadvantages. Nothing is more difficult than to repair an act of stupidity..." [78]

General von Seeckt was dismissed in 1926 because he had permitted a son of the Crown Prince to take part in army manœuvres without any previous information of the minister of defence. In the previous year Field-Marshal von Hindenburg had been elected President of the Republic: he considered himself the real Commander-in-Chief of the army and was not content with the modest rôle to which President Ebert had been relegated by General von Seeckt, determined to exclude any civilian interference with the army. The officer corps now looked towards the new President and put its confidence in him;[79] but it continued to remain a State within the State, hostile towards the republican form of government. Its sympathies were with the parties of the Right.[80] This was admitted in 1931 by the Minister of Defence, General Wilhelm Groener:

"Seeckt's convictions remained riddles to his own subordinates, and some of them will have thought a certain amount of right-wing radicalism suitable to get into the good books of the highest chief, in spite of his sharp orders to the contrary... which nobody took seriously. Under General Heye matters did not improve because... he permitted the lieutenants to dance on his nose... Unfortunately the commanders still imagine that anyone is a grand chap if he is recommended by the bosses of the nationalist associations..." [81]

In the following year the Chief of the Army Command, General Kurt von Hammerstein-Equord, declared in front of his generals:

"we all stand ideologically on the Right..." [82]

General Groener, a south-German and a commoner, with a more reasonable attitude towards the republic, tried to remedy matters, but in vain. He himself became instrumental in further undermining the foundations of the republican government, mainly through the influence of one of his subordinates, General Kurt von Schleicher.[83] In the autumn of 1930 even General Groener went so far as to say:

"In the political happenings of Germany no stone must be moved any longer without the word of the Reichswehr being thrown decisively into the balance..."[84]

In the spring of 1930, when President von Hindenburg thought of entrusting the Social Democratic Chancellor Hermann Müller with semi-dictatorial powers, Groener declared through von Schleicher that this was an impossibility.[85] The generals then suggested to the ancient President Heinrich Brüning as the new chancellor; he had found favour in their eyes through his energetic defence of the military budget of 1928-9 in parliament, and even more so through his distinguished service as a company commander at the front in the Great War.[86] In this amateurish way the last republican government which had a parliamentary majority was overthrown, and the period of semi-dictatorial government was inaugurated. During the last four years of his life General von Schleicher continued to conduct politics in the same amateurish fashion. For several years he was the real power behind the throne, now occupied by an octogenarian Imperial field-marshal, who by habit listened more to soldiers than to civilian ministers.

The attitude adopted by General von Schleicher and many other officers towards the rising Nazi Party was more than equivocal: it was, after all, although not led by gentlemen, a party which shared many of the ideas of the officers, their opposition to Versailles, their determination to strengthen Germany through rearmament, their nationalism, their opposition to the parliamentary system. As early as October 1930 von Schleicher told the assembled army commanders that among other groups, many people belonged to the Nazis from "circles which stand close to us;" the Nazis' foreign political programme, although not practicable at the moment, was, he said, welcome to the army, as was their fight against pernicious influences in the cultural and political life of Germany.[87] In the following year von Schleicher informed the chancellor, Brüning, that his government must orientate itself more towards the Right if homogeneity was to be preserved between government and Reichswehr.[88] In March 1932 he wrote to General Groener:

"After the events of the last days I am rather glad that in the form of the Nazis there exists a counter-weight" (namely to the Social Democrats' power in Prussia), "although the Nazis are not very honourable brethren either, and have to be treated with the utmost caution. If they did not exist, one really would have to invent them. Under these circumstances, your course, strictly neutral, is in my opinion the only correct one . . ."[89]

A few weeks later, however, General von Schleicher had lost confidence in Groener's ability to handle the complicated internal situation and began intriguing against his own chief, who was simultaneously attacked with fury by the Nazis because he had dissolved their storm troops. Von Schleicher first advised Groener to take sick leave, and later suggested to him he should resign to ease the atmosphere inside the army. The Chief of the Army Command, General von Hammerstein-Equord, followed Schleicher's lead "like a well-trained spaniel" and went so far as to say: "old Groener has become senile!"[90] Thus the army leaders forced Groener to hand in his resignation; this was followed during the same month by the resignation of the Chancellor, Brüning, brought about by similar intrigues in which von Schleicher played the major part. Brüning's successor was the candidate of General von Schleicher, Franz von Papen, hitherto almost unknown in German politics. The new cabinet was von Schleicher's cabinet, and he himself became the new Minister of Defence.[91] As a recent German study of these years puts it:

"The leadership of the Reichswehr, a State within the State since the foundation of the Republic, had undermined the political key positions; it thought to have degraded the Republic to its appendix . . ."[92]

Von Papen's government, however, only lasted for a few months. It fell because it was without any popular support and was not even able to gain that of the Nazis. The man who for so many years had intrigued behind the scenes, who had been responsible for the downfall of so many governments, became the new Chancellor: General Kurt von Schleicher. But his government only lasted for two months: it was overthrown by the same intrigues in which the general seemed past-master, this time carried on behind his back by von Papen with Hitler. The result was the formation of the Hitler–Papen government on 30th January 1933. It has been widely believed that in this hour of emergency the generals von Hammerstein and von Schleicher contemplated armed resistance to the appointment of the Hitler government.[93] It has more recently been asserted in works published in this country that the generals contemplated armed resistance to *achieve* the appointment of Hitler.[94] It seems more likely that on this occasion the generals were politically as helpless as during the previous years; they were above all concerned that the army should not be used in a direct political sense, that is in a civil war against Left and Right, which would endanger its usefulness as a military instrument.[95] This opinion is confirmed by a memoir of General von Hammerstein written in 1935, and recently published for the first time: in this he strongly denied that the army had any intention of a *Putsch*; but he does admit that its leaders made strong representations to President von Hindenburg against another Papen government, which in their opinion would result in the dreaded civil war.[96]

Thus the army leaders, by their intrigues and their deep-rooted antipathy to parliamentary government prepared the way, first for a series of non-parliamentary semi-dictatorial governments ruling through the authority of the President, and finally for an entirely despotic government, which destroyed the political parties, parliament and the constitution. In 1932 Colonel von Blaskowitz, later to become one of Hitler's field-marshals, told his officers:

"The political parties are Germany's calamity. Through their sectarian interests they prevent all stable and useful work of the government . . . Therefore the government has to be freed from the chains of parliamentarianism, to be able to work independently, basing itself on the confidence of the Reich President and the power of the Reichswehr . . ."[97]

The curses had come home to roost. The political power of the generals disappeared with the parliamentary system which they had undermined so assiduously. General von Schleicher himself was one of the first victims of the régime which, through his intrigues and his plots, he had helped so much to put into the saddle.

At the end of his review of Professor Craig's book on *The Politics of the Prussian Army*, Mr A. J. P. Taylor asks:

"Substitute 'British admirals' for 'German generals', and is the story very different?" [98]

My answer would be: very different indeed; especially in home affairs the influence of the British Navy has been negligible. The whole political tradition of the Prussian army does not exist in this country. Naturally, a navy does not have such opportunities as an army for interfering with internal affairs, for becoming the power behind the throne, for opposing the existing political régime. It is much more difficult to say whether other large armies, that of France, that of Tsarist Russia, that of Japan, did not play a part similar to that of the Prussian army. What is easy to see is that its tradition was *not* that of the *coup d'état*, of the pronunciamento, of directly entering the field of party politics. The individual soldier and officer was not permitted to engage in political activities, and if he did so, he was dismissed, and might even be put in trial.[99] But the army as a whole wielded not only political influence, but political power: it was much more successful than the armies of other countries in making its weight felt. The political ambitions of French generals time and again were successfully curbed by the existing constitutional régime, even during the First World War. The Prussian officer corps was also much more successful than any other officer corps in preserving its solidarity, its traditions, its spirit almost unchanged in a changing world. It saw itself as the rock on which the waves of radicalism were breaking, until it was broken itself by the greatest wave of radicalism Germany had ever seen. It remains to be seen whether this tradition and this spirit have been able to survive the catastrophe of the Second World War.

NOTES

[1] See, for example, *Denkwürdigkeiten aus dem Leben des General-Feldmarschalls Kriegsministers Grafen von Roon*, 4th edition, i, Breslau, 1897, p. 398; ii, Breslau, 1897, pp. 30, 151.

[2] Gordon A. Craig, *The Politics of the Prussian Army, 1640–1945*, Oxford, 1955.
[3] Gerhard Ritter, *Carl Goerdeler und die deutsche Widerstandsbewegung*, Stuttgart, 1954, p. 146.
[4] Compare the view expressed by A. J. P. Taylor, *The English Historical Review*, lxxii, 1956, p. 291; "The German generals ... did what they were told, when faced by a resolute civilian, whether Bismarck or Hitler."
[5] The best biography of Scharnhorst is still that written by Max Lehmann, 2 vols., Leipzig, 1886–7. Two interesting recent studies are: Rudolf Stadelmann, *Scharnhorst – Schicksal und geistige Welt*, Wiesbaden, 1952, unfortunately a torso; and Reinhard Höhn, *Scharnhorsts Vermächtnis*, Bonn, 1952.
[6] Höhn, op. cit., pp. 56–7. In November 1810 Scharnhorst put it this way: "Not the greater talents of the French generals brought about victory ... In Holland, in Germany, in Italy, in Spain, in the Vendée, everywhere it was the spirit of the military, the great mass of better educated leaders, the union of all classes, of all grades of education in the armies, which triumphed": '*Vier Denkschriften Scharnhorsts aus dem Jahre 1810*,' *Historiesche Zeitshrift*, lviii, 1887, p. 105.
[7] Stadelmann, op. cit., pp. 72–3; Höhn, op. cit., pp. 157–8.
[8] Stadelmann, op. cit., pp. 72–3.
[9] Höhn, op. cit., pp. 180–2, quoting a draft of Scharnhorst's of 15th March 1808.
[10] Höhn, op. cit., pp. 187, 191, quoting a memorandum of Neidhardt von Gneisenau of August 1808.
[11] Höhn, op. cit., pp. 178, 372, 385.
[12] Ibid., p. 372.
[13] Ibid., pp. 276–7.
[14] Karl Demeter, *Das Deutsche Offizierkorps in seinen historisch-soziologischen Grundlagen*, Berlin, 1930, p. 34; Johannes Ziekursch, *Politische Geschichte des neuen deutschen Kaiserreiches*, i, Frankfurt, 1932, p. 30.
[15] *Denkwürdigkeiten des General-Feldmarschalls Alfred Grafen von Waldersee*, edited by Heinrich Otto Meisner, ii, Stuttgart, 1922, p. 354.
[16] Demeter, op. cit., pp. 258–9, printing an essay of Prince Frederick Charles of 3rd January 1860 on the "Origins and Development of the Spirit of the Prussian Officer, its Characteristics and Effects".
[17] Von Roon, op. cit., i, pp. 130, 135, 142, 247. Even Helmuth von Moltke's utterances were not very different; Rudolf Stadelmann, *Moltke und der Staat*, Krefeld, 1950, pp. 105, 110–11.
[18] Demeter, op. cit., pp. 158–9; Ziekursch, op. cit., i, p. 67.
[19] Craig, op. cit., p. 137, quoting Carl Schmitt, *Staatsgefüge und Zusammenbruch des Zweiten Reiches – Der Sieg des Bürgers über den Soldaten*, Hamburg, 1934, p. 10.
[20] This mixture of motives, political, military and emotional, emerges clearly in the memorandum on army reform which General von Roon submitted to the king in 1858: von Roon, op. cit., ii, pp. 521–72.
[21] Ibid., ii, p. 47.
[22] Ibid., ii, p. 24: letter of 18th June 1861.
[23] Ibid., ii, pp. 58–9; *Prinz Friedrich Karl von Preussen – Denkwürdigkeiten aus seinem Leben*, edited by Wolfgang Foerster, 4th edition, Stuttgart, 1910, i, p. 269: letter to von Roon of 17th December 1861. Similar views were expressed by Edwin von Manteuffel and many other generals: Craig, op. cit., pp. 154–8; Ziekursch, op. cit., i, p. 67.
[24] *Prinz Friedrich Karl von Preussen – Denkwürdigkeiten aus seinem Leben*, i, p. 268.

[25] VON ROON, op. cit., ii, pp. 81, 87, 93, 120, 304.
[26] DEMETER, op. cit., pp. 216–17; CRAIG, op. cit., pp. 236–8.
[27] VON ROON, op. cit., iii, p. 390: letter of 4th February 1874.
[28] DEMETER, op. cit., p. 159.
[29] VON WALDERSEE, op. cit., i, p. 177: entry of 3rd June 1878.
[30] Ibid., i, p. 181: entry of 19th October 1878.
[31] GENERALOBERST VON EINEM, *Erinnerungen eines Soldaten*, Leipzig, 1933, p. 67.
[32] Ibid., p. 82.
[33] VON WALDERSEE, op. cit., ii, 1922, pp. 377, 388, n. 1: entries of 25th November 1896 and 20th February 1897.
[34] Ibid., ii, p. 388: on 22nd January 1897.
[35] Ibid., ii, p. 381: entry of 30th December 1896.
[36] Ibid., iii, 1923, pp. 207, 218: entries of 21st February and 1st July 1903.
[37] For details see CRAIG, op. cit., pp. 267–72.
[38] VON WALDERSEE, op. cit., i, pp. 349–51; ii, pp. 13, 48: entries of 1st, 7th and 12th January 1888, 1st November 1888, and 15th April 1889.
[39] Ibid., ii, p. 118: entry of 17th March 1890.
[40] Ibid., ii, pp. 353, 404, 407, 418: entries of 19th July, 30th August and 12th December 1897, and 16th August 1898.
[41] Ibid., iii, pp. 69, 215: entries of 9th December 1900 and 1st June 1903.
[42] Ibid., ii, p. 126: entry of 4th May 1890.
[43] Ibid., ii, p. 131: entry of 25th July 1890; similarly on 12th January 1896: ibid., p. 364.
[44] Ibid., ii, p. 364: entry of 12th January 1896.
[45] Ibid., ii, p. 250: entry of 21st July 1892.
[46] STADELMANN, *Moltke und der Staat*, p. 138.
[47] CRAIG, op. cit., p. 196. This view Moltke maintained in later years: STADELMANN, op. cit., pp. 203–4, 206.
[48] CRAIG, op. cit., pp. 191, 200–1, 204.
[49] VON WALDERSEE, op. cit., i, pp. 95, 103–4, 117: entries of 9th September, 23rd October and 26th December 1870; *Prinz Friedrich Karl von Preussen – Denkwürdigkeiten aus seinem Leben*, ii, pp. 285–90; STADELMANN, op. cit., pp. 227–9, 239–40; CRAIG, op. cit., pp. 205–8.
[50] VON WALDERSEE, op. cit., i, p. 163; STADELMANN, op. cit., pp. 247–52, 503–6; CRAIG, op. cit., pp. 212–15.
[51] VON WALDERSEE, op. cit., i, p. 163: entry of August 1871; ZIEKURSCH, op. cit., i, p. 356; STADELMANN, op. cit., pp. 223–4, 255, 262–3, 507–8; CRAIG, op. cit., p. 215.
[52] VON WALDERSEE, op. cit., i, pp. 341, 350: entries of 7th December 1887 and 7th January 1888; CRAIG, op. cit., pp. 268–72.
[53] See the scathing comment of the Kaiser's favourite, Philipp Eulenburg, quoted by CRAIG, op. cit., p. 241.
[54] GERHARD RITTER, 'Nemesis der Macht?', *Frankfurter Allgemeine Zeitung*, 20th April 1955, p. 6.
[55] CRAIG, op. cit., p. 252.
[56] RITTER, loc. cit., p. 6. The legend of the "Iron Hindenburg" was so firmly believed that it survived the defeat and the revolution: in 1925 he was elected President of the Republic.
[57] ARTHUR ROSENBERG, *The Birth of the German Republic, 1871–1918*, London, 1931, p. 117. Rosenberg's description of "the dictatorship of Ludendorff" is the best picture of Germany during the Great War.
[58] ROSENBERG, op. cit., pp. 124–9, 173–4, 203–4, 226–9; CRAIG, op. cit., pp. 316–27, 340–1.

[59] GENERAL FRIEDRICH VON RABENAU, *Seeckt – Aus seinem Leben, 1918–1936*, Leipzig, 1940, pp. 118–19. Rabenau's work is the main authority on von Seeckt.
[60] Ibid., p. 143.: letter of 6th February 1919 (italics by the author).
[61] Ibid., p. 275.
[62] Ibid., p. 325; OTTO-ERNST SCHÜDDEKOPF, *Das Heer und die Republik – Quellen zur Politik der Reichswehrführung 1918 bis 1933*, Hanover and Frankfurt, 1955, p. 117.
[63] VON RABENAU, op. cit., p. 199.
[64] Ibid., p. 493.
[65] Ibid., p. 563.
[66] SCHÜDDEKOPF, op. cit., p. 104, and VON RABENAU, op. cit., pp. 221–2, give somewhat different versions of this speech, but the differences are slight. Compare also Noske's own version: GUSTAV NOSKE, *Von Kiel bis Kapp*, Berlin, 1920, p. 209.
[67] VON RABENAU, op. cit., p. 227, who calls it an event such as the military history of Prussia-Germany had hardly ever seen.
[68] DOROTHEA GROENER-GEYER, *General Groener – Soldat und Staatsmann*, Frankfurt, 1955, p. 147; WOLFGANG SAUER, 'Die Reichswehr', in: KARL DIETRICH BRACHER, *Die Auflösung der Weimarer Republik*, Stuttgart and Düsseldorf, 1955, p. 249: the method used was to create an artificial difference between *Befehlsgewalt* and *Kommandogewalt* and to limit the authority of the Minister of Defence to the former; VON RABENAU, op. cit., p. 244.
[69] SAUER, loc. cit., p. 256, and n. 92, quoting the recollections of several former generals.
[70] VON RABENAU, op. cit., p. 342; SCHÜDDEKOPF, op. cit., p. 119.
[71] SCHÜDDEKOPF, op. cit., p. 120, n. 368.
[72] VON RABENAU, op. cit., pp. 355, 366–7, 370; SCHÜDDEKOPF, op. cit., p. 120, n. 368, p. 166, n. 466, p. 188: letter of von Seeckt of 5th November 1923.
[73] VON RABENAU, op. cit., p. 387, n. 2.
[74] Ibid., pp. 239–40: decree of 18th April 1920.
[75] Ibid., pp. 316–17: memorandum of September 1922.
[76] On the relationship between the Reichswehr and the Red Army, see HELM SPEIDEL, 'Reichswehr und Rote Armee', *Vierteljahrshefte für Zeitgeschichte*, i, 1953, pp. 9 ff.
[77] VON RABENAU, op. cit., pp. 407, 418, 420–2, 430; SCHÜDDEKOPF, op. cit., p. 120, n. 368.
[78] VON RABENAU, op cit., pp. 418, 420: letters of 2nd July and 4th October 1925.
[79] GROENER-GEYER, op. cit., p. 246.
[80] THILO VOGELSANG, 'Neue Dokumente zur Geschichte der Reichswehr', *Vierteljahrshefte für Zeitgeschichte*, ii, 1954, pp. 398–9. General von Schleicher himself told the assembled army commanders on 25th October 1930: "the criticisms of the right-wing press are dangerous because the army – especially the younger part of the officer corps – believes that whatever comes from this quarter must be correct...": ibid., p. 403.
[81] GROENER-GEYER, op. cit., p. 279: letter of 26th April 1931.
[82] VOGELSANG, loc. cit., p. 421: on 27th February 1932.
[83] "The man at the helm was neither Hindenburg, nor Groener, but Schleicher": VOGELSANG, loc. cit., p. 399. On Groener see the biography written by his daughter, from which extracts have been quoted above. Groener was looked at as an outsider by the officer corps; they never forgave him his attitude at the time of the collapse of the monarchy in November 1918.
[84] VOGELSANG, loc. cit., p. 409, n. 39.
[85] VON RABENAU, op. cit., p. 651.

⁸⁶ BRACHER, op. cit., pp. 300, 307-8; VOGELSANG, loc. cit., p. 399.
⁸⁷ VOGELSANG, loc. cit., p. 406; SCHÜDDEKOPF, op. cit., pp. 308-9: on 25th October 1930.
⁸⁸ SCHÜDDEKOPF, op. cit., p. 311.
⁸⁹ Ibid., p. 342: letter to Groener of 25th March 1932.
⁹⁰ GROENER-GEYER, op. cit., pp. 316, 325-6, based on Groener's own notes; BRACHER, op. cit., pp. 490-8; VOGELSANG, loc. cit., pp. 423-4, prints General von Hammerstein's own explanations as given to the army leaders on 21st May 1932.
⁹¹ BRACHER, op. cit., pp. 511-18, 520-5, 532-3; VOGELSANG, loc. cit., p. 426.
⁹² BRACHER, op. cit., p. 532.
⁹³ HERMANN FOERTSCH, *Schuld und Verhängnis – Die Fritsch-Krise im Frühjahr 1938 als Wendepunkt in der Geschichte der nationalsozialistischen Zeit*, Stuttgart, 1951, pp. 26-8; SCHÜDDEKOPF, op. cit., p. 356, n. 911.
⁹⁴ JOHN WHEELER-BENNETT, *The Nemesis of Power – The German Army in Politics, 1918-45*, London, 1954, pp. 281-6; CRAIG, op. cit., pp. 461, 466; for a discussion, see SCHÜDDEKOPF, op. cit., p. 357.
⁹⁵ VOGELSANG, loc. cit., pp. 430-1; BRACHER, op. cit., p. 662, n. 39.
⁹⁶ BRACHER, op. cit., pp. 733-4.
⁹⁷ Letter of the later Major-General Helmuth Stieff, executed by the Nazis on 8th August 1944, of 21st August 1932: *Vierteljahrshefte für Zeitgeschichte*, ii, 1954, p. 297.
⁹⁸ TAYLOR, loc. cit., p. 291.
⁹⁹ See, for example, the famous case of the three lieutenants Scheringer, Ludin, and Wendt, who were tried by the German Supreme Court at Leipzig in October 1930: see the documents in Schüddekopf, op. cit., pp. 289-305. This trial aroused grave dissatisfaction in the officer corps because the matter was not settled behind closed doors, and because the officers were arrested in front of their units: see VOGELSANG, loc. cit., pp. 401-2: General von Schleicher addressing the army commanders on 25th October 1930.

14

THE HISTORICAL ROOTS OF NATIONAL SOCIALISM

I do not believe that National Socialism was an 'accident' in the course of German history, or a 'strange aberration'—any more than Bolshevism was an 'accident' in the course of Russian history. Any movement able to seize and to hold power for any length of time must have roots linking it firmly with the specific historical development of the nation in question, must give expression to the aspirations and to the longings of millions of people, must be able to mobilise them for its aims and retain their active or passive allegiance. Otherwise no government, however perfect its machinery of terror, could maintain itself in power for more than a few months. The National Socialist dictatorship was not alien to the German people, nor was Germany an 'occupied country' (although this has been alleged), but National Socialism grew on German and Austrian soil. Professor Bracher is entirely right when he calls his last book: *The German Dictatorship*.[1]

On the other hand, I do not believe that National Socialism was the inevitable outcome of a long historical process which started with Martin Luther and his reliance on the authority of the German princes. Nor do I think that the Germans—preconditioned by centuries of absolute government—are fundamentally unsuited to democratic government and longing for a firm, paternal hand to guide them. After all, Germany possessed in the Hanseatic towns, the Free Imperial Cities and the Assemblies of the Estates ancient self-governing institutions able to hold their own with those of any other country, institutions, moreover, which in many cases could look back upon an unbroken tradition from medieval to modern times. Yet such views were widely held, especially in the countries allied against Germany in the last war, and were propounded with all the airs of pseudo-scientific knowledge. In the middle of the war, in 1941, Sir Robert Vansittart, the permanent under-secretary in the Foreign Office, gave a series of famous broadcasts which were published under the title 'Black Record—Germans Past and Present'. There he likened Germany to a butcher-bird 'steadily destroying all its fellows': 'Well, by hook and by crook—especially crook—

the butcher-bird got three wars before 1914.'[2] Vansittart went back to the deeds of the Germanic tribes and of the Teutonic Order to show that 'Germany as a whole has always been hostile and unsuited to democracy'. He compared the activities of the Hanseatic League to those of the *Auslandsdeutsche* of the twentieth century; he stated boldly that the dictatorship of Hitler derived from the authoritarian system of Bismarck and the autocracy of the Kaiser, that 'No other race could have managed to idolize such people'.[3]

Vansittart thus subconsciously adopted some of the racialist theories and fantasies of the man he was fighting against. But professional historians too, in the years of the war, saw in Hitler the logical outcome of the German past, and 'the Germans' as ardent supporters of Hitler's policy of conquest. In the same year in which Vansittart was holding forth on Germany's Black Record, Mr. Rohan Butler stated in his book, *The Roots of National Socialism*:

> This achievement of national socialism is a great and original tour-de-force, but it does not alter the fact that national socialist theory is almost entirely derived from the common elements in traditional German thought during the past hundred and fifty years. For that line of thought which leads from Herder to Hitler is traditionally and typically German...[4]

Mr. Butler also considered that the socialism of the founder of German Social Democracy, Ferdinand Lassalle, was national socialism and that the object of his policy was dictatorship;[5] while another Oxford historian, Mr. A. J. P. Taylor, wrote at the end of the war in an attempt to show the deep roots of the German dictatorship:

> During the preceding eighty years the Germans had sacrificed to the Reich all their liberties; they demanded as reward the enslavement of others. No German recognized the Czechs or Poles as equals. Therefore every German desired the achievement which only total war could give. By no other means could the Reich be held together. It had been made by conquest and for conquest; if it ever gave up its career of conquest, it would dissolve....[6]

What I object to particularly in these sweeping generalisations are the words 'every German', 'typically German', and the claims that 'no German' recognised the Slav peoples as equals: As if other European nations had not produced their racialist writers—the French, for example, Gobineau, and the English Houston Stewart Chamberlain—, as if there was no other tradition in German political thought but that leading to Hitler, as if there had not been a wave of pro-Polish thinking and writing in Germany in the first half of the nineteenth century, as if wars of conquest were only waged by Germans, as if the wave of terror unleashed by Hitler in 1933 was not for several years solely and entirely directed against Germans! It is, of course, understandable that views such as those quoted above were held during the years of the Second World War, but today saner opinions should prevail.

No one can seriously doubt that Hitler was carried to power by a colossal wave of nationalist fervour, fed by years of propaganda against the 'shame' of Versailles and by the infamous stab-in-the-back legend. As early as November 1918—only a few weeks after the revolution which caused the collapse of the German Empire and the flight of the Kaiser—a German officer wrote:

> In the most difficult moment of the war ... the revolution, prepared for a long time, has attacked us from the rear.... I do not know of any revolution in history which has been undertaken in so cowardly a fashion and which—what is much worse still—has necessarily aggravated the dire plight which has befallen us; perhaps it will lead to a complete catastrophe ...[7]

The man who wrote this was then a junior officer; but he was destined to become the chief of the German general staff, to resign in protest against Hitler's plans of aggression against Czechoslovakia, and to die by his own hand on 20 July 1944, the day when the plot against Hitler's life miscarried. In the years after 1919 the stab-in-the-back legend became one of the most potent weapons in Hitler's armoury—and millions of Germans believed him only too willingly.

German nationalism—like most European nationalisms—came into being in the course of the nineteenth century. More precisely, it was born at the very beginning of the century, at a time when the Germans had been deeply humiliated by the victories of Napoleon and the French occupation of wide stretches of Germany. Hence German nationalism was virulently, passionately anti-French. The Corsican conqueror was hated as the scum of humanity, as the arch-fiend. The poet Heinrich von Kleist exclaimed:

> Dam the Rhine with their corpses,
> let it, jammed with bones,
> foam, flow around the Palatinate, and
> thus form the frontier!
> A pleasure hunt when the shooters
> track the woolf!

> Kill him! the last judgement
> will not ask you for the reasons![8]

At the same time another poet, one of the leading lights of the Prussian Reform movement, Ernst Moritz Arndt, tried to explore the reasons why the French had become 'such a heartless, perfidious, sly and vain people', and he discovered the principal source of their 'depravity' in their *Mischmasch* (mixed race) and bastardisation. In his opinion it was the greatest misfortune of the French 'that the capital and the centre of the whole state and the entire French life developed in the most bastardized districts of France, for this centre was the pernicious cancer which corroded all that was healthy and strong in the other parts of the country...' The Germans, on the other hand, so Arndt found, had not been bastardised by other peoples, were not of mixed origin, and had remained, to a larger degree than many other nations, in a state of 'natural purity': they were blessed because they were 'an original people'.[9] Considering that Arndt himself came from the Baltic island of Rügen, where the descendants of Slavonic tribes formed the bulk of the local population, a very strange assertion indeed! Such an admixture of Germans and Slavs had taken place all over eastern Germany in the course of the Middle Ages—in the very areas where the kingdom of Prussia was to grow. Nothing is further removed from the historical truth than the alleged racial 'purity' of the inhabitants of Prussia, Brandenburg, Pomerania and Silesia—but perhaps this was a particularly strong reason for asserting this purity in the face of all the evidence.

Arndt also was the first to write about the 'Northern Man'—later a famous slogan of National Socialist propaganda. He echoed Kleist by declaiming:

> Kill all the French!
> Kill all knaves!

A very close associate of Arndt in the struggle against the French, the famous founder of the German sports and gymnastics movement, Friedrich Ludwig Jahn, stated in a lapidary fashion: 'the purer a nation, the better; the more mixed, the more like bandits'. Even after the defeat of Napoleon he declared publicly: 'Whoever has his children learn French... errs, whoever persists in this, sins against the Holy Ghost. But if he has French taught to his daughters, this amounts to teaching them prostitution.'[10] Jahn also tried to imitate ancient Germanic customs by sporting a colossal beard and wearing allegedly Germanic clothes. His ideal was the Germanic hero, Arminius or Hermann, who had defeated Varus' legions in the year 9 in the Teutoburg forest—the hero too of a famous play by Heinrich von Kleist. If German nationalism and racialism were born together at the time of the War of Liberation against Napoleon, yet another trait appeared at the same time—not so much on the side of the Reformers and Patriots, but on the side of their conservative opponents in Prussia; for the Junker Ludwig von der Marwitz accused the chief minister of Prussia of transforming the kingdom into 'a Jewish state' because he favoured Jewish emancipation.

Arndt and Jahn aimed at the creation of a Greater Germany which was to include not only the Austrian lands, but also the Netherlands, Denmark and Switzerland. Its new capital, so Jahn demanded, should be built on the Elbe and be called 'Teutonia'.[11] In Arndt and Jahn, not in the other Reformers of the early nineteenth century, all the elements are present which were to be characteristic of National Socialist ideology more than a century later: veneration of the *Volk*, of racial purity and all things Germanic, extreme hatred of foreign nations, virulent nationalism, anti-semitism, and Pan-Germanism, which aimed at uniting not only those speaking German, but also several other 'Germanic' nations. One may consider them cranks—and many did so then and later—but a direct line runs from them to the *völkisch* enthusiasts of the later nineteenth century, and from them to Hitler; and the youth of Germany was permeated by their ideas. It is no accident that their selected writings were re-issued to the *Wehrmacht* in the Second World War. This honour they shared with another 'prophet', Paul Bötticher, who called himself Paul de Lagarde.

Lagarde was born in 1827, the son of a teacher at a Berlin *Gymnasium*, and as a teacher too the son had to earn his living until he succeeded, at the age of forty-two, in obtaining a chair at the University of Göttingen—by that time he was a well-known orientalist. But side by side with his academic work he published a series of *Deutsche Schriften* which even in his own day became the bible of the nationalist student corporations and later exercised a profound influence on generations of young Germans. The gospel Lagarde preached was a fantastic combination of racialism, anti-semitism, Pan-Germanism and expansionism. As early as 1853— when he was only twenty-six years old and long before the unification of Germany—Lagarde demanded the incorporation in Germany of Russian Poland, as well as Alsace and Lorraine. He considered that Magyars, Czechs and 'similar nationalities living under the sceptre of Austria' were 'a burden to history'; as their territories were thinly populated, German emigration was to be directed, systematically and according to a carefully worked-out plan, into Istria, Bohemia, Galicia, Posnania, Silesia and the Slovak and Magyar districts of Hungary. Simultaneously the Polish and the Austrian Jews were to be transferred to Palestine; even if they were willing to Germanise themselves they could not be suffered to remain: 'it is impossible to tolerate a nation within the nation'. Lagarde considered the Germans 'far too soft a material' to be able to withstand the Jews who were hardened by years of Talmudic training.[12]

In his later writings these schemes were worked out in greater detail. Austria's only task, Lagarde postulated in 1875, was to become a colonial state of Germany. All the nationalities of the Habsburg Empire—with the only exception of the Southern Slavs—were 'politically valueless: they are only material for new Germanic creations'.[13] A few years later he repeated that the only feat worthy of the German nation was the Germanisation of the countries bordering on Germany in the east; territory for German settlements was to be gained to the east of Poland and to extend to the Black Sea, and further German colonies were to be formed in Asia Minor: 'we suffocate from education and the liberalism of the bureaucrats'.[14] Austria could only be preserved through 'ruthless Germanization': 'we must not play up to the Czechs and similar people: they are our enemies and have to be treated accordingly'.[15] Territory was to be gained from Russia; if Russia proved unwilling to cede it, 'we will be forced to start expropriation proceedings, that means war'. But the Germans, Lagarde added, were a peaceful nation; 'yet they are convinced of their right to live, namely as Germans, and convinced that they have a mission for all the nations of the world: if they are prevented from living as Germans, prevented from carrying out their mission, then they are entitled to use force'.[16] As to the Jews, Lagarde stated in 1881: 'The *alliance Israélite* is nothing but an international conspiracy for the promotion of Jewish world power, similar to the Freemasons, in the semitic field the same as the Jesuit Order in the catholic area.... Every foreign body within a living organism creates discomfort, illness, often festering sores and death.' The Jews as foreigners were 'nothing but the carriers of putrefaction'.[17] These and many other statements of the Göttingen professor could be taken straight from the pages of *Mein Kampf*. In the twentieth century the ideas of the German mission in the world, of the need to gain living space in the east became the common coinage of German nationalism.

In the later nineteenth century anti-semitism was wide-spread in Germany, partly in academic circles, partly among the lower middle classes, which were hit hard by the rapid economic changes of the time, the advance of capitalism and the severe economic crisis of 1873, due to over-production and over-speculation in the years after the Franco-Prussia war. Severely anti-semitic were the writings of the composer Richard Wagner on artistic and religious topics in which he accused the Jews of invading German cultural life and corrupting the German language: in the end no one would be able to understand his own word. 'The Jew', so Wagner alleged, had taken over German intellectual work and created 'a repulsive caricature of the German spirit' which he presented to the German people as a 'pretended reflection'.[18] To Wagner, the Jews were 'the plastic demon of the decay of humanity'; their 'triumphant security' they owed unfortunately to the favours of liberal princes.[19] In 1879 the famous historian Heinrich von Treitschke wrote in the very conservative journal *Preussische Jahrbücher* that people of the highest education, men who would indignantly repudiate any idea of religious intolerance or of national arrogance, were exclaiming 'as with one voice: the Jews are our misfortune!'[20] Treitschke's lectures at Berlin University, inspired by his fervent nationalism and Pan-Germanism, found an enthusiastic echo among a multitude of students. From the universities these slogans penetrated into the market place. An Anti-semitic Party was formed in 1886 which gained five seats in Hesse in the *Reichstag* elections of 1890; its leader was a librarian at Marburg University, Otto Böckel. In the *Reichstag* elections of 1893 the Anti-semites polled 263,000 votes and obtained sixteen seats; in 1898 their votes rose to 284,000 while the number of their deputies dropped to twelve.[21] In the elections of the early twentieth century, however, the influence of the Anti-semites declined.

Yet the decline was deceptive, for meanwhile there had come into being perhaps the most important annexationist and anti-semitic organisation of pre-war Germany, the *Alldeutscher Verband* (Pan-German League). It was founded in the 1890s and originally was chiefly preoccupied with imperialist propaganda, with Germany's need to acquire a much larger colonial empire. By 1901 it had 22,000 active members, in addition to numerous organisations which were corporate members of the League, among them a very large union of white-collar workers, the *Deutschnationale Handlungsgehilfenverband*. In the *Reichstag* dozens of deputies belonged to the Pan-German League, mainly from the Conservative and National Liberal parties. Officially the Pan-German League was not anti-semitic, but from 1908 onwards a new and energetic leader, Heinrich Class, a pupil of Treitschke, gave to its propaganda a much more aggressively expansionist and anti-semitic tune. In that year Class began a campaign against the Jews as the carriers of materialism: they were to be treated as foreigners, to be excluded from certain professions and to be forbidden to acquire property. Class maintained close contacts with powerful economic organisations and many influential politicians, usually preferring to work behind the scenes. The Pan-German League was one of the most influential pressure groups in Imperial Germany.[22]

Class was strongly influenced, according to his own testimony, by Lagarde and by another racialist writer, born in 1855 as the son of a British admiral, Houston Stewart Chamberlain. Chamberlain finally married a daughter of Richard Wagner, settled in Bayreuth and became the arch-priest of the Wagner cult; at the end of his life he became an equally ardent admirer of Adolf Hitler. At the very end of the nineteenth century Chamberlain published two massive volumes, *The Foundations of the Nineteenth Century*—a far more substantial exposition of racialist theory than Lagarde had ever produced. Chamberlain interpreted the whole course of European history from the moment of the appearance of the Germanic tribes 'as a struggle between Teuton and non-Teuton, between Germanic conviction and anti-Germanic sentiment'. 'Among all mankind,' he claimed, 'the Aryans stand out physically and spiritually; therefore they are by right ... the lords of the world.'[23] According to him, the Indo-Europeans had opened the doors to the Jews for idealistic reasons: 'like an enemy the Jew broke into the gap, stormed all positions and planted—I do not want to say on the ruins, but on the breach of our genuine singular character— the flag of his features which are eternally alien to us'. To achieve their domination the Jews, while remaining themselves racially pure, were infecting the Indo-Europeans with Jewish blood by putting out thousands of small sideshoots: 'if this continued for several centuries, there would be left in Europe only one racially pure people, that of the Jews; all the rest would be a herd of pseudo-Hebraic half-castes, that is beyond any doubt a people degenerate physically, mentally and morally'.[24] All these fantasies were clothed in a mass of scientific, learned jargon, not likely to appeal to the masses, but to the educated and semi-educated; as early as 1912 *The Foundations of the Nineteenth Century* went into its tenth edition.

For two decades Chamberlain lived in Vienna, and there he was in close touch with a far more successful propagandist of the Pan-

German and anti-semitic cause, Georg Ritter von Schönerer, the son of a successful railway builder who had been ennobled for his services to the Monarchy. In Vienna too, anti-semitism received a strong impetus from the economic crisis of 1873 which caused the failure of leading banks, and great misery among the small people of the capital. It was easy to find a scapegoat in the Jews who were very prominent in Vienna's cultural and economic life. Schönerer started his political career as an admirer of Bismarck's Germany, and the 'Watch on the Rhine' was the favourite song of the Austrian student corporations among whom he found his most enthusiastic pupils. From German nationalism Schönerer soon moved to anti-Habsburg propaganda and anti-semitism. As a member of the Austrian parliament, the *Reichsrat*, he proposed in 1887 the adoption of a new law which was to prohibit the immigration of foreign Jews and was to be a preliminary to another law directed against Austrian Jews. As Schönerer put it: 'the customs and ways of life of these alien parasites are hostile to the Aryan descent of the German nation and to its Christian culture.'[25] On another occasion Schönerer exclaimed: 'I hold reconciliation with the Slavs to be a useless effort.... One hears of equality between Germans and Slavs. It is as if one compared a lion to a louse because both are animals.'[26]

Schönerer engaged in strident propaganda against the Catholic Church and urged his followers to leave the Church and to become Protestants. But he also tried to revive Germanic customs and festivals. Celebrations were organized to commemorate the battle of Noreia, where the Cimbri had defeated the Roman legions in the year 113 B.C., as well as the battle of the Teutoburg forest of the year 9, which Kleist had celebrated eighty years before. A new Germanic calendar was to start with the year of the battle of Noreia, the year 1888 becoming the year 2001, and Germanic names were to replace the Latin months of the Christian calendar. One of Schönerer's favourite slogans was:

> 'Without Juda, without Rome,
> We will build Germania's dome!'

We are told that this was the slogan which the young Hitler put framed over his bed.[27] But anti-Catholicism was not popular in Austria. In Vienna itself Schönerer's popularity was soon overshadowed by that of another anti-semitic politician, Dr. Karl Lueger, who at the end of the nineteenth century became Vienna's most popular mayor and the founder of the Christian Social Party. His anti-semitism was less violent than that of Schönerer whose followers sported a badge depicting a Jew hanging from the gallows.

Lueger was a non-racialist, and always remained a loyal Catholic and pro-Habsburg.

In the early twentieth century the main area of Schönerer's influence shifted from Vienna and Lower Austria to the German-speaking districts of northern Bohemia which were more industrialised. There the position and the standard of living of the German population were threatened by the influx of Czech workers who were seeking employment in the growing industries of the area and were willing to accept lower wages than the German workers. In opposition to the Czechs a *Deutsche Arbeiterpartei* was founded there in 1904 by German workers from Bohemia and Moravia and some Austrian towns: the party programme combined nationalist with radical social demands and was strongly opposed to Marxist 'international' Social Democracy. A few months before the collapse of the Habsburg Monarchy the party adopted the name of German National Socialist Workers' Party; it was comparatively strong in northern Bohemia, but much weaker elsewhere.[28] It was the first National Socialist party, but—needless to say—this fact was never acknowledged by Hitler. As early as December 1919 the 'National Socialists of Greater Germany' held their first common deliberations in Vienna which were attended by representatives of the National Socialist parties of Austria, Czechoslovakia and Germany, parallel with a party conference of the Austrian National Socialists. A representative from Bohemia, Hans Knirsch, spoke on 'the future of Germandom in the unredeemed lands'. Among the groups represented at the conference, those from Bohemia clearly were by far the strongest.[29] There the seed sown by Schönerer had germinated—but it also germinated in the mind of another Austrian, Adolf Hitler, who in *Mein Kampf* expressly acknowledged his debt to Schönerer and to Lueger. It was the fierce national struggle between Germans and Slavs in the Habsburg Monarchy which gave rise to National Socialism in its original form and very deeply influenced the young Hitler.

Anti-semitism acquired a new lease of life when, with the end of the world war and the creation of an independent Poland, many thousands of Jews migrated from Galicia and Posnania to Vienna and to Berlin. They feared the uncertainty and the strong anti-semitism of Poland and preferred, usually speaking German, to settle in German surroundings; yet after the lost war the conditions prevailing in Vienna and Berlin were extremely unsettled, and violence was never far from the surface. One year after the outbreak of the revolution the Viennese police noted in a comprehensive report that anti-semitism was becoming more and more marked:

'The exasperation with the eastern Jews who either engage in food-smuggling and overcharging or do nothing whatever grows daily; so does the hatred of the Jewish Communists....'[30] In December 1918 a socialist newspaper reported that Jews and Christians who looked like Jews had been publicly assaulted in Berlin. A leaflet distributed in Berlin at that time claimed that the seat of the executive committee of the workers' and soldiers' councils was the synagogue in the house of deputies, and its private address was to be found in the Jewish quarter behind the Alexanderplatz, 'for short: in Jewish Switzerland'.[31] In February 1919 the leaders of the Pan-German League founded a new mass organisation, the *Deutschvölkischer Schutz und Trutzbund*, to take up the fight against the Jews on a larger scale, to eliminate their influence and thus to 'save' German culture. Within eighteen months this new League had almost 100,000 members and had attracted into its ranks many of the older *völkisch* organizations.[32]

With the collapse of the Hohenzollern and Habsburg monarchies Jews for the first time acquired ministerial office in Germany and Austria. The new government of People's Representatives in Berlin had two Jewish members, Haase and Landsberg; also Jewish were the prime minister of Prussia, Hirsch, and the prime minister of Bavaria, Eisner, as well as several prominent members of the new Austrian cabinet, for example Bauer and Deutsch. Jewish too were very prominent leaders of the nascent Communist parties, such as Rosa Luxemburg and Paul Levi. Perhaps even more striking to the public mind was the fact that, when Soviet Republics were proclaimed in Budapest and Munich in the spring of 1919, the leaders in both cases were almost exclusively Jewish. The slogan of the 'Jewish World Conspiracy', the slogan first coined by Lagarde, acquired a new and sinister meaning. The fear of Bolshevism became rampant among the middle and lower middle classes—until Hitler was able to ride to power in exploiting this fear. The fact that the new Communist parties of Germany and Austria were extremely weak and very easily defeated, that the Munich Soviet Republic only lasted for a few weeks, counted for little. These were conspiracies hatched by alien elements in which no good German could possibly participate—although in reality many good Germans, and even many good Bavarians, did participate in such ventures. The right-wing propagandists too made no difference between Communists and Social Democrats; to them they were all birds of a feather—although in reality Jewish Social Democrats, Landsberg in Germany and Bauer and Deutsch in Austria, took a very determined stand against Communist adventures and attempts at a *coup d'état*, which were very quickly suppressed. In the process many of the most prominent Jewish leaders of the extreme left were murdered, such as Luxemburg and Jogiches in Berlin and Landauer and Leviné in Munich. Murdered too was the Bavarian prime minister, Eisner, when on his way to the Diet to which he intended to submit his resignation.

Political violence indeed became rampant in central Europe. The world war had elevated violence to a patriotic duty: the killing of as many enemies as possible became the aim of every good soldier. After the end of the war the psychology of trench warfare could be transmitted to political life, and the 'internal enemy' became the object of similar violent action. There were many thousands of professional officers and NCO's who were unable to return to civilian life, and for whom there was no employment in the much reduced armies of the vanquished states. They were only too eager to continue the good fight, be that against the Communists at home, or against the Poles and Russians on the eastern frontiers. It was from these elements that the Free Corps were recruited; they committed political violence on a scale hitherto unknown, by no means only against Communists. Some of the most notorious Free Corps wore the swastika, the symbol of 'Aryan' Germanism, painted on their steel helmets and were openly anti-semitic. As early as March 1920 the Ehrhardt Brigade felt strong enough to resist a government order for its dissolution and to march into Berlin with the aim of deposing the government which had to escape to the south. Officers of the Ehrhardt Brigade in 1921 murdered a former minister, Erzberger, and in 1922 the Foreign Minister Rathenau, a Jew. Officers of the same brigade were used in the early 1920s to organise and to train Hitler's Storm Troopers in Munich. It was from the Free Corps and their successors that the National Socialist Party gained many of its earliest and most enthusiastic recruits. Among a random sample of men who joined the party between the years 1925 and 1927 as many as 20 per cent had been active in the Free Corps.[33] In Austria the same part was played by the *Heimwehren* which sprang up like mushrooms in the countryside in the years after 1918.

The fight of the Free Corps against the Poles in Upper Silesia and against the French in the Ruhr became a heroic legend, potent far beyond the circles of the extreme right. A Free Corps officer, Albert Leo Schlageter, who was shot by the French for sabotage, became a national martyr whose name was venerated by hundreds of thousands and exploited for purposes of early National Socialist propaganda. Hundreds of thousands hoped that the French occupation of the Ruhr would lead to another 'war of national liberation', like the war hailed by Arndt and Jahn one hundred and ten years before. When Hitler in November 1923 started his *Putsch* in Munich, not so much against the French as against the allegedly Marxist government in Berlin, it was a Bavarian Free Corps, *Oberland*, that marched together with his Storm Troopers and lost several of its members in the shooting at the Felderrnhalle. Although Hitler never acknowledged this, he and the rapid growth of his party owed a tremendous debt to the Free Corps, and equally to the earlier *völkisch* organisations.

In general the rise of the National Socialist Party was greatly facilitated by the strident and aggressive nationalism which permeated the Germany of the Weimar Republic. This affected all classes of the population, and even the Communist Party, which in 1930 published a programme 'for the national and social liberation of the German nation', in which national came first, and social only second.[34] This nationalism affected in particular the university students and secondary school teachers and their pupils, and the ex-servicemen of the world war, many thousands of whom joined the para-military associations, such as the *Stahlhelm* and the *Jungdeutscher Orden*. At many a Prussian secondary school even the one republican holiday, 'Constitution Day', was converted into an event to commemorate the great victories over the French, Rossbach and Sedan. Nationalism was particularly rampant in the German Nationalist People's Party, whose leaders so greatly aided Hitler's rise and combined with him in violent political campaigns, in particular against the acceptance of the Young Plan, against the Prussian government, and in the presidential election of 1932. And the German Nationalist Party was a party of the respectable middle class, of academics and industrialists: its support made Hitler acceptable. German nationalism was, of course, fanned by the terms of the Treaty of Versailles and by the virulent propaganda directed against it. But German nationalism had been extreme ever since the years of French domination under Napoleon. German unification under Bismarck had not abated it, but in the Second German Empire its voice became louder and shriller. In a country defeated and humiliated, plagued by one crisis after the other, it surpassed itself. That Stresemann successfully dismantled the terms of Versailles, that Germany again became a great power and a member of the League of Nations, made no impact on the masses. 'The Chains of Slavery' must be broken, and the very real achievements of the Republican governments counted for nothing.

The lost war and the revolution of November 1918 destroyed not only the old order, but at the same time the stability and security which it had guaranteed. This was a system in which everybody knew his place, in which the lower classes were firmly kept down, a hierarchical order, as it had existed for centuries. Indeed, the old ruling class, the nobility, kept its leading position at court, in the army and in the bureaucracy which occupied the commanding heights of society up to 1918. Members of the middle classes gradually penetrated into the leading groups, but did not dispute power with them and were rather assimilated and absorbed by them. There was a successful intermarriage between the owners of the broad acres and the industrial barons. Now this whole order seemed threatened by upstarts from the working class, such as Ebert who had been a mere saddler's apprentice. In the eyes of respectable bourgeois Germans Ebert cut a ridiculous figure, and it was a liberal middle-class illustrated paper which published on its front page a photograph of Ebert in bathing outfit to reinforce that impression. Although the Social Democrats, in both Germany and Austria, lost their position in the government as early as 1920, and re-entered it only for very short periods during the following years, there was 'red' Prussia where the SPD remained the leading party in the government until Papen's *coup d'état* of July 1932; and in Austria there remained 'red' Vienna whose surrender had to be forced by artillery fire two years later. As long as they existed 'red' Prussia and 'red' Vienna were equated with the dangers of Bolshevism by an assiduous propaganda. They personified to the middle classes a working-class victory achieved in November 1918, achieved as Hitler put it, by the 'November criminals'.

In general, of course, democracy was far from popular. The governments of the post-war period were extremely weak and ever-changing. There was no important statesman to give a lead, no leader to inspire any enthusiasm. The slow inflation of the mark destroyed whatever confidence in the government there might have been, and deprived the middle and the lower middle classes, the pensioners and all those who had something to lose, of the remnants of their security. These *déclassés* blamed the Republic for their loss of social status. It was a miracle that the Weimar Republic survived the crisis of 1923 when slow inflation became galloping inflation, when the printing machines could not keep up with the demand for more and more notes of ever greater denominations, when 'emergency money' had to be issued by countless local authorities, only to lose its value over night, when houses and whole streets could be bought for a few dollars. It is not surprising that eighteen months after the end of the inflation the Germans elected as their new president not a politician, but the old Field-Marshal von Hindenburg, who had liberated East Prussia from the Russians in 1914, a father figure, who might, after all, one day hand over the throne to a new Emperor. Not that monarchism was all that strong in the Germany of the 1920s: much more potent was the longing for a strong and paternal leader, who would lead the Germans back to the days of strength and glory, of order and stability, who would do away with the squabbling of the political parties. The French, in a very similar situation after their defeat of 1870, turned to the father figure of Marshal MacMahon and elected him as their president. That both marshals had been defeated, did not seem to affect the issue.

Hindenburg no doubt represented to most Germans the forces of the old Prussia. The 'day of Potsdam', when the new German parliament was ceremoniously opened by Hitler in the Garrison Church of Potsdam, where the Prussian kings lay buried, seemed to symbolise the union of the old Prussia with the new order of National Socialism. Hindenburg, in the resplendent uniform of an Imperial field-marshal, and many other former generals in dress uniform lent their image to the great occasion. Yet in reality National Socialism owed comparatively little to the old Prussia, and comparatively little to so-called Prussian militarism—except perhaps the love of so many Germans for military uniforms which affected even the political left. The leaders of the German army, the *Reichswehr*, certainly did not welcome the National Socialists with open arms, although some generals were much more sympathetic towards them than others. What might be said, however, is this. Centuries of absolute government—not only in Prussia, but in most German principalities—and the continuation of semi-absolute methods of government after 1871 had not permitted the slow growth of a genuine parliamentary tradition. There were many parliaments in Germany from the early nineteenth century onwards, but the governments were not responsible to parliament but only to the local prince. The leaders of the political parties did not learn how to wield political responsibility and did not share in political power. When power fell into their lap through the collapse of the old régime, not through their own efforts, they were totally unprepared for it and totally at a loss how to handle the reins of government. A glance at the protocols of the meetings of the government of People's Representatives of 1918–19 shows how pathetic the new 'rulers' were, how totally helpless, how dependent on the senior civil servants and the generals of the old régime. This in a way was the worst legacy which the old Prussia and the Empire left to the

Social Democrats and to the leaders of other political parties who soon joined them in a coalition government.

It is not surprising then that in these conditions democracy was unable to strike root in Germany, that the anti-democratic forces soon recovered from the shock, that the three democratic parties were never able to gain a majority in a general election after the year 1919. The first German republic suffered from fatal weaknesses, defects created at its birth, which permitted its enemies to destroy it. Among these enemies were not only the National Socialists, but also the old conservatives and nationalists, Pan-Germans and Völkische, who all combined forces against the hated republic. Many of them were to realise later what régime they had helped to create, but by then it was too late. The roots of National Socialism reach far back into the nineteenth century, but not into the dim Germanic or medieval past. I have tried to show here that they are manifold, that there is no single cause to which this historical phenomenon can be attributed, and that has been the purpose of my paper.

NOTES

1. Karl Dietrich Bracher, *Die deutsche Diktatur*, Cologne-Berlin, 1969. English transl. London, 1971.
2. Sir Robert Vansittart, *Black Record: Germans Past and Present*, London, 1941, pp. 1–2.
3. Ibid., pp. 21–3.
4. Rohan D'O Butler, *The Roots of National Socialism, 1783–1933*, London, 1941, p. 283.
5. Ibid., p. 134.
6. A. J. P. Taylor, *The Course of German History*, London, 1945, pp. 213–14.
7. Wolfgang Foerster (ed.), *Ein General kämpft gegen den Krieg—Aus nachgelassenen Schriften des Generalstabchefs Ludwig Beck*, Munich, 1949, p. 12: letter of 28 November 1918.
8. *Heinrich von Kleist's gesammelte Schriften*, Berlin, 1891, ii, p. 613: 'Germania an ihre Kinder'.
9. Ernst Moritz Arndt,, *Volk und Staat*, Selected writings ed. by Paul Requadt, Stuttgart, s.a., pp. 81, 92: written in 1815–16.
10. The quotations according to Günther Scholz, 'Patriotische Klimmzüge auf der Hasenheide: Friedrich Ludwig Jahn', in Karl Schwedhelm (ed.), *Propheten des Nationalismus*, Munich, 1969, pp. 23, 31.
11. Bracher, op. cit., p. 26; for Arndt see: Gabriele Venzky, *Die Russisch-Deutsche Legion in den Jahren 1811–1815*, Wiesbaden, 1966, p. 69.
12. Paul de Lagarde, 'Über die gegenwärtigen Aufgaben der deutschen Politik' (1853), *Deutsche Schriften*, Göttingen, 1886, pp. 27, 31, 34.

13. 'Über die gegenwärtige Lage des deutschen Reichs' (1875), ibid., pp.111–12.
14. 'Die Finanzpolitik Deutschlands' (1881), ibid., p. 308.
15. 'Programm für die konservative Partei Preussens' (1884), ibid., p. 359.
16. 'Die nächsten Pflichten deutscher Politik', ibid., pp. 390-1.
17. 'Die Stellung der Religionsgesellschaften im Staate' (1881), ibid. pp. 255–6.
18. Richard Wagner, 'Was ist deutsch?' (1865), *Ausgewählte Schriften über Staat und Kunst und Religion (1864–1881)*, Leipzig, s.a., p. 206.
19. 'Erkenne dich selbst' (1881), ibid., p. 358.
20. Heinrich von Treitschke, 'Unsere Aussichten', *Preussische Jahrbücher*, November 1879, quoted by Gerd-Klaus Kaltenbrunner in Karl Schwedhelm (ed.), *Propheten des Nationalismus*, p. 50.
21. Peter Pulzer, *The Rise of Political Anti-Semitism in Germany and Austria*, New York and London, 1964, pp. 109, 112, 121, 190.
22. For details see Pulzer, op. cit., pp. 227–9, 305–6; George L. Mosse, *The Crisis of German Ideology*, New York, 1964, pp. 219–24; Alfred Kruck, *Der Alldeutsche Verband, 1890–1939*, Wiesbaden, 1954.
23. Houston Stewart Chamberlain, *Die Grundlagen des 19. Jahrhunderts*, 2nd ed., Munich, 1900, pp. 503, 520.
24. *Ibid.*, p. 324. An English translation, *The Foundations of the Nineteenth Century*, was published in 1911.
25. There is no good published work on Schönerer and the Austrian Pan-Germans. But there is a very interesting London Ph.D. thesis of June 1963: J. C. P. Warren, The Political Career and Influence of Georg Ritter von Schönerer, from which the above quotation is taken.
26. Quoted by Arthur J. May, *The Hapsburg Monarchy 1867–1914*, Cambridge, Mass., 1960, p. 211.
27. Joseph Greiner, *Das Ende des Hitler-Mythos*, Zürich-Leipzig-Vienna, 1947, p. 81.
28. For all details see Andrew G. Whiteside, *Austrian National Socialism before 1918*, The Hague, 1962; and his 'Austria' in Hans Rogger and Eugen Weber (eds.), *The European Right—A Historical Profile*, Berkeley and Los Angeles, 1965, pp. 308 ff.
29. Details in *Deutsche Arbeiter-Presse—Nationalsozialistisches Wochenblatt*, Folge 49, Vienna, 6 December 1919. A copy in Landesregierungsarchiv Tirol, Innsbruck, Präsidialakten 1920, XII.77. The issue of 24 December 1919 contains the speeches of two other representatives from Czechoslovakia, Dr. Schilling and Rudolf Jung, as well as the speech of the Austrian 'leader', Dr. Walter Riehl, a Viennese lawyer. For Riehl see the unpublished Vienna Ph.D. thesis of Rudolf Brandstötter, Dr. Walter Riehl und die Geschichte der nationalsozialistischen Bewegung in Osterreich, Vienna, 1969.
30. Police report, 17 November 1919, signed Schober: Verwaltungsarchiv Vienna, Staatsamt des Innern, 22/gen., box 4860.
31. Hermann Müller, *Die November-Revolution*, Berlin, 1931, p. 109; Emil Eichhorn, *Über die Januar-Ereignisse—Meine Tätigkeit im Berliner Polizeipräsidium*, Berlin, 1919, p. 14.
32. For all details see Uwe Lohalm, *Völkischer Radikalismus—Die*

Geschichte des Deutschvölkischen Schutz—und Trutzbundes, Hamburg, 1970, pp. 15, 20–2, 81, 84, 89, 176–7.

33. Theodore Abel, *Why Hitler came into Power—An Answer based on the Original Life Stories of Six Hundred of his Followers*, New York, 1938, p. 81. A very large number of the top-ranking party and SA leaders had served in the Free Corps.

34. *Programmerklärung zur nationalen und sozialen Befreiung des deutschen Volkes*, issued by the Zentralkomitee der Kommunistischen Partei Deutschlands, 24 August 1930.

15

BISMARCK AND THE PRUSSIAN LIBERALS

In the revolution of 1848 to 1849 the German Liberals failed to unite Germany. The National Assembly at Frankfurt, after many months of deliberation, had worked out a constitution; it envisaged a smaller Germany, without Austria, and with the Imperial dignity hereditary in the House of Hohenzollern. But when the Imperial crown was offered to King Frederick William IV of Prussia by a delegation of the Frankfurt Assembly, be declined to accept a Crown 'baked of dirt and clay'. Dislike of popular sovereignty caused him to turn down an offer that, if accepted, would have solved the German problem in a liberal sense. The popular risings in favour of the constitution that broke out in many parts of Germany during the spring of 1849 were defeated by the Prussian army, under the command of the king's brother, William, later the Emperor William I. The rump of the National Assembly was dissolved by force. Thus ended the dreams of a Germany united by popular effort under the black, red and gold colours and liberal leadership.

This defeat of liberal aspirations was brought about not only by Prussian military strength, but also by disunity among the Liberals themselves. The large majority of the Liberals at Frankfurt were moderates, aiming at the foundation of a German constitutional monarchy, and not at social and political revolution; but there was a minority of radicals and revolutionaries whose policy of provoking revolts and mutinies frightened the rest. Their policy drove the majority towards the right and inclined it to seek a compromise with the forces of the old order. These fears among the moderates, although hardly justified, were one of the fundamental causes of the defeat of the revolution in 1849.

It was a defeat that had lasting consequences. Many people were beginning to doubt whether it was possible to achieve unity and liberty together: if this should prove impossible, might not liberty have to be sacrificed to unity? The moderates no longer believed in their own strength and were looking towards Prussia to provide the leadership which Germany lacked. In contrast with the period before 1848, Prussia now possessed a constitution, and the king of Prussia was no longer an absolute ruler. It is true that the rights of the Prussian *Landtag* were closely circumscribed and that ministers were not reponsible to it, but to the king. Yet the second chamber, elected on the basis of a franchise that strongly favoured the propertied classes, served as a platform for the expression of liberal demands and aspirations. If the king of Prussia would make some concessions and reform the Prussian government and administration according to the needs of the time, he could create conditions in which Prussia might take the lead in Germany and unite the country through her example.

Politically, there was much wishful thinking in this conception of the Prussian monarchy, for the Prussian constitution was little more than a fig-leaf of absolutism. The state was still ruled by the bureaucracy, and its commanding positions were still occupied by members of the Prussian nobility. This applied especially to the Prussian army, which had successfully weathered the storms of 1848. The officers formed an 'exclusive special caste, the first Estate in the country', as a liberal deputy put it in 1861. The guards regiments were officered exclusively by noblemen; so were ninety per cent of the cavalry, and seventy per cent of the infantry regiments. Over ninety per cent of the generals were nobles. This state of affairs was likely to continue, since most of the future officers were educated in the cadet schools, where all liberal influences were eradicated and the spirit of superiority over mere civilians was inculcated in the pupils.

Liberal hopes wer particularly unrealistic with regard to the king, whom they expected to initiate the reform of the Prussian state. After the shock of March 1848, the policy of Frederick William IV had become openly reactionary. The course adopted by the ministry of Otto von Manteuffel, which dominated the last years of the reign, was a mixture of arbitrary police measures with intrigues and infringements of the law and the constitution. Therefore – as so often in the course of Prussian history – liberal hopes concentrated on the person of the heir to the throne, the king's brother William. His accession was hailed as the beginning of a 'new era', the name given to the ministry he appointed in place of that of von Manteuffel. Yet there was little justification for these soaring hopes. William, as a second son, had not been expected to become king, nor educated to fill that position, but had received his training in the army: he was first of all a Hohenzollern, and then an army officer. Military affairs was the only field in which he trusted his own judgment. He did not understand politics; the aspirations of the Liberals were and remained as alien to him as they had been in 1848, when he belonged to the extreme reactionaries. He was convinced that he ruled by divine right and was determined to preserve his powers, among which the absolute control of the armed forces held pride of place.

In a different sphere, however, Prussian leadership of Germany was daily being realized: that of economic development. Through the decision of the Great Powers, taken at the Congress of Vienna, Prussia had acquired large provinces on the Rhine and the Ruhr, where in the eighteenth century she had owned only small and scattered territories.

Soon the coming of the industrial revolution transformed these regions beyond recognition and created an arsenal of modern industry greater than anywhere else on the Continent; meanwhile, in Berlin and other eastern towns, too, industrialization was making rapid progress, especially in the 1850's and 1860's. In the Prussian Saar, the output of coal multiplied eighteen times between 1820 and 1860. Railway construction forged ahead equally quickly in Prussia, the length of the line open to traffic multiplying by seven between 1844 and 1860. The industrial spirit even invaded the domains of noble power, the 'knights' estates', on many of which sugar refineries, breweries, brick kilns, saw mills, flour mills, etc., were established. Clearly a 'new era', in a sense quite different from the meaning given to it in 1858, had dawned in Prussia.

Yet is was precisely with this new industrial and bourgeois spirit that William was most out of tune. The society of the old, rural Prussia he was able to understand; he loved the simple, patriarchal relationships between the landlords and the peasants, who had but recently emerged from serfdom. This God-given order of things, of which he was the divinely appointed guardian, must be defended against the new spirit of Mammon and criticism. While the king knew many prominent members of the middle classes, he remained surrounded by noblemen, such as his adjutants, von Alvensleben and von Manteuffel, whose feudal and anti-liberal views influenced him strongly. To them, all Liberals were revolutionaries and 'reds' who aimed at the overthrow of the monarchy. Yet the mere fact that a new ministry was appointed by William when he became regent in place of his insane brother, and that this new ministry did not attempt to influence the elections of 1858, resulted in a sweeping victory for the moderate Liberals. They gained with 210 seats a large majority in the second chamber, while the right-wing Conservatives declined from 236 to 59 seats, hardly more than the 58 of the Catholics. This liberal victory had been won on the basis of the three-class franchise: the respectable bourgeois and property owners – only those paying direct taxes were entitled to vote – had voted liberal, not the famous 'rabble' beloved of all reactionaries. The following years saw the outbreak of an open conflict between the Crown and the majority of the second chamber.

The conflict was caused by a bill for the reform of the Prussian army which was submitted to parliament by the government in 1860. It was a project dear to the heart of Prince William, intended to increase the size of the regular army in proportion to the growth of the population, and to make it more efficient from the military point of view. According to the Army Act of 1814, the recruits had to serve for three years with the Line and, after that, for two years with the reserve. They were then transferred to the *Landwehr*, a separate reserve army with its own officers, which in case of mobilization was to supplement the regular army, but as independent units. Thus General von Boyen, the author of the Army Act, had hoped to associate the people with the army and to create a citizens' force, to keep alive the feeling of patriotism and the spirit of the War of Liberation. The *Landwehr* was a more democratic force than the regular army, and its officers – in contrast with those of the army – were mainly of middle-class origin, hence popular with the Liberals, but looked down upon by the professional soldiers. In addition, when mobilized in 1849 on account of the revolutionary disorders in the west and south of Germany, the *Landwehr* units had proved much less reliable than those of the Line. In the opinion of General von Roon, the Minister of War, the *Landwehr*, therefore 'lacked the true, real, strong military spirit . . . this bellicose ardour, this fire, this warmth for the earnest execution of their bloody and painful duty in case of war . . .'

The bill for the reform of the army proposed to abolish the separate status of the *Landwehr* and its officer corps, the members of which were to become officers of the reserve. Service with the Line, which had been reduced from three to two years in 1833, was to be restored to three, and that with the reserve extended from two to five years. The number of recruits to be called up annually for the service with the regular army was to be increased from 40,000 to 63,000. This increase and the extension of the period of service would make it possible to eliminate the *Landwehr* units from the front-line army and to leave the older classes at home in case of mobilization; the army would become more reliable, more suitable for the conduct of an offensive war. Yet the reform entailed an increase of the total annual expenditure by one-third, a sum of nine million thalers, and of another five million at the outset. The government used the mobilization caused by the war of 1859 between Italy and Austria to start the reform measures, and submitted to the Prussian parliament a budget envisaging the continuation of the reform in 1860. In that year a bill for the reorganization of the army was also introduced, but the second chamber only passed a provisional budget, granting the necessary means for one year. In 1861 the second chamber again emphasized that it had not accepted the plan of military reorganization and had only granted the required means provisionally.

The Liberals did not object to the proposed increase of the army, but to the change in the rôle and importance of the *Landwehr* and to the disappearance of its separate officer corps, to which they were strongly attached for political and sentimental reasons. The real issue was not whether the army should become more efficient, but whether it should continue to be a stronghold of reaction, divorced from the liberal tendencies of the age: traits that were to be enhanced by the planned reorganization. For the Prussian nobility this was a vital question. Since the eighteenth century, its younger sons used to serve as officers, for noble estates were entailed and no other suitable career was open to young noblemen. Most of the noble families were far from rich and depended on the government to uphold their economic and social position. The army conflict in Prussia was at the same time a social conflict between a rising middle class and a declining nobility. This was clearly perceived at the time. Thus the historian of the foundation of the German Empire of 1871, Professor von Sybel, said in 1862: 'in internal affairs, the great conflict of our time is not a conflict between Crown and parliament, but one between the excessive privileges of the nobility and the free right of merit.' Another moderate Liberal declared: 'it is a struggle about principles . . . a struggle of the burghers versus the Junkers.'

To give a lead to the liberal and national hopes of the middle classes, the German Progressive Party was founded in 1861. It was inspired by the achievement of Italian unity in the preceding years and aimed at a liberal solution of the German question. It was not opposed to the king and the monarchy, nor was it anti-Prussian, as was clearly stated in its programme: 'The existence and greatness of Prussia depend upon the firm unification of Germany, which cannot be brought about without a strong central power exercised by Prussia and without a representation of the people . . .' One of its leaders, Max von Forckenbeck, in an election speech, expressly denied 'that the Progressive Party has striven for a government by the majority of the second chamber or has wanted to infringe upon the rights of the king. Under the entirely different social conditions of Prussia a government by parliamentary majority as in England is neither possible nor desirable for freedom.' Only some of the more radical Liberals aimed at the introduction of ministerial responsibility. The Progressive Party was not a radical but a moderate party, nor was it opposed to a compromise on the military issue. Its leaders perceived that, by 'provisionally' granting the means for the reorganization of the army, they had taken their stand on weak ground; for, meanwhile, the new regiments had been established, the officers had been commissioned, and the *Landwehr* units had been broken up. This could not be undone without severe damage to the military strength of Prussia, and without completely antagonizing the king, who regarded the reorganization of the army as falling entirely within his field of competence. It was only after all attempts at a compromise had failed that the second chamber in 1862, for the first time, refused to sanction any means for the reorganization of the army and approved military expenditure only to the extent it had been granted before the reforms.

The king and his advisers were more sharply opposed to any compromise than the majority of deputies. As early as 1860, William was accusing the deputies of lack of patriotism because they were against his military reforms. He regarded them as 'enemies and revolutionaries . . . because they are aiming at the limitation of the highest attribute of royalty, the war command'. When, in April 1861, some of the liberal ministers urged the king to make certain concessions in the constitutional field, General von Roon, the Minister of War, wrote to him that the parliamentary antecedents of these ministers imposed party duties upon them that were incompatible with their duties towards His Majesty: he should make his royal will felt and thus 'break the chains of the eagle; the king by the grace of God remains, at the head of his people, the centre of gravity in the state, master of the country, unfettered by ministerial guardians and parliamentary majorities . . .'

Three times in the course of two years the government resorted to a dissolution to break the deadlock between Crown and parliament and to redress the parliamentary balance in its favour. Each time the Progressives were returned as the strongest party, possessing, together with their liberal allies, an overwhelming majority in the second chamber. The pro-government Conservatives, on the other hand, were reduced to the size of a splinter party, with but ten seats in 1862 and 38 in 1863, this increase being due to political and social pressure in the rural areas: teachers and officials were threatened with disciplinary measures unless they voted conservative, and people were censured, fined or dismissed from their appointments on political grounds. It was of no avail. The overwhelming majority voted liberal, whether they were Protestants or Catholics, Germans or non-Germans, living in towns or villages. 'The result of the elections in Pomerania', General von Roon was informed by his nephew after the election of 1861, 'was decided solely by the peasants, who . . . take an attitude most decidedly *against us* . . . The meetings were stormy everywhere – they hardly listened to me, they were like people enchanted! . . .' This is remarkable, indeed, if one remembers how strongly to the right the rural areas of Prussia voted in later years.

The largest group among the deputies were the legal officials, followed closely by the landowners; third in importance came the other officials, and fourth merchants and industrialists; all other groups were of minor importance. Members of the leading social groups of the old Prussia, the civil servants and the land-owners, were the leaders of the movement for liberal reform and German unity. Prominent among them were liberal noblemen, judges and university professors. Yet the Progressive Party was not merely a party of notables, but enjoyed mass support among workers as well as peasants. There were many popular societies, singing and cultural associations, sports and rifle clubs, which provided the party with a mass basis. The singers' festival of September 1859 was attended by about twelve hundred singers and twenty to twenty-five thousand visitors, among them many peasants and other country people. There was much 'excited political discussion' that centred around one subject: 'national party, reform of the *Landtag*, unity under the leadership of Prussia'.

In spite of their numerical strength, the Progressives had no idea how to achieve their aims against a determined government, and no realistic means of gaining victory. They rejected the weapon that might have brought success: refusal to pay taxes. On the contrary, the economic progress of Prussia was so quick that mounting tax returns facilitated the work of the government and paid for the reorganization of the army. After the experiences of 1848, the Liberals abhorred revolution on principle. As Professor von Sybel put it in 1863 in a letter to a friend: 'You would not find in the whole of Prussia anyone who did not regard open violence as foolish and criminal, since it would be suppressed immediately.' And in another letter: 'the régime will last until the army declares for the constitution, or until it is defeated in a foreign war – unless the same luck happened to us that happened to the English in 1688 with the Prince of Orange: dissension within the highest circles, for example, a declaration of the Crown Prince in favour of the constitution.' It is true that the Crown Prince disapproved of the anti-liberal policy of the government; but he was far too obedient and respectful towards his father, far too conscious of his duty as a Hohenzollern and an officer, ever to speak publicly in favour of a change of government. It was, indeed, a broken reed on which these hopes were pinned. True enough, a defeat abroad would probably have led to the collapse of the autocratic régime at home – as it had done in 1806. This time, however, there was no Napoleon to defeat the Prussian army, but victory followed upon victory, and these victories sealed the fate of the Liberals.

Before this occurred, startling changes took place on the domestic front. King William, who was thinking of abdicating in favour of his son, was finally prevailed upon by General von Roon to appoint Otto von Bismarck as Prime Minister of Prussia. In 1848 Bismarck had been conspicuous for his reactionary views; a self-appointed spokesman of the extreme right, he had intended to march on the revolutionary capital at the head of his peasants. According to his version, the king, when Bismarck's appointment as a minister was suggested by a reactionary group at the royal court, had written against his name: 'only suitable when the bayonets rule without any limitations'. Later, Bismarck had held various diplomatic posts, but never a high government office. King William, cautious and legitimist by nature, deeply distrusted his revolutionary aims in the field of foreign policy: to him, Bismarck was a Jacobin. During the decisive interview in September 1862, he attempted to make Bismarck agree to a programme that would have tied his hands. This Bismarck had no intention of accepting. He explained to his master that the only real issue was 'rule by the king, or parliamentary government', a formula with which William fully agreed. He was entirely won over by Bismarck's declaration of allegiance: 'I would rather go under with my King than leave Your Majesty in the lurch in the fight against parliamentary domination.' No concessions to the majority: Bismarck undertook, if need be, to govern against the second chamber and without a budget. As he declared in one of the committees of the *Landtag* a week after his appointment: 'the great questions of the time are not decided by speeches and majority resolutions – that was the great mistake of 1848 and 1849 – but through iron and blood.' One of his chief opponents, von Forckenbeck, sorrowfully wrote to his wife: 'Bismarck-Schönhausen, that means: government without budget, rule of the sword at home, war abroad. I believe him to be the most dangerous minister for Prussia's freedom and happiness.'

Although the Prussian constitution stated quite unequivocally that the budget had to be fixed annually by law and to be passed by the two houses of parliament, Bismarck claimed that, if agreement between the Crown and parliament was not reached, the constitution did not contain any provision as to what was to happen. Thus there was a gap. The second chamber had just voted against the budget proposed by the government and had passed one that eliminated all expenditure for the reorganization of the army. This had been duly rejected by the first chamber in which government influence was paramount, so that no budget existed at all. Yet the government continued to levy taxes and to spend the money collected on the reorganization of the army and other purposes, just as if a budget had been voted. Judges and other officials opposed to this policy were disciplined or dismissed. Censorship was imposed upon the press – a decree that the *Landtag* by an overwhelming majority declared to be unconstitutional. In September 1863 – one year after Bismarck had taken office – the *Landtag* was once more dissolved. Strong government pressure was brought to bear upon the electors to obtain a favourable result; but only 38 deputies loyal to the government were elected, while the Liberal opposition mustered 253, hardly less than in the previous year. The police regime instituted by Bismarck had not achieved the hoped-for results. A few weeks later, at the beginning of 1864, the session of the *Landtag* was closed. Clearly, different methods were required to bring about a change of the political climate.

This was achieved by the two wars that Bismarck fought in 1864 and in 1866, against Denmark and against Austria. The wars not only brought victory and thus justified the reorganization of the Prussian army from a military point of view, but they showed the way to the solution of the German problem 'through iron and blood'. Austria was expelled from Germany and the North German Confederation was founded, entirely dominated by Prussia, with King William as its president and Bismarck as its chancellor: the precursor of the German Empire of 1871. These events completely changed the internal political situation in Prussia. On the day of the battle of Sadowa, new elections were held which resulted in a severe defeat of the Progressives and their liberal allies; they lost 105 of their 253 seats, while the Conservatives increased their's from 38 to 142. At new elections, held in 1867, the liberal defeat was even more catastrophic: the opposition succeeded in retaining only 70 seats, while the number of Conservatives grew from 142 to 181.

What is even more important, a new liberal party, the National Liberals, was formed which supported Bismarck's solution of the German question and throughout remained more national than liberal. At the elections of 1867, this new party gained 55 seats in the old Prussian provinces and 46 in the newly annexed ones, in both cases considerably more than the Progressives, who only mustered a total of 48 deputies. National enthusiasm triumphed over liberal and constitutional aspirations. In September 1866, after the conclusion of the war against Austria, the *Landtag* passed an indemnity law which sanctioned the measures taken by Bismarck's government during the preceding years; it consented, after the event, to the state expenditure of the years without a budget, and therewith to the reorganization of the army that had been undertaken against the decisions of parliament. Thus the *Landtag* admitted that it had been at fault, while Bismarck had been justified in pursuing his anti-parliamentary policy. Bismarck was the victor in the constitutional conflict, and parliament was forced to admit it.

The political climate of Prussia changed quickly and completely. As early as 1864, the Hanoverian political leader, Rudolf von Bennigsen, reported full of misgiving: 'In the north [of Germany] agreement with Bismarck – that is the adulation of military power and diplomatic success – grows in a frightening way.' Another observer wrote at the end of the year: 'In Berlin the population on the whole shares the views of Herr von Bismarck. They are intoxicated with military glory, and the spirit of voracity which has been long dormant is awakening.' Three successful wars within seven years brought about a veneration of martial glory and military might such as Prussia had never seen. From Prussia this spirit began to spread into the others parts of Germany. Upon the conquest of Germany by Prussia, there followed a spiritual conquest, the effects of which were to last into the twentieth century.

The Liberals desired the unification of Germany so ardently that they were willing to forego their political ambitions when Bismarck gained unification at the point of the sword. The foundation of a strong German Empire opened such vistas of economic expansion that the middle classes were reconciled to Bismarck's methods and to their own political defeat. Having to choose between unity and liberty they chose unity – to their own economic advantage. German liberalism never regained the strength that it had possessed in 1848 and in the early 1860's. It remained split into a number of minor parties that either accepted Bismarck's masterful leadership or remained in doctrinaire opposition. Many of the former liberal leaders – such as the famous historians von Sybel and Treitschke – made their peace with Bismarck and became his most ardent prophets and propagandists.

Why was the collapse of the liberal opposition so sudden and so complete? That this was not due to official pressure and persecution is proved by the fact that such measures had been successfully withstood for several years, and that in spite of them the opposition had gained victories in open elections, without a ballot. Nor was the collapse due to disunity among the Liberals – as in 1848–49, when the moderates had been driven to the right by the super-radicalism of the small extreme left. In the 1860's, the Progressives were united and not threatened by a radical movement. Ferdinand Lassalle's German Workers' Party was as yet too small to present such a threat, and unable to wield any influence so long as the three-class franchise lasted. It is true that Bismarck toyed with the idea of allying with Lassalle to defeat the Progressives, of playing off the lower against the middle classes. Yet this never materialized, and there is no evidence that the workers were willing to swallow the bait if it had been offered. On the contrary, Bismarck's policy of repression succeeded in uniting the opposition against his arbitrary policy. When it became clear, however, that it was Bismarck, not the Liberals, who was achieving German unity, they were confronted with the choice of either remaining in doctrinaire opposition or of accepting what he was presenting to them. The majority then chose the latter course, and only a minority remained faithful to their principles. Faced with a similar alternative, the Liberals of any other European country might have made the same choice. It has also to be remembered that Prussian liberalism was of very recent growth, with strong roots only in certain provinces, especially in the Rhineland, which had become Prussian only fifty years earlier. The existence of an absolute government with strong powers of police control, and the existence of serfdom until the early nineteenth century, had stifled the growth of an independent middle class. Hence there was no real liberal tradition. When Bismarck took a leaf out of their book and fulfilled at least part of their programme, only the very faithful Liberals – and perhaps the less realistic – refused to accept the gift that he was offering.

16

AUGUST BEBEL

FOR three-quarters of a century the German Social-Democratic Party, the SPD, has been one of the strongest political parties in Germany. For many years—between 1912 and 1932—it was the strongest party in the Reichstag, to be eclipsed in the latter year by the rising Nazi party, as it has been in post-war Germany by the ruling Christian Democratic party. The political influence exercised by the SPD during the early years of the Weimar Republic, when the president as well as most ministers were moderate socialists, was stronger than that of any other party; it bears much of the responsibility for the failures as well as the achievements of the Weimar Republic. It withstood the onslaught of Nazism more successfully than any other party, retaining to a large extent the loyalty of its followers. Its leaders actively participated in the resistance to Hitler during the war years, and to the imposition of communist control in Berlin and East Germany after the war, thus proving anew their fidelity to democratic principles. Yet when in power in the years after 1918 the SPD was curiously ineffective and weak; and it abdicated power to the forces of reaction without even a show of resistance and thus shared in the inglorious dissolution of the Weimar Republic.

No other person had such a profound influence on the development of the SPD, being responsible alike for its successes and its weaknesses, as August Bebel, its uncontested leader from its foundation until his death in August 1913. To the present day Bebel enjoys the almost unique distinction of being acclaimed in West as well as in East Germany.[1] The famous historian Theodor Mommsen, who was certainly no political friend of Bebel's, wrote: 'Everybody in Germany knows that a dozen of the Eastalbian Junkers, if collectively fitted out with a head such as Bebel's, would shine among their peers'.[2] When a Swiss newspaper erroneously reported that Bebel had died, Marx, in a letter to Engels, declared this to be 'the greatest disaster for our party!' He considered him unique (*eine einzige Erscheinung*) within the German, and even the European working-class movement,[3] and he was probably right.

In contrast with so many other socialist leaders, Bebel was not an intellectual and was entirely self-educated. Born in 1840, the son of an n.c.o. in the Prussian army, he attended only an elementary school and

---

[1] See, for example, the articles by Dieter Fricke, 'August Bebel heute', *Zeitschrift für Geschichtswissenschaft* (East Berlin), 1963, pp. 1045, 1252, commemorating the fiftieth anniversary of the death of 'the great leader of the German workers'.

[2] Mommsen in *Die Nation*, xx, 13 December 1902; quoted by Fricke, *Zeitschrift für Geschichtswissenschaft*, 1960, p. 278.

[3] *Briefwechsel zwischen Friedrich Engels und Karl Marx*, ed. A. Bebel and E. Bernstein, iv (Stuttgart, 1919), p. 478.

would have followed his father's career if he had not been pronounced unfit for military service on account of his poor health. He thus became a turner and got to know his country during years of wandering as a journeyman in search of work. He then settled in Saxony which was industrially more advanced and had a much stronger liberal tradition than the neighbouring Prussia. In Leipzig he became active in the workers' educational movement, trying to arouse the interest of his fellow-workers in the betterment of their status. At a time of the growth of the liberal and national movement he also became interested in politics. At that time, the *Arbeitervereine* (workingmen's clubs) were a part of the general liberal movement which aimed at German unification through a German Parliament, as had been unsuccessfully attempted in 1848.

From the outset, Bebel stood on the left and radical side; he was in favour of a German republic and democratic unity, opposed to a constitutional monarchy and the unification of Germany by Prussia. His views were identical with those of the south German democrats, but he was also critical of their lack of courage. He remained an inveterate enemy of Bismarck's policy, which to him was not German, but Great Prussian, ' aiming at winning mastery over the whole of Germany and at imbuing Germany with a Prussian spirit and Prussian principles of government—which are the mortal enemy of all democracy.' After the foundation of the North German Confederation by Bismarck, Bebel, as a deputy in the Reichstag, publicly protested against a federation ' that makes Germany a large barracks and destroys the last remnant of freedom and popular rights '. The outbreak of the Austro-Prussian war of 1866 he considered a catastrophe and called for an uprising of the people to resist the peace-breaker, Prussia. To him, an Austrian victory was preferable to Prussia's because in that case ' the ministry of Bismarck and the rule of the Junkers which to the present day oppress Germany like a nightmare would have been swept away '.[4] Many years later, in 1912, he still remembered: ' It was one of the saddest days of my life when it became known in 1866 that Austria was expelled from the German Confederation '.[5] The majority of the German liberals, on the other hand, and many German socialists too, were won over by Prussia's military victories and now put their hopes in a Prussian leadership of Germany. Bebel's enmity to Ferdinand Lassalle and the rival socialist party founded by him had its roots, above all, in their differing attitudes towards Prussia and the German state founded by Bismarck.

IN the same year in which Prussia defeated Austria and expelled her from Germany, Bebel became a member of the First International, the International Working Men's Association. It had been founded with

---

[4] August Bebel, *Aus meinem Leben*, 7th ed. (Stuttgart, 1922), i, pp. 117, 153, 165; ii, pp. 3, 108, 145.
[5] *Victor Adler, Briefwechsel mit August Bebel und Karl Kautsky* (Vienna, 1954), p. 547.

the active participation of Marx, but Bebel at that time knew virtually nothing of Marx's writings. As he himself describes it, he tried to read the *Critique of Political Economy*, but soon gave up the attempt. It was only some years later, during one of his many spells of imprisonment, that he found the time to read the first volume of *Das Kapital*. Even the *Communist Manifesto* and other more popular writings of Marx were not known to the German social-democrats at that time. Much better known were the writings of Lassalle, and these seem to have converted Bebel to socialism in the first instance. During his whole life-time Bebel was not much influenced by socialist theory; he was above all a tribune of the people.

Bebel's great hour came with the outbreak of the Franco-Prussian war in 1870. Germany was gripped by anti-French fervour, and war against Bonaparte once more became the rallying cry that united the country. Even many social-democrats joined in the bellicose and nationalist outbursts. Yet in the North German Reichstag Bebel and his close friend Wilhelm Liebknecht refused to vote for the war credits demanded by the government, 'because this would be a vote of confidence in the Prussian government which has prepared the present war by its actions in the year 1866.... As foes of every dynastic war, as social republicans and members of the International Working Men's Association which opposes all oppressors without difference of nationality ... we cannot declare ourselves either directly or indirectly in favour of this war and therefore abstain from voting ...' This attitude met with sharp criticism even from high party officials, who branded it as Saxon particularism and almost caused a split in the party ranks. In November 1870—after the overthrow of the Second Empire and the proclamation of the French Republic—Bebel and Liebknecht went further. They voted against the new war credits and urged the government to conclude an immediate peace with France and to renounce any annexation of French territory. To them, the war had become 'a war against the French people, not a war of defence, but a war of conquest, not a war for the independence of Germany, but a war for the subjugation of the noble French nation ...' Throughout Germany the party organised meetings against the annexation of Alsace and Lorraine and for an honourable peace with France. Its leaders were virtually the only Germans who realised that the annexation did 'not bring peace but war', as it created the continuing danger of another war, and that within Germany it strengthened the forces of military reaction.[6] History has justified this policy of the young and weak party.

The German constitution of 1871 was sharply criticised by Bebel in the Reichstag. On 25 May he attacked it as 'sham constitutionalism' and 'naked ceasarism' so that the chairman intervened and prevented him from continuing his speech. Bebel also bravely defended the

[6] Bebel, *Aus meinem Leben*, ii, pp. 179, 186, 194–96; *Der Hochverrats-Prozess wider Liebknecht, Bebel, Hepner vor dem Schwurgericht zu Leipzig vom 11. bis 26. März 1872*, 2nd ed. (Berlin, 1911), pp. 312–13, 414–18.

Commune of Paris which had been brutally suppressed by the troops of the Versailles government, with the indirect help of Bismarck. In another Reichstag speech on 8 November 1871 he reminded his listeners 'that the battle in Paris is but a small encounter of outposts, that the main action in Europe is still to come and that, before many decades have passed, the battle-cry of the Parisian proletarians "war to the palaces, peace to the cottages, death to want and idleness!" will have become the battle-cry of the entire European proletariat'. No wonder that Bebel quickly earned the hatred of the respectable middle-class citizens and of the authorities of Bismarck's Germany. In the Leipzig treason trial of 1872, in which these and other speeches figured prominently in the indictment, he was sentenced once more to a term of imprisonment lasting two years. Some years later, when the Reichstag at Bismarck's insistence voted the law against the socialists, a renewed and more severe wave of persecution was unleashed against the social-democrats, leading to repeated banishments and expulsions of the leaders from their places of residence. These petty police measures undermined the existence of many party functionaries, but they kept alive the spirit of rebellion and the solidarity among the party members, who were treated like potential criminals by the authorities and looked at like pariahs by society. They were not part of the nation, but outside it.

Among the social-democrats this created an attitude of permanent protest and hostility to the state and its organs. It also created, as the members' loyalty never faltered and the party continued to grow, an almost touching belief in the masses and an easy optimism as to the future, ideas which remained characteristic of the leaders of the German Left. But there was considerable friction and disagreement among the party leaders, and in 1881 Bebel wrote to Engels: 'Fortunately the masses, as always, are better than the leaders and one day they will march ahead without taking notice of them ... To me it is incomprehensible that one can look into the future with anything other than hope considering our state of affairs ...' Two years later he reaffirmed his belief that 'only the best was to be hoped for' from the masses.[7] At the party congress at Erfurt in October 1891 he again proclaimed, this time as an argument against the moderates in the party, his 'great confidence in the good sense and the revolutionary instincts of the masses'. Against those who feared that the masses were not mature enough to make proper use of political power if it fell into the party's hands, Bebel argued at the Dresden party congress two years later, 'that in every great popular movement the right men have been found at the right time'; and he pointed to the work done by party members in the trade unions, in social insurance, in arbitration courts for trade disputes, and in parliament, as evidence of what working men could achieve. Yet this was a question which the critics were only too justified in putting. In 1918 power fell to the social-democrats, and the task of governing

[7] *Aus meinem Leben*, iii, pp. 169, 252.

Germany found them completely unprepared. The problems of political power and its use had never been discussed, and subconsciously the party leaders did not believe that power would fall to them within the foreseeable future.

EQUALLY vague were Bebel's ideas about the methods which the SPD was going to use to achieve its aims. In 1870 he wrote: 'Whether the working class, following the example of the feudal nobility and the bourgeoisie, will use the same violent means ... and will confiscate the private property of the bourgeoisie and transform it into common property ... that is difficult to establish. The course of this development depends on the intensity with which the participating groups are drawn into the movement; it depends on the resistance which the movement encounters among its enemies.... There are two ways to achieve our goal. The first consists in the gradual displacement of the private entrepreneurs through legislation after the establishment of the democratic state. This route would be followed if the adversaries of the Social-Democratic movement in good time saw sense.... The other, much shorter, but also more violent route would be that of forcible expropriation, the elimination of the private entrepreneurs at one blow, by whatever methods. Accordingly, the outcome of the crisis depends on the capitalist class itself, the character of the crisis is determined by the ways in which it uses the means of power it possesses....'[8]

Twenty years later, at the party congress of 1891, Bebel officially renounced the use of force, the building of barricades, in his opinion the means of the bourgeois party, and proclaimed: 'Bougeois society works so assiduously towards its own demise that we have merely to await the moment when we can pick up the power that is sliding from its hands.... Yes, I am convinced that the realisation of our ultimate goals is so near that only a few present in this hall will not see those days....' In his opinion, 'a party which has millions behind it must operate more cautiously than a sect without any importance and any responsibility', like an 'army fighting against a vastly superior enemy that could not take its position by a frontal assault without bashing in its heads. It thus must advance inch by inch, pace by pace against the enemy until it can risk the decisive battle ...'[9] These two pronouncements are difficult to reconcile with each other. If the enemy was 'vastly superior', how could the realisation of the socialists' ultimate goals be that near? How could they be certain that the capitalists would dig their own graves so that the socialists simply had to wait for the day when power would slide from the grasp of the bourgeoisie? No answer to these questions was attempted. Nor did Bebel and Liebknecht have

---

[8] Bebel, *Unsere Ziele*, 14th ed. (Berlin, 1919), pp. 19, 50.
[9] *Protokoll über die Verhandlungen des Parteitages der SPD, abgehalten zu Erfurt* (Berlin, 1891), pp. 57, 172.

a ready answer to the rhetorical question of the public prosecutor at their Leipzig trial whether the accused really believed that the princes would amicably descend from their thrones, that the civil servants would readily join the republican party, and that the commanding officers would voluntarily absolve the soldiers from their oaths of allegiance? [10]

Yet in other respects Bebel was a political realist. When, after the experiences of the Russian revolution of 1905, the Left in the SPD advocated the use of the general strike, especially to prevent the outbreak of war, Bebel replied: 'You have no idea of the situation that existed in 1870 at the outbreak of war. It is true that meanwhile we have become stronger; but the power at the disposal of our adversaries has also grown tremendously. . . . Who can believe that it is possible to organise a mass strike at a time when enormous excitement, a fever, grips the masses and stirs up the lowest depths, when the danger of a colossal war with its frightful misery faces us? That is a naive idea. At the outbreak of such a war five million men are called up in Germany the first day, among them many hundreds of thousands of party comrades. . . . If the party leaders were so rash as to proclaim on such a day a general strike, a state of siege would be declared throughout Germany together with general mobilisation, and then not the civil courts, but courts-martial would have the power of decision. . . .' [11]

If, however, Germany were attacked by another power, the social-democrats, Bebel declared at the Erfurt congress, were as ready as any other party to defend the country. If Russia, ' the incarnation of cruelty and barbarism, the enemy of all human culture ', should attack Germany, ' we are as much and more interested than those who are ruling Germany and we shall oppose the aggressor. . . . If then we should fight side by side with those who today are our enemies, we would do this not so as to save them and their political and social order, but so as to save Germany, that is ourselves, and to free our soil from a barbarian who is the greatest enemy of our endeavours and whose victory would mean our defeat as social-democrats. . . .' [12] Words such as these, pronounced as early as 1891, were to have fatal consequences nearly a quarter of a century later when a Russian army penetrated into Germany. There is little doubt, on the other hand, that even with these utterances Bebel was much closer to the German masses than many intellectuals who were dreaming of a general strike and revolution.

BEBEL was on equally firm ground when he declined to use the weapon of the general strike to unhinge bourgeois society. He steadfastly maintained that the task of the SPD was to fight for concrete rights which were vital to the working class. If, for example, an attempt

---

[10] *Der Hochverrats-Prozess wider Liebknecht, Bebel, Hepner*, p. 546.
[11] *Protokoll über die Verhandlungen des Parteitages der SPD, abgehalten zu Mannheim vom 23. bis 29 September 1906* (Berlin, 1906), pp. 240–41.
[12] *Protokoll über die Verhandlungen des Parteitages der SPD, abgehalten zu Erfurt*, p. 285.

was made to abolish the universal franchise, then SPD resistance could reckon with a good deal of sympathy in bourgeois circles. 'Apart from that, we possess far more power when defending a right that we have had for decades than when we want to conquer a new right.' If the authorities violated the right to form trade unions, to hold meetings or found political associations, and perhaps if the question of eliminating the Prussian three-class franchise became acute, then the weapon of the general strike might be used.[13] What Bebel advocated was a defensive, not an offensive strategy; it was not a strategy in the fight for socialism, but in defence of certain democratic rights. Quite logically, he was prepared to support all genuine liberal demands put forward by the representatives of the bourgeoisie. 'That we have done in the past and will do in the future, and it will be entirely agreeable to me and to my party comrades if we are often put into the position of giving support to demands of the bourgeois parties....'[14]

Yet Bebel was against coalitions with bourgeois parties because he was convinced 'that not the social-democrats, but the bourgeois parties would be the gainers and we the losers. It is a political law that, wherever the Right and the Left combine, the Left loses and the Right gains....'[15] Although this may not be a political law, Bebel's maxim was in many ways confirmed by the experiences of the SPD after 1918 when it formed coalition governments with non-socialist parties. When the principles of the party were at stake Bebel would not make any concessions, not even to attract voters. When the Bavarian social-democrats under Georg von Vollmar, who had to work in a country still largely agrarian, urged that the wishes of the peasants should be taken into account, Bebel replied in 1894 at the Frankfurt SPD congress: 'consideration for the peasants and similar backward elements must not influence us; if the peasants will not be convinced we need not bother about them. Their prejudices, their ignorance, their limitations must not induce us to relax any of our principles. You [turning to the Bavarian delegates] are not the representatives of the Bavarian peasants, but of the intelligent industrial workers, and you have to preserve our programme pure and undiluted. If the peasants do not come to us as it is, the difficulties of the time will teach them to think anyway....'[16] With this basic attitude, the SPD—under Bebel as well as after him—was never able to penetrate into circles outside the industrial working classes, nor did it ever show any interest in the problems of land reform and dividing the large estates of the nobility. The party remained a working-class party and could not gain a majority.

---

[13] *Protokoll über die Verhandlungen des Parteitages der SPD, abgehalten zu Jena vom 17. bis 23. September 1905* (Berlin, 1905), pp. 308–09.
[14] Bebel to Haussmann, 7 October 1909; quoted by Fricke, *Zeitschrift für Geschichtswissenschaft*, 1960, p. 289.
[15] *Protokoll über die Verhandlungen des Parteitages der SPD, abgehalten zu Magdeburg vom 18. bis 24. September 1910* (Berlin, 1910), p. 252.
[16] *Protokoll über die Verhandlungen des Parteitages der SPD, abgehalten zu Frankfurt vom 21. bis 27. Oktober 1894* (Berlin, 1894), p. 118.

Bebel was also determined to ward off any attack on the principles of the party from within. In his opinion, these came chiefly from Eduard Bernstein and his supporters on the right wing, who aimed at transforming the SPD into a party of social reform. That, Bebel wrote, amounted to giving up the name of Social-Democrats and becoming Social-Liberals, and this he could not support ' because I cannot go along with it as it is contrary to all my convictions '. Those who in truth no longer belonged to social-democracy should leave the party. Some months later he still believed that a reconciliation was impossible and a breach with the reformers inevitable.[17] Yet here Bernstein saw more clearly than Bebel. The SPD had never been a revolutionary party, as the Bolsheviks and Rosa Luxemburg's Polish Socialist party were. In reality, no principles were at stake between Bebel and Bernstein; hence a compromise was possible, and no breach occurred. For the later development of the SPD Bernstein's theories proved more important than the slogans of the past, which dated from the years of struggle with the police and of persecution under the law against the socialists. In Bebel's time the SPD remained a party of revolutionary slogans and reformist practices and tried above all to improve the lot of the working classes within the existing society. With the outbreak of the first world war the radical slogans of the past, too, were assigned to limbo.

HOW little Bebel was at home in the world of the east European revolutionary parties is shown by a curious intermezzo which took place in 1904–5. The faction fights among the Russian and Polish socialists occupied the attention of the International Socialist Bureau and of the International Socialist Congress which met in Amsterdam in 1904. While, in addition to the Bolsheviks and Mensheviks, the Russian Socialist-Revolutionaries were accepted as members of the International, the same privilege was refused to the Jewish Socialist *Bund* which had its main strength in Russian Poland. There two rival Polish parties were fighting each other: Pilsudski's Polish Socialist party, the PPS, and Rosa Luxemburg's Social-Democratic party of the Kingdom of Poland and Lithuania. Representatives of Ukrainian, Latvian, and Armenian socialist groups had also appeared in Amsterdam. The chaotic conditions in the Russian revolutionary movement at a time of growing internal tension and Russian defeats at Japanese hands made it appear doubtful whether the revolutionary forces could ever be co-ordinated for attacks upon the Tsarist regime, which at this juncture were more promising than ever before. Hence the leaders of the Socialist International tried to bring about a reconciliation among the warring factions. In October 1904 Bebel wrote to the Menshevik leader Axelrod and suggested that 'those Russian socialist factions which are so close to each other that a common cooperation is possible' should meet at

---

[17] *Victor Adler, Briefwechsel mit August Bebel und Karl Kautsky*, pp. 268–69, 309.

a conference to discuss measures of cooperation and unification. Among these groups Bebel mentioned the followers of Lenin, the Jewish *Bund*, the Poles, and the Latvians. Above all, however, Axelrod's friends should agree to the plan, as Bebel did not want to start an enterprise which was 'utterly hopeless'. Neither the participation of the Socialist-Revolutionaries nor of the PPS was envisaged, probably because the objections of the other Russian and Polish groups were considered too strong.[18]

Yet even in this truncated form the plan did not prosper. At the end of 1904 Bebel reported that Axelrod, whose participation was vital, was 'curiously reticent, half yes, half no'. He did not want to take the initiative, but was willing to come if Bebel called the conference. The latter believed 'that the attempt must be made to bring the hostile parties together, for everything about which they quarrel and disagree is mere rubbish (*Quark*) compared with what is in practice at stake and what should be worked for. If these people cannot now master the situation they are acting irresponsibly. . . .' At the beginning of 1905 Bebel tried to arrange that the conference should meet in Zürich in the course of January and asked the Austrian socialist leader Victor Adler to arrange for the invitation of certain Polish and Ukrainian groups. But Axelrod still objected to the participation of the Socialist-Revolutionaries and the PPS on grounds which Bebel considered very threadbare (*besonders fadenscheinig*), and soon also to the invitation of Lenin.[19] Rosa Luxemburg, on the other hand, was violently opposed to Adler as a mediator because he protected the PPS, and she reproached Axelrod for consenting at all to the summoning of the conference. In her opinion, Bebel and the Germans had not 'the faintest idea' about the differences among the Russian parties and were inclined to 'agreements made out of thin air'. Amidst this confusion, Bebel had to give up the whole plan.

But this was not the end of his attempts at mediation. A few weeks later he once more wrote, this time only to the Mensheviks and the Bolsheviks, that the split had caused 'great dismay and lively disapproval' among the socialists of other countries; he hoped it would be possible, in view of the developments inside Russia, 'to find common ground for the struggle against the common enemy'. The rival parties should accept the decision of an arbitration court of five which would meet in Zürich under Bebel's chairmanship.[20] This time the Mensheviks accepted Bebel's suggestion, but Lenin refused: in his opinion, the split in the Russian party was a fact that could not be decided upon by foreign comrades, but only by a Russian party congress. Lenin's refusal

---

[18] D. Geyer, 'Die russische Parteispaltung im Urteil der deutschen Sozialdemokratie', *International Review of Social History* (Amsterdam), 1958, pp. 418–20.
[19] Bebel to Adler, 28 December 1904, 4 and 8 January 1905: *Victor Adler, Briefwechsel mit August Bebel und Karl Kautsky*, pp. 446, 452.
[20] Luxemburg to Axelrod, 9 January 1905; Bebel to the Mensheviks, 3 February 1905: Geyer, *loc. cit.*, pp. 426–27, 430.

was upheld by other Bolshevik representatives abroad, who referred to the views held by the local groups in Russia which were allegedly repudiating all attempts at reconciliation and demanding the summoning of a party congress.[21] When the congress met in London at the end of April 1905 it was a Bolshevik affair, while the Mensheviks simultaneously held their own counter-conference at Geneva. The outcome was a deepening of the split, the creation of separate organisations of the two groups. Bebel commented acidly to Axelrod: 'It must be said openly that the influence of the emigrés on the Russian movement, effective as it has once been, is at the moment merely disastrous and damaging. . . . It is a case which has never occurred previously that, in the midst of a revolution, the leaders abroad manage to hold a congress which ends in the exacerbation of the conflicts. Such an action amounts almost to unscrupulousness and complete incapacity to be the leaders of the movement. . . . ' Bebel was now determined not to 'lift a finger any more in the whole affair unless the hostile parties put forward a *common* proposal'; he thought it ridiculous to thrust upon them the idea of 'a conciliation conference with which the parties in question will have nothing to do'.[22] The plan was never revived.

Bebel's approach to these involved factional struggles, partly political, partly personal, was that of common sense. He was the leader of a democratic mass party in which such conflicts were openly discussed and if need be voted upon, but did not lead to splits. To him the issues at stake between Bolsheviks and Mensheviks, between them and the different Polish groups, and among the latter, must have appeared incomprehensible and due to personal animosities. In a letter to Adler he wrote: 'The split among the Poles is as *unqualifizierbar* (irrational, impossible to define) as that among the Russians. . . .'[23] Nobody at that time could foretell that the splits were destined to make world history.

During his life-time Bebel was venerated by the German workers 'like a king', as Helmuth von Gerlach put it in 1909; 'no one is loved so fervently by so many as he is'.[24] Yet half a century after his death it seems difficult to recapture that spirit. His writings seem curiously old-fashioned, a period piece rather than living socialist thought. Clearly, it was the man that counted, his honesty, his sincere convictions, his courage, his faculty of keeping together the party and invigorating it with his spirit. None of the later SPD leaders—neither Friedrich Ebert, nor Otto Wels, nor any of the post-war leaders—possessed these gifts. None of them was so universally recognised and respected, none so deservedly popular as Bebel.

---

[21] O. Pjatnizki, *Aufzeichnungen eines Bolschewiks* (Berlin, 1930), pp. 88–89.
[22] Geyer, *loc. cit.*, pp. 437, 440–41.
[23] Bebel to Adler, 30 May 1905: *Victor Adler, Briefwechsel mit August Bebel und Karl Kautsky*, p. 455.
[24] Quoted by Fricke, *Zeitschrift für Geschichtswissenschaft*, 1963, p. 1047.

17

THE FORERUNNERS
OF NATIONAL SOCIALISM IN AUSTRIA

'Forerunners of National Socialism in Austria' is a large subject that makes it necessary to go back to the period before 1918, to the time of the severe national conflicts in the Habsburg Monarchy in the later 19th century. The *Ausgleich* of 1867 had brought the Magyars autonomy and important privileges, but it had not solved the problems of the Slav nationalities who formed the majority of the inhabitants of the Dual Monarchy. On the contrary, Poles, Czechs, Slovenes and Croats now demanded rights similar to those which had been granted to the Magyars in 1867. While these until 1918 successfully preserved their position in the kingdom of Hungary against the pressure of the Slav nationalities and Magyarized many thousands of Slavs without arousing strong opposition, the position in the Austrian half of the Monarchy was quite different. There the German-speaking inhabitants still occupied a disproportionate share of the leading posts in the army and the bureaucracy, and German remained the official language without a knowledge of which it was impossible to get an important post; but even according to the official statistics the Germans only formed a good third of the population. And their share did not grow as did that of the Hungarians in their Kingdom, but it slowly declined: from 36.8 per cent of the total in 1880 to 35.8 per cent in 1900, while that of the Slavs grew correspondingly.[1]

The German minority found itself clearly on the defensive. It defended positions which could not be held for ever; it felt itself threatened by real and by imaginary dangers. It clang to privileges which were out of date, instead of giving way to the promptings of the Slav nationalities and seeking a genuine *Ausgleich* with them. Thus the well known Linz Programme of the German Liberals of 1882 demanded that only those should be permitted to hold official posts who spoke fluent German, that in the public administration only German should be spoken, and the same should apply to parliament and the army. The intellectual fathers of the Linz Programme were two men who later became leading Socialists, and were certainly not the protagonists of an exaggerated German nationalism, Victor Adler and Engelbert Pernerstorfer; and apart from them a third man who is far

---

[1] The figures for 1880, 1890, 1900 and 1910 are given by R. A. Kann, *A History of the Habsburg Empire 1526–1918*, Berkeley-London, 1974, p. 607.

more important for this theme: Georg Ritter von Schönerer.[2] It was due to his prompting that three years later another sentence was added to the Linz Programme: 'To carry out the envisaged reforms it is indispensable to eradicate the Jewish influence from all spheres of the public life.'[3]

The Austrian Germans felt threatened not only by the advance of the Slavs and their demands for equal rights, but also by the growing influence of the Jewish minority which occupied leading positions in the economic and cultural life of Vienna. All that has to be mentioned here is the vital importance of Jewish bankers such as the Rothschilds or the high percentage of Jewish students and teachers at the University of Vienna, especially in the legal and medical faculties. It is true that the large majority of the Jewish students and teachers felt they were Germans and were in favour of assimilation; but that did not diminish the feeling of threat and competition among their non-Jewish colleagues. While in Hungary the Jews were successfully Magyarized, barriers against them began to be erected at the Austrian universities. This applied in particular to the student corporations, the *Burschenschaften*, which since their foundation in the early 19th century had been strongholds of German nationalism and liberalism and had hitherto accepted Jewish students without any difficulty. But in the eighteen-seventies some *Burschenschaften* began to refuse to accept Jews or baptized Jews as members – a rule which was soon extended to students who were only partly of Jewish origin. The German nationalist and anti-semitic student corporations soon provided Schönerer with his most enthusiastic followers, and it seems that it was under their influence that he became a racial anti-semite. The *Burschenschaften* had always been decidedly 'national' in their views, for German unity "from the Meuse to the Memel, from the Adige to the Belt", and their colours had always been the black, red and gold of a united Germany. This clearly included the German parts of the Habsburg Monarchy, and also crown lands in which the population was not entirely German as well as some where the Germans were only a minority. That posed the question what the frontiers of a united Germany were to be. As is shown by the quotation from the *Deutschlandlied*, most Germans were only too inclined to draw them very extensively. Above all, in their view Bohemia and Moravia – in spite of their Czech majority – must form part of a united Germany: an opinion which was shared even by Marx and Engels.

The history of the 19th century seemed to have repudiated these longings, for the German Empire of 1871 was a smaller Germany –

---

[2] For Schönerer see above all: A. G. Whiteside, *The Socialism of Fools – Georg Ritter von Schönerer and Austrian Pan-Germanism*, Berkeley-London, 1975; and as an important collection of sources, E. Pichl, *Georg Schönerer*, 6 vols., Oldenburg, 1938.

[3] Pichl, op. cit., i, p. 115.

without Austria and Bohemia, the Netherlands and German Switzerland. In the German Empire Bismarck's solution of the German question was generally accepted, but not so by the German nationalists of Austria. On the contrary, the powerful Bismarckian Empire acted like a magnet, and the favourite song of the Austrian *Burschenschaften* was 'The Watch on the Rhine', which at least after 1815 was no longer a concern of Austria. The German Empire appeared immensely strong and united, without any real conflict, if compared with the Dual Monarchy with its bitter national struggles and its continuous internal unrest. As early as 1879, before he became an anti-semite, Schönerer exclaimed in the Austrian Parliament: 'If only we would belong to the German Empire!' Or as he put it later in a more poetic form:

> In the great year Seventy,
> There sounded the Watch on the Rhine;
> Germania has arisen –
> Never to sleep again . . .
>
> Germania, let sound your bugle
> Far and wide, so that
> The sons of the Eastern March
> Can build their German house![4]

A strong German nationalism was an ideology popular in the German parts of the Dual Monarchy, by no means only on the political Right. What distinguished the Schönerer movement was its racial anti-semitism and its anti-clericalism: traits which were to reappear in the later *völkisch* and National Socialist organizations. The general form of anti-semitism, in Germany as well as in Austria, was not racialist. Jews who converted to Christianity could rise to the highest positions in state and church, they were frequently ennobled or married into old noble families. This widely spread anti-semitism was more social in its connotation and differentiated between the assimilated Jews who had long been domiciled in Vienna or other towns and the non-assimilated Eastern Jews. It found its poignant expression in the famous phrase of Karl Lueger, the popular mayor of Vienna: 'I decide who is a Jew.' Like Schönerer Lueger had originally been a German Liberal, and later he became an anti-semite and a clerical – as it seems because he thought that this would attract the masses more strongly than liberalism. In any case in the late 'eighties Lueger supported the anti-semitic initiatives of Schönerer in the Austrian Parliament and demonstrations of sympathy with Schönerer outside parliament.

What distinguished Schönerer's anti-semitism from that of Lueger was his racialism which discriminated against people who were only

---

[4] Ibid, i, p. 70; ii, p. 542. Later the National Socialists too referred to Austria as 'the Eastern March'.

partly of Jewish origin and stressed the superiority of the 'Germanic race' over all other human races. In 1887 the *Erste Wiener Turnverein* changed its bylaws so that in future only Germans 'of Aryan descent' could become members; soon eight local gymnastic clubs in Austria followed this example. In 1902 the *Deutsche Turnerbund* had 133 associated clubs in Austria with about 13,000 members. The printed bylaws of all these clubs prescribed that only Germans 'of Aryan descent' could be accepted as active or passive members.[5] In 1888, 407 local communes of the Waldviertel, where Schönerer's castle of Rosenau was situated, sent a petition to the government which was clearly written under his influence: 'But we have no intention to show cosmopolitan politeness to immigrant Asiatic foreigners and we demand, of course, that posts in offices and schools in our old German district are not to be given to people who not only have an insufficient command of the German language, but who are totally foreign to German ways and customs and German sentiment . . . In reality the Jews are a foreign nation and foreign race who are not inclined to show humanity and toleration towards us, but who consider it their tribal right to exploit us through lying and cheating and if possible completely to subjugate us . . .'[6] In his journal *Unverfälschte Deutsche Worte*, Schönerer wrote in 1883 he believed that it was easier to mix with Slavs and Latins than with Jews because the former were 'as Aryans tribally related to us', while the latter had nothing in common with the Germans.[7]

In addition Schönerer venerated all things Germanic, which expressed itself in the rejection of the Christian calendar and the Christian way of dating. Germanic names were to replace those of the Latin months, and the year 1 was to start not with the birth of Christ, but with the victory of the Cimbri and Teutonici over the Romans at Noreia in Styria in the year 113 B.C.[8] Schönerer's followers sported 'Germanic ornaments' or figures of hanged Jews in silver dangling from their watch chains. His picture adorned pocket knives, beer mugs, pipes and cigarette holders. Yet the movement created by him never became a mass movement, although it had numerous enthusiastic adherents among the students and the lower middle class of Vienna, as well as in the countryside, especially in Lower Austria. Out of a total of 3260 men who signed Schönerer's electoral address of 1883, more than a quarter worked in agriculture, and there also were many academics and others with a secondary education, and many craftsmen and artisans.[9] Exactly the same social groups fifty years later were to furnish the National Socialists with an enthusiastic following.

[5] Ibid., ii, pp. 381–2; P. G. J. Pulzer, *The Rise of Political Anti-Semitism in Germany and Austria*, New York, 1964, p. 223.
[6] Pichl, op. cit., i, pp. 353–5.
[7] Ibid., ii, p. 59.
[8] Ibid., ii, pp. 428–9.
[9] For details see D. van Arkel, *Antisemitism in Austria*, Leiden, 1966, pp. 136–44.

The growth of the Schönerer movement into a mass party was prevented in the first place by the fact that the general situation in the Habsburg Monarchy until 1914 remained relatively stable, in spite of all conflict and unrest, and that economic growth continued in spite of many crises, that there was no inflation and no mass unemployment. Furthermore, Schönerer possessed no integrating or charismatic personality, but he constantly quarrelled even with his most faithful disciples; one after the other of them left his party or was expelled from it, so that soon there were several 'Pan-German' or 'Free-Pan-German' parties. Schönerer also committed serious tactical mistakes, for example when he made a violent physical attack on the staff of the *Neues Wiener Tagblatt*, in consequence of which he was sentenced to rigorous imprisonment of four months and the loss of his parliamentary seat.[10] His most serious tactical error probably was – in a strictly Catholic country – his slogan of 'Break with Rome', his rejection of the Old Testament as the 'Jew Bible', and his propaganda for conversion to Protestantism. In 1913 Schöner proudly claimed that more than 70,000 men and women had left the Catholic Church. But this was a minute number, and it seems likely that many of them had left the church out of their socialist conviction and not on account of Pan-German propaganda. His anti-Catholicism earned Schönerer the bitter enmity of the Catholic Church, in contrast with the Christian Social movement of Lueger, which was also anti-semitic but developed into a mass party thanks to the support of the clergy. Even one of his most loyal adherents, the deputy Dr. Eisenkolb, warned Schönerer that their 'evangelical cause' suffered damage because the *Unverfälschte Deutsche Worte* wrote so often of the 'Jew Bible'.[11] But Schönerer could not be induced to change his line. As he expressed it himself in 1903, the 'Pan-Germans' could well become a mass party if they renounced certain basic programmatical demands: 'that would produce a large party, but also bring about the end of the German people.'[12] In general, it seems questionable whether the movement could have become a mass party in the conditions of pre-1914; it would have had to overcome the competition of the Christian Social and Social Democratic parties, and this would have been very difficult.

Yet one should not for that reason underestimate the importance of the Schönerer movement. It influenced the *Burschenschaften* and other sections of the academic youth, and many of them rose to leading positions in the bureaucracy and in economic and academic life. Ardent followers of Schönerer can be found later not only in the nationalist Grossdeutsche Party, but also in the Heimwehren and other right-wing

---

[10] For details see Whiteside, op. cit., pp. 132–7.
[11] Pichl, op. cit., vi, pp. 385–8.
[12] Ibid., vi, p. 56.

organizations, and above all among the National Socialists. As Professor Adam Wandruszka has written: 'In the last period of the Monarchy almost all young people of the national camp were strongly influenced, at least for a time, by the 'Pan-German' ideology of Schönerer . . . Now [i.e. in the 1930s] in their riper age . . . the ideals of their youth appeared to be brilliantly confirmed by the successes of National Socialism in the German Empire. Thus often a kind of intoxication . . . permeated the older generation to which National Socialism was in the first instance often brought by the younger generation, so that the fathers adopted the political views of their sons in the conviction that they were experiencing a second youth.'[13] These words were written from personal experience, and they clearly reflect the great importance of Schönerer in preparing the way for National Socialism. Certainly, there were also many youngsters who did not belong to the 'national camp', but this comprised many elements of the first importance.

The *völkisch* ideology which influenced these youngsters was totally unrealistic. It peopled the world with Germanic gods and with devils, with races destined to rule and superior to all other races, and with others whose ultimate destiny was slavery and subjugation. It was a backward-looking and romantic ideology which repudiated anything modern in art and literature, thought longingly of the greatness of the Middle Ages and of the Holy Roman Empire of the German Nation, and dreamt of repeating the deeds of the Nibelungen and the Teutonic Knights, of replacing Slav by Teuton. In spite of this – or perhaps because of it – it influenced many thousands. At the beginning of the 20th century it seemed as if anti-semitism and the *völkisch* ideology were losing their influence, in Austria as well as in Germany. But the great catastrophies of the First World War, the collapse of the monarchies and the vast inflation were to give them a new lease of life and provide them with the mass basis which they had been lacking.

Apart from these forerunners of National Socialism in the *völkisch* camp, there also existed a direct progenitor of Austrian National Socialism: the German Workers' Party founded in 1904 by German-speaking trade unionists at Trautenau in Bohemia. In the industrialized districts of northern Bohemia a sharp social and national conflict developed in the late 19th century between the native German workers and immigrating Czech workers who in the opinion of the Germans were willing to work for lower wages than the Germans. The skilled German workers in the mines, printing works, textile factories and on the railways, felt themselves threatened by the Czechs whose standard of living was lower than their own. In 1898 the representatives of several thousand workmen met and founded the association of unions

[13] A. Wandruszka, 'Österreichs politische Struktur', in: H. Benedikt (ed.), *Geschichte der Republik Österreich*, Vienna, 1954, p. 405.

of German journeymen and workmen, which was to represent their interests, only accepted 'Aryans' as members and recognized Schönerer as their patron. In the following year, the first German workers' congress met at Eger; it was attended not only by delegates from the industrial areas of northern Bohemia, but also from Vienna and Graz, Munich and Berlin. The demands put forward by the congress were partly national and anti-Czech, and partly social, such as the nationalization of large-scale industry, the mines and railways. The weaver Hans Knirsch, who later became a leading National Socialist, moved that a greeting address be sent to Schönerer, 'the leader of the German people of the Eastern March', which was unanimously accepted. In 1901 the association had 82 member unions with about 14,000 members.[14] The *völkisch* unions were an important political feature of Bohemia and Austria in general; they and the *völkisch* gymnastic clubs were later to offer a choice recruiting ground to the National Socialists and to provide many of their officials.

The German Workers' Party was a product of these *völkisch* trade unions and was founded by prominent union members. In its programme of 15 August 1904 the new party declared that, in contrast with Social Democracy, it was not 'a narrow minded class party', but 'a liberal and national party which opposes with all its might the reactionary tendencies, the feudal, clerical and capitalist privileges and any influence of alien *völkisch* groups'. It demanded the introduction of the equal, general and direct franchise, the right of free association and assembly, freedom of speech and the press, and far-reaching political self-government.[15] These were radical, democratic demands, as they were also put forward by the left-wing parties. Added to these were in the later party programmes *völkisch* and anti-capitalist slogans. Thus the programme adopted in 1913 declared: 'The working class has a very special interest in the position of power, the preservation and expansion of the living space of its people . . . Austrian Social Democracy is a child of the German party, and its international principles were to undergo here their decisive test. Under the impact of reality the whole dogmatic edifice collapsed ignominiously. Only the poor comrades of the 'German tongue' have remained loyal to them – to their own detriment. They who created Social Democracy with their contributions were pushed out of their work-places in many districts by the heartily welcomed Slav comrades. The German entrepreneur took on the cheaper Slav workman . . . We have recognized the pernicious results of the international dogmas for our own nation and the duplicity

---

[14] For details see A. G. Whiteside, *Austrian National Socialism before 1918*, The Hague, 1962, pp. 38, 49, 52, 60–3; Pichl, op. cit., vi, pp. 219, 226–7.

[15] A. Ciller, *Vorläufer des Nationalsozialismus*, Vienna, 1932, p. 135; A. G. Whiteside 'Nationaler Sozialismus in Österreich vor 1918', *Vierteljahrshefte für Zeitgeschichte*, ix, 1961, pp. 333–4.

of Social Democracy, led by Jews and inter-twined with the mobile big capitalists.' The programme further demanded the 'socialization of the monopolies', the 'prohibition of all income without work', and called for a struggle against 'interest slavery', capitalism, Marxism and the Jews.[16] This was the first time that certain slogans appeared which after the war were to figure in the programme of the NSDAP; it was to show the same characteristic mixture of *völkisch*, nationalist, radical and socialist demands.

Before the collapse of the Habsburg Monarchy, in August 1918, the German Workers' Party changed its name to 'German National Socialist Workers' Party' – several years before the use of that name in Munich. At the same time yet another party programme was published which combined *völkisch* with certain socialist demands: 'the transfer of all large capitalist enterprises in which private management is damaging the common weal into the possession of the state . . . or the commune . . . Elimination of the predominance of the Jewish banks in economic life'. There also figured a clearly imperialistic slogan: 'unification of the whole area of German settlement in Europe (!) in a democratic and social German Empire', as well as the fight against 'the parasitic power of the Jewish and free-trading spirit in all spheres of public life'. The party was small, but in 1911 it succeeded in gaining 31,000 votes and three seats in the Austrian Parliament against Social Democratic rivals; in 1914 the *völkisch* trade unions had, according to their own figures, 45,000 members in Austria.[17] These figures were not all that low, even compared with the much stronger Free trade unions. In any case, the party founded in Bohemia in 1904 had a much stronger claim to the name of a 'workers' party' than the party founded in Munich fifteen years later, which was above all a party of the lower middle classes. But in the opinion of the convinced Pan-Germans of the Schönerer school the German Workers' Party was 'black and yellow', i.e. its aim was not the destruction of the Habsburg Monarchy and union with Germany. As we have seen, its ideology was nevertheless strictly *völkisch* and German imperialist, and it was a direct forerunner of National Socialism.

The collapse of 1918 brought it about that the Austrian National Socialists found themselves distributed among three states: German Austria, Czechoslovakia and Poland. Of these, the party in Bohemia was by far the strongest. At the 'deliberations of the National Socialists of Greater Germany' which took place in Vienna in December 1919, the party in Bohemia was accorded four votes, compared with two for the party in Austria, and one each for smaller groups in Germany and in Polish Silesia. The leader of the Austrian National Socialist Party, Dr Walter Riehl, also came from Bohemia; he had a flourishing legal

[16] Whiteside, 'Nationaler Sozialismus in Österreich vor 1918', pp. 344–6.
[17] Ciller, op. cit., pp. 90, 96, 140–2.

practice in Vienna, was the grandson of a radical deputy in the German Parliament of 1848, and as a young man had been an active Social Democrat. At the party conference of the Austrian National Socialists, which took place simultaneously with that of 'the National Socialists of Greater Germany', the officials of two German trade unions spoke on the subject of 'Party and Union', and several German trade unions were represented.[18] The close links between these unions and the party had been preserved, as had been the social composition of the party. But among its leaders men with academic degrees or the title of engineer prevailed; and the most important among the *völkisch* trade unions was the *Deutschnationale Handlungsgehilfenverband*, a white-collar union, which was also strong in Germany and provided several of the early leaders of the NSDAP. The social composition of the Austrian party was rather mixed, and it was a purely urban party without any influence among the peasantry. A police report on the foundation of the party group in Innsbruck from the year 1920 mentioned as members 'circles of the intelligentsia, people with fixed salaries, office workers, railway employees and servants':[19] a classification which probably also applied to other local groups.

What helped National Socialist propaganda and gave it an echo in large circles of the population was the wave of fierce anti-semitism which permeated Central Europe after the collapse of 1918. This was closely connected with the widespread fear of Bolshevism which seemed ready to engulf Central Europe, above all after the proclamation of the Hungarian Soviet Republic in March 1919. In Austria, and especially in Vienna, there existed at the same time a strong movement of workers' and soldiers' councils and a dangerous agitation of Communist emissaries from Hungary in favour of the proclamation of an Austrian Soviet Republic. The council movement and 'Bolshevism' could easily be identified, and there was also a 'Jewish danger', seemingly proved by the fact that in Moscow as well as in Budapest Jews were very prominent among the leaders of the new Soviet governments. In Austria too, Jews for the first time occupied prominent government posts, such as Otto Bauer, the Foreign Minister, or Julius Deutsch, the Minister of Defence. That it was due to them in particular that the danger of communist revolution receded was intentionally overlooked.

In Vienna there lived at the end of the war about 20,000 Eastern Jewish refugees, and their number was swollen during the first months of peace by some thousands of Polish Jews who escaped from pogroms, in all perhaps 25,000 Jewish refugees in a city of over 1,800,000

[18] *Deutsche Arbeiterpresse – Nationalsozialistisches Wochenblatt*, no. 49, 6 December 1919.
[19] Police report, Innsbruck, 3 January 1920: Tiroler Landesarchiv, Präsidialakten 1920, xii 77.

inhabitants, one and a half per cent of the population. In view of the growing shortage of food and living accommodation it was easy to unleash an anti-semitic mass progaganda, directed especially against the Eastern Jews. As many of them could not find regular employment in the conditions of the post-war period, they were collectively classified as black market profiteers and usurers. What made this propaganda so dangerous was that it was spread not by wild *völkisch* agitators, but by highly respectable bourgeois deputies of the Christian Social and German Nationalist (*Grossdeutsch*) parties which were both represented in the government. Thus the German *Volksrat* for Vienna and Lower Austria organized in September 1919 a mass meeting in the town hall of Vienna. There the nationalist deputy Dr Ursin demanded the dissolution of the Jewish banks and the expropriation of Jewish property. He exclaimed that 'all nations were paying tribute to the Jews, Jewry had conquered at the present time a position of power such as had never existed previously', and even the reparations 'were accruing to the Jewish-American milliardairs'. At the end the meeting unanimously adopted a resolution demanding the expulsion of all Eastern Jews within ten days. A few weeks later another meeting took place in the town hall, called by the Anti-Semitic League, which again demanded the expulsion of the Eastern Jews. One speaker claimed that they 'had immediately started to engage in black market activities, had acquired riches and bought palaces, while the entire population had to starve'. The journalist Anton Orel and a National Socialist demanded the expulsion not only of the Eastern Jews, but of all Jews, 'to prevent the threatening ruin of Vienna at the last moment'.[20]

On 26 September 1919 the Christian Social *Reichspost* published a leader according to which the Jewish question was 'the question of fate for the Republic': in the Eastern March 'six millions of Germans are dominated by a small percentage of members not only of a different nation, but even of a different race'; the decisive question for the present and for the future was whether Austria was to be 'a Jewish Republic or a German Republic'.[21] One of the principal speakers at this and later meetings was the prominent Christian Social deputy Leopold Kunschak who spoke from the same platform as Dr Ursin and Dr Riehl. In October 1919 Kunschak demanded in a meeting of the Christian Social workers' clubs 'amidst strong applause' a 'separate Jewish register and a separate Jewish curia' for elections; Jewish children were to go to Jewish schools and Jews were to be excluded from all public offices; Jews who converted to Christianity were to be treated as

---

[20] Vienna police reports of 25 September and 5 October 1919: Verwaltungsarchiv Vienna, Pol. Dir. Wien, Berichte 1919. The figures of the Jewish refugees are taken from A. Staudinger, in *Jahrbuch für Zeitgeschichte 1978*, Vienna, 1979, p. 28.

[21] Quoted by Staudinger, loc. cit., p. 30.

Jews and to be completely separated from the Germans.[22] Further still went the demands of the Tyrolese Anti-Semitic League which was founded about this time in Innsbruck. On 30 November a mass meeting held there demanded that the Jews must be declared a nation; all people who had but one Jewish great grandmother or great grandfather were to belong to it; the professions of soldier, official, judge, professor and teacher were to be closed to Jews; textbooks written by Jews were no longer to be used; the buying of property in the Tyrol, the cattle and timber trades were to be prohibited to Jews – and all that although the number of Jews in the Tyrol was extraordinarily small. Violent attacks were launched on the Minister of Defence, Deutsch, as 'a member of that race which during the war could not be seen at the front but only in the rear lining its own pockets'.[23]

Perhaps the most extreme utterances of racial anti-semitism appeared at the end of 1918 at Innsbruck in the *Neue Tiroler Stimmen*, a daily paper with close connections to the Christian Social Party. There an engineer H.R. (probably Hans Reinl, later a prominent SA leader) published four long pieces on 'The racial-political causes of the collapse', which not only contained violent attacks on Bolshevism, but accused the Jews of aiming at world power. 'The real victor in this war everywhere was Jewry. Everywhere it has known how to exploit the economic and political conditions to the last and to gain power through war profits, usury and imposing slavery . . .' Reinl's special enemies were 'the men of the revolution' of 1918. According to him, 'all these characters with their thick lips, fanatical eyes, bent legs, unkempt beards and grizzly hair – from the mulatto face of Liebknecht to the primitive mongol type of Ebert – belong rather to the anthropological department of a waxworks than to the cabinet table of the German Empire'. Yet neither Ebert nor Liebknecht was of Jewish origin, and Liebknecht was never a member of any German government. Reinl, however, found that the revolution of 1918 could be explained quite simply: 'The lower races are once again trying to rise. The Jewish pied piper has summoned them from their century-long slumber and leads them to the attack against all which is to be understood under the symbol of the cross . . . hordes of slaves, a hundred times deceived . . .'[24] What seems important in all these quotations is that large bourgeois newspapers and representatives of the largest Austrian party were preaching racial anti-semitism and racialist ideology. In January 1919 even the later leader of the party, Dr Ignaz Seipel, spoke of the 'Bolshevist danger' as a 'Jewish danger', for the Jews had become 'an

---

[22] Ibid., p. 31.
[23] Tiroler Landesarchiv, Präsidialakten 1919, xii 76e. Deutsch had served at the front as an officer during the war.
[24] *Neue Tiroler Stimmen*, 9, 10, 30 December 1919 and 2 January 1920.

element of disintegration' which, 'wherever its waves penetrate, corrodes and destroys the rock of the nation'; he thought the danger was that 'the real Germans would be pushed out of the positions of influence and would fall completely under Jewish sway'.[25]

At the anti-semitic mass meetings of 1919 in Vienna the National Socialists cooperated closely with other right-radical and *völkisch* groups and parties, which enabled them to reach a much larger audience. This cooperation continued during the following years. In 1923 and 1924 mass demonstrations against the peace treaties of St Germain and Versailles were held in Vienna, in which above all the *völkisch* gymnastic clubs and the Ex-Servicemen's League participated, apart from contingents of the *völkisch* trade unions and students' and pupils' associations, the Grossdeutsch party and the National Socialists. In 1924 the latter numbered about 1500 among about 13,000 participants, a small minority.[26] Above all, it was anti-semitic rioting which offered an opportunity to the National Socialists to cooperate with other larger organizations. When an international Zionist congress was to be held in Vienna in August 1925 the Anti-Semitic League, the Pan-German League, the *völkisch* gymnastics clubs and the National Socialists formed an 'Anti-Semitic Fighting Committee', which was rather surprisingly joined by the Christian gymnastics clubs and the Christian Social *Reichspost*, to prevent the holding of the congress. In their negotiations with members of the government and the police commissioner the members of the committee stated repeatedly they would not permit the congress to meet in 'this Aryan city of Vienna', but the government remained firm. On the day of the opening of the congress many thousands rioted in the streets of the inner city which became the scene of ugly clashes. More than a hundred of the rioters were arrested by the police.[27]

By far the most important and largest of the right-wing organizations of these years were the *Heimwehren* which under different names came into being in 1919 in the different Austrian provinces on a local basis and were supported by the two large bourgeois parties. In the south – Styria and Carinthia – the struggles against the Yugoslavs led to the formation of paramilitary defence units. But they also developed in the provinces which were not threatened from outside, and their ideology was from the outset directed against 'Red Vienna', 'Marxism' and the 'Bolshevist danger' which to them seemed synonymous. Added to it was a strong anti-semitism. Thus the

---

[25] Quoted by Staudinger, loc. cit., p. 18.

[26] Vienna police report, 28 September 1924: Polizeiarchiv Vienna, Schober papers, box 50.

[27] F. Berg, *Die weisse Pest*, Vienna, 1926, p. 69; R. Brandstötter, 'Dr Walter Riehl und die Geschichte der nationalsozialistischen Bewegung in Österreich', Vienna Ph.D. thesis 1969, pp. 226–7.

Forerunners of National Socialism in Austria 267

Tyrolese Heimwehr leader, Dr Richard Steidle, exclaimed in May 1919 at an assembly of the Peasant League: 'People of the Tyrol, guard your domestic rights! Peasant, burgher and worker, those of you who are Tyrolese, do not allow yourselves to be ordered about by foreigners and to be pushed into misery. You especially, you peasants, help to create order in your own land, and then hold out your hands to your brothers in the other Alpine lands to fight Vienna's Asiatic rule. The German Alpine lands can only be saved by a thorough settling of accounts with the spirit of Jewry and of its helpers.'[28] In Vorarlberg and Tyrol as well as in other provinces the Heimwehren cooperated closely with the Bavarian right-wing paramilitary Orgesch (Organization Escherich), which channelled large amounts of money and weapons into Austria. With the weapons there came Bavarian officers and – after the defeat of the Kapp Putsch in Germany – German officers who had to escape from Germany. One of them was Captain Waldemar Pabst, an accomplice in the murder of Rosa Luxemburg and Liebknecht, who was employed as chief of staff of the Tyrolese Heimwehren. Another was Colonel Max Bauer, Ludendorff's adjutant, a strong protagonist of *völkisch* ideas, who established close links with the Heimwehren and the National Socialists. The Heimwehr emblem in Styria was the swastika as a *völkisch* symbol.

How close were the links between the Heimwehren and the German right-wing extremists was also proved by the person of the Upper Austrian (later Austrian) Heimwehr leader, Prince Ernst Rüdiger von Starhemberg. In 1921 he went to Upper Silesia as a member of an Innsbruck student group to take part in the battles of the German Free Corps against the Poles. After his return to Innsbruck he became the leader of a local group of the Bavarian Free Corps *Oberland* which had fought in Upper Silesia and extended its activities into Austria, and as such he participated in the Hitler Putsch in Munich in November 1923. Fifteen years later he wrote in his memoirs of his vision of Adolf Hitler: 'Like hundreds of thousands I was fascinated. He captivated me as an orator, and irresistible were his words and demands in their naturalness and apparently compelling logic.' To Starhemberg, 'Munich in 1923 was the great hope of the national patriots of Austria and Germany',[29] and thousands of young Austrians thought the same.

The 'great hour' of the Heimwehren came with the burning of the Vienna Palace of Justice in July 1927; that was the hour for which they had waited and they succeeded within a few days in breaking the general strike proclaimed by the trade unions. Now they became mass organizations, far stronger than the National Socialists who competed

[28] Reports in *Tagespost*, Graz, 27 and 29 May 1919.
[29] 'Lebenserinnerungen des Fürsten Ernst Rüdiger von Starhemberg von ihm selbst verfasst im Winter 1938/39 in Saint Germain', MS. in Institut für Zeitgeschichte, Vienna.

with them. But in spite of very considerable help from Hungary and Fascist Italy they did not succeed in achieving their cherished goal, political power, and not even in removing the hated Social Democrats from the town hall in Vienna. In May 1930 Dr Steidle and other Heimwehr leaders tried to establish greater unity among the squabbling Heimwehr leaders by making them take an oath to Fascism as a unifying ideology; but this attempt also misfired, and instead of leading to greater unity the oath only caused renewed conflict and growing disunity within the movement. The admonitions of Mussolini, who wanted to see deeds for his money and his arms, were in vain. Only in Styria the local Heimwehr leader, Dr Walter Pfrimer, tried to seize power in September 1931 by a Putsch, but he was not supported by the other leaders and the enterprise very quickly collapsed. The result of all these failures was widespread disappointment and embitterment among the Heimwehr members which was to benefit the National Socialists.

Even before 1931 more or less close contacts existed between the Styrian Heimwehren and the German National Socialists. After the failure of the Putsch they became considerably closer. The rise of Hitler and National Socialism in Germany convinced many Heimwehr leaders that Hitler had much greater chances of success and the taking over of power than the Heimwehren with their for ever bickering leaders. Before the general election of November 1930 prominent Heimwehr leaders negotiated with Hitler about an electoral alliance with the National Socialists. But the negotiations broke down because Hitler insisted on absolute parity, while the Heimwehr leaders were only willing to concede parity for the first ten mandates and after that a proportion of two to one in their own favour.[30] But in 1931 – after the failure of the Pfrimer Putsch – the Styrian Heimwehren and the National Socialists formed a common 'battle front'. In a mass meeting of their uniformed members in Graz in October Hitler's emissary, the German deputy Theo Habicht, exclaimed that the political leader of the German people was 'only and solely Adolf Hitler. The first precondition of a collaboration between Heimatschutz and National Socialists is the avowal of Adolf Hitler . . .' The Styrian Heimwehr leader Hanns Rauter replied that their aim too was 'the union of all Germans', therefore they had several times been in touch with Hitler and had sought 'close cooperation'. 'We all', Rauter stated, 'desire a German dictatorship, our eyes and our hopes are directed towards the German Empire.' At the end of the meeting Habicht was able to announce that 'the Styrian Heimatschutz has given the expected answer to all principal and decisive questions . . . NSDAP and Heimatschutz will', he concluded amid thunderous applause, 'fight shoulder to shoulder against this system and for the Great Third German Empire.' Officially the Styrian Heimwehren and the National Socialists

---

[30] *Der Panther – Steirische Heimatschutzzeitung*, Folge 29, 15 November 1930.

remained separate organizations, but the members fraternized amidst scenes of enthusiasm and their leaders proclaimed 'that the two organizations are marching shoulder to shoulder in the fight against Bolshevism, Marxism and parliamentary democracy'. The 'Twelve Principles of the Styrian Heimatschutz' of 1932 laid down that 'the highest regard for Germanic racial consciousness is for the Heimatschutz the natural precondition of *völkisch* policy'; only 'Aryan national comrades' who accepted these principles could be members.[31] On 1 May 1933 Hitler – now the German chancellor – received the leaders of the Styrian Heimwehren in his Berlin chancery and they vowed unconditional loyalty to him. In the same year the SA and the Heimwehr units in Styria were amalgamated and common leaders were appointed locally.[32]

When the National Socialists rose against the Dollfuss government in July 1934 the units of the former Heimwehren in the south of Austria bore the brunt of the fighting and proved themselves the best trained formations. In the whole of Austria, the Heimwehren lost many of their members to the quickly growing National Socialist Party, and the same was true of other nationalist and right-wing organizations. Most strongly this National Socialist magnetism was felt by the nationalist party, the *Grossdeutsche*, who felt themselves the true heirs of Schönerer. Before the elections of April 1932 they offered to the National Socialists an electoral alliance in Vienna, so that 'no *völkisch* votes would be lost, while in the other case (*sic*) a gratifying victory of the *völkisch* cause would be assured'. But the proposal was turned down by the National Socialists certain of their coming victory, and the result justified their refusal. At the simultaneous elections in four Austrian provinces[33] they obtained about twenty per cent of the vote – to a large extent at the expense of the Grossdeutsche and the Heimwehren. In May 1932 the leaders of the Grossdeutsche discussed this catastrophic result. All speakers opposed a dissolution of their own party although, as they admitted, their followers 'were deserting them in spite of all party resolutions'.[34] The majority of local councillors and other mandatories elected on the Grossdeutsch lists transferred about this time to the National Socialists. In Vorarlberg the local Grossdeutsch organization recommended to its members in May 1933 to join the NSDAP 'because this movement upholds the principal demands of the Grossdeutsche Party, especially that for an *Anschluss* with Germany and anti-semitism'. Twelve months later, in May 1934, the Grossdeutsche finally signed an

[31] Idem, 2. Jahrgang, Folge 45, 7 November 1931; Police reports, 1–2 November 1931: Verwaltungsarchiv Vienna, Bundeskanzleramt, 22/gen., box 4869.

[32] *Der Panther*, 4. Jahrgang, Folge 17, 29 April 1933; agreements of 22 April and 23 November 1933: Bundesarchiv Koblenz, Sammlung Schumacher, no. 277.

[33] Carinthia, Lower Austria, Salzburg and Styria.

[34] Habicht to Strasser, 2 June 1932: Bundesarchiv, Sammlung Schumacher, no. 305 i; meeting of 4 May 1932: Verwaltungsarchiv Vienna, Grossdeutsche Partei, box 16.

agreement of common action with the National Socialists, jointly to oppose the Dollfuss government.[35] This meant in practice the end of the party which had contributed so much to the spread of the Pan-German, *völkisch* and anti-semitic ideology. In 1936 the Directorate of Public Security stated that 'the former Grossdeutsche Party, which has lost its followers almost completely to the National Socialists, is condemned to total inactivity.'[36]

If we finally ask what was the historical importance of the different forerunners of National Socialism in Austria, one answer is certain: it was fed by a number of very different sources, exactly as in Germany. One of the most important among them was anti-semitism, which was very marked in Austria already before 1914, but it was not the only one. What seems very important to me are the fears widely spread among the middle and lower middle classes, the feeling of being threatened, be it by the Jews or the Slavs, by Marxism or Bolshevism, by economic catastrophies or by the rise of new social classes, the working class whose leaders occupied leading positions after the revolution. These fears seemed to be confirmed by the events of 1919, for Bolshevism established itself for a short time not far from the gates of Vienna and seemed to threaten Austria in the form of the workers' and soldiers' councils. This threat – whether real or imaginary – could be used by unscrupulous politicians for their own purposes, and it was much enhanced by economic crisis and inflation.

Yet the roots of the *völkisch* ideology and of racial anti-semitism go back far into the 19th century. The ideology found its first fierce expression in Schönerer's Pan-German movement, which was the most important forerunner of National Socialism. As Josef Greiner, Hitler's friend in the early years, recounts, he found framed over his bed the Schönerer slogans 'Without Juda, without Rome, we will build Germania's dome!' and 'We look freely and openly, we look all the time, we look full of joy to the German Fatherland!'[37] There can hardly be a better proof of the great importance of Schönerer for the growth of the *völkisch* ideology. In this particular case the line of transference seems to have been a very direct one. That the same is also true of much larger circles is proved by the example of the 'national' youth of the 1930s; its 'intoxication' infected the older generation which had been influenced by Schönerer and whose older ideals now seemed to be realised. If Schönerer in the late 19th century had been unable to create a mass movement this came into being in the very different conditions of the post-war period.

[35] *Vorarlberger Tagblatt*, 8 May 1933; the German Minister in Vienna to the Auswärtige Amt, 18 May 1934: Bundesarchiv Koblenz, Reichskanzlei, R 43 ii/1475.

[36] Generaldirektion für die öffentliche Sicherheit, 4 April 1936: Haus-, Hof- und Staatsarchiv Vienna, Liasse Österreich 2/21, file 468.

[37] J. Greiner, *Das Ende des Hitler-Mythos*, Zürich-Leipzig-Vienna, 1947, p. 81. Ibid., pp. 50, 79–80, further evidence for Schönerer's influence on the young Hitler.

18

ROSA LUXEMBURG, FREEDOM AND REVOLUTION

Among the rather unimaginative and slow-moving leaders of the German Social Democratic Party of the early twentieth century – who were occupied with the task of achieving better living conditions for the workers and passing high-sounding resolutions against the evils of bourgeois society (which did not oblige anybody to take any action) – one was entirely different: a fiery woman of Jewish-Polish origin, small and slender, slightly lame from a childhood disease, an orator who could sway the masses, a professional revolutionary who seemed to belong to the Russian world from which she came rather than to modern Germany. Rosa Luxemburg was born on 5 March 1871 in the small Polish town of Zamość near Lublin into a fairly prosperous Jewish middle-class family. Her span of life coincided almost exactly with that of the German Empire which Bismarck had founded at Versailles a few weeks before her birth; its collapse in November 1918 she out-lived only by some weeks. Her family sympathised with the aspirations of the Polish national movement, and at the age of sixteen Rosa Luxemburg joined an underground revolutionary socialist group called *Proletariat* and participated in its clandestine activities among the workers of Warsaw. In 1889, when threatened with arrest and imprisonment, she was smuggled out of Poland by her comrades and went to Zürich, the centre of the Russian and Polish political émigrés. There she studied at the university and took part in the intense political and intellectual life of her fellow socialists, in the heated discussions where the battles of the coming Russian revolution were fought out in advance.

Her political activities remained intimately connected with Poland. She was a co-founder of the Social Democratic Party of the Kingdom of Poland and Lithuania in 1894 and a chief contributor to its paper published in Paris. She was opposed to the slogan of independence for Poland, which was advocated by another Polish socialist party, the PPS; instead she advocated the overthrow of the tsarist autocracy in alliance with the Russian working class as the primary task of the Polish revolutionary movement. She aimed at the establishment of a Russian democratic republic within which Poland would merely enjoy cultural autonomy. To Poland she returned during the revolution of 1905 to participate in the revolutionary struggle. There her party had become a mass party which issued papers and leaflets in several languages, organised trade unions and strikes, and co-operated closely with the

Russian Social Democratic Workers Party. After a few months of great poltical activity, however, Rosa Luxemburg and her lifelong friend Leo Jogiches were arrested. She was kept in prison for four months, but was then released on account of her Germany nationality (she had contracted a *pro forma* marriage with a German comrade so as not to be hampered in her political work) and expelled from Poland, never to return.

It was in Germany that she made her home at the end of the nineteenth century; there she worked together with Karl Kautsky, the editor of the theoretical weekly of the German Social Democrats, *Die Neue Zeit*, and the propounder and populariser of Marxist theories. In the columns of this paper and at German Party congresses she crossed swords with Eduard Bernstein, who had just published his articles on 'Problems of Socialism', emphasising the evolutionary transition from capitalism to socialism and 'revising' orthodox Marxism in a Fabian sense.[1] In the columns of *Die Neue Zeit* Rosa Luxemburg soon crossed swords with another redoubtable figure of the international socialist movement, V. I. Lenin, on the question of the organisation of Russian Social Democracy and the powers of the central committee of the party, which showed that she was well aware of the dangers threatening the revolutionary movement from within. There too she commented vigorously on the Russian revolution of 1905 and discovered in it a new weapon of primary importance, the political mass strike, which she attempted to transfer to Germany. Her close association with Kautsky came to an end after some years during which she learned to distrust his Marxist jargon and to doubt the readiness of the Social Democratic leaders to accompany their revolutionary works by similar deeds.

During the years preceding the outbreak of the First World War Rosa Luxemburg became the acknowledged theoretical leader of a left wing within the German Social Democratic Party, whose adherents claimed that they were the only true heirs of Marx's revolutionary ardour. She also published her most important theoretical work, *The Accumulation of Capital*,[2] in which she tried to demonstrate that capitalism could expand only so long as it had at its disposal non-capitalist, colonial markets: with their progressive absorption and their conversion to capitalism through the division of the world among the imperialist powers the system was bound to reach its 'final phase':

Imperialism is simultaneously a historical method of prolonging the existence of capitalism and the most certain means of putting an end to its existence in

---

[1] Rosa Luxemburg's attack on Bernstein was published in 1900 as a pamphlet with the title *Sozialreform oder Revolution?*

[2] English translation, London, 1951.

the shortest possible time. This does not imply that the final goal must be reached inevitably and mechanically. Yet already the tendency towards this final limit of capitalist development expresses itself in forms which will make the last phase of capitalism a period of catastrophes.[3]

She maintained in conclusion that

the more capital, through militarism, in the world at large as well as at home, liquidates the non-capitalist strata and depresses the living conditions of all working people, the more does the daily history of capital accumulation in the world become a continuous chain of political and social catastrophes and convulsions which, together with the periodic economic catastrophes in the form of crises, will make the continuation of capital accumulation impossible . . . even before capitalism has reached the natural, self-created barriers of its economic development.[4]

In Rosa Luxemburg's opinion capitalism was doomed and its final crisis was inevitable: a point on which she differed from Lenin, whose *Imperialism, the Highest Stage of Capitalism*, written a few years later, contained certain analogies with her analysis of imperialism, but avoided any definite pronouncement on the 'inevitability' of capitalist collapse.[5]

It is not, however, on economic theories such as these that Rosa Luxemburg's fame as a socialist writer rests. This is, above all, due to her uncompromising stand against war and militarism. In February 1914 she was arrested and sentenced to twelve months imprisonment on a charge of inciting soldiers to mutiny because she had declared publicly: 'if they expect us to murder our French or other foreign brothers, then let us tell them: "No, under no circumstances!"' At the outbreak of war in August 1914 the German Social Democratic Party – like most other socialist parties – decided to support the fatherland and to grant the war credits demanded by the government; this decision was opposed only by a small minority in the party caucus and by not a single deputy at the decisive vote in the Reichstag on 4 August. Rosa Luxemburg from the outset hotly attacked this policy and never forgave the party's leaders for their betrayal of the ideals to which they had once subscribed:

With the 4 August 1914 official German Social Democracy and with it the International have miserably collapsed. Everything that we have preached to

---

[3] Rosa Luxemburg, *Die Akkumulation des Kapitals, Gesammelte Werke*, VI, Berlin, 1923, p. 361.
[4] *Ibid*, pp. 379–80.
[5] Hence Rosa Luxemburg has always been criticised by her 'Marxist' commentators: see, for example, the remarks of the Marx-Engels-Lenin-Institut beim Z.K. der SED in Rosa Luxemburg, *Ausgewählte Reden und Schriften*, I, Berlin, 1951, p. 408.

the people for fifty years, that we have proclaimed as our most sacred principles, that we have propounded innumerable times in speeches, pamphlets, newspapers, and leaflets, has suddenly become empty talk. The party of the international proletarian class struggle has suddenly been transformed as by an evil spell into a national liberal party; our strong organisations, of which we have been so proud, have proved to be totally powerless; and instead of the esteemed and feared deadly enemies of bourgeois society we are now the rightly despised tools of our mortal enemies, the imperialist bourgeoisie, without a will of our own. In other countries more or less the same breakdown of socialism has occurred, and the proud old cry: 'Working men of all countries, unite!' has been changed on the battlefields into: 'Working men of all countries, slit each other's throats!'

Never in world history has a political party become bankrupt so miserably, never has a proud ideal been betrayed so shamefully.[6]

She explained why German Social Democracy was able to change its policy so quickly and successfully, without encountering any major opposition inside the party:

It was precisely the powerful organisation, the much-lauded discipline of German Social Democracy, which proved their worth in that the whole organism of four millions allowed itself to be turned round within twenty-four hours at the behest of a handful of parliamentarians and let itself be joined to a structure, the storming of which had been its lifelong aim . . . Marx, Engels, and Lassalle, Liebknecht, Bebel, and Singer educated the German working class so that Hindenburg can lead it. The better the education, the organisation, the famous discipline, the building-up of trade unions and party press is in Germany than it is in France, the more effective is the war effort of German Social Democracy in comparison with that of the French.[7]

Soon Rosa Luxembourg and her circle of friends, intellectuals like herself, began to organise opposition to the war and to issue clandestine anti-war leaflets, signed with the pen-name of Spartacus: hence their group came to be known as *Spartakusbund* (Spartacus League). Thus they remained faithful to the resolution that had been voted for the first time by the Congress of the Socialist International at Stuttgart in 1907 at the suggestion of Rosa Luxemburg, Lenin, and Martov:

If the outbreak of war threatens, the workers and their parliamentary deputies in the countries in question are obliged to do everything to prevent the outbreak of war by suitable means . . . If war should nevertheless break out, they are obliged to work for its speedy termination and to strive with all their might to use the economic and political crisis created by the war for the

---

[6] Underground leaflet of the Spartacus League of April 1916: *ibid.*, II, Berlin, 1951, p. 534.
[7] *Die Internationale*, No. 1, 1915: *ibid.*, II, p. 521.

mobilisation of the people and thus to hasten the overthrow of capitalist class rule.[8]

Their underground activities soon landed most of the leaders of the Spartacus League in prison. Rosa Luxemburg was arrested in February 1915 and, with the exception of only a few months, spent the remaining years of the war in various German prisons – until she was freed by the revolution of November 1918. In prison she wrote her most eloquent denunciation of the war, in which she clearly established the responsibility of the German Imperial government because the Austrian ultimatum to Serbia had been issued with its consent, because it had assured Austria in advance of German support in case of war, and because it had given Austria 'an entirely free hand in its action against Serbia'. *The Crisis of Social Democracy*, written under the pen-name of Junius, bitterly condemned the war and even more bitterly condemned the policy of the German Social Democrats:

This world war is a relapse into barbarism. The triumph of imperialism leads to the destruction of civilisation – sporadically during a modern war, and finally if the period of world wars which has now been started should continue without hindrance to the last sequence. We are today faced with the choice, exactly as Frederick Engels predicted forty years ago: either the triumph of imperialism and decline of all civilisation, as in ancient Rome, depopulation, desolation, degeneration, one vast cemetery; or the victory of socialism, that is the conscious fight of the international working class against imperialism and its method: war . . .

Yes, the Social Democrats are obliged to defend their country during a great historical crisis; and this constitutes a grave guilt on the part of the Social-Democratic Reichstag fraction, that it declared solemnly on 4 August 1914: 'We do not desert the fatherland in the hour of danger'; but it denied its own words at the same moment, for it *has* forsaken the fatherland in the hour of its greatest peril. The first duty towards the fatherland in that hour was to show it the real background of this imperialist war; to tear away the tissue of patriotic and diplomatic lies which surrounded this attack on the fatherland; to proclaim loudly and clearly that for the German people victory or defeat in this war is equally disastrous; to resist with all force the muzzling of the fatherland by the state of siege . . . finally, to oppose the imperialist war aims of the preservation of Austria and Turkey – that is of reaction in Europe and in Germany – by the old truly national programme of the patriots and democrats of 1848, the programme of Marx, Engels, and Lassalle: by the slogan of the united, great German republic. That is the banner that should have been raised, a banner that would have been truly national, truly liberal and in conformity with the best traditions of Germany, as well as of the international class policy of the working class.[9]

[8] *Internationaler Sozialisten-Kongress Stuttgart 1907*, Berlin, 1907, p. 102: Thursday, 22 August 1907.
[9] *Ausgewählte Reden und Schriften*, I, pp. 270, 372–73.

Rosa Luxemburg's voice became the symbol of opposition to the war, but it remained a cry in the wilderness. Although many Germans became war-weary on account of mounting casualties and increasing hunger, the Spartacus League never mustered more than a few hundred members, and the non-revolutionary, pacifist Independent Social Democratic Party became the mass opposition party in the later years of the war. Although the Spartacists joined this party, its leaders were men far removed from Rosa Luxemburg's revolutionary idealism, men like her old enemies Eduard Bernstein and Karl Kautsky. Even after the revolution of 1918 it was the Independent Social Democratic Party which became the mass party of the radicalised section of the German working class; while the newly founded German Communist Party, the successor of the Spartacus League, remained a small sect.

It was in prison, too, that news reached Rosa Luxemburg first of the February and later of the October revolution in Russia: her revolutionary ideals seemed at last to have reached the realm of reality, if not in Germany then at least in Russia. And it was in prison too that she wrote what must remain the most important testimony to her independence of spirit, a trenchant criticism of Lenin's policy after the October revolution.[10] As early as 1904, at the same time and for the same reasons as George Plekhanov, she had criticised Lenin for his advocacy of

a ruthless centralism, the chief principles of which are on the one hand the sharp distinction and separation of the organised groups of the avowed and active revolutionaries from the surrounding, if unorganised, yet revolutionary active circles, and on the other hand the strict discipline and the direct, decisive intervention of the central authority in all activities of the local party groups. It is sufficient to remark that according to this conception the central committee is authorised to organise all local committees of the party, therefore also empowered to decide upon the personal composition of each Russian local organisation, from Geneva and Liège to Tomsk and Irkutsk, to impose upon them its own local rules, to dissolve them altogether by decree and to create them anew, and thus finally to influence indirectly even the composition of the highest party organ, the party congress. Thus the central committee appears as the real active nucleus of the party and all other organisations merely as its executive tools.[11]

Against Lenin's formula that the revolutionary Social Democrat was nothing but 'a Jacobin who was inseparably linked with the organisation of the class-conscious proletariat', Rosa Luxemburg emphasised that it was in a conspiratorial organisation of the type created by Blanqui that tactics and activity were worked out in

[10] *Die russische Revolution*, ed. Paul Levi, Berlin 1922.
[11] 'Organisationsfragen der russischen Sozialdemokratie', *Die Neue Zeit*, XXII, Stuttgart, 1904, pp. 486–87.

advance, according to a fixed plan, that its active members were but the executive organs of a higher will which was formed outside their sphere of action, and blindly subordinated to a central authority which possessed absolute powers. In her opinion, the conditions of Social Democratic action were entirely different,

not based on blind obedience, nor on the mechanical subordination of the party militants to a central authority; and it is equally out of the question to erect an absolute partition between the nucleus of the class-conscious proletariat, which is organised in firm party cadres, and the surrounding sections which are already engaged in the class struggle and are being drawn into the process of class education.

According to her, Lenin's ideas amounted to

a mechanical transfer of the organisational principles of the Blanquist movement of conspirators into the Social Democratic movement of the masses of the workers.

Social Democracy was not 'linked' with the organisation of the class-conscious workers, but was 'the proper movement of the working class', so that Social Democratic centralism had to be of an entirely different quality from that of Blanqui. Local organisations had to have sufficient elbow-room so that they could deploy their initiative and make use of the existing opportunities to further the struggle; while the ultra-centralism advocated by Lenin was designed to control, channel, and regiment the activity of the party.[12]

Thus Rosa Luxemburg realised at a very early stage the dangers inherent in the Bolshevik type of organisation; but this did not prevent her from co-operating with Lenin during later years and from welcoming the Russian revolution as 'the most tremendous fact of the world war'. Her criticisms of Lenin's policy after the October revolution were above all directed against his agrarian policy and against the anti-democratic, dictatorial tendencies inherent in Bolshevism. Lenin, at the time of the October revolution, had taken over the agrarian programme of a non-Marxist party, the Social Revolutionaries, which sanctioned the division of the expropriated estates of the nobility among the peasants and created a strong class of peasant proprietors. Rosa Luxemburg predicted that this policy would

create for socialism a new and powerful class of enemies in the countryside, whose opposition will be much more dangerous and tenacious than that of the noble landlords had ever been

and that

[12] *Ibid.*, pp. 488–89, 491–92.

an enormously enlarged and strong mass of peasant proprietors will defend their newly acquired property tooth and nail against all socialist attacks. Now the question of a future socialisation of agriculture, and of production in Russia in general, has become an issue and an object of struggle between the urban workers and the peasants.[13]

How right she was, the years of Stalin's forced collectivisation were to show; but she did not consider whether, in the conditions of 1917, Lenin, if he wanted to seize and to retain power, had any alternative but to sanction occupation of the land by the peasants, which was proceeding spontaneously and independently of his orders and wishes. On this point she was more orthodox than Lenin.

Far more weighty was Rosa Luxemburg's criticism of the antidemocratic policy of Lenin and Trotsky, of their suppression of free political life, of their establishment of a dictatorship not of the masses, but over the masses. She declared quite unequivocally that

it is an obvious and indisputable fact that without a free and uncensored press, without the untrammelled activity of associations and meetings, the rule of the broad masses of the people is unthinkable.[14]

And she prophesied correctly that

with the suppression of political life in the whole country the vitality of the Soviets too is bound to deteriorate progressively. Without general elections, without complete freedom of the press and of meetings, without freedom of discussion, life in every public institution becomes a sham in which bureaucracy alone remains active. Nothing can escape the working of this law. Public life gradually disappears; a few dozen extremely energetic and highly idealistic party leaders direct and govern; among them in reality a dozen outstanding leaders rule, and the élite of the working class is summoned to a meeting from time to time to applaud the speeches of the leaders and to adopt unanimously resolutions put to them; *au fond* this is the rule of a clique – a dictatorship it is true, but not the dictatorship of the proletariat, but of a handful of politicians, that is a dictatorship in the bourgeois sense.[15]

Rosa Luxemburg had not become an adherent of 'bourgeois democracy', nor was she against dictatorship. She stood on the platform on which Marx had stood in 1848; dictatorship of the broad masses of the people was to her the same as revolutionary democracy, a dictatorship against the small minority of capitalists and landlords, but not against the people.

---

[13] Rosa Luxemburg, *Die Russische Revolution*, ed. Paul Levi, Berlin, 1922, pp. 86–87.
[14] *Ibid.*, p. 108.
[15] *Ibid.*, p. 113.

Dictatorship, certainly! But dictatorship means the way in which democracy is used, not its abolition; it means energetic, resolute interference with the acquired rights and economic conditions of bourgeois society, without which there can be no question of a socialist revolution. But this dictatorship must be the work of the class, and not of a small, leading minority in the name of the class; i.e. it must originate from the continuous active participation of the masses, must be directly influenced by them, must be subordinate to the control of the whole people, and must be borne by the increasing political education of the masses.[16]

These masses must participate actively in political life and in the shaping of the new order, 'otherwise socialism will be decreed and imposed from above by a dozen intellectuals'.[17]

The masses, however, cannot acquire political education and experience without political freedom: it is here that Rosa Luxemburg realised the deep gulf which separated her libertarian socialism from totalitarian socialism:

Freedom only for the supporters of the government, only for the members of one party – however numerous they may be – that is not freedom. Freedom is always freedom for the man who thinks differently.[18]

It is proof of her political genius that she could write these words a few months after the inauguration of the Bolshevik dictatorship. The essay was not published in her lifetime, however, but only some years after her death by her pupil Paul Levi (who succeeded her in the leadership of the German Communist Party) after he had broken with Moscow.

The German revolution of November 1918 freed Rosa Luxemburg from prison. She spent the remaining few weeks of her life in feverish activity, exhorting the masses to revolutionary action, pouring scorn on the moderate Social Democratic leaders who suddenly found themselves in power, writing numerous articles for the communist paper, *Die Rote Fahne*, which she edited together with Karl Liebknecht. In contrast with the majority of communists, she considered it necessary to participate in the elections to the German National Assembly which were to take place in January 1919; but she did so for reasons entirely at variance with those of the large mass of German socialists, who put their faith in the introduction of parliamentary democracy, and not in the continuation of violent revolution. She wanted to use parliament as a revolutionary platform, as a means of furthering the cause of revolution:

Now we stand in the midst of the revolution, and the National Assembly is a counter-revolutionary fortress which has been erected against the revolutionary

[16] *Ibid.*, pp. 116–17.
[17] *Ibid.*, p. 111.
[18] *Ibid.*, p. 109.

proletariat. It is thus essential to besiege and to reduce this fortress. To mobilise the masses *against* the National Assembly and to summon them to battle: for this the elections and the platform of the National Assembly must be used.

It is necessary to participate in the elections, not in order to pass laws together with the bourgeoisie and its mercenaries, but to chase the bourgeoisie and its partisans out of the temple, to storm the fortress of the counter-revolution and to hoist on it victoriously the flag of the proletarian revolution. To do this a majority in the National Assembly would be required? That only those believe who render homage to parliamentary cretinism, who want to decide upon revolution and socialism through parliamentary majorities. It is not the parliamentary majority *inside* which decides the fate of the National Assembly itself, but the working masses outside in the factories and in the streets . . .

The elections and the platform of this counter-revolutionary parliament must become a means to educate, rally and mobilise the revolutionary masses, a step in the struggle for the establishment of the proletarian dictatorship.[19]

Although the masses of the German workers proved more than reluctant to follow the communist lead, Rosa Luxemburg never lost her faith in them. The day before she was murdered by counter-revolutionary thugs, on 15 January 1919, she wrote in her last article which contained an appraisal of the attempted seizure of power by the extreme left in Berlin, the so-called Spartacist rising:

The masses are the decisive element, they are the rock on which will be built the final victory of the revolution. The masses have stood the test; they have made out of this 'defeat' one link in the chain of historical defeats which constitute the pride and the power of international socialism. And this is why out of this 'defeat' victory will be born . . . Tomorrow already the revolution will arise again in shining armour and will frighten you with her trumpet-call: I was, I am, I shall be![20]

The course of the German revolution was to show how unjustified her faith in the masses and her revolutionary optimism had been, and when the masses in Germany moved, they moved in a direction totally different from that which she had so confidently predicted.

A few weeks before Rosa Luxemburg was murdered, the German Communist Party was founded in Berlin. In its programme, published in December 1918, Rosa Luxemburg once more gave expression to the ideas which had inspired her criticism of Lenin's policy after the October revolution, to her clear refutation of the rule of a minority over the working class and of all putschist tactics (which so tragically came to a head in the Spartacist rising of January 1919):

The proletarian revolution requires no terror to achieve its aims, it hates and despises murder . . . It is no desperate attempt of a minority to fashion the

[19] Article in *Die Rote Fahne* of 23 December 1918: *Ausgewählte Reden und Schriften*, II, pp. 652–53.
[20] Article in *Die Rote Fahne* of 14 January 1919: *ibid.*, p. 714.

world according to its own ideals, but the action of the many millions of the people, which is called upon to fulfil its historical mission and to transform historical necessity into reality . . . The Spartacus League is not a party which wants to seize power over the working class or through the working class . . . The Spartacus League will never seize power unless it be through the clear, positive wish of the large majority of the working masses in Germany, never otherwise than on the basis of their conscious approval of the views, aims and political methods of the Spartacus League . . . Its victory stands not at the beginning, but at the end of the revolution: it is identical with the victory of the many millions of socialist workers.[21]

It was a tragedy, not only for itself, that the new party did not heed this advice of its founder; throughout its history it remained devoted to putschist tactics, and when it finally came to power, it did so as a clique ruling over the workers and maintained in power by the bayonets of a foreign army.

In the new party programme Rosa Luxemburg also emphasised what in her opinion constituted the essential features of socialism:

The essence of a socialist society consists in this, that the great working mass ceases to be a regimented mass, but lives and directs the whole political and economic life in conscious and free self-determination . . .

The proletarian masses must learn to become, instead of mere machines employed by the capitalists in the process of production, the thinking, free, and active directors of this process. They must acquire the sense of responsibility of active members of the community which is the sole owner of all social wealth. They must develop zeal without the employer's whip, highest productivity without capitalist drivers, discipline without a yoke, and order without regimentation. Highest idealism in the interest of the community, strictest self-discipline, a true civic spirit of the masses, these constitute the moral basis of a socialist society.[22]

It is in ideas such as these, in her searching criticism of the conceptions of Lenin, in her emphasis on the moral and democratic basis of socialism that the lasting value of Rosa Luxemburg's thought can be found. Her theory of the inevitable collapse of capitalism, her blind faith in the masses and in revolution as such, her vast optimism as to the future of socialism have been disproved by events which she did not live to see. Yet enough remains to make her one of the outstanding exponents of modern socialist thought. It is no accident that she has been classified as a heretic in Eastern Europe and that the only recent edition of her writings omits all that is truly important among them. For Rosa Luxemburg, socialism and freedom were inseparable: those who have abolished freedom have no use for her ideas.

[21] *Was will der Spartakusbund?* ed. Kommunistische Partei Deutschlands (Spartakusbund), Berlin, 1919, pp. 17, 22–23.
[22] *Ibid.*, pp. 16–17.

19

REVOLUTIONARY SITUATIONS IN EUROPE

1917–1920

As we all know, at the end of the first world war revolutions occurred in a number of European countries – in contrast with the second world war at the end of which there was no such revolution: with the possible exception of Yugoslavia where the revolution was the result of the guerilla war of the Partisans against the German occupation. It took place during the war rather than at its end, and it was a civil war rather than a revolution of the older variety. The revolutions of 1917-1920, moreover, all occurred in *defeated* countries, first in Russia and then in Central Europe. There may have been revolutionary situations in some of the victor states, above all in Italy, but if so they did not lead to the outbreak of a revolution. The assumption of power by the Italian Fascists in 1922 hardly deserves that name, and not even that of a counter-revolution. It was only in the defeated countries that the regime which had led the country into war and failed to bring about a negotiated settlement was so discredited, that the masses were so war-weary and hungry, that they turned against the monarchical government which was responsible for their misery and overthrew it. The February revolution in Petrograd and the great January strikes in Austria-Hungary and Germany started with bread riots or because the bread ration was cut drastically by the authorities. In these countries, too, even before the actual outbreak of the revolution the armed forces showed dangerous signs of disintegration and mutiny; the authorities were no longer able to rely on their unconditional obedience. Mass desertion from the Russian armies began even before the February revolution. Mutinies broke out in the German navy in August 1917 and in the Austrian navy in February 1918. Smaller mutinies occurred in several units of the Austrian army in May 1918, mainly caused by prisoners of war returned from Soviet Russia who refused to return to the front. Above all, tens of thousands of soldiers deserted from the Austro-Hungarian army and formed the 'green cadres' of the Balkans and other less accessible mountain areas, as Professor Plaschka and his collaborators have shown in a recent detailed study.[1] In the German army, on the other hand, there were no mutinies of any size prior to the revolution, in spite of all Russian efforts to promote fraternization. In all the armies, the soldiers fighting at the front were much less affected by revolutionary ideas than the sailors or the units in the rear, perhaps because the relationship between officers and men was considerably better at the front than it was in the hinterland or on board the battleships.

In Russia as well as in Central Europe revolution actually broke out when it became clear that the war was lost, when troops ordered to take action against striking workers or mutinous sailors refused to do so, when the government no longer found the defenders willing to protect it. The decisive event was the fraternization of soldiers and workers: these two social groups carried the revolutionary movement to victory within a very short time, and the old order collapsed ignominiously. It is indeed surprising how few people were willing to sacrifice their lives for the preservation of the Romanov, Habsburg and

---

1. Richard G. Plaschka, Horst Haselsteiner and Arnold Suppan, *Innere Front – Militärassistenz, Widerstand un Umsturz in der Donaumonarchie 1918* (Graz/Cologne, 1975). For the mutiny of Cattaro, see Richard G. Plaschka, *Cattaro – Prag* (Graz/Cologne, 1963).

Hohenzollern dynasties, how quickly the ruling social groups gave up all hope of resistance to the revolutionary movements. In Russia, in Hungary and in Germany there was civil war, but this broke out much later. Nor did the existing left-wing parties play any conspicuous part in bringing about the revolution. In Russia, prior to 1917, the socialist parties led a precarious underground existence and had no mass influence. In Austria and Germany, the social-democratic parties supported the war and were opposed to all but constitutional changes in the existing order of things. The extreme left, the later Communists, were extremely weak and possessed no influence among the war-weary masses. The German Independent Social Democrats were a large left-wing party and opposed to the continuation of the war, but they had no revolutionary aims, did not organize a revolutionary movement and were completely surprised by the events of November 1918. So were the leaders of the other political parties. In November 1918 a prominent Social Democrat from Saxony remarked that it was "a remarkable fact that not only the old authorities were pushed back in the first attack by the new workers' and soldiers' councils, but also the old parties. Even the Social-Democratic Party for a few days ceased to exist...."[2]

This quotation points to another factor which the revolutions in Russia and in Central Europe had in common: the spontaneous formation of workers' and soldiers' councils which quickly, within a few hours, assumed a position of great authority. In Petrograd, on February 27, 1917, a Soviet of Workers' Deputies was hurriedly constituted in the Tauride Palace and on the same day transformed into a Soviet of Workers' *and* Soldiers' Deputies by a fusion with the revolutionary soldiers of the capital. This was prior to the formation of the Provisional Government in a different wing of the same palace. As one of the founder members of the Soviet put it: the Soviet was "the only organ capable of guiding the movement into one channel or the other, ... the only organ now wielding any real power in the capital".[3] In Berlin, on November 10, 1918, a mass meeting of the newly elected workers' and soldiers' councils confirmed the new government in office – or as some will have it elected this new government – a coalition government of the two social-democratic parties. The meeting also insisted on parity of these two parties within the government, and equally on parity within the Executive Committee of the workers' and soldiers' councils that was elected by the same meeting. The Executive Committee claimed the right to control the actions as well as the composition of the new government which for the time being depended on the support of the workers' and soldiers' councils.[4] In Russia as well as in Germany, their national congress was – until the meeting of a constituent assembly – the sovereign constitutional organ in whose hands lay the decision about the political future of the country: a sovereign authority created by the revolution.

In the Habsburg monarchy, on the other hand, the revolutionary movement assumed national forms and was directed by "National Councils" quickly set up in Budapest, Prague and the other capitals. Even in Vienna, the initiative for revolutionary action did not come from the soldiers or the workers, but from the German deputies of the *Reichsrat* who, on October 21, 1918, constituted themselves as "the Provisional Assembly of the independent German-Austrian State" and elected an executive committee which took over the power of government. Here the initiative came almost entirely from the three major political parties – the Social Democrats, Christian Social and German Nationalist parties – who formed a coalition government. In the Austrian army, soldiers' councils were formed quickly, but workers' councils only appeared somewhat later. In Hungary too, workers' and soldiers' councils came into being after the outbreak of the revolution, and their power slowly increased parallel with the decline of that of the government of Count Károlyi. In Hungary as well as in Russia the authority of the new

---

2. Dr. Gradnauer on Nov. 25, 1918: Erich Matthias (ed.), *Die Regierung der Volksbeauftragten 1918-1919* (Düsseldorf, 1969), I, no. 30, p. 192.
3. N.N. Sukhanov, *The Russian Revolution 1917* (London, 1955), p. 119 (March 1, 1917).
4. For a discussion of these events, see Eberhard Kolb, introduction to *Der Zentralrat der deutschen sozialistischen Republik* (Leiden, 1968), pp. xiii-xv; F.L. Carsten, *Revolution in Central Europe 1918-1919* (London/Berkeley, 1972), pp. 39-40.

government was slowly eroded by the growing influence of the workers' and soldiers' councils. In Austria and in Germany, the opposite was the case. Both governments were supported by new military forces which were created from the remnants of the old armies, and after a few months their authority was more or less firmly established. If there was an equilibrium it did not last, and soon the old authorities, especially the bureaucracy, reasserted themselves. So did the established political parties and, according to the Saxon Social Democrat whom I have already quoted, "the proven forces of the trade unions", and that was only two weeks after the outbreak of the revolution.[5]

In Russia, in the spring of 1917, the development was entirely different. As early as March 9/22 – ten days after the February revolution – the War Minister Guchkov wrote to General Alexeyev: "The Provisional Government possesses no real power and its orders are executed only in so far as this is permitted by the Soviet of Workers' and Soldiers' Deputies, which holds in its hands the most important elements of actual power, such as troops, railroads, postal and telegraph services. It is possible to say directly that the Provisional Government exists only while this is permitted by the Soviet of Workers' and Soldiers' Deputies. Especially in the military department it is now only possible to issue orders which do not basically conflict with the decisions of the above mentioned Soviet."[6] Nor was the situation any better in the civil sphere as the old administrative machinery ceased to function and the Provisional Government failed to create any new organs to take its place. In the country districts, the commissars nominated to succeed the former governors "possessed little power except that of persuasion", as one well known authority on the Russian revolution has put it, and the new committees elected by the peasants "paid little attention to instructions from the centre."[7] Already on March 4/17 the French ambassador Paléologue noted in his diary: "The Provisional Government has not long been in capitulating to the demands of the socialists. At the Soviet's command, it has actually come to the following humiliating decision: the troops which have taken part in the revolutionary movements will not be disarmed but will remain in Petrograd".[8]

It was not really the case that "dual power" was established in Russia as it has so often been said, but power was increasingly taken over by the Soviets, especially that of Petrograd which "more and more became the centre of Russian political life".[9] Sukhanov, one of our most reliable witnesses of the Russian revolution, has emphasized: "When it entrusted the power to the first cabinet of the revolution the Soviet was only just going into battle – for the army and the real source of authority in the State. By April 17th...... it had won this battle and become the master of the situation in another sense.... Now the Soviet had in its hands a strongly organised, spiritually united army; now ten million bayonets were the obedient instrument of the Soviet, which with them had in its hands the totality of all state power and the entire fate of he revolution". And again: "All real power and authority was in the hands of the Soviet. The many millions of the army submitted to it; hundred and thousands of democratic organizations acknowledged it; the masses obeyed it".[10] Only two days after the outbreak of the revolution the Petrograd Soviet issued an order to the armed forces which established its authority over all units "in all political matters" and instructed them to carry out the orders of the Military Committee of the Duma "only in those cases in which they did not run contrary to the orders and decisions of the Soviet of the Workers' and Soldiers' Deputies".[11] In April this decree was reinforced by an instruction to the Petrograd garrison not to demonstrate in the streets with arms "without a summons from the Executive Committee of the Soviet"; the committee further claimed that it alone was entitled to issue orders in such matters to the units.[12]

---

5. Dr. Gradnauer on Nov. 25, 1918: *loc. cit.*
6. Letter of Mar. 9/22, 1917, quoted by William Henry Chamberlin, *The Russian Revolution 1917-1921* (New York, 1965) I, p. 101.
7. *Ibid.*, pp. 100-101.
8. Maurice Paléologue, *An Ambassador's Memoirs* (London, 1973), p. 834.
9. Chamberlin, *op. cit.*, I, p. 110.
10. Sukhanov, *op. cit.*, pp. 296, 326.
11. Order no. 1, Mar. 1, 1917: Valentin Gitermann, *Geschichte Russlands* (Zürich, 1949), III, p. 633.
12. Paul Miliukov, *Political Memoirs 1905-1917* (Ann Arbor, 1967), p. 450.

In military and other matters power was slipping from the hands of the Provisional Government and transferred to the Soviets, at the centre as well as in the provinces. At first the Soviets only controlled the existing authorities. Later they took over more and more administrative tasks and themselves assumed the local power. In a small way this started immediately after the outbreak of the revolution. Sukhanov recounts that on March 2/15 the telephone rang at the Petrograd Soviet, and the caller, speaking on behalf of the Council of Representatives of the Petrograd banks, asked for permission for the banks to reopen. Permission was readily granted once it was established that the employees were also in favour of reopening. A week later, the Soviet reached agreement with the manufacturers' association on new and improved working conditions, the introduction of the eight-hour day, and the establishment of factory and central conciliation boards for cases of labour conflicts.[13] As no large legal trade unions or factory committees existed in Russia, the local Soviets took over many of their functions and special departments of labour were founded by the more important Soviets. In Kiev the Soviet committee charged with this task settled 65 labour conflicts during the early months of the revolution. In Nizhni Novgorod the Soviet curtailed the 'export' of bread; in Krasnoyarsk it introduced a rationing system for vital commodities. Elsewhere the Soviets organized a workers' control system which was responsible for the allocation of raw materials and fuel; other Soviets supervised sales and wage scales.[14] In the textile centre of Ivanovo-Voznesensk "the Soviet authority was far-reaching and effective long before there was any question of a Soviet regime on the national scale."[15] These examples could easily be multiplied.

The movement in the industrial towns was paralleled by a similar quite spontaneous movement in the villages. The primary motor of this was of course the enormous land-hunger of the Russian peasantry which had erupted with elementary force during the revolution of 1905. In 1917 agrarian disorder quickly reappeared in many districts. The peasants were firmly convinced that the land belonged to the people who tilled it and used every means to freeze out the landowners. They demanded wages for their labour which the landlords were unable to pay. The volost committees often forbade the villagers to work on the estates: "We won't give them any labourers; then they will all starve like cockroaches", they said.[16] At the end of April Countess Lamoyska told the French ambassadoor that on her family estate in Podolia the peasants simply stood about making arrangements how to divide the land. "One of them will affect to want the wood by the river; another puts in for the gardens and proposes to turn them into folds. They go on talking like that for hours and do not stop even when my mother, one of my sisters or myself go up to them".[17] To another landowner near Voronezh the peasants simply explained "that she had, of course, got to lose her land".[18] Public committees and local Soviets took over from the old autorities which, as a member of the Provisional Government put it, "abolished themselves".[19] Peasant Soviets were also formed on the district and provincial levels, parallel with those of the workers and soldiers. In May the first all-Russian congress of peasant deputies met in Petrograd. It was attended by 1115 deputies about half of whom belonged to the Socialist Revolutionaries and only 14 to the Bolsheviks.[20]

Indeed this whole process — the loss of authority by the Provisional Government, the disappearance of the old administrative authorities, the assumption of more and more power by the Soviets and the growing exercise of public functions by them — seems to have had very little to do with Bolshevik propaganda. Obviously, all these changes eventually played into their hands, but in the early months of the revolution they were

---

13. Sukhanov, *op. cit.*, pp. 136, 188, 211.
14. Oskar Anweiler, *Die Rätebewegung in Russland 1905-1921* (Leiden, 1958), pp. 138, 168-169, 170-171.
15. Chamberlin, *op. cit.*, I, p. 114.
16. Michael T. Florinsky, *The End of the Russian Empire* (New York, 1961), pp. 233-234.
17. Paléologue, *op. cit.*, p. 923.
18. Bernard Pares, *My Russian Memoirs* (London, 1931), p. 461.
19. Miliukov, *op. cit.*, p. 426.
20. Anweiler, *op. cit.*, p. 150.

too weakly represented in the Soviets to exercise a significant influence on these developments; while the other socialist groups which predominated in the Soviets considered the revolution a 'bourgeois' one and were for that reason alone opposed to any takeover of power. Not even the disintegration of the Russian armies which so often has been attributed to Bolshevik propaganda was primarily due to their influence. More important, surely, was the effect of the shattering defeat of the Kerenski offensive in July 1917 and above all, the ardent desire of the peasant soldiers to participate in th partition of the land which took place in their native villages. They voted with their feet; they were sick and tired of the war and no longer willing to sacrifice their lives for a lost cause.

The element of spontaneity which for several months was predominant in the Russian revolution was equally predominant eighteen months later in Central Europe. At the outset, the revolution in Austria and in Germany was a revolt of sailors and soldiers, but it quickly spread to the industrial workers. Exactly as in Russia, workers' and soldiers' councils were formed in all major German towns, but they nowhere replaced the old authorities which continued to function as before.

On the day of its formation, November 12, 1918, the new social-democratic government of Prussia expressly asked all state authorities and officials to carry on with their official duties, so as "to contribute to the preservation of law and order in the interest of the fatherland".[21] Ten days later even the Executive Committee of the workers' and soldiers' councils appealed to all local councils not to interfere with the processes of administration and to let the old administrative authorities which accepted the new regime conduct their business unhindered. The local workers' and soldiers' councils were empowered to exercise control over the old authorities and "to consolidate the revolutionary achievements",[22] but this was a vague formula and the control never became real. No "dualism" ever developed. Indeed, in many towns the workers' and soldiers' council merely functioned as a rubber stamp for the actions of the existing local authorities.

The new social-democratic ministers were convinced that they were unable to master the severe problems arising from the lost war, the armistice, the demobilization, the lack of food and raw materials, the undefined frontiers of the German republic, without the support of the skilled bureaucrats who had administered the country in the past. Except at the top, there were very few changes of personnel. Even at the top the undersecretaries of state for foreign affairs, justice, finance, labour, posts and telegraphs, and the navy were left in office; so was the Prussian minister of war, General Scheüch, whose post was of vital importance as there was no German war ministry. The Social Democrats believed that no qualified socialists or democrats were available to replace the conservative and monarchist higher civil servants. They were afraid to make any radical changes in the complex machinery of government at a time of great stress and acute shortages. As Ebert, the chairman of the Council of People's Representatives, put it on November 25: "We were obliged, after we had taken over political power, to see to it that the machinery of the Reich did not collapse; we had to see to it that the machinery continued to run so that our food supply and the economy could be maintained. . . . . Therefore we appealed urgently to all Reich offices to continue with their work until further notice. Only thus were we able to prevent the collapse. . . ."[23]

The same policy prevailed in a sphere of even greater political importance, the military one. It has often been said that as early as November 10, 1918 an "alliance" was concluded between Ebert and General Groener who telephoned Ebert from army headquarters; speaking in the name of the High Command, he put himself and his fellow-officers "at the disposal of the government" as Groener wrote in his diary.[24] Yet the

---

21. Decree of Nov. 12, 1918: Gerhard A. Ritter and Susanne Miller (eds.), *Die deutsche Revolution 1918-1919* (Frankfurt, 1968), no. 4d, p. 94.
22. Proclamation of the Executive Committee of Nov. 23, 1918, printed in Richard Müller, *Vom Kaiserreich zur Republik* (Vienna, 1925), II, p. 255.
23. Speech at the conference of prime ministers of the German states on Nov. 25: Matthias (ed.), *op. cit.*, no. 30, pp. 180-181.
24. Entry of Nov. 10, 1918, quoted by F.L. Carsten, *Reichswehr und Politik* (Cologne, 1964), p. 20, n. 16.

agreement reached on that day was a strictly utilitarian one. The new government in Berlin believed that it needed the services of the skilled military technicians to bring the armies back safely from the vast occupied territories in west and east and to carry through their demobilization as well as the provisions of the armistice with the Entente. The officer corps in its turn needed the support of the government to maintain "order and discipline in the army", which threatened to break down as they had already broken down in the navy. Many years later General Groener wrote in his memoirs that he had also told Ebert on November 10 that "the officer corps expected from the government a fight against Bolshevism"; but there is no proof that words such as these were used by him over the telephone.[25]

In the eyes of the generals, discipline and order in the army were theatened above all by the soldiers' councils which were elected by all units and demanded radical changes in the structure of the army, for example, the election of officers, a participation in the officers' power to issue orders, and the abolition of the officers' epaulettes and other insignia of rank. Such radical demands were anathema to the officer corps. Only four weeks after the telephone conversation between Ebert and Groener the High Command thus demanded that the officers' power of command must be fully restored and that the soldiers' councils must disappear from the army; they were to be replaced by mere trustees who would only be entitled to inform the officers of the grievances of the other ranks. But the demands of the High Command were not limited to the military field and included the immediate summoning of a National Assembly and the exclusive conduct of affairs "by the government and the legal organs of administration":[26] demands clearly directed against the influence of the workers' and soldiers' councils and caused by fear that through that influence the election of a National Assembly might be delayed. In reality the opposite was the case. At their national congress in mid-December 1918 the workers' and soldiers' deputies decided with an overwhelming majority to hold the elections as early as the 19th of January 1919. In general too the large majority of the local councils stood under the influence of the right-wing Social Democrats and were in favour of early elections. In other words, they voted themselves out of power, for the elections did not produce a socialist majority.

Three weeks before the elections, in late December 1918, the coalition of right-wing and left-wing Social Democrats broke up when Ebert and his colleagues ordered troops loyal to the High Command into Berlin in an attempt to evict a 'red' sailors' unit from the palace. The sailors considered themselves the legitimate defenders of the revolution which they had started by their mutiny, and there had been clashes between them and the government. Actually, it was once more General Groener who telephoned Ebert and *demanded* from him that he should accept the protection of the High Command, otherwise it would cease to support him.[27] Thus within a few weeks what started as an understanding with a strictly limited purpose became not precisely an "alliance", but a relationship in which the military could put forward their demands in the form of an ultimatum, which the weak government then accepted. When Groener was heard under oath as a witness in the so-called Stab-in-the-Back trial in Munich in 1925 he declared that he and Ebert had also agreed that the Independent Social Democrats should be pushed out of the government, and this was certainly achieved.[28] When one of the experts attached to the court asked Groener against whom the "alliance" of the 10th of November was directed, Groener without any hesitation replied "against the danger of Bolshevism and against the system of councils":[29] like so many other Germans he completely identified the two.

---

25. Wilhelm Groener, *Lebenserinnerungen* (Göttingen, 1957), p. 467, Cp. the comment by Ulrich Kluge, *Soldatenräte und Revolution* (Göttingen, 1975), p. 144, the most recent study of this important topic.
26. Letter of Hindenburg to Ebert, composed by Groener, Dec. 8, 1918: quoted by Carsten, *op. cit.*, p. 22.
27. Entry in Groener's diary of Dec. 23, 1918: quoted by Kluge, *op. cit.*, p. 451, n. 277.
28. *Der Dolchstoss-Prozess in München/Oktober-November 1925* (Munich, s.a.), p. 225.
29. *Ibid.*

About the same time that the fight for the palace in Berlin ended in a draw at Christmas 1918 the government began with the recruitment of "reliable" volunteer units or Free Corps. These came under the orders of the High Command and those of professional officers. There were no soldiers' councils in the new units, while those functioning in the units of the old army lost their *raison d'être* with the return of the front-line units and the progress of their demobilization. Whatever left-wing or republican formations had come into being in the early months of the revolution were either dissolved or transformed into police forces. The new army which was eventually recruited from the Free Corps and similar units no longer knew any soldiers' councils. Their early disappearance also led to a fatal weakening of the workers' councils which became more and more isolated. Many of the local authorities rendered passive resistance to the councils' claims of supervision; in many cases the funds and facilities granted to the workers' councils by the authorities were withdrawn. After the election of the national assembly and of state parliaments and local councils on the basis of universal franchise the majority of the workers' councils themselves considered that their functions were terminated and many dissolved themselves. The whole council movement which had begun with such high hopes of democratization and participation reached its end in the early months of 1919. It is true that the authorities did their level best to bring the movement to an early end, but by that time it had lost is fighting spirit and the will to resist. It revived briefly at the time of the Kapp Putsch in March 1920, but only in certain parts of Germany, especially in Saxony and the Ruhr: proof that many left-wing workers still put their trust in the workers' councils as a means to prevent a comeback of the old ruling forces and a reactionary *coup d'état*. In the Ruhr a veritable Red Army came into being on that occasion, further evidence of quite spontaneous working class action, as a recent study has shown.[30] But these were the last sparks of a dying movement, and they too were quickly suppressed. In Germany there was no longer a revolutionary situation.

The question might, of course, be asked whether such a situation existed in November 1918. My answer would be an emphatic 'yes', but it only lasted a very short time. The total collapse of the Hohenzollern Empire within a few days, the vast spontaneous movement of the sailors, soldiers and workers which led to the formation of the workers' and soldiers' councils, the take-over by the new government and similar revolutionary governments in all the German states, the radical break with the monarchical and semi-feudal past, are in my opinion the best proof that there was a real revolutionary situation. Germany went 'red' but only for a brief period. There was a break with the past, but it remained limited to the constitutional field and did not extend to the social one; the social structure remained virtually unchanged. Soon the old ruling groups, the bureaucracy, the officer corps, the large landowners, the industrialists, regained much of their former strength. As it was expressed by a popular novel, *"Der Kaiser ging, die Generale blieben"* (the Emperor went, the generals remained); and the generals were not the only group that retained its power. In Germany the bourgeois revolution came very belatedly and it was not complete. Perhaps it remained incomplete because the middle classes did not fear a return of the old order, but feared 'Bolshevism' or what they understood under that label. This fear was shared by the leaders and the majority of members of the Social-Democratic Party. It was that fear too which, fifteen years later, helped Adolf Hitler into power. But it was not a fear based on reality, for the German Communists, even in 1932-33, were weak and did not constitute a serious threat to the existing order.

If we ask the question: why did the German revolution, in contrast with the Russian one, so quickly lose its impetus, some of the answers are very obvious. In Russia, the revolutionary movement became more and more radical because the Provisional Government did not solve any of the burning issues of the day. Under war-time conditions, the elections to the Constituent Assembly proceeded very slowly and it finally met *after* the Bolshevik assumption of power, only to be dispersed by military force. As there was no Constituent Assembly, no decision was taken on the vital issue affecting the large majority

---

30. George Eliasberg, *Der Ruhrkrieg 1920* (Bonn, 1974): Vol. 100 in a series edited by the Friedrich Ebert Stiftung.

of the population: the land question; and meanwhile the peasants solved it by seizing the land of the big landowners and appropriating it. A vast agrarian revolution engulfed Russia. The Provisional Government not only failed to conclude an armistice with the victorious Germans, but in the summer of 1917 launched a large offensive which ended in complete failure and caused new mass desertions from the army. The Russian masses desired nothing more than peace and land, and the February revolution brought them neither. In all three respects the German revolution took the opposite course. The National Assembly was elected two months after the outbreak of revolution and met soon after.

There was no agrarian revolution, and no attempt to seize the estates of the Junker families in the east of Germany. The peasants were only drawn into the council movement on any scale in Bavaria, and Bavaria had very few large estates. The German Social Democrats failed signally to mobilize the peasantry and there was no land-hunger on any scale, perhaps because of the rapid growth of industrial towns. At the national congress of the workers' and soldiers' councils in Berlin in December 1918 only one delegate pleaded in favour of the partition of the large estates and the creation of smaller farms to increase production – and he was not a socialist.[31] No one else spoke on this vital issue. Two Independent Social Democrats advocated the socialization of the land, and especially of the latifundia, and the moderate Social Democrats ignored the issue.[32] There could be no clearer evidence of their total lack of interest in a question so decisive for the future of Germany. Finally, the armistice between Germany and the Entente was concluded two days after the outbreak of the revolution: the longing of the war-weary masses for peace was satisfied by the new government. That the peace settlement would bring new hardships and unleash a violent nationalist agitation in Germany could not be foreseen. The revolutionary impetus evaporated quickly with the overthrow of the monarchy, the election of a new government of left-wing tendencies, and the conclusion of the armistice. When the extreme left two months later, in January 1919, tried to force the German revolution on to a more radical course it was defeated with ease by the Free Corps. But the brutality used by them in supressing the extreme left caused further polarization and drove masses of socialist workers to the left. It was only then that a serious Communist danger began to appear. If the Free Corps had been created to "combat the Bolshevik danger", their actions certainly increased it. But the slogan "All power to the Soviets!" never caught on in Germany.

It seems much more doubtful whether a revolutionary situation existed in Austria in November 1918, or at any time in 1919. As already stated the new Austrian government was not a social-democratic one but a coalition of the three major parties in which Social Democrats held only a few posts. This government was not responsible to any workers' and soldiers' councils but to parliament. Soldiers' councils quickly came into being, but they remained isolated because workers' councils were only formed later, and they never supervised the government or the administration. Their first national conference only took place in March 1919, six months after the revolution. At this conference only the industrial areas of Upper and Lower Austria and of Styria were represented in any strength, for most of Austria was still rural and conservative. A speaker from Linz emphasized that it was impossible to win the large and medium peasants to the cause of socialism. He was seconded by a speaker from Leoben who declared that, if the workers' council was to be a revolutionary organ, "peasant councils would dilute it; most peasants are reactionary"; it would be pointless to put any hope in the peasantry.[33] Thus the workers' councils remained isolated in Vienna and a few industrial areas and from the peasantry, which Otto Bauer considered "a determined enemy of the working class".[34] There was no land-hunger among the peasants and, although there were large estates,

---

31. *Allgemeiner Kongress der Arbeiter – und Soldatenräte Deutschlands vom 16. bis 21. Dezember 1918, Berlin, s.a. (1919)*, col. 327.
32. *Ibid.*, cols. 319, 339.
33. (Karl Heinz), "Die Geschichte der österreichischen Arbeiterräte", MS. in Arbeiterkammer Wien, pp. 66, 70.
34. Thus Bauer on Nov. 1, 1918: *Protokoll des Parteitages des sozialdemokratischen Srbeiterpartei,* Oct. 31-Nov. 1, 1918, p. 111: Parteiarchiv Wien.

they consisted mostly of woods and land unsuitable for agriculture. The Austrian peasants were catholic, conservative and law-abiding, and any rural surplus-population seems to have been absorbed by the growth of Vienna and industrial towns, while in Russia the opposite was the case.[35]

In military affairs, the development was very different from Germany, for the old Austro-Hungarian army simply disintegrated into its national components. The High Command and the general staff did not survive the revolution. In Vienna and other parts of Lower Austria the Social Democrats succeeded in creating a fairly efficient new army, the *Volkswehr*, in which soldiers' councils played a prominent part and officers had to be approved by the units in which they exercised the command. But in the provinces where the Social Democrats were weak their influence within the *Volkswehr* was very limited, and so was that of the soldiers' councils. The whole council movement, inside and outside the army, met with the bitter hostility of the provincial governments, the bourgeois parties which had a clear majority in the Constituent Assembly,[36] and the middle and lower middle classes in general. It was rightly identified with the Social-Democratic Party and its stronghold in Vienna and thus had no chance ever to become a national movement. When the *Volkswehr* was transformed into the new regular army all social-democratic efforts to preserve the structure of the soldiers' councils were defeated by the bourgeois majority. Indeed, this was one of the causes leading to the break-up of the coalition government, and the Social Democrats moved into permanent opposition. As Austria was much less industrialized than Germany, the working-class movement was considerably weaker.

In Vienna the left-wing movements received a considerable impetus in the spring of 1919 when the Hungarian Soviet Republic was proclaimed, followed a few weeks later by the proclamation of a *Räterepublik* in Munich. It appeared that Vienna – and Austria in general – might form the bridge between 'red' Hungary and 'red' Bavaria. But the Council Republic in Munich lasted only a few weeks; it aroused but little enthusiasm in rural and catholic Bavaria and was suppressed by government troops at the end of April. This, however, did not end the Hungarian efforts to spur the rather reluctant Austrian Communists into action. The leaders of the Austrian party were removed by an emissary sent from Budapest, and in May 1919 a new 'directory' was appointed at his prompting which was to proclaim a Soviet Republic in Vienna. In mid-June the attempt was made, but it ended in miserable failure, for the ever-watchful Austrian police on the evening before the planned rising arrested the assembled Communist leaders. On the day itself, the demonstrators were dispersed by a volley of police shots, and the Vienna *Volkswehr* succeeded in preserving law and order without much difficulty.[37] Even if the attempt had succeeded in Vienna – and that was extremely unlikely against the opposition of the Social Democrats – 'red' Vienna would have been surrounded by a totally hostile countryside and cut off from all supplies of food and other necessities. But even in Vienna there was no revolutionary situation in June 1919;[38] and the Austrian Communists were much weaker still than their German comrades, partly because Austrian Social Democracy was further to the left than the German party. In Germany, the most revolutionary situation during this period probably existed in the days after the Kapp Putsch when the whole left was suddenly united in resisting a reactionary military Putsch; but even their motor was absent in Austria. There the end of the Hungarian Societ Republic in August 1919 marked also the end of all efforts at communist revolution.

The question arises whether there was a revolutionary situation in Hungary when the Societ Republic was proclaimed there by a united action of Social Democrats and

---

35. See Harry T. Willetts, "The agrarian problem", *Russia Enters the Twentieth Century* (London, 1971), p. 136.
36. On Feb. 16, 1919 the Social Democrats only gained 40 per cent of the vote and 69 out of 159 seats.
37. For details see F.L. Carsten, *Revolution in Central Europe 1918-1919* (London, 1972), pp. 231-234.
38. This against the opinion of Hans Hautmann and Rudolph Kropf, *Die österreichische Arbeiterbewegung vom Vormärz bis 1945, Sozialökonomische Ursprünge ihrer Ideologie und Politik* (Vienna, 1974), pp. 133, 197.

Communists in March 1919. There too, workers' and soldiers' councils were formed after the outbreak of the revolution in October 1918, and their power grew while that of the new government declined. Exactly as in Russia, this new government was unable to solve the land question, and in Hungary – in contrast with Austria – there were many thousands of land-hungry peasants. When the government did not carry out the promised scheme of land reform many large estates were forcibly occupied by peasants and agricultural labourers: there was an incipient agrarian revolution. In some counties, the administrative officials were chased away or forced to resign; in others, the local administration was taken over by new 'directorates'.[39] The government was unable to resist the occupation of the large estates because it had no reliable force at its disposal. Peasant councils took an active part in these developments. In short, the situation in Hungary in the early months of 1919 began to approximate to that in Russia two years earlier. Similar too was the semi-feudal state of society which made the peasants and the agricultural labourers a revolutionary class in both countries.

Yet the actual establishment of the Soviet Republic was caused not by a revolution, but by the ultimatum of the Allies handed to President Károlyi which demanded a further withdrawal of the Hungarian army and the occupation of more Hungarian territory by the Romanians. The government resigned rather than accept the ultimatum, and the "dictatorship of the proletariat" was proclaimed by the united Social Democrats and Communists in Budapest with the consent of the workers' council. At first an outburst of Hungarian nationalism worked in favour of the Soviet Republic and enabled the Red Army to conquer large areas which had belonged to the former kingdom, especially in Slovakia. Yet for doctrinaire reasons the revolutionary government did not distribute the land to the peasants and was thus unable to secure their loyalty. Disloyalty turned into hatred when punitive expeditions were organized against the peasantry to enforce deliveries and to crush all opposition. If Lenin thought it necessary to adopt the agrarian programme of the Socialist Revolutionaries and to sanction the take-over of the land by the peasants, this lesson was not learned by his Hungarian disciples. With regard to the land question, Communists could be as rigid and doctrinaire as German Social Democrats. It seems likely that, even if the Károlyi government had not resigned in March 1919 on account of the ultimatum, its authority would have declined further and a more left-wing government would have finally taken its place. But whether it would have been able to stay in power is a very different question. As it was the Allies were responsible both for the establishment and for the overthrow of the Soviet Republic.

In Italy, finally, a semi-revolutionary situation existed not in October 1922 when the Fascists marched on Rome, but two years earlier. In September 1920 the workers occupied the factories in Milan and Turin. 600,000 workers participated in the occupation, but it only took place in northern Italy and it ended in complete failure. The Italian Socialists were completely surprised by this spontaneous action and did not know what attitude to adopt towards it. The prime minister, Giolitti, suggested a compromise by which the workers received a small wage increase and the empty promise of workers' control in industry; and the factories were evacuated after some weeks of occupation.[40] About the same time an incipient agrarian revolution took place in many parts of Italy, especially in Emilia, Umbria, the Marches and Tuscany. Landless labourers and small-holders seized large areas of land belonging to big estates, land that was often badly farmed or not farmed at all. This again was a spontaneous movement not led by the Socialists or any other party. But it was unable to overcome the deep antagonism between small-holders, leaseholders and labourers who often clashed violently. The strikes and boycotts of the agricultural labourers were broken by the landowners, partly by offering some of them better conditions and even small plots of land, partly by the

---

39. For details see F.T. Zsuppan, "The Early Activities of the Hungarian Communist Party", *Slavonic and East European Review*, no. 101, (June 1965), pp. 331-334.
40. Denis Mack Smith, *Italy – A Modern History* (Ann Arbor, 1959), pp. 338-339; Erwin v. Beckerath, *Wesen und Werden des fascistischen Staates* (Berlin, 1927), p. 4; Robert Michels, *Sozialismus und Faschismus in Italien* (Munich, 1925), pp. 201 ff.

Revolutionary Situations in Europe, 1917-1920

use of armed fascist squads. This movement too ended in failure, and it offered to the Fascists the opportunity to establish their control in certain provinces, as a recent study of Fascism in Ferrara has shown.[41] As far as the Italian left was concerned, it was a tale of missed opportunities; but this does not mean that a dictatorship of the proletariat could have been established in Italy, for Socialist strength was concentrated in the north while the other regions and the Church were hostile to it.

The March on Rome itself can hardly be classified as a revolutionary seizure of power. It is true that some 25,000 Fascists were assembled in four columns in the neighbourhood of Rome, many of them unarmed, wet and hungry, to occupy the city. Meanwhile Mussolini waited in the safety of Milan for the royal summons, and this duly came after the king had refused to sign a decree proclaiming martial law. Thus Mussolini was able to arrive at Rome station in a sleeping car and *before* his men, and at the invitation of the king to form a constitutional government.[42] Recently Professor Renzo de Felice has maintained that Fascism was "revolutionary because it mobilized the masses for the first time and actively involved them. . . . in the day to day functioning of the system."[43] But in the twentieth century many regimes have succeeded in the mobilization and involvement of the masses: must they therefore all be called revolutionary? If this were so, then in the words of Denis Mack Smith's reply to this claim, "we shall have to find a new word for the events of 1789 and 1917".[44]

What, then, caused a revolutionary situation in Europe in the years after the first world war? In the first place, clearly military defeat which discredited the government and made it unable to resist demands for radical change. Military defeat also caused mutiny or near mutiny in the armed forces. Either they started the revolutionary movement, or they fraternized with the masses protesting against the continuation of the war and the misery which it had created. The old armies soon disintegrated under the impact of defeat and revolution. Their place had to be taken by new force more or less loyal to the revolutionary government. The revolution itself was not organized or prepared by any left-wing party, but it was a spontaneous mass movement in which the workers joined hands with the soldiers: their alliance was an essential element for the victory of the revolution. So was the support of the peasantry. In a Europe which was still largely agricultural the attitude of the peasants was of decisive importance. Where they turned against the revolution – as in Bavaria, Austria and Hungary – its achievements proved shortlived. The peasants could withhold vital supplies and force the revolutionary government to its knees. Everywhere the support of the urban working class provided too small a social basis, and the working class usually was deeply disunited. The attempts by radical minorities to push the revolution on to a more extremist course were doomed to failure from the outset, whether undertaken in Berlin, Munich, Vienna or Budapest. Especially in Munich and in Budapest these attempts prepared the way for counter-revolution, and ultimately for the rise of Fascism. In Russia, on the other hand, the revolutionary situation deepened in the course of 1917 because the Provisional Government continued a disastrous war and refused to sanction the expropriation of the land by the peasants, because the Soviets became more powerful than the government which possessed neither a military force nor an administrative machinery on which it could rely. These very exceptional circumstances played into the hands of the Bolsheviks: they did not create this situation, but they exploited it to the full.

---

41. Paul Corner, *Fascism in Ferrara 1915-1925* (Oxford, 1975).
42. For details see Mack Smith, *op. cit.*, pp. 365-372.
43. Michael Ledeen, in the *Times Literary Supplement* (Jan. 9, 1976), p. 36.
44. Mack Smith, *ibid.*, (Jan. 16, 1976), p. 58.

20

ARTHUR ROSENBERG:
ANCIENT HISTORIAN INTO
LEADING COMMUNIST

Among the German historians of the period before the second world war, Arthur Rosenberg occupies a unique place, not only because he stood very much on the left, but also because he was very active in politics, as a deputy in the Reichstag as well as a leading functionary of the KPD (Communist Party of Germany) and the Comintern (Communist International). There were a few other left-wing historians (the vast majority of German historians were fairly far to the right), for example Gustav Mayer and Eckart Kehr; but they took no prominent part in political life and were satisfied to make their mark through their writings; their politics, too, were much more moderate than those of Rosenberg, who was not only a leading communist, but also for some time a leader of the ultra-left wing of the party. It is also true, however, that he wrote the books by which he is remembered today—*The Birth of the German Republic*, *A History of Bolshevism*, *A History of the German Republic*, and *Democracy and Socialism*—after he had broken with the KPD and communism, and had ceased to play an active part in politics.

Curiously enough, there was nothing in the first thirty years of Rosenberg's life to indicate a trend to the left or a strong interest in politics. He was born in Berlin in 1889, the son of a Jewish businessman and, up to the outbreak of the revolution in November 1918, he led a conventional middle-class life, hardly disturbed even by the first world war and the rise of a radical anti-war movement in Germany. He went to a Berlin *Gymnasium*, and then studied history and classical philology at Berlin University, devoting most of his time to ancient history. In 1911 he gained his doctorate with a thesis on 'Investigations into the

Roman Centuriate Constitution'. Two years later, at the age of only twenty-four, he established himself as an unpaid university lecturer (*Privatdozent*) with a second thesis on 'The State of the old *Italici*: Constitution of the *Latini*, *Osci* and *Etrusci*'. After the outbreak of war in 1914 Rosenberg had to join the army but spent most of the war years in the War Press Department, and only a short time with the German army of occupation in France. He also did intelligence work for General Ludendorff, Quarter-Master General of the army, whom he greatly admired—Rosenberg's admiration for the efficiency and valour of the German army remained alive until his years of exile in the second world war. During the first war Rosenberg's strong German patriotism even led him to join the extreme right-wing *Vaterlandspartei* when it was founded in 1917, and remain a member until 1918.[1] In 1917 he published an entirely conventional introduction to a new edition of Johann Gustav Droysen's *History of Alexander the Great*, which showed no trace of political interest or any sign that a war was then in progress the effects of which were much vaster than all the campaigns of Alexander.[2]

It was only after the outbreak of the German revolution that Rosenberg became a member of the only large left-wing party, the Independent Social Democrats (USPD); but he took no prominent part in its activities; rather he continued to write on subjects of ancient history. At the end of 1920 the Independent Social Democrats split, owing to Russian intervention and pressure, and Rosenberg—with the party's left wing—joined the KPD, to become as early as 1921 one of the elected communist town councillors of Berlin. His speeches at the Communist party conferences of December 1920 and August 1921 were full of revolutionary enthusiasm, unmarked by any sense of reality. At a time when the strong radical trend of the years 1918–19 had been replaced by a marked trend to the right, not only in Germany, but above all in Italy, he exclaimed: 'Comrades! The world-revolutionary situation today is such that the wave is reaching

[1] Information kindly supplied by Professor Hans Rosenberg, University of California at Berkeley.

[2] Johann Gustav Droysen, *Geschichte Alexanders des Grossen*, introduction by Dr Arthur Rosenberg (Berlin 1917). For Rosenberg's early life and career see Helmut Schachenmayer, *Arthur Rosenberg als Vertreter des historischen Materialismus* (Wiesbaden 1964), 15–16; Hermann Weber, *Die Wandlung des deutschen Kommunismus*, II (Frankfurt 1969), 262.

Central Europe. Italy and Germany are becoming ripe for the decisive battle, a decisive battle that will have to be waged by us with similar tactics in both countries.' He stated that the Italian government had not dared to attack the factories occupied by the workers because they were well armed, and clearly considered that similar methods should be adopted in Germany.[3]

At the next party conference eight months later Rosenberg still envisaged 'great periods of fierce struggles' which would lead to 'heavy clashes with the state authorities', without even mentioning the fact that these tactics had just been tried in the ill-famed March Action of 1921 and had led to a catastrophe for the German communists. He admitted, however, that 'the large majority of the German workers at the moment are still following Menshevik parties'; but he got over this disagreeable fact by maintaining 'that almost every simple workman at heart is a communist in his feelings (*gefühlsmässig*)' and only did not quite believe yet that communism could be realized.[4] Like so many other enthusiastic communists, Rosenberg was convinced that a revolutionary situation existed, and even the new defeat of the German communists in the autumn of 1923 was unable to shake this conviction. On the contrary, within the KPD he joined the left opposition around Ruth Fischer and Arkadi Maslov which rejected the 'opportunist' course of Brandler and other party leaders; and it was in Rosenberg's house in Berlin that the left oppositionists secretly met leaders of the Russian Workers' Opposition, such as Shlyapnikov and Lutovinov, who had been banished to Berlin after their defeat at the tenth party congress of the Bolshevik party. Both groups rejected Lenin's New Economic Policy and the consequent move to the 'right' in the policy of the Comintern, which in their opinion marked a 'degeneration' of communism.[5] Hence Rosenberg rose to real prominence in the KPD only after the defeat of 1923 and the take-over of the party by the left opposition. In 1924 he became a member of the party directorate for the district of Berlin-Brandenburg and was made a member of the central committee at the party conference held at Frankfurt in April of the same year. In July, at the Fifth World

[3] *Bericht über die Verhandlungen des Vereinigungsparteitages der USPD (Linke) und der KPD (Spartakusbund)* (Berlin 1921), 143-44.
[4] *Bericht über die Verhandlungen des 2. Parteitages der Kommunistischen Partei Deutschlands*, 22-26 August 1921 (Berlin 1922), 346.
[5] Schachenmayer, op. cit., 23-24; Weber, op. cit., II, 262-63.

Congress of the Comintern, Rosenberg was even elected a member of its Executive Committee (ECCI) and of its Presidium. In May he became a deputy of the Reichstag, which he remained until the general election of 1928.

Within the KPD, Rosenberg—together with Werner Scholem—soon emerged as the leader of the ultra-left opposition to Ruth Fischer and Maslov, but nevertheless remained a member of the central committee. In the spring of 1926, however, he took an attitude different from that of the ultra-left and soon after he began to support the new party leadership under Thälmann.[6] By the autumn of 1925 his attitude had become much more realistic than it had been only recently. In an article on the internal party discussions published in November he clearly stated that the KPD could command the allegiance only of a minority of the proletariat and that this minority exercised only a minimal influence on the rest of the working class; that the large majority of the German working class followed the SPD, the Catholics and the Black-White-Reds (Nationalists); 'of the peasants we have only won over a few per cent, not to mention the lower middle class and the intellectuals.' He added quite unequivocally that the masses of the workers were for the social-democrats (SPD) because they were convinced that in a non-revolutionary situation the SPD represented their interests better than the KPD, because they considered the communists 'a herd of confused concocters of theses, rowdies and putschists'. The party, he continued, had not yet developed a serious, sober style of work: 'with us the revolution has been in general "organized" in as slovenly a way as the accounts of our literature sales', and he demanded a programme with simple, concrete demands which everybody could understand, especially on the local level, such as increased benefits for the unemployed and old age pensioners, distribution of food, clothes, and coal to the needy by local communal organizations, the procuring of cheap living accommodation: these were demands which the masses could understand;[7] but they were in glaring contrast to current KPD methods.

In the Reichstag Rosenberg spoke frequently for his party on a variety of subjects, especially on matters of taxation, customs and

---

[6] Schachenmayer, op. cit., 25–26; Weber, op. cit., II, 263.

[7] Arthur Rosenberg, 'Einige Bemerkungen zur Parteidiskussion', *Die Internationale* (Berlin), 1 November 1925, 693–96.

reparations, on foreign policy and Germany's entry into the League of Nations, and in protest against the one-sided verdicts of the German courts in political cases, against 'class justice'. On most occasions, his speeches were not particularly distinguished and they did not differ from the current party line. Thus he opposed Germany's attempt to join the League with the argument that it was 'nothing but an instrument of power of French capitalism'—a remark which earned applause not only from the communists but also from the national socialists. Therefore, Rosenberg continued, Germany should not make any effort to become a part of this power apparatus of the French big capitalists, and he found it 'monstrous' that a large party should have put forward a motion to that effect. 'The only possible national policy', he proclaimed, was for 'the proletariat to constitute itself as the nation' and to carry out the liberation of the working masses, 'and in this sense a national policy in Germany will begin only when the revolution is carried through'.[8] Ten months later Rosenberg repeated that the League of Nations was an instrument for the coming war against Soviet Russia; if Germany became a member she too would become a tool used in support of a war of intervention; it was particularly regrettable that the SPD supported such dangerous tendencies and lent its hand to plans which brought a real danger of war, and this merely because of that party's hostility to Russia and the KPD.[9]

There were occasions, however, when Rosenberg was able to make use of his great historical knowledge to confound his political critics. In an attack on the German tax on turnover he defended the Roman system of taxes which had not known any tax on wages, which had distributed bread free to the poor and charged them no rent for one year; and he offered his adversary a private tutorial on ancient history, when the latter called out that the turnover tax had been invented by the Emperor Augustus.[10] Even more trenchant was Rosenberg's intervention on the issue of the huge indemnities which were to be paid to the former German princely houses—the occasion of a plebiscite in favour of their expropriation organized by the left-wing parties which

[8] *Verhandlungen des Reichstags*, 25 July 1924, Stenographische Berichte, vol. 381, 682, 688.
[9] Ibid., 20 May 1925, vol. 385, 1974.
[10] Ibid., 3 August 1925, vol. 387, 3906.

mobilized many millions but was in the end unsuccessful. In June 1926 Rosenberg reminded the Catholic Centre Party, the leading party in the government which was strongly in favour of the proposed indemnities, that the German princes had made their profits whenever there was a revolutionary change: at the time of the Reformation a large number of princes converted to Protestantism only so as to be able to seize the monasteries and other possessions of the Church: 'It is an irony of fate that the bishops with their authority have solemnly come out in defence of the legality and the conservation of this robbery of the Catholic Church'. The second period of systematic appropriation of other people's property by the princes had been the time of Napoleon, when the Imperial Diet carried out the reorganization of Germany and when the dynasties which now demanded compensation—Hohenzollern and Wittelsbach, Wettin and Württemberg—used this opportunity to usurp vast lands in central and southern Germany.[11] But the Centre was not to be swayed by arguments which were historically correct but seemed to violate the cherished principle of private property.

BY FAR THE MOST IMPORTANT parliamentary activity of Arthur Rosenberg was his prominent participation in the work of the committee appointed by the Reichstag in 1925 to investigate the causes of the German collapse in 1918. This was the fourth parliamentary committee charged with the same task; but it was only during the years after 1925 that real progress was made in the work, and that in particular the 'stab-in-the-back' legend was very closely investigated and at least in part demolished. On 2 December 1925 Rosenberg used the opportunity of his nomination as an expert reporter to the committee to deliver a lengthy lecture on the political currents on the German left during the war years. He emphasized that there had been not only two currents—one in favour of measures of defence and supporting the war effort (the SPD), and the other opposed to them (the USPD and Left Radicals); the latter two were only too often identified. In reality, however, there had been three main groupings in the working-class movement which had to be clearly distinguished: a right wing represented by the SPD, a centre consisting of the Independent Social Democrats, and a left wing

[11] Ibid., 29 June 1926, vol. 390, 7692.

consisting of the Spartacus League as its nucleus as well as several other groups. He went on strongly to deny the allegations, mainly put forward by naval officers, that the Independents had undermined the navy by their agitation in 1917–18, had instigated the outbreak of the naval mutiny and therewith the collapse of the front, for the Independent Party was not in principle opposed to defence measures and was not a revolutionary party. The Left Radicals, on the other hand, had no influence on the events of 1917–18 in the navy, and the mutinous sailors had not even known of the existence of groups to the left of the Independents; their demands were very moderate and showed no trace of Spartacist influence; the sailors were children, not revolutionaries. The revolution of November 1918 started from Kiel, Hamburg, and Munich, towns where the Left Radicals had virtually no followers; 95 per cent of the soldiers' councils supported the SPD; neither the Independents nor the Left Radicals had exercised an influence worth mentioning among the soldiers' councils. National resistance was no longer possible in November 1918, not even in alliance with Soviet Russia, for the German people were physically exhausted and the situation at the front was desperate on account of the lack of reserves, and no government could have changed this state of affairs.[12]

The chairman of the committee, Dr Philipp, a member of the Nationalist Party, commented after this exhaustive lecture that Dr Rosenberg had as it were split his personality and that a clear division ran through his report: first he spoke in strictly scholarly fashion as an academic, but at the end came his personal political judgment; and the report clearly exercised a marked influence on some of the witnesses.[13] When another expert, the very conservative archivist of the *Reichsarchiv* E. O. Volkmann, noted that in Berlin a revolutionary committee had been formed in October 1918, Rosenberg was quick to point out that this committee was unable to act on account of its internal differences, that it was completely overtaken by events, that by the time it decided to do something the whole of Germany was already engulfed by revolution, so that Berlin had to follow suit. When the committee's chairman and Dr Volkmann blamed the revolution for bringing

[12] *Die Ursachen des Deutschen Zusammenbruchs im Jahre 1918*, Zweite Abteilung IV (Berlin 1928), 91 ff.
[13] Ibid., 333.

about chaos at the eastern front and the dissolution of the army, which allegedly caused the loss of Posnania, West Prussia and other districts, Rosenberg countered by stating that the war was already lost; a compromise peace was out of the question, and an eastern frontier a little more favourable to Germany did not mean very much at a time of such world-shaking events. Their opinions, he continued, amounted in practice to giving up the 'stab-in-the-back' accusation against the revolutionaries; what was decisive was the fact that the Entente had proclaimed as one of its war aims the 'Restitution of Poland with free access to the Sea'; unfortunate for Germany, too, was the accident that the coastal district to the west of Danzig was purely Polish. Thereupon another deputy interrupted: 'They are Cassubians!' To which Rosenberg replied that the inhabitants considered themselves Poles and in all elections to the Reichstag and the Prussian Diet voted for Polish candidates, so that the Poles were able to extend their state and to include in it this coastal area.[14]

At a later meeting of the parliamentary committee Rosenberg developed for the first time his new theory, subsequently expounded in *The Birth of the German Republic*, that the real revolution in Germany occurred in *October* 1918 when the military High Command collapsed and Ludendorff resigned, when power was taken over by the large middle strata of the German nation, which were opposed to Ludendorff's dictatorship and to that of the agrarians and the bourgeoisie but did not aim at social revolution. He even went so far as to declare that what happened in November 1918 was of importance only as an accessory (*Beiwerk*), that there had been two revolutions during the war, the first in 1916, with the establishment of military dictatorship, and the second in October 1918 with its collapse, but none in November.[15] Thus he ignored entirely the elemental revolutionary process of November–December 1918, when workers' and soldiers' councils sprang up like mushrooms all over Germany and took over political power, in favour of a rather legalistic constitutional interpretation—a strange attitude for a professed revolutionary marxist. Rosenberg also quite correctly indicated the basic weakness of Bismarck's German Empire: its 'birth mark' was 'that this large modern industrial state was built

[14] Ibid., V (Berlin 1928), 215–22.
[15] Ibid., VII, i (Berlin 1928), 261.

upon a feudal aristocratic base', that it 'was burdened with the tremendous ballast of the old feudal system', 'a piece of the Middle Ages which as it were projected into modern bourgeois society'.[16] There is no doubt that Rosenberg learned an enormous amount during his work for the parliamentary committee of enquiry, that he was able to study many confidential documents—knowledge which he later put to good use. His contributions to the committee's work were so highly valued by his parliamentary colleagues that after his resignation from the KPD he was asked to continue as a member, although now without a vote.[17]

AFTER HE LEFT THE KPD Rosenberg continued as a Reichstag deputy, but only to the end of the legislative period in the spring of 1928. When speaking on the subject of 'class justice' and political amnesty in July 1927, he clearly outlined his attitude to the party he had just left:

> It is absolutely not the case that the official KPD constitutes any real danger to the existing state. On the basis of my knowledge of the Communist party I can emphasize with all stress: there is no responsible communist who thinks in any way of deeds of violence or actions against the law, even in the slightest way. What remains is only a certain romantic phraseology which does not constitute the slightest real threat to the existing political order. The danger, the unpleasant side of this romanticism, lies in a different field. Through this romanticism millions of workers are prevented from pursuing their interests in a realistic and factual way. The fight against romanticism causes the other tendencies and groups of the working class movement to squander their energies to an extraordinary extent.[18]

This was one of the very few occasions when Rosenberg spoke publicly about his reasons for leaving the KPD. He clearly recognized that it was the split in the working-class movement and the resulting in-fighting which absorbed all its energies. Officially he motivated his resignation in April 1927 by the complete failure of the Comintern in China (at the time of the beginning civil war between Kuomintang and Chinese commun-

---

[16] Ibid., V, 223; VII, i, 251.
[17] Schachenmayer, op. cit., 22.
[18] *Verhandlungen des Reichstags*, vol. 393, 1181.

ists) and a turn to the right in Soviet policy, which meant that the Comintern had become a drag on it and ought to be dissolved.[19] But the reasons given in his Reichstag speech seem less far-fetched and more realistic. In fact Rosenberg ceased to be a revolutionary romantic and turned to the serious writing of recent history. In the following year his first major book, *The Birth of the German Republic*, was published in Berlin, very largely the fruit of his work as a member of the parliamentary committee of enquiry into the causes of the German collapse. Four years later there followed his *History of Bolshevism*, the first serious academic treatment of the subject, again partly based on his personal experience.

Rosenberg retired from active political life and did not join any other party. But in fact he moved closer to the SPD and began to write for several of its journals, especially *Die Gesellschaft*, edited by Rudolf Hilferding. There he published critical essays on 'bourgeois' historians, such as Treitschke and Delbrück. When Delbrück died in 1929 Rosenberg wrote very appreciatively of his work, which he considered 'an important possession for socialist, proletarian research'. While Delbrück sometimes came close to the marxist interpretation of history, he had never accepted it; he would never have subscribed to the interpretation of a materialist historian that the basic fact of German history in the eighteenth century was the class conflict between the nobility and the serfs, and that compared with this the wars between Frederick the Great and Maria Theresa were 'a small domestic quarrel within the ruling class'.[20] When writing on 'Treitschke and the Jews' in 1930—a truly burning problem at a time of rising anti-semitism at the German universities—Rosenberg tried to explain the prevalence of anti-semitism in German academic circles by the ideology which they required to defend their social position. 'The enmity towards the Jews which was characteristic of a large section of German academics already before the war, was part of the aristocratic ideal of life which these men were searching for. The nobility by birth felt at heart much more secure. It did not need such an ideological buttress.'[21] In these and other interpretations Rosenberg tried to uphold an orthodox marxist point

---

[19] Weber, op. cit., II, 263; Schachenmayer, op. cit., 27.
[20] 'Hans Delbrück', *Die Gesellschaft*, September 1929, 252.
[21] 'Treitschke und die Juden', *Die Gesellschaft*, July 1930, 82.

of view, and he also preserved a positive attitude towards the Bolshevik revolution. In 1932 he considered the Bolsheviks' teachings and methods as 'tremendously progressive for the Russia of the tsars', and what the Bolsheviks accomplished in the course of the revolution as 'an immortal historical achievement'. But what was progressive for Russia was reactionary for the developed industrial countries of the West, where the bourgeois revolution had been by and large completed, and where the peasantry no longer constituted the majority of the population.[22] Although he never joined the SPD, Rosenberg was fairly close to its left wing; he not only lectured to appreciative audiences at Berlin University but also gave courses to the leaders of the SPD youth organization.[23]

In March 1933 Rosenberg left Germany for good. In the same month the University of Berlin, in a report to the Prussian Ministry of Education, stated that his *History of Bolshevism* was clearly designed to glorify Bolshevism; and in September he was deprived of the *venia legendi*.[24] During the years 1934–37 he lectured at the University of Liverpool, and then went to the United States; until his death on 7 February 1943 he was a professor at Brooklyn College, New York. During these years he continued to write for social-democratic periodicals, above all the *Zeitschrift für Sozialismus*, published by the emigré leadership of the SPD, on historical and political topics. In the same publishing house of the Sudeten German Social Democrats, Graphia at Karlsbad, there also appeared in 1935 what was perhaps Rosenberg's most important book, his *History of the German Republic*. Thus his links with the SPD remained close even during the years of emigration. Whether he would have resumed a more active political role after the end of the war is, of course, impossible to say.

Rosenberg's *History of the German Republic* covers only the years 1918 to 1930: he deliberately excluded the years of the Brüning, Papen, and Schleicher governments. As he put it in the introduction: 'From the point of view of historical development January 1933 has brought nothing in Germany that is new in

---

[22] *Geschichte des Bolschewismus* (Berlin 1933), 231.
[23] Information by the late Fritz Erler, who attended one of the courses, held shortly before Hitler's seizure of power.
[24] Schachenmayer, op. cit., 32, 34.

principle, but has only emphasized by way of an extraordinary exacerbation the same tendencies which had been dominant ever since Brüning's emergency decrees of 1930.' The book itself would prove that its author had been justified in concluding his narrative with the year 1930 when Brüning became Chancellor.[25] Almost two years after the establishment of Hitler's dictatorship Rosenberg was unable to see that it was something new in principle, that, while Brüning might have used semi-dictatorial methods, he had been neither a dictator nor a fascist. In truth Germany in the years 1930–32 was not a totalitarian country; on the contrary it saw violent clashes between a multitude of political parties and three general elections in which these were absolutely free in their political propaganda, and in which even the KPD could score considerable successes.

In 1934 Rosenberg published, again in the Sudeten German Social-Democratic publishing house, a substantial pamphlet on *Fascism as a Mass Movement*, in which his somewhat strange views on the subject were explained in detail. There he distinguished not only two but three forms of German fascism: the National Socialists; the old German Nationalists who were opposed to any kind of socialism and unconditionally defended private capitalism; and thirdly the so-called *Volkskonservativen* or the Brüning tendency, 'who had no sizeable following either among the masses or among the capitalist upper class, but were able on account of favourable circumstances to exercise power in Germany during the years 1930–32'. Even the Cuno government of 1923 was classified as 'the victory of legal fascism'. He claimed that fascism originated neither among the youth nor among the lower middle classes; it represented 'the counter-revolutionary capitalist, the born foe of the class-conscious working class. Fascism is nothing but a modern, popularly masked form of bourgeois capitalist counter-revolution'. In other words Rosenberg identified any reactionary dictatorship or semi-dictatorship, any authoritarian capitalist government with fascism, and hence naturally could maintain that National Socialism had added nothing that was new in principle to the picture of modern class conflicts.[26]

[25] *Geschichte der Deutschen Republik* (Karlsbad 1935; English trans. London 1936), 6.
[26] Historikus, *Der Faschismus als Massenbewegung* (Karlsbad 1934), 7, 51, 59, 75.

Throughout these years Rosenberg's strong marxist views did not change, and it is from this angle that his curious interpretation of fascism can best be understood. His last book, on *Democracy and Socialism*, was in reality a vindication of Marx's pronouncements on the subject of democracy, based in particular on the writings of the young Marx and on the correspondence between Marx and Engels.[27] Rosenberg came to marxism not in his youth but comparatively late, when already fully established as an ancient historian, and marxism provided the inspiration for his activities as a politician as well as a historian; but his particular form of marxism also prevented him from assessing new developments. It is difficult to explain his sudden change from an extreme right-wing to an extreme left-wing position in the year 1918. Unexplained, too, remains the curious contradiction of the mid-1920s when he not only became a leading communist but moved to the ultra-left wing of the German party, while at the same time retaining his sound historical judgment and his mastery in grasping the complex events of the German collapse of 1918. His books on the history of Bolshevism and of the Weimar Republic remain remarkable achievements and have found a strong echo among the younger generation of German historians, exactly like the essays of Eckart Kehr. It is a great pity that neither of them was able to exercise a personal influence on this younger generation, which would have found Rosenberg's great political experience and his learning particularly attractive. Today Arthur Rosenberg no longer occupies an isolated position; his views are echoed by many academics and especially by the younger generation.

[27] Arthur Rosenberg, *Demokratie und Sozialismus—Zur Geschichte der letzten 150 Jahre* (Amsterdam 1938; English trans. London 1939).

21

'VOLK OHNE RAUM'

A NOTE ON HANS GRIMM

Of all the political slogans current in Germany in the 1920s and 1930s, none exercised a stronger influence on the youth of the country in school and university than that which proclaimed that Germany needed more space, that the nation – to be able to live – required more *Raum*. Deprived of its colonial empire by the Treaty of Versailles without any justification – thus the young were taught in the German schools – the Germans had become a *Volk ohne Raum*, a nation without living space. They were pressed together in a narrow and overpopulated country; like plants in an overgrown field they had no chance to develop and to grow; but the other European nations possessed enormous empires which could absorb the energies of the young and the ambitious and offered them vast opportunities not available to young Germans. In a country where the position of the middle and lower middle classes was undermined by the consequences of the war and the defeat and, above all, by the inflation of the mark which deprived millions of their savings and their property, these slogans found a ready echo. Many thousands ardently believed that all that Germany needed was more 'space'. But the great propaganda effect of the phrase *Volk ohne Raum* was more than anything else due to a novel with that title first published in 1926. Its author was Hans Grimm, hitherto a little known writer, then 51 years old; he had spent the decisive years of his early manhood in British South Africa as a trader, but had returned to Germany in 1910. His long novel, running to well over 1200 pages, had a vast success. Within a few years it sold hundreds of thousands of copies; before the Second World War the sales had reached half a million, and by 1964 more than 700,000, showing that its influence is continuing in post-war Germany.

This success was not due to the novel's literary merits – it is poorly written and full of digressions – but to its political content, its message to the Germans. This indeed seems to be the purpose of the whole book which is patently political and propagandist. Its story, briefly told, is that of a young German born in the later nineteenth century into a peasant family unable to make a living on its small farm near the Weser. Hence the father of the family, and later his only son too, is forced to seek work in industry – symbolizing the road of millions of Germans from the land into the factory. The son, however, rebels against this fate, which deprives him of the possibility of marrying the love of his youth, and eventually – under the influence of his only friend – joins the social-democrats. In consequence he is dismissed from his job, first in a Bochum metal works, later in a Ruhr mine where he becomes involved in a mining disaster which he is unable to avert. Sentenced to a short term of imprisonment for his inflammatory speech at the graves of his comrades, he emigrates to South Africa where he begins to prosper through his industry and skill. At the outbreak of the Boer War he – like many other Germans – volunteers for the Boer army, is wounded in one of the first battles and taken prisoner. After years of imprisonment by the British on the island of St Helena he returns to South Africa; but he finds life more and more unbearable in a British colony, where the Germans find themselves treated as second-class citizens, and decides to try his luck in the new German colony of South-West Africa. There he takes part in the fight against the Hottentots, then together with a cousin buys a large farm, and again makes good, thanks to his hard work and ability, but also because of his fortuitous participation in the diamond rush which engulfed the colony. The outbreak of the First World War, however, destroys his newly-found prosperity, and that of the whole colony. He has to leave his farm on account of difficulties with the British occupying force and finds refuge on the farm of a friend; there he pursues and in self-defence kills the leader of a band of marauding bushmen. For this deed he is arrested by the British authorities, tried and sentenced first to death and then to a long spell of imprisonment. Escaping from prison after the German collapse he succeeds in making his way as a fugitive to Portuguese Angola, where he is rearrested at British behest but finally shipped back to Europe. Arriving in the defeated Germany of the early 1920s he in vain tries to arouse his countrymen to a consciousness of their political situation, of their confinement within too narrow a space, while the colonial powers enjoy all the advantages of their empires. During one of his propaganda tours he is attacked and killed by a political enemy. It is only the writer Hans Grimm who (figuring prominently in the novel) is able to understand the message given by this man when they meet near their native villages on the Weser; the vast majority of his listeners remain indifferent, considering the hero of the story a cross between a quack and an itinerant preacher.

Hundreds of thousands of Germans certainly did not remain indifferent to Grimm's novel, which became a best-seller on its publication in 1926 in 'the month of fog of that year, in the confused days of Locarno'.[1] This success cannot be explained by its artistic merit or by the writer's skill in telling a long and involved story, but by its immediate appeal to the political prejudices of masses of fairly unpolitical Germans. Grimm told them what they wanted to hear, what they consciously or subconsciously believed, what helped them to compensate the sense of humiliation created by the defeat of 1918 and the Treaty of Versailles. He confirmed to them that they were 'the cleanest and most decent and most honest and most efficient and most industrious nation of the earth' (p. 1110); and that 'the most numerous and most skilled and most productive white nation of the earth, through its own responsibility and that of its ancestors, lives within too narrow frontiers' (p. 1073).

At times this assurance is deliberately put into the mouth of non-Germans. Thus a Portuguese officer tells the hero after Germany's defeat:

The world has suffered a vast misfortune through the strangling of Germany. When the German men-of-war were still afloat with their brilliant flag, and when there still was a German army and a German emperor, freedom was still upheld among the nations (p. 1182).

This German mission in the world is repeatedly emphasized, by the hero of the novel as well as by others:

We must go to ourselves, we must, we must, we must. Otherwise the forces of rejuvenation will be diverted from Germany and will be

---

[1] *Volk ohne Raum*, p. 1299. All references are to the unabridged edition in one volume, 341st to 365th thousand (Munich, s.d.).

sucked away! And, when we are completely finished, there certainly will never be any help for the world! (p. 595).

'Germany with its peace and its love of foreigners and its diligence and its distinguished leaders and its victories'[2] was superior to the other nations, in spite of the defeat and the decline in the years after 1918.

As a race, too, the Germans were better than their neighbours if only they remained pure and did not mix with 'inferior blood'. Of a peasant family from the Weser Grimm writes:

> His children were slim and blond, as if they had grown up in the forest among the beeches; and it was quite clear that neither Celt nor Slav, neither Frenchman (*Welscher*) nor Jew had adulterated their Lower Saxon blood (p. 45).

To this pure group of course also belonged the hero, who had grown into 'a tall youngster with a long, fine face, as it belongs to a Lower Saxon of untainted blood' (p. 83). Among the British, on the other hand, Grimm distinguishes those who belong 'to the rarer English Germanic type' and hence are the more decent, and those who 'belong to the stupidly proud, usual mixed Britondom (*Mischbritentum*)' and only want to instruct others (p. 513). In general Grimm had come to dislike the British during his long stay in South Africa – perhaps because the 'germanic type' was so rare among them. They had grabbed an empire and refused to share it with others; but they also suffered from other faults:

> With the British there exists a special trait: they have to see the enemy, that means whom they make into their enemy, outwardly too in dirt and filth; then they can feel superior and chosen; and on this their sluggish fantasy then feeds (p. 1032).

Throughout the book the British are cast in the role of the villain, not the French or the Dutch whose colonial empires were equally vast. It was Britain which deliberately prevented German expansion in Africa, which deliberately humiliated and maltreated Germans (and Boers), and which possessed the space in four continents which Germany needed in order to live. British misdeeds during the Boer War are recounted in detail, but not one

---

[2] p. 191. Needless to say, this was a reference to the Germany of William II, not that of the Weimar Republic.

word is said about the similar German deeds of the Herero War in South-West Africa. The explanation is quite simple:

> The women and children [of the Boers] were white; and that is still different from Hereros and Hottentots, and this remains a different thing no less before God than it is before man (p. 605).

It was thus only British perfidy which put the hero on trial for the killing of a mere Hottentot.

All this was the violent German nationalism and racialism that was only too common in Weimar Germany – in 1932 Grimm pronounced solemnly: 'I have one sole passion and its name is Germany.'[3] But there was something more he emphasized. There was the secret alliance between Germany's enemies abroad and their helpers inside Germany. The latter were, above all, the social-democrats, and in the second instance the Jews, and many of the socialist leaders happened to be Jews. As a German officer serving in South-West Africa puts it in a talk with the hero:

> ... but the awful thing is that the material for the impertinent fairy tales of the bad German has been supplied for many years by born Germans and always originates in the stupid German internal political struggle. From Marx and Moses Hess and Engels and Liebknecht and Jacoby and Pfau, if you know all the names, to Harden, you can read what the mischiefmakers in the world repeat against us; and formerly they said Prussia, and later they said the Prussianized Germany and the Emperor.[4]

The theme of the collusion between the British and the social-democrats is repeated again and again, for example in the description of a socialist meeting in Saxony where the speaker holds forth for two hours on the 'suppression of the Prussian worker', the 'strangling of democracy in the Reich', the 'subjugation of the world', and the 'rule of Junkers and generals'. The meeting is presided over by 'comrade Siegfried Katz, lawyer Dr Siegfried Katz', who 'did not belong to those without any property' but confirmed the speaker's valuable remarks. 'Accidentally a travelling British expert on Germany took part in the meeting.... He wrote

---

[3] Quoted from a pamphlet published in 1932 by Edgar Kirsch, *Hans Grimm und der nordische Mensch* (Munich, 1938), p. 14.

[4] *Volk ohne Raum*, p. 931. The majority of the names mentioned are those of Jews.

an article: "Germans amongst themselves. – The true meaning of Prussian militarism. – A brutal Confession." ... Through the good offices of Reuter's News Agency this article was sent out into the English-speaking world' (p. 368). There are three components of the conspiracy against Germany: the social-democrats, the Jews, and the British, all acting together if only unintentionally.

The Jews, in Grimm's opinion, were unable to understand the essence of Germanhood, hence their hostility to anything German. As a German doctor explains to the hero:

I tell you more than half of all that is written and said in Germany is written and said against Germany by men who use the German language and live in German towns, but who have not understood the tribes which constitute the Germans and the German Reich, the Lower Saxons and Frisians, the Swabians and Bavarians, the Franconians and Thuringians, and will never understand them and cannot possibly understand them (p. 515).

That this is not an opinion ascribed to others but Grimm's very own is evident from a pamphlet which he wrote more than twenty years later, after the collapse of the Third Reich. There he re-affirms that 'a definite Jewish circle had its special share in the vexatious tales told about Prussia-Germany', but maintains simultaneously that he had never been an anti-Semite.[5] In the novel Jewish activities are only too often identified with those of the British, especially in the economic field. One speaker uses the words 'the banks and the stock exchange and the Jews' three times within one paragraph (p. 869), a phrase similar to Hitler's identification of the Jews with 'grasping' capital. In general there is a striking parallel between the story of the sinister Jewish World Conspiracy, which figured so prominently in national-socialist propaganda, and the collusion between the British, the Jews, and the social-democrats which Grimm emphasizes. The one is more polite and less primitive than the other, and for that reason could be all the more easily believed.

It is true, of course, that the political message of the novel reflected the ideas current in the Germany of the time. But it would be to underestimate the influence exercised by one of the most popular German writers to be satisfied with this truism. Grimm was a writer who strongly influenced public opinion,

---

[5] Hans Grimm, *Rückblick* (Göttingen, ca. 1950), p. 15.

especially among the middle and lower middle classes, and to a large extent helped to mould it. The success of the national-socialists in capturing the lower middle class and the youth of the country must largely be attributed to those who prepared the ground. The preparation of the ground included the insidious attacks on the social-democrats, at a time when they occupied leading posts in the governments of Germany and of the major German states. If the leaders of this party had cooperated with the national enemy before the First World War when they were in opposition, what might they not accomplish against the national interest in the powerful positions which they held in the 1920s? The German middle classes deeply distrusted all Reds and Marxists: Grimm and others of his kind told them why they were justified in doing so. As the social-democrats had taken a leading part in the creation of the Weimar Republic, this propaganda naturally affected the existence of the republic itself.

Yet the major importance of Grimm's novel undoubtedly lies in the creation of the legend of the *Volk ohne Raum*, of the nation which needed more space if it wanted to survive. It is true that Grimm aimed at gaining that space in Africa at the expense of Britain, while Hitler sought it in eastern Europe, especially in Poland. Yet this seems largely a tactical difference. If millions of young Germans were brought up in the belief that more space was the nation's primary need – and this was a marked trait of the instruction in the secondary schools from the 1920s onwards, and even more so after 1933 – then one day they would be willing to die for this idea. Their graves are to be found from the Arctic Circle to the Caucasus, but Hans Grimm lived to deny vociferously any responsibility for the events of the Third Reich. It is true that he was not a national-socialist and differed from them in certain matters. Rather he was an extreme nationalist. In Germany nationalism of a violent and anti-western type has a much stronger tradition than national-socialism; this kind of fervent nationalism is much more likely to stage a come-back than Hitler's brand of a German fascism.

22

RADICAL NATIONALIST OFFICERS CONTRA HITLER[1]

Nearly twenty years after the attempt on Hitler's life by Claus Count Schenk von Stauffenberg one of the best known German newspapers published an article with the headline 'Embarrassment about Stauffenberg'.[2] A biography of the Count published at the same time stated regretfully: 'In West Germany – the only country to be mentioned – one makes an embarrassed detour around Stauffenberg. One does not love him.'[3] It is true that the Bendlerstrasse in Berlin – the seat of the Army High Command, where Stauffenberg made his plans to overthrow the tyrant and where he was shot in the evening of 20 July 1944 exclaiming 'Long live our Holy Germany!' – has been renamed Stauffenbergstrasse. But in West Germany there is much stronger sympathy with the conservative heads of the conspiracy – Carl Goerdeler, Ludwig Beck, Ulrich von Hassel or Johannes Popitz – or with the moderate Social Democrats who collaborated with them – Wilhelm Leuschner, Julius Leber, Carlo Mierendorff – than with the hotblooded, reckless, fanatical young colonel, whom Goerdeler called 'wrong-headed' and a man who wanted 'to play a part in politics'.[4]

How can this attitude to Stauffenberg be explained, and what were his political ideas and plans? We know that originally he was, like so many young men of his generation, rather uncritical of Hitler and National Socialism. As one of his biographers writes, 'certainly, Stauffenberg did not object from the beginning . . . For a long time he saw in Hitler a symbol of the resurrection of the nation.'[5] Hitler's nationalism, stressed time and again, his fulminations against the 'chains of Versailles', his promises to make Germany again great and strong, the 'national uprising' he inaugurated, won over large numbers of young Germans, and among them many young officers. There is even a report by a fellow officer that on 30 January 1933, when an enthusiastic crowd celebrated the National Socialist victory in the streets of Bamberg, Stauffenberg took part in the demonstration; when

---

[1] 'Radical nationalist' is an attempt at the translation of the German term 'nationalrevolutionär' which indicates extreme right-wing views with a revolutionary connotation, in some ways more radical than those of the National Socialists. This essay was written for the 20th anniversary of the bomb plot, but during the past twenty years political attitudes in West Germany have not changed all that much.
[2] *Die Zeit*, no. 12, 20 March 1964.
[3] Bodo Scheurig, *Claus Graf Schenk von Stauffenberg*, Berlin, 1964, p. 90.
[4] Goerdeler's memorandum of November 1944, quoted by G. Ritter, *Carl Goerdeler und die deutsche Widerstandsbewegung*, Stuttgart, 1954, p. 527, note 46.
[5] Scheurig, op. cit., p. 91.

he was reprimanded by a superior officer he is said to have remarked to his comrades that the great soldiers of the War of Liberation against Napoleon would have had more of 'a feeling for such a genuine popular revolt'.[6] The young count – he was then 25 years old – a lieutenant in the 17th Bavarian cavalry regiment, felt closer to the spirit of the War of Liberation than to the 'office generals' of the Bendlerstrasse who commanded the Reichswehr. The army of 100,000 men stipulated by the Treaty of Versailles felt isolated from the people by its very structure, separated from the nation. Would not the National Socialist movement be able to build the bridge to the people? Could not the Reichswehr thus be freed from its isolation?

Ideas such as these were held by many young army officers. As early as 1929 Lieutenant Henning von Tresckow – later one of the leaders of the military opposition to Hitler – gave an approving lecture in the officers' mess at Potsdam on the 'Breaking of the Shackles of Interest', one of the National Socialist propaganda slogans; in other ways too he tried to influence the officers of his regiment, the aristocratic 9th Prussian infantry regiment, in favour of National Socialism.[7] Similar ideas were current among the lieutenants of another Potsdam regiment, the 4th Prussian cavalry regiment, which like the other had a large percentage of noble officers.[8] In 1929 leaflets circulated in the army which were written by young officers and began with the terse statement: 'The spirit in the Reichswehr is dead.' All officers who desired the victory of the 'national revolution' must join hands and must achieve 'that the Reichswehr does not fire on a national popular uprising, but makes common cause with the uprising and becomes the nucleus of the future army of national liberation.'[9]

When the authors of this leaflet were tried before the highest German court at Leipzig – they had established links to National Socialist leaders – another young lieutenant, Helmuth Stieff, who was to become one of the conspirators against Hitler, wrote to his fiancée: 'What they [the accused] say has unfortunately for the most part to be accepted, and you will read many things which have so often aroused my indignation. That perhaps is the good side of the whole affair, that the eyes of the chaps on top will be opened to the enormous discontent in the officer corps . . .' And two weeks later: 'Undoubtedly the accused have acted wrongly and have infringed the principle of subordination. But are not their tribulations also ours? All these things I

---

[6] H. Foertsch, *Schuld und Verhängnis*, Stuttgart, 1951, p. 22; but see J. Kramarz, *Claus Graf Stauffenberg, 15 November 1907–20 Juli 1944*, Frankfurt, 1965, pp. 42–3.

[7] H. Teske, *Die silbernen Spiegel*, Heidelberg, 1952, p. 31, and 'Analyse eines Reichswehr-Regiments', *Wehrwissenschaftliche Rundschau*, 1962, p. 260.

[8] M. von Faber du Faur, *Macht und Ohnmacht*, Stuttgart, 1953, pp. 127–8.

[9] R. Scheringer, *Das grosse Los unter Soldaten, Bauern und Rebellen*, Hamburg, 1959, p. 179, with the quotation from the leaflet of 1929.

have told you often enough, and at least 90 per cent of the officer corps think the same . . .'[10]

Added to the national enthusiasm of the young officers was their total rejection of the political parties of whatever colour, of the revolution of 9 November 1918 and of the 'system' of the Weimar Republic, which had been founded as a result of this revolution. This was clearly expressed in Stieff's letters on the occasion of the trial at Leipzig: 'In this way one cannot win adherents to the present system, and that regrettable excesses occurred is solely the responsibility of the parties which support this system of vexation. But the harsh reproach must be levelled against our own top leaders that out of indolence they did not obtain any redress (. . .) and that they adopted the point of view of the beneficiaries of November [1918] who do not have our conception of honour (probably from considerations of parliamentary tactics) . . .' And later in the same letter: 'That we cannot organize a defence of the frontiers together with the *Reichsbanner* [the pro-Republican paramilitary organization] because these scoundrels would betray everything, even you will see. We alone are too weak and must collaborate with circles who are opposed to disarmament.'[11] This was written at a time when the official policy of the army leadership aimed at cooperation with the *Reichsbanner* for the defence of Germany's eastern frontiers, especially against Poland.

With regard to this and to other controversial issues there developed 'within the officer corps a rift between the monarchist pre-war officers and the younger officers which was wider than what by a law of nature usually separates different generations.'[12] The older officers remained loyal to their monarchist convictions; they had confidence in the ancient field-marshal who was now the president of the Republic, and saw in him a kind of viceroy of the House of Hohenzollern – until the day when the latter would be able to reoccupy its proper place. The more intelligent among them realized of course that there was little chance of this happening in the foreseeable future, but this did not influence their basic attitude. It was therefore no accident that in the circles of the military opposition, already before the war, plans were made to arrest Hitler and to proclaim the eldest son of the crown prince, Prince Wilhelm of Prussia, regent. During the war the plans became more concrete. As Prince Wilhelm had fallen in France in May 1940, it was now the second son of the crown prince, Prince Louis Ferdinand of Prussia, who was to become regent, or as a preliminary solution, the crown prince himself.[13] In this sense General Beck and Goerdeler

---

[10] Letters of 25 September and 7 October 1930: Institut für Zeitgeschichte, Munich, 1223/53.
[11] Letter of 11 October 1930, ibid.
[12] L. Freiherr Geyr von Schweppenburg, *Gebrochenes Schwert*, Berlin, 1952, p. 54.
[13] For details see Ritter, op. cit., pp. 189, 290–2, 479–80, 504–5.

sounded officers who had joined the conspiracy, among them Stauffenberg; but he rejected the plan, and the same can be assumed of the younger officers in general.[14] Yet their reservations against the intentions of Goerdeler went much further. Stauffenberg suspected him and the other 'civilians' of wanting to reinstate the 'republican-democratic-parliamentarian system'. In April 1944 Goerdeler therefore sent a lawyer friend to explain to Stauffenberg Goerdeler's 'constructive new ideas', and 'it was agreed that the old state of affairs was not to be resuscitated in any way'.[15] Two months later a conflict broke out between Goerdeler and Stauffenberg because the colonel, without consulting Goerdeler, had established connections with leading Social Democrats – presumably to win their support against Goerdeler's restaurative plans – while Goerdeler 'did not think that such negotiations belonged to the sphere of the military'.[16]

Very similar was the attitude of another young officer, Lieutenant Peter Count Yorck von Wartenburg, who cooperated closely with Stauffenberg. Yorck considered men such as Goerdeler and Popitz 'too old and reactionary so that no durable government could be expected from them'. They aimed, as he put it, at an obvious 'Kerensky solution'; their plans would lead 'to a markedly reactionary regime which inevitably would bring about the restauration of the old trade unions and parties and would reproduce the conditions of 1932'. Like Stauffenberg Yorck desired 'a much broader basis ... with the inclusion of the working class to the left wing of Social Democracy'.[17] But when an old Social Democrat informed Stauffenberg of the plans of the trade unions the latter expressed strong misgivings:[18] no wonder because their intentions were also 'restaurative', in favour of the revival of the old unions and· parties which was rejected by the younger officers.

In the discussions with the same Social Democrat Stauffenberg in the winter of 1943–1944 developed his own political ideas. He considered 'a certain new social order necessary', but at the same time he expressed his wish 'that the traditional values should not be thrown overboard and that the historical achievements of the nobility should be respected'. He also submitted an exposé of his social-political ideas, which was so vague 'that his true political intentions could not be recognized'.[19] For a 'revolutionary' officer who has been suspected of

---

[14] Kaltenbrunner's report to Bormann, 5 September 1944: *Spiegelbild einer Verschwörung – Die Kaltenbrunner-Berichte an Bormann und Hitler über das Attentat vom 20. Juli 1944*, Stuttgart, 1961, p. 352.

[15] Kaltenbrunner's report on the testimony of Rechtsanwalt Wirmer, 14 August 1944: ibid., p. 212

[16] Kaltenbrunner's report of 1 August 1944: ibid., p. 118.

[17] Kaltenbrunner's reports of 18–19 August 1944: ibid., pp. 257, 264.

[18] Kaltenbrunner's report of 12 August 1944 (testimony of H. Maas): ibid., p. 205.

[19] Ibid.

sympathies with Bolshevism and Soviet Russia these were rather conservative opinions. Gerhard Ritter has expressed the view that what Stauffenberg wanted to express was his opposition to any land reform and the partition of the large estates.[20] With all his radicalism this scion of an ancient noble family was also very conscious of traditional values, as shown by his remark of 1933 about 'the great soldiers of the War of Liberation'; only that he was loyal to a tradition which differed from Beck and Goerdeler whose political conception was determined by the values of the Hohenzollern Monarchy.

Compatible with this basic attitude is what has been told by a fellow conspirator, Gisevius, who was fundamentally critical of Stauffenberg[21] and saw him with his eyes sharpened: 'On one thing he was clear and determined: Stauffenberg did not want that Hitler should involve the army which was threatened by mortal danger in his catastrophe; to him, a soldier above everything, the salvation of the fatherland and the salvation of the army were identical.'[22] Two different traditions had long existed in the Prussian army: the national and revolutionary one of Scharnhorst, Gneisenau and Boyen who had fought for internal and external liberty, and the strictly conservative one of Roon and Moltke which Seeckt and Beck had inherited. 'The young colonel cannot deny his ideological and professional background. What he dreams of is the salvation of Germany by political officers who renounce corruption and mismanagement.'[23] This, however, did not mean that he favoured an alliance with the Soviet Union against the West as Seeckt and other Reichswehr generals had done in the 1920s. The idea attributed to Stauffenberg by Gisevius 'of the common victorious march of the grey-red armies against the plutocracies'[24] is not confirmed by any witnesses or any other evidence and differs completely from what we know of his plans. What the conspirators intended in reality was 'immediately after taking over power ... to send negotiators to Moscow as well as to London'; they wanted 'to establish connections simultaneously with East and West'.[25] It was Stauffenberg who, according to the findings of the Gestapo, 'was unteachable in his conviction that an agreement with England or with the English military leaders must be possible for a common front against Soviet Russia', although other conspirators tried to convince him that this was quite unrealistic.[26] Stauffenberg was not a National Bolshevist, neither in his ideas on foreign policy nor in his

[20] Ritter, op. cit., p. 528 note 46.
[21] Cp. P. Hoffmann, *Widerstand, Staatsstreich, Attentat*, Munich, 1970, p. 773 note 6.
[22] H.-B. Gisevius, *Bis zum bittern Ende*, Zürich, 1946, ii, p. 276.
[23] Ibid., p. 302.
[24] Ibid., p. 319.
[25] Kaltenbrunner's report to Bormann, 21 November 1944: *Spiegelbild einer Verschwörung*, p. 493.
[26] Kaltenbrunner's reports 8 August, 7 September and 29 November 1944: ibid., pp. 174, 367, 506–7.

internal political programme. Nor was he impressed by the proclamations of the 'National Committee for a Free Germany', which had been founded in Russia by communist exiles and German prisoners of war.[27]

But what was Stauffenberg's internal political programme? As several other young noblemen of his generation he certainly was 'an officer with an interest in social problems'.[28] But, as the Social Democrats soon established, he was not a socialist, and not even a Christian socialist, as has been claimed.[29] This is also proved by the draft of an oath which he composed in case Germany should be partitioned by the victorious powers. It ran: 'We aim at a new order which makes all Germans the upholders of the state, and which guarantees to them law and order and justice, but we despise the lie of equality, and we bow before the ranks established by nature. We want a nation which, rooted in the soil of the homeland, remains close to the natural powers, which finds happiness and satisfaction in the given ways of life, and proudly overcomes the low impulses of envy and jealousy. We desire leaders who, coming from all sections of the people, linked with the heavenly powers, are an example to others by their good sense, discipline and sacrifices.'[30] The sharp rejection of 'the lie of equality' and the emphasis on 'the ranks established by nature' show how far removed Stauffenberg was from the world of democratic socialism. The text confirms his romantic and tradition-based nationalism and idealism rather than adherence to any modern ideology.

Similar ideas were held by other young officers who belonged to the circle of the conspirators. In the summer of 1941 Lieutenant-Colonel Stieff wrote to his wife: 'But the conviction has taken root in me ever more firmly that nations are best led and governed wherever groups tied by bonds of tradition exercise the power of government, not upstarts and autocrats free from all inhibitions.'[31] This included not only a clear reference to Hitler and other dictators, but also to 'the men of November' whom the writer had denigrated ten years previously. A return to the 'system' of the Weimar Republic was also rejected by Stauffenberg. While the older generation of officers and civilians considered a monarchy the best state, Stauffenberg and the younger officers did not know what to put in the place of a constitutional state and the modern mass organizations of parties and trade unions. They dreamt of a state to be led in patriarchal fashion by a natural, traditional élite; according to their origin they saw this élite above all in the old noble and

[27] Kaltenbrunner's reports of 8 August and 29 November 1944: ibid., pp. 174, 507; Kramarz, op. cit., pp. 177–8.
[28] Kaltenbrunner's report of 22 October 1944: *Spiegelbild einer Verschwörung*, p. 465; Kramarz, op. cit., p. 137.
[29] Thus W. Venor, in *Die Zeit*, no. 12, 20 March 1964.
[30] Scheurig, op. cit., p. 59; Kramarz, op. cit., p. 200.
[31] Letter of 2 August 1941: *Vierteljahrshefte für Zeitgeschichte*, ii, 1954, no. 5, p. 301.

military families. But would these be able to build the new state and to govern it, and would the lower classes in the 20th century be willing to be guided by the nobility? And that in a country in which all bonds of tradition had been destroyed by the revolution of 1918, the inflation and economic crisis, and the National Socialist dictatorship. These questions do not seem to have occurred to the officers.

In fact the marked élitism, the aristocratic exclusiveness, the contempt for the bourgeois world and the modern plebeians, the romantic nationalism, the acceptance of certain Prussian traditions reflected the ideas which had been generally popular in German nationalist circles and those of the youth movement. They seem to owe a great deal to the writings of Ernst Jünger: less to the Jünger of the Second World War who had retired to an isolated observation post, and much more to the Jünger of the 1920s who was a political activist and deeply influenced the younger generation of German nationalists. Until 1923 Jünger had been a Reichswehr officer; he was very close to the younger officers in his whole ideology and way of thinking, even if they were not all aware of this affinity.

This was the world of ideas in which Stauffenberg and other radical officers moved – a world with which they were far more familiar on account of their origin and environment than that of socialism and communism, democracy and parliamentarianism. It is not at all surprising that some of their fellow conspirators thought they were revolutionaries who perhaps even flirted with the East. In reality they stood politically on the Right, but not in the camp of the established right-wing parties. Their views did not exercise any influence on political developments in post-war Germany; but the same would probably have happened if the coup d'état of July 1944 had been successful. No new state could be built on the ideas expressed by Stauffenberg in his oath of 1944. Forty years after his execution in the courtyard of the Bendlerstrasse he remains a somewhat enigmatic and controversial figure: not surprisingly because we know so little about his plans for the future and his political convictions. What we have to admire are his courage, his patriotism, his willingness to take the risk in spite of his severe physical handicaps, his impetuous activism without which the attempt would never have been made. Although the prospects of success were almost nil, he risked everything. He was no cunctator, and for these qualities he deserves an honourable place in the annals of German history.

23

INTERPRETATIONS OF FASCISM

Twenty years ago George L. Mosse, in the first issue of the *Journal of Contemporary History*, boldly stated: 'In our century, two revolutionary movements have made their mark upon Europe: that originally springing from Marxism, and fascist revolution... but fascism has been a neglected movement,' while many historians and political scientists had occupied themselves with the left-wing parties and revolutions.[1] Today fascism can no longer be called a neglected subject. Indeed, there is a large volume of books and articles, not only dealing with the fascist movements of individual countries but also many comparative studies, trying to establish the differences as well as the similarities between the various movements which have been called 'fascist'. This is partly due to the industry and devotion of Professor Ernst Nolte who in 1963 published one of the fundamental studies of the problem, a comparison of the Action Française, Italian fascism, and German National Socialism;[2] he has since then written several more books on the fascist movements[3] and has edited a volume of source material, assembling theories put forward by a large variety of writers on the subject of fascism during the past half-century.[4] His example has inspired many others, and the development of the New Left has provided another impetus to the study of fascism. No doubt some of the interest in the subject is purely political and polemical; but even on a more scholarly level the volume of recent publications seems to justify a survey of the theories, old and new, and a preliminary answer to the question to what extent they are new or merely restating older views, and what may be the most fruitful approaches to a further study of the problem. This paper does not pretend to be exhaustive but hopes to stimulate further discussion, by historians, political scientists, sociologists, and social psychologists, for the study of fascism invites a cooperative effort of several academic disciplines: a cooperative effort which is not always easy to achieve. This survey will largely neglect publications devoted to one country and concentrate above all on comparative and more general contributions to the subject.

One of the problems which from the outset occupied the attention of political analysts – and indeed remains one of the central issues of any analysis of fascism – was: where did the mass following of the fascist parties come from, and which social groups tended to support them? Clearly, it was not the industrial working class, which by and large followed the Marxist parties, nor was it the bourgeoisie proper which even numerically could not have provided a mass following. Hence the answer given by Italian critics of fascism as early as the early 1920s was that this mass support came from the *piccola borghesia*, the lower middle classes in town and country. Thus Giovanni Zibordi wrote in 1922 that Italy was 'a country which has a surplus of the lower middle classes, and it is they who, under the influence of special circumstances and favoured by them, have made as it were their own revolution, combining it with a counter-revolution of the bourgeoisie.' Zibordi observed at the same time that, among the followers of the fascists, 'those declassed by the war are particularly numerous: the youngsters who went to the front before they were twenty years old and came back at the age of 23 or 24, being neither able nor willing to return to their studies or their places of work in a regular fashion; the petty bourgeois from a very modest and inferior background who during the war became officers or NCOs ... and who today cannot get reconciled to go back to their modest occupations.'[5] Zibordi's opinion was echoed in 1923 by Luigi Salvatorelli who stated 'that the petit-bourgeois element not only predominates numerically, but in addition is the characteristic and directing element ... Thus fascism represents the class struggle of the lower middle class which exists between capitalism and proletariat as the third [group] between two combatants.' But he added that the lower middle class was not 'a true social class with its own strength and functions, but a conglomerate living at the margin of the capitalist process of production'.[6]

These views have since been echoed by numerous writers, Italian as well as non-Italian. Thus Palmiro Togliatti, leader of the Italian Communist party, wrote in 1928: 'The social basis of fascism consists of certain strata of the petty bourgeoisie in town and country ... In the towns too fascism leans above all on the lower middle classes: partly workmen (artisans), specialists and traders, partly elements displaced on account of the war (former officials, cripples, 'arditi', volunteers).'[7] Another prominent Italian left-winger, Angelo Tasca, stated a few years later: 'This petty and middle bourgeoisie ... formed the backbone of fascism in Italy and everywhere else. But the expression "middle class" must be given a wider meaning, to include the son of a family waiting for a job or for his inheritance to *déclassés* of all kinds, temporary or permanent, from the half-pay officer to the *Lumpenproletarier*, from the strike-breaker to the jobless intellectual.'[8] Similarly social psychologists like Erich Fromm and Wilhelm Reich wrote during the Second World War: 'Nazi ideology was enthusiastically welcomed by the lower sections of the *Mittelstand*, small shopkeepers, artisans, white collar workers and *Lumpenproletarier*'[9] and: 'The *Mittelstand* began to move and, in the form of fascism, became a social force.'[10] More recently a well-known American sociologist, Seymour Lipset, maintained: 'The thesis that fascism is basically a middle-class movement representing a protest against both capitalism *and* socialism, big business *and* big unions, is far from original ... Data from a number of countries demonstrate that classic fascism is a movement of the propertied middle classes, who for the most part normally support liberalism.'[11]

At a conference in Reading some years ago, several speakers held that the lower middle classes were particularly prone to the fascist appeal. Thus Professor Kogan said: 'The lower-middle class, rejecting proletarian egalitarianism as socially degrading, while not having a secure position itself, would be most vulnerable to the fascist appeal.' And Dr Solé-Tura: 'Fascist movements came about as an expression of discontent in the lower middle classes of both town and country.'[12] Professor Nolte, on the other hand, has tried to define more precisely what sections of the lower middle class belonged to the original fascists: 'the cadres of its shock-troops were not formed from "the" petty bourgeoisie, but from certain fringe sections of the petty bourgeoisie, the "mercenaries" and the academic youth with its irrational inclinations.'[13] A more recent German study of the origins of fascism emphasizes that it was above all the economic and social threat to the existence of the Mittelstand which made it susceptible to fascist propaganda; 'a precondition of fascism is the economic threat to one or several groups of the Mittelstand and the capitalist bourgeoisie. If capitalism were "harmonious", "free from crises" ... there would be no need of fascism.'[14] Thus the view that certain sections of the middle classes – whether propertied or threatened, lower-middle or middle, urban or rural – provided the first cadres and the mass following of fascism is widely held to the present day. It seems only a variant of this view if a well-known German historian, Martin Broszat, emphasizes that 'the fascist movements in all these countries (Germany, Italy, Hungary, and Rumania) discovered and used the national and political potential of the small peasants and agricultural labourers ... Often the small peasants above all voted for the fascists because the latter were the first national party whose propagandists came into the villages and identified themselves with the interests and the feelings of the peasants.'[15] Yet fascism practically everywhere was a movement that started in the towns and was later carried from the towns into the villages; that is true even of eastern Europe where the rural character of the fascist movements was more pronounced than in the more western countries, and where the neglect of the peasantry by the traditional political parties was proverbial.[16]

Apart from the peasants, who indeed were particularly prone to listen to fascist propaganda, two other social groups were extremely prominent among the earliest followers of fascist parties, and indeed provided them with their first semi-military squads or storm troops (and both were very largely of lower middle-class origin): former officers and soldiers, especially ex-servicemen of the First World War, and university students and young graduates; during the first years after 1918 these two groups overlapped. Again Zibordi was one of the first to make this point.[17] It has been repeated more recently by Stuart Woolf, who, discussing the effects of the First World War, has pointed out that it 'created

Interpretations of Fascism 329

vast masses of ex-combatants who were to form the most fertile seedbeds of nascent nationalistic and fascist movements.'[18] And on the other side of the Atlantic, Professor Sauer has found: 'It may even be said that a distinct interest group was formed within the fascist mixture by what might be called the military desperadoes, veterans of the First World War and the postwar struggles, who had not been reintegrated into either the civilian society or the armed forces.'[19] Similarly a German historian has recently stated: 'It was no accident that ex-servicemen who had not been socially reintegrated formed the nucleus of the fascist movements.'[20]

Perhaps the enthusiastic participation of university students in the fascist movements, above all in central and eastern Europe, has been stressed less often. Especially the Iron Guard started as an organization of Romanian students, and in Germany and Austria the universities became strongholds of National Socialism many years before the so-called 'seizure of power'. Here it was in the first instance bitter economic distress and the dismal prospects of ever obtaining a post, but even more so the fervent nationalism and anti-bolshevism of the post-war years that drove many thousands of students into the Free Corps and the paramilitary formations of the right, and then into the fascist camp. From Finland to Spain, from Flanders to Italy, students were among the most ardent and convinced fighters in the fascist cause. Indeed, at least one recent writer has gone further and finds in 'the mass rush into the fascist movements above all the signs of an aggressive and violent revolt of the young'.[21] This seems to be too wide and too vague a formulation, for we would still like to know from what sections of the population these youngsters came; and it takes too little account of the many older men among the leaders as well as among the followers of the fascist movements.

All the writers quoted so far seek the social basis of the fascist parties in the middle class or certain sections of it. Quite different is the interpretation of those who believe that these parties were able to attract followers from *all* sections of society, but especially the uprooted and declassed elements. Again this interpretation was formulated as early as the early 1920s and has been frequently restated since. Curiously enough, it apparently was first put forward by a well-known communist, Clara Zetkin – an interpretation which differs considerably from later communist pronouncements on the subject. 'The carrier of fascism,' she stated in 1923, 'is not a small caste, but broad social groups, large masses which reach far into the proletariat . . . Masses of many thousands flocked to fascism. It became a refuge for those without a political home, for the socially uprooted, for those without an existence and the disappointed.'[22] And some years later a dissident communist theorist, August Thalheimer, wrote: 'Parasitic elements of all classes which are uprooted economically and socially, excluded from the direct process of production, are the natural elements, the natural tools of the "executive power which has made itself independent"' – a definition which he applied to Bonapartism as well as to fascism.[23] This definition was then taken up and developed further by another Marxist writer with a similar intellectual background, Paul Sering (Richard Löwenthal), who found

> that this [fascist] party recruits itself from members of all classes, while within it certain groups are prevalent and form its nucleus, groups which have been called 'middle groups' in a confusing terminology. The bourgeoisie is represented, but only the bourgeoisie which is in debt and needs support; the working class is represented, but only the workers who are chronically unemployed and unable to fight, living in distressed areas; the urban lower middle classes join, but only the ruined lower middle classes, the rentiers are included, but only the rentiers expropriated by the inflation; officers and intellectuals lead, but only ex-officers and bankrupt intellectuals. These groups form the nucleus of the movement – it has the character of a true community of bankruptcy – and this allows the movement to expand beyond its nucleus into all social classes parallel with the crisis because it is socially interlinked with all of them.[24]

These views have been echoed more recently by several historians. Thus a German-American historian has stated: 'Historical evidence shows that support of fascism may not be confined to the classical elements of the lower middle class . . . but may extend to a wide variety of groups in the large field between the workers on the one hand and big business, the aristocracy, and the top levels of the bureaucracy on the other.'[25] Another American professor agrees: 'The component sectors of both fascism and nazism could not be reduced to lower middle classes and Lumpenproletariat; an assorted variety of social categories took an active part in fascist movements: war veterans, unemployed, young people, peasants. A common trait was recognized in all groups – their uprootedness.'[26] And a British survey concurs: 'Fascist parties, then, had a fairly uniform doctrine, but extremely varying social composition. From whatever class the support came, it was invariably made up of the chronically discontented ... Poor aristocrats and gentry, ex-service or junior officers, unemployed or under-employed university graduates and students, ambitious small businessmen and aspiring youths from the lower middle and working classes, all became prominent as the élite of the élitists.'[27] There can be little doubt that this analysis is basically correct, that the term 'lower middle class' is too general and too vague to explain the wide differences in social background of the fascist leaders and followers (and the participation of large numbers of the working class). The element of uprootedness, of social insecurity, of a position threatened and assailed, of loss of status, is of vital importance for the problem; and in this century the greatest uprooter, the greatest destroyer of security was the First World War with its aftermath of revolution and civil war. This would also explain why no mass fascist movement arose in the aftermath of the Second World War, which was not followed by revolutions, civil war, and vast economic crises but by a great effort of economic reconstruction.

If violent opposition to socialist or proletarian revolution was one of the primary causes of the growth of fascism, it is also true that the fascist movements only developed *after* these revolutionary forces had been decisively defeated, when the threat had already disappeared.[28] In Italy the occupation of the factories by the workers ended in their evacuation and a signal defeat of the left, which was badly split and disunited. In Germany the left-wing risings of the early 1920s were defeated by the Free Corps and the army, and in the vast slump of the early 1930s the working-class movement was thrown onto the defensive and totally unable to act. In Hungary and Finland the fascist movements grew after the end of the civil war and decisive defeats of the local communists from which they were unable to recover. Again, the first to point this out, as far as Italy was concerned, was Zibordi who wrote in 1922: 'Fascism is . . . the instrument of a counter-revolution against a proletarian revolution which did exist only in the form of a programme and a threat.'[29] And, after the Nazi victory in Germany, Otto Bauer pointed out: 'But in reality fascism did not triumph at the moment when the bourgeoisie was threatened by the proletarian revolution: it triumphed when the proletariat had long been weakened and forced onto the defensive, when the revolutionary flood had abated. The capitalists and the large landowners did not entrust the fascist hordes with the power of the state so as to protect themselves against a threatening proletarian revolution, but so as to depress the wages, to destroy the social gains of the working class, to eradicate the trade unions and the positions of power gained by the working class.'[30] Recently a young German left-wing analyst has once more emphasized this point: 'Fascism is preceded by an attempt at proletarian revolution which largely ended in failure or by revolution-like risings of the proletariat (as in Italy). These revolutionary attempts of the proletariat were supported by sections of the lower middle class and semi-proletarian groups.' Preconditions similar to these, he continues, also existed in Austria, Hungary, and Spain before the establishment of conservative dictatorships.[31]

Was the threat then purely imaginary, the fear of proletarian revolution unjustified – or to put it more crudely, was it deliberately exaggerated by an unscrupulous propaganda? This, on the whole, is not the opinion of the modern historians. Thus Professor Trevor-Roper has stated: 'For fascism, as an effective movement, was born of fear. It might have independent intellectual roots; it might owe its form, here and there, to independent national or personal freaks; but its force, its dynamism, sprang from the fear of a new, and this time "proletarian" revolution.'[32] And Renzo de Felice has spoken of a double fear: 'The winning fascist faction accepted a compromise with the existing order, because of the fear of revolution that haunted the ruling classes in Italy. But the basic motivation of this faction was also fear of revolution, a fear

Interpretations of Fascism 333

of the left-wing fascists mobilizing and taking power.'[33] A younger German writer of the New Left has made this point in much more general terms: 'The fact that capitalist industrial society cannot be overlooked and the experience of being without any power, of being the prisoner of anonymous forces produce a fear which then seeks a firm support . . . In fascism there assembled above all the sections of the bourgeois middle classes which were declassed or immediately threatened with becoming déclassés. By their votes for fascism they protested against this threat.'[34] Yet relatively few historians have ventured into this field which they may feel belongs more properly to the social psychologists.

Indeed, social psychologists, social scientists, as well as historians, have stressed much more the loss of prestige and of social security which affected the masses after the First World War. This point was made in its classical form by Erich Fromm in 1942 and has been repeated often ever since:

The authority of the monarchy had been uncontested and, by leaning on it and identifying themselves with it, the members of the lower middle classes gained a feeling of security and of self-admiring, narcissistic pride . . . There was the lost war and the overthrow of the monarchy. The state and the princes had been secure rocks on which – seen psychologically – the petit bourgeois had built his existence; their downfall and the defeat shook the foundation of his existence . . . Not only the economic situation of the lower middle classes, but their social prestige too declined rapidly after the war. Before the war they could believe that they were something better than the worker. After the war the social prestige of the working class rose, and that of the lower middle class sank correspondingly. There was no one any longer on whom they could look down, a privilege which had always been one of the strongest positive factors in the life of the philistine.[35]

This interpretation has been restated by political scientists and others. Thus Professor Germani has told us: 'It is widely recognized that "disequilibration" had caused loss of status (in terms of prestige as well as in terms of power and wealth) for the urban middle class. Such loss had taken place both in relative and in absolute terms: decreasing distance because of the advance of the working class, absolute downward mobility in terms of unemployment, inflation, decreasing income, and decreasing political influence... The advance of the working class was resented as an "invasion" or "usurpation" of status.'[36] And a German writer has spoken emphatically of the 'fear of decadence' and added: 'Blind fear of decline has been one of the most powerful roots of fascist tendencies, and not only in Germany.'[37] There can be no doubt that these fears were not imaginary but largely justified, that the middle and the lower middle classes, the 'little man', had lost their stable place in society, their security and prosperity, that they felt helpless in the new order of things after the war, the victims of forces which they could not understand.

The social psychologists have pointed to other traits in the fascist make-up which had an important influence in attracting the masses. Thus Erich Fromm has enumerated the 'veneration of the strong' and the 'hatred of the weak', 'the longing to submit, and the lust for power';[38] and Wilhelm Reich wrote at the same time: 'The fascist mentality is the mentality of the "little man", suppressed, longing for authority and at the same time rebellious... The fascist is the sergeant in the vast army of our deeply ill civilization, the civilization of big industry.'[39] Reich also emphasized that the fascists strongly identified themselves with their Leader: 'every National Socialist felt himself, in spite of his dependence, like a "little Hitler".'[40] Fromm equally stressed another form of identification which worked strongly after the Nazi seizure of power:

A further impetus to loyalty towards the Nazi régime became operative after Hitler had come into power: for many millions, the majority of the population, Hitler's government was identical with 'Germany'. As soon as he had formed the government, 'to oppose him' meant no less than to exclude oneself from the community of the Germans... Apparently nothing is more difficult for the average person to bear but the feeling not to be at one with a larger group. Even if German burghers were strongly opposed to the Nazi principles, as soon as they had to choose between standing alone and belonging to Germany the large majority chose the latter.[41]

Such ideas have been fruitful in stimulating modern historians to accept terms and views imported from a different discipline. Thus Professor Mosse found: 'In under-developed countries, the stress upon the end to alienation, the belief in the organic community, brought dividends – for the exclusion of the workers and peasants from society had been so total that purely economic considerations could take second place.'[42] And the sociologist Dr Barbu stated:

One of the most fruitful approaches was to conceive of the party as a type of primary community, a corporate morality, which tried to reinforce the feeling of belonging to something, the primary emotional involvement of the individual ... In an industrializing society it might appeal to the lower middle class, in a transitional society to the people who became available through a primary mobilization process, the peasants who left the villages to come to the towns. But the problem remained the same all the time: the fascist movement appealed to people who needed strong bonds ... The fascist party offered a type of solidarity; it appealed to people who suffered from the disintegration of traditional or any kind of social solidarity.[43]

A young German historian wrote more recently of the 'salvation [found] in the submission to a strong authority. This can express itself in the identification either with a powerful collective – the state, the nation, the enterprise – or with the personality of the Leader: the "authoritarian-masochistic character" projects its ego-ideal onto a Leader figure with which he identifies himself unconditionally.'[44] Indeed, there seems no reason why such a process should only be at work 'in under-developed countries', for in modern industrial societies too the alienated might join a party with which they can totally identify themselves, all the readier if that party stands in total opposition to society and state and seeks to destroy them. This, of course, need not be a fascist party, but under certain political and social conditions, and as far as certain social groups are concerned, it would be a fascist party and Leader with whom the masses could identify most easily, to whose promise of reintegration they would most readily listen. The 'people's community' (*Volksgemeinschaft*) promised by the leaders of the Third Reich did not materialize, but millions were longing for it.

In the early stages of the rise of fascist movements, a very similar mechanism was operative on the local level. As Dr Adrian Lyttelton has found for Italy,

The origins of many squads are to be found in a loose, informal relationship between a group of adolescents, somewhat resembling that of a youth gang ... Primary ties of kinship or friendship were important in creating a feeling of camaraderie among the *squadristi*. The existence of this 'small group solidarity' served to protect the Fascist from the feelings of impotence and ennui common among those in the grip of large, impersonal bureaucratic organizations; they seemed to allow the individual to achieve both integration and independence. At the same time, of course, the violence which was the essence of *squadrismo* allowed an outlet for aggression.[45]

Exactly the same could be said of the 'gangs' of local stormtroopers, or indeed of their predecessors, the Free Corps and uniformed paramilitary associations in Germany.

There was another psychological factor, important for both Germany and Italy (but not for some of the other countries where fascist movements grew): the feeling of national shame which affected millions on account of defeat and, what was in their eyes, an ignominious peace settlement. This is most obvious for the countries defeated in 1918, Germany and Hungary; but it is also true of Italy, where the crushing defeat of Caporetto caused the same sense of shame, where the ultimate victory over the Austrians was 'mutilated' by the peace settlement, and where 'the war was won but the peace lost'.[46] This feeling directly inspired the first fascist enterprises and above all Gabriele d'Annunzio's expedition to Fiume, the dress rehearsal for the march on Rome. Recently a younger German historian has drawn our attention to 'the groups of enemies against which fascism directs the wrath of the masses'; he believes that 'those social groups are especially suited as objects of aggression which are distinguished from the large majority by their looks or their behaviour and which therefore can easily be recognized. Racial, national or religious minorities ... thus function only too often as objects of aggression. They have the additional advantage that they are rather defenceless so that the mob can discharge its aggressions without risk and punishment. Violence and murder ... committed against members of the minorities are looked upon not only as permitted but even as an honourable national service.'[47] Admittedly, all these factors cannot be measured by statistics and defy a more precise definition, but they seem important in any assessment of the roots of fascism, and helpful in any attempt to answer the question why fascist movements were able to attract vast crowds and to perpetrate deeds which any normal society would classify as criminal. Here again the primary catalyst would seem to be the First World War which accustomed millions to the use of violence and elevated it to the rank of a patriotic duty.

This once more is not a new perception but it was recognized as early as 1928 by the Italian socialist Filippo Turati (who had been a pacifist during the war): 'The war ... accustomed the youngsters as well as the grown ups to the daily use of usual and unusual weapons ... it praised individual and collective murder, blackmail, arrest, the macabre joke, the torturing of prisoners, the "punitive expeditions", the summary executions ... it created in general the atmosphere in which alone the fascist bacillus could grow and spread.'[48] Turati also thought that this spirit in particular affected the youngsters who, because of their age, had been unable to participate in the war but were all the more eager to win military laurels, especially in a situation where their lives were no longer at stake.[49] Because the Italian (and German) governments were notoriously weak and unable to cope with the ever-worsening economic crisis, there was 'a growing longing for a strong government', a 'yearning for peace and order', for 'a strong hand at the helm'.[50] The willingness of large masses to accept a Leader, who would overcome misery and strife and lead them to a glorious future, can partly be explained by the social and economic distress of the post-war period. As Professor Vierhaus has pointed out, 'sections of the population which politically and socially were without any orientation had a need of strong authority; they acclaimed the leaders in whom the masses not seldom put semi-religious hopes of salvation, to which the leaders and their propaganda replied with the vague but all the more effective promise of a general improvement, a better, proud national future.'[51] Indeed, fascist rallies often had the atmosphere of a revivalist assembly, and the masses shouted: 'The Leader is always right!'

Several historians have stated that – in contrast with all other parties and political movements – the Leader of a fascist party needed charisma, but very little effort has been made to define this charisma, or the social and psychological conditions under which it became effective. Thus Professor Seton-Watson has written: 'An obviously important feature of fascism which often gets left out . . . is the charismatic leader. Mussolini, Degrelle, and José Antonio Primo de Rivera were clearly men of outstanding abilities. Szálasi and Codreanu were complex personalities combining ruthlessness with strange flashes of nobility of character. Hitler still defies analysis.'[52] Yet it was Hitler before whom battle-hardened generals trembled, who was able to arouse the masses to a fever pitch, whose decisions were unquestioningly accepted by his enthusiastic followers. In a more general form Professor Vierhaus maintains: 'The Leader taking his stand on the basis of the plebiscite can only legitimize himself by his charisma, i.e. the fact that he stands above the ordinary and commonplace, by his personal authority. This has to rely on proving itself every day by deed and success; hence the ever-repeated public appearances of the Leader with a ceremonial which is cunningly adapted to different situations.'[53]

It has often been said that without Hitler there would have been no National Socialism, or that at least National Socialism would have been very different without him. This again seems a field where the historian or the political scientist might have to rely on the help of the social psychologist. A well-known psychologist has recently defined Hitler 'as the quintessential embodiment of Germany's and Austria's many defeat-shattered, uprooted "little men", craving for the security of belonging, for the restoration of power and glory, and for vengeance.' He gave expression 'to a state of mind existing in millions of people, not only in Germany'.[54] This is true, but it does not get us much further.

If the psychological factors which conditioned fascism are difficult to define and have to a large extent defied a more precise analysis, the same need not apply to the social preconditions of its growth. More than fifty years ago, in 1923, Luigi Salvatorelli, who understood fascism as a movement of the lower middle classes, thought that fascism developed in Italy because Italy was economically backward and thus had a particularly numerous petty bourgeoisie.[55] Ten years later the sociologist Franz Borkenau, who understood fascism in the same sense, added that its victory in Italy was due to 'the absence of a politically and economically adequate industrial bourgeoisie'. As fascism destroyed those sections of the working-class movements which were willing to reach a compromise with the bourgeoisie, 'the bourgeoisie of the most developed capitalist countries cannot afford such a policy. In countries where up to 75 per cent of the population belong to the proletariat in the proper sense of the term, democracy, reformism and free trade unions are virtually indispensable factors for the preservation of the status quo. To do without them is only feasible in countries where the proletariat is still weak enough simply to be suppressed ... In more developed conditions this is not a question of advantages and disadvantages, but the destruction of the modern working-class movement is a total impossibility.'[56] When these lines were published Hitler had already been appointed chancellor of Germany.

Some years later Otto Bauer attempted another analysis of fascism from a Marxist point of view, which in his opinion rested on a social equilibrium:

> The fascist dictatorship comes into being as the result of a peculiar equilibrium of the social classes. On one side there is the bourgeoisie which controls the means of production and circulation and the power of the state ... On the other side stands the working class which is led by reformist socialists and the trade unions. Reformism and trade unions have become stronger than the bourgeoisie is willing to accept ... Exactly as the absolutism of the early capitalist epoch ... developed on the basis of the equilibrium of the forces of the feudal nobility and the bourgeoisie ... so the new fascist absolutism is the result of a temporary equilibrium when the bourgeoisie could not force the proletariat to accept its will by the old legal methods, and the proletariat was unable to liberate itself from the rule of the bourgeoisie; and thus both classes fell under the dictatorship of the violent mob which the capitalists used against the proletariat until they themselves had to submit to the dictatorship.[57]

Bauer's opinion has more recently been restated by Dr Solé-Tura: 'Fascism is the solution found for the contradictions caused by the development of capitalism at a characteristic point of fundamental class equilibrium.'[58] Yet Bauer's comparison with the period of absolutism can hardly be maintained: the seventeenth century was a period when the feudal economy had long disintegrated, when the power of the nobility was no longer as strong as it had once been, when a new economic order based on the towns and the urban middle classes was developing: hence there could be a time of equilibrium when the princes were able to play off one group against the other. But it would be vastly overestimating the strength of social democracy and the trade unions to say that it balanced that of the bourgeoisie; the very ease with which social democracy was destroyed in Central Europe proves that this strength was more imaginary than real.

There is, however, another theory which may be more helpful in explaining why certain countries have been more prone to produce fascist mass movements than others. Professor Nolte has suggested a geographical classification combined with an approach based on social structure, 'the path of growing industrialization and a declining share of the agrarian population, which in Albania and Yugoslavia around 1930 comprised around 80 per cent of the total but in England counted for hardly more than 10 per cent. It could obviously be held that in the former group the social preconditions of fascism did not yet exist, while in the last group they existed no longer, that only in the centre of Central Europe fascism found the preconditions for a full development.' Although Nolte then proceeds to point to the obvious difficulties in accepting this interpretation, he concludes that 'the view which sees the primary cause of fascist movements in a certain mixture of social forces remains noteworthy and important.'[59] Indeed, it seems that societies undergoing a rapid social and economic transformation from a pre-industrial to an industrial society proved a favourite breeding ground of the fascist movements, that members of certain social groups found it particularly difficult to adjust themselves to social change, to accept a lower social status or the rise of a new social force, that the period of quick transition was the most difficult one: when the process of industrialization was more or less complete a new equilibrium was established, and with it greater social security, for the individual as well as for the group as a whole. Yet this theory, while it seems worth exploring in greater detail, still does not answer why the fascist movements developed in the 1920s and 1930s, and why they became mass movements in certain countries but not in others. Other factors to be considered here obviously are the stability or instability of political institutions, the strength or weakness of democratic and liberal traditions, the popularity or unpopularity of parliament and the political parties, the marked differences in the political and social structures of the European countries. Perhaps little headway can be made in this field until many more detailed studies have become available.

Another, much more tangible, precondition for the *success* of the fascists was their alliance with certain ruling circles and with the political right, and there does not seem to be any disagreement among the historians on this issue, irrespective of their political views. Thus more than ten years ago Nolte stated unequivocally: 'Hardly less than Hitler's oratorical gifts and passion, the German army, the connections of Dietrich Eckart and the protection offered by the director of [the Munich] police Pöhner contributed to make the National Socialist Party into what it was in 1923... The collaboration of the state and of leading circles in society became at least as important for the development of National Socialism as for that of fascism' in Italy.[60] More recently another German historian has written: 'In reality National Socialism like other fascist movements could only reach power in alliance with the traditional Right, and it received its support because its attacks were to a very large extent directed against the political Left.'[61] From the political left a younger German writer agrees with this thesis: 'The system of rule established by Italian fascism too can be defined as an alliance between the fascist movement and the social upper strata. Yet the balance was different from the German form. Already during the period before the seizure of power Italian fascism had been unable to gain such a strong mass basis as German fascism. The result was that there the fascist movement, even after its "seizure of power", did not obtain the same position of strength in its coalition with the social upper classes as it did in Germany.'[62] Similar is the statement of an American historian: 'The general conclusion one can make from the rise to power of Mussolini and Hitler seems to be this: The radical Right had its best chance in societies where older but still powerful élites see their values and interests eroded by rapid and modernizing social change, change which generates a massive liberal and left threat to "old ways". When this happens conservatives, ultra-conservatives and reactionaries of differing ideologies and classes tend to unite and strike back "by any means necessary".[63]

Indeed, one can go further and say: if a fascist party disregards the forging of a firm alliance with the forces of the old order and of the state and tries to seize power relying entirely on its own strength, the attempt is doomed to failure. This is the lesson which Hitler drew from his Munich putsch of 1923 when he aimed at drawing the Bavarian government and army onto his side but ultimately failed to achieve this end; when he came to power in 1933 he was appointed chancellor by the ancient field-marshal, he had the support of the army and of the bureaucracy, and he formed a coalition government with the right-wing German Nationalist party. When Horia Sima, the leader of the powerful Iron Guard, tried to sieze power in Bucharest at the beginning of 1941 he failed because the government of Marshal Antonescu and the Romanian army turned against him. Szálasi, the leader of the Arrow Cross movement, was unable to form a firm alliance with the traditional right in Hungary and the government of the Regent Horthy, hence he was excluded from power until he was raised to the position of a puppet leader by the Germans at the end of the war. Here a striking difference exists between the seizure of power by a fascist party and by a movement of the extreme left.

In spite of these facts, political commentators, historians, and political scientists seem to be agreed in using the term 'fascist revolution', while they are also aware that the fascist movements contained counter-revolutionary elements. Thus Zibordi wrote as early as 1922: 'It seems to me that fascism is at the same time the following: a counter-revolution of the true middle class against a "red" revolution... a revolution, or rather a convulsion of petty bourgeois, declassed and discontented sections, and a military revolution.'[64] The German former National Socialist Hermann Rauschning in 1938 coined the slogan of 'The Revolution of Nihilism' and declared: 'National Socialism has not only eliminated the positions of power held by the working class, which could justify the verdict that it is a counter-revolutionary movement, but it has equally destroyed the middle class, the political and social positions of the middle class, and of the old, leading social strata... The German revolution therefore is at least both: a social revolution and a counter-revolution.'[65] And from the German left it was stated at about the same time: 'The fascist revolution is thus a genuine revolution insofar as it presents an important scissure in the development of bourgeois society which necessarily is taking place in revolutionary forms and is caused by economic developments. Its typical results are: 1. a new higher form of the organization of the state; 2. a new reactionary form of social organization; 3. a growing check to economic development by reactionary forces which have usurped the power of the state.'[66]

Most modern historians concur that the fascist movements were revolutionary. Thus Professor Mosse speaks of the 'two revolutionary movements' of the twentieth century, of the 'fascist revolution', which in his opinion in the West 'was primarily a bourgeois revolution'.[67] Professor Sauer has stated in the *American Historical Review:* 'There is virtual agreement among scholars that fascist movements contained, contrary to the Marxist thesis, a true revolutionary potential.'[68] And Professor Bracher has written: 'An interpretation which sees in fascism and National Socialism only the final stage of a reactionary counter-revolution and denies it any revolutionary character amounts to an incorrect simplification of complicated processes. All four basic currents which have contributed to the ideologies of fascism and of National Socialism are simultaneously determined by revolutionary and by reactionary forces.'[69] But there are a few dissentient voices. Thus the American editor of an anthology on fascism maintains: 'Fascism cannot be understood if it is viewed as a revolution. It was a counter-revolution. Its purpose was to prevent the liberalization and radicalization of Italy and Germany. Property and income distribution and the traditional class structure remained roughly the same under fascist rule. What changes there were favoured the old élites or certain segments of the party membership.'[70] A similar view is held by a German left-wing analyst: 'As the beginning of a fascist dictatorship one must see the transfer of power to, or the taking over of power by the most reactionary forces existing which aim at the establishment of a rule of unlimited violence so as to secure the interests of the native, or maybe a foreign, monopoly capitalism. This need not necessarily be fascist parties, but could be the military, or leaders of conservative reactionary parties, or representatives of the higher clergy.'[71]

The issue seems to be confused by the fact that fascist parties – in Germany and in Italy – only came into power through an alliance with conservative and reactionary forces, but an alliance that did not last. Also, in both countries, the opposition of more radical, 'revolutionary' fascist groups had to be overcome before the dictatorship was securely established. Yet it would be silly to deny that there were genuine revolutionary elements in the fascist movements, especially so in central and south-eastern Europe, and that important changes in the existing social structure were introduced by the German – but less so by the Italian – dictatorship. As there were only these two fascist régimes, any generalization becomes very difficult. Perhaps the cautious statement by Professor Bracher that revolutionary as well as reactionary elements were present in the fascist ideologies might be extended to the fascist movements as such, and the proportions naturally varied from country to country. Wherever social conditions were particularly antediluvian and radical social reform was urgently necessary, for example in Hungary and Romania, the revolutionary elements would be stronger, and vice versa.

As the basic elements of fascist ideology, Professor Bracher has identified four currents: national imperialism, étatism, populist socialism, and racialism.[72] To these might be added two more: a kind of national romanticism, glorifying the agrarian and pre-industrial past and military virtues,[73] and corporativism,[74] which had little influence in Germany, but a much stronger one in Italy, Austria, and Spain. Whatever other elements we might add to this list, it seems clear that most of these components were traditional or reactionary, and that only very few could qualify as 'revolutionary'. There were no doubt 'populist' traits in the fascist movements, as several historians have recently emphasized, but the comparison with the *Narodniki* of tsarist Russia seems far-fetched and untenable – precisely because the *Narodniki* were a genuine revolutionary group inspired by a revolutionary creed.[75] In any case, very few historians and political scientists would today accept, without any qualification, Richard Crossman's assertion of 1939: 'In Central Europe, where the economic interpretation of history was the myth of the working-class movement, Racialism became the revolutionary philosophy of a discontented German middle class.'[76] The roots of German racialism went back far into the nineteenth century, and racialist ideas formed part of the traditional armoury of the right.

Discarded too has been the view which so intelligent an historian as Arthur Rosenberg held in 1934 that fascism is 'the counter-revolutionary capitalist, the born foe of the class-conscious working class. Fascism is nothing but a modern, popularly masked form of the bourgeois-capitalist counter-revolution.'[77] This view corresponded to that propounded at the same time by the Communist International that 'fascism is the open and terrorist dictatorship of the most reactionary, chauvinist and imperialist elements of the finance capital.'[78] It has been restated since in exactly the same form in Germany: 'The basic trait of fascism is – in the summarizing and still valid definition of Dimitrov – "the open and terroristic dictatorship of the most reactionary, most chauvinist and most imperialist elements of the finance capital."'[79] But the mere repetition of an old cliché does not make it any more correct or fitting a very complex reality. A critic of this view from the New Left was completely justified when he pointed out: 'Not the direct support by big capitalism caused the rise of fascism, but the economic crisis immanent in the capitalist system drove the frightened masses, above all the lower middle classes threatened by proletarianization, into the fascist camp ... Only when fascism had become a mass movement support by big capitalists began to a larger extent.'[80] Indeed, large numbers of finance and other big capitalists and many members of the old aristocracies were frightened by the semi-proletarian and pseudo-revolutionary character of the fascist movements – and not without reason.

There can be little doubt that, under the fascist régime, the old ruling circles were partly replaced by 'a new political class',[81] drawn above all from the leaders of the fascist party whose origins were considerably lower down on the social scale than those of the older groups. This again was the case much more in Germany than in Italy where the old bureaucracy continued to rule almost unchallenged. And even in Germany those party leaders who entered the bureaucracy seem to have taken on its traditional attitudes and to have adopted its standards to a surprising degree.[82] But so far little research has been done in this field, and any more general conclusion must await further investigation. As Professor Schapiro has pointed out, Hitler engaged in bitter and prolonged conflicts with the bureaucracy (from which he often emerged victorious), while 'so far as Mussolini was concerned, he did not succeed in making very serious inroads into the state.'[83] It seems that there is a need here of more comparative studies. It may be the case that National Socialism against its will carried through a modernization of the administrative structure which the Weimar Republic had failed to obtain, while this was not achieved in Italy. It may well turn out, in any case, that the similarities between the two fascist régimes were as pronounced as the differences between them.

What are the conclusions of this brief survey? It seems that no fundamentally new interpretations of fascism have been put forward by the modern historians and political scientists, but that they have taken up and discussed – in one form or the other – the old interpretations of the twenties and thirties. Especially the views and ideas of Italian writers from the early 1920s, formulated from a close observation of the Italian scene, have to a large extent been confirmed by later research. But, in spite of the large volume of modern research and the many dozens of monographs and Ph.D. theses on the subject, a great deal of work remains to be done and in particular there is still a great shortage of good comparative studies. As we have seen, many modern historians are prepared to accept ideas from, and to cooperate with, social psychologists and sociologists, and this may produce more valuable results in the future. If this survey has not produced anything startlingly new, it hopes at least to stimulate further cooperation and research; for fascism remains one of the fundamental issues of the twentieth century and deserves the attention of all concerned about the fundamental traits in the development of our society. Today it is fashionable to call every dictatorship from Greece to Latin America 'fascist': a clear definition of what fascism was and what constituted a fascist movement would eliminate much confused talk and clarify the minds of many students. To equate the terms 'reactionary' and 'fascist', or to identify military dictatorship with fascism, is to misunderstand the nature of fascism.

Postscript

This essay was written more than ten years ago. It stated at the beginning that, in more recent years, numerous books and articles on fascist movements in individual countries as well as many comparative studies had been published, that fascism was no longer 'a neglected movement'. The intervening years have brought a new flood of such studies, and it therefore seems appropriate to mention at least some of the more important ones, especially those which offer new conclusions or indicate new approaches to further research. This flood of new studies is proof of the vitality of a subject which is important not only for our understanding of recent history but seems relevant to certain problems of our present society.

Many of the recent studies discuss the social basis of different fascist movements, and there a certain consensus seems to have been reached. In Germany as well as in Italy some social groups were more inclined to follow the fascist appeal than others; this applied in particular to the old and the new Mittelstand, the self-employed, white-collar workers, lower-grade officials, as well as to students and members of some of the professions, such as teachers and doctors. It also applied, at least in certain areas, to peasants and landowners, although their support of fascism was less certain than that of the urban middle groups. The upper and the working classes, on the other hand, were considerably less inclined to accept fascist propaganda. These conclusions were reached by several German historians who contributed papers to the thirtieth congress of German historians held in October 1974 and now available in book form: Wolfgang Schieder (ed.), *Faschismus als soziale Bewegung – Deutschland und Italien im Vergleich*, which contains three essays on Italian fascism and three on National Socialism.[84] In spite of its title, the book does not make any comparisons between Germany and Italy, but apparently the reader is left to draw his own inferences from the details supplied. Similar conclusions with regard to the social basis of National Socialism are reached by Professor Childers in a contribution to the tenth anniversary issue of the *Journal of Contemporary History*, based on an analysis of voting patterns in the late 1920s and early 1930s.[85] But his conclusion that the 'old' middle class was more receptive to National Socialist propaganda than the 'new' seems somewhat doubtful and would need more detailed confirmation.

A certain amount of agreement seems also to have been reached on the issue of the relationship of the traditional upper classes and the fascists. Professor Henry A. Turner's detailed researches into the connections of German capitalists with National Socialism have cleared the air with regard to a topic obfuscated by partisanship and political bias.[86] A younger German historian has recently emphasized that the relationship between the upper classes and fascism was not necessarily a positive one. Especially in Hungary and in Romania the upper classes did not conclude an alliance with the fascists because this seemed too dangerous to them and because they did not want to disturb the social peace.[87] The result was that in Romania the Iron Guard was defeated by the army; and in Hungary the Arrow Cross only came into power at the end of the Second World War thanks to German support. In Italy and in Germany, however, the fascist 'seizure of power' was only made possible by the alliance with the established upper classes, with the army and the higher bureaucracy. Wherever a revolutionary 'seizure of power' was attempted and met with firm resistance by the army and the state authorities, it failed, be that in Germany or in Romania.

A question much discussed in recent contributions to the subject of fascism is whether it was an expression of anti-modernism, whether the fascist leaders were in reality modernizers, and whether fascism in the two countries where it achieved power resulted in a modernization of state and society. Again it was Professor Turner who opened the discussion in an essay on 'Fascism and Modernization' in which he posed these questions without attempting a definite answer.[88] A Canadian historian, Alan Cassels, has distinguished 'two prototypes of fascism': one in advanced industrial societies which was 'nihilistic and backward-looking', the other in under-industrialized societies which was forward-looking and modernizing and used corporative ideas to achieve this end.[89] In Germany, Dr Wippermann has pointed to the example of Romanian and Hungarian fascism which both tried to promote the modernization of an antiquated social structure and aimed at the consolidation and integration of the nation through the elimination of the Jews and other foreign elements.[90] Yet it seems impossible to construct two different types of fascism by the use of this model, for all fascist movements contained elements of a protest against modernization and urbanization as well as tendencies towards a restructuring of society in a more modern sense. The mixture may have differed according to the relative backwardness and development of the country in question, but the tendency towards modernization was present even in the most developed countries. For Germany, this has long been shown by Ralf Dahrendorf[91] and David Schoenbaum,[92] whatever Hitler's intentions may have been. If National Socialist ideology was backward-looking and tried to revive medieval ideas and social relations, Mussolini's quest for a new Roman Empire and a return to the soil was not precisely forward-looking either. But the relationship between these different and often contradictory elements clearly requires more detailed research. So does the relationship between fascist ideology and social reality on which little work seems to have been done in recent years.

In general, the emphasis of much recent research has been on the differences, rather than on the similarities, between different fascist parties and régimes. A point made by several historians is that the relationship between the bureaucracy and the ruling party was dissimilar in Italy and in Germany. In Italy, Mussolini's well known circular to the prefects of 5 January, 1927 assigned to them control over the party and made even the party's federal secretaries subordinate to the prefects who were empowered to remove 'undesirable elements' from the fascist organizations.[93] There is no parallel to this from Germany, and during the war the tendency there was in the opposite direction. On the other hand, if the fascist party in Italy in the 1930s no longer had any political functions and became a mass organization of careerists and public functionaries,[94] its later role in Germany was perhaps not all that different. Although the opposite has been asserted recently, there seems to be no evidence that fascism in Italy – or for that matter in Germany – 'involved them [the masses] . . . in the day to day functioning of the system.'[95]

Another point that has emerged from the recent studies of fascism is that there is no generally accepted theory of fascism which could apply to the many countries in which fascist movements developed in the 1920s and 1930s. Indeed, several historians have stated that fascism cannot be explained by one simple formula,[96] that National Socialism was 'qualitatively different in its substance from Italian fascism',[97] that 'it seems unwise to continue with studies of fascism that start with the assumption that there must have been such a generic phenomenon.'[98] In short, the present trend among the historians is towards more detailed studies of single fascist parties or movements, and away from any generalization. If this leads us to new research and new monographs on individual countries this trend is very welcome; if it should lead to the neglect of comparisons and more general interpretations, this writer at least would regret it. Whether we study 'fascism' or 'fascisms' a comparison, bringing out the differences as well as the similarities, remains of vital importance, not only to the professional historian.

Notes

1. George L. Mosse, 'The Genesis of Fascism', *Journal of Contemporary History*, vol. I, no. 1 (1966), p. 14.
2. Ernst Nolte, *Der Faschismus in seiner Epoche* (Munich, 1963).
3. Above all, *Die faschistischen Bewegungen* (Munich, 1966), and *Die Krise des liberalen Systems und die faschistischen Bewegungen* (Munich, 1968).
4. *Theorien über den Faschismus* (Cologne and Berlin, 1967).

5. Giovanni Zibordi, *Critica socialista del fascismo* (Bologna, 1922), quoted by Nolte, *Theorien über den Faschismus*, pp. 80, 85.

6. Luigi Salvatorelli, *Nationalfascismo* (Turin, 1923), quoted ibid., pp. 130, 131, 135.

7. P. Togliatti, *A proposito del fascismo* (1928), quoted by Renzo de Felice, *Le interpretazioni del fascismo* (Bari, 1969), p. 181. The 'arditi' were Italian shock troops of the First World War.

8. A. Rossi (Angelo Tasca), *The Rise of Italian Fascism*, 2nd ed. (New York, 1966), p. 340 (first published in 1938).

9. Erich Fromm, *Die Furcht vor der Freiheit* (Frankfurt, 1966), p. 206 (written in 1942).

10. Wilhelm Reich, *Die Massenpsychologie des Faschismus* (Cologne, 1971), p. 68 (written in 1942).

11. Seymour Martin Lipset, *Political Man – The Social Bases of Politics* (New York, 1960), pp. 134, 174.

12. N. Kogan and J. Solé-Tura, in S. J. Woolf (ed.), *The Nature of Fascism* (London, 1968), pp. 13, 43.

13. Ernst Nolte, *Die faschistischen Bewegungen* (Munich, 1966), p. 65.

14. Manfred Clemenz, *Gesellschaftliche Ursprünge des Faschismus* (Frankfurt, 1972), pp. 147, 228. Compare another more simplified German view which has been put forward recently: 'their [the intellectuals'] arguments would never have brought fascism to power. This was achieved by the support of a whole social class, the lower middle class and the so-called new middle class. The lower middle class, above all the small "independent" shopkeeper, the enemy of the big concerns, was backward-looking, and was ultimately disappointed with fascism': Otto-Ernst Schüddekopf, *Fascism* (London, 1973), p. 132.

15. Martin Broszat, 'Soziale und psychologische Grundlagen des Nationalsozialismus', in E. J. Feuchtwanger, ed., *Deutschland – Wandel und Bestand* (Munich, 1973), p. 166 (English trans. [London, 1973], p. 138).

16. See especially Eugen Weber, 'The Men of the Archangel', *Journal of Contemporary History*, vol. I, no. 1 (December 1965), pp. 111, 114, 117.

17. See the quotation in n. 5.

18. S. J. Woolf, introduction to *European Fascism* (London, 1968), p. 4.

19. Wolfgang Sauer, 'National Socialism: Totalitarianism or Fascism?', *American Historical Review*, vol. LXXIII (1967), p. 411.

20. Heinrich August Winkler, 'Extremismus der Mitte?', *Vierteljahrshefte für Zeitgeschichte*, vol. XX (1972), p. 187. The article is above all a criticism of the fascism interpretation by Seymour Lipset.

21. Martin Broszat, in *Deutschland – Wandel und Bestand* (Munich, 1973), p. 170. (I am unable to find this quotation in the English translation, *Upheaval and Continuity – A Century of German History*, ed. E. J. Feuchtwanger [London, 1973], p. 134 ff.)

22. Clara Zetkin, 'Der Kampf gegen den Faschismus', protocol of the Enlarged Executive of the Communist International (12–13 June 1923), quoted by Nolte, *Theorien über den Faschismus*, pp. 89, 92.

23. August Thalheimer, 'Über den Faschismus' (1930), in Wolfgang Abendroth, ed., *Otto Bauer, Herbert Marcuse, Arthur Rosenberg u.a. – Faschismus und Kapitalismus* (Frankfurt and Vienna, 1967), p. 22.

24. Paul Sering, 'Der Faschismus', *Zeitschrift für Sozialismus*, pp. 24–5 (September–October 1935), p. 781. This analysis, published in the theoretical journal of the exiled SPD, was the first serious attempt at a Marxist analysis of the problem after Hitler's seizure of power.

25. Wolfgang Sauer, in *American Historical Review*, vol. LXXIII (1967), p. 410.

26. G. Germani, 'Fascism and Class', in S. J. Woolf, ed., *The Nature of Fascism* (London, 1968), p. 72.

27. Michael Hurst, 'What is Fascism?', *Historical Journal*, vol. XI (1968), p. 179.

28. This has been emphasized by Nolte, *Der Faschismus in seiner Epoche* (Munich, 1963), p. 397.

29. Giovanni Zibordi, *Critica socialista del fascismo*, quoted by Nolte, *Theorien über den Faschismus*, p. 80.

30. Otto Bauer, *Zwischen zwei Weltkriegen? Die Krise der Weltwirtschaft, der Demokratie und des Sozialismus* (1936), in Wolfgang Abendroth, ed., *Otto Bauer, Herbert Marcuse, Arthur Rosenberg u.a. – Faschismus und Kapitalismus*, pp. 153–4.

31. Manfred Clemenz, *Gesellschaftliche Ursprünge des Faschismus* (Frankfurt, 1972), pp. 213–14.

32. H. R. Trevor-Roper, 'The Phenomenon of Fascism', in S. J. Woolf, ed., *European Fascism* (London, 1968), pp. 23–4.

33. R. de Felice, in S. J. Woolf, ed., *The Nature of Fascism* (London, 1968), p. 250.

34. Reinhard Kühnl, *Formen bürgerlicher Herrschaft – Liberalismus-Faschismus* (Reinbek bei Hamburg, 1971), pp. 89–90.

35. Erich Fromm, *Die Furcht vor der Freiheit*, pp. 208–10.

36. G. Germani, 'Fascism and Class', op. cit., p. 89.

37. Wilhelm Alff, *Der Begriff Faschismus und andere Aufsätze zur Zeitgeschichte* (Frankfurt, 1971), pp. 124 ff., 141.

38. Fromm, op. cit., pp. 207–8.

39. Wilhelm Reich, *Die Massenpsychologie des Faschismus* (Cologne, 1971), p. 17.

40. ibid., p. 100.

41. Fromm, op. cit., pp. 205–6.

42. George L. Mosse, 'The Genesis of Fascism', *Journal of Contemporary History*, vol. I, no. 1 (1966), p. 21, with special reference to the Iron Guard and the Hungarian Arrow Cross.

43. Z. Barbu, in S. J. Woolf, ed., *The Nature of Fascism* (London, 1968), pp. 111–12.

44. Kühnl, op. cit., p. 89.

45. Adrian Lyttelton, *The Seizure of Power – Fascism in Italy 1919–1929* (London, 1973), p. 244.

46. These points have above all been made by Adrian Lyttelton, especially during a recent panel discussion at Oxford on 'fascism'. Cf. ibid., pp. 28, 30.
47. Kühnl, op. cit., p. 94.
48. Filippo Turati, *Fascismo, Socialismo e Democrazia* (1928), quoted by Nolte, *Theorien über den Faschismus*, p. 144.
49. ibid.
50. ibid., p. 149; L. Villari, *The Fascist Experiment*, p. 41, quoted by Paul Hayes, *Fascism* (London, 1973), p. 148.
51. Rudolf Vierhaus, 'Faschistisches Führertum', *Historische Zeitschrift*, vol. 198, no. 3 (June 1964), p. 629.
52. Hugh Seton-Watson, 'Fascism, Right and Left', *Journal of Contemporary History*, vol. I, no. 1 (1966), p. 194.
53. Vierhaus, op. cit., p. 629.
54. Henry V. Dicks, 'Deadly Fantasies', *New Statesman*, 16 February 1973, p. 235.
55. Luigi Salvatorelli, *Nationalfascismo* (1923), quoted by Nolte, *Theorien über den Faschismus*, pp. 135-6.
56. Franz Borkenau, 'Zur Soziologie des Faschismus', *Archiv für Sozialwissenschaft und Sozialpolitik*, vol. LXVIII (February 1933), pp. 513-47; quoted ibid., pp. 165, 170-71. The argument is further developed ibid., pp. 179-80.
57. Otto Bauer, *Zwischen zwei Weltkriegen? Die Krise der Weltwirtschaft, der Demokratie und des Sozialismus*, pp. 155-6.
58. J. Solé-Tura, 'The Political "Instrumentality" of Fascism', in S. J. Woolf, ed., *The Nature of Fascism* (London, 1968), p. 49.
59. Nolte, *Die faschistischen Bewegungen*, pp. 189-90. Cf. the geographical subdivision made by Wolfgang Sauer, in the *American Historical Review*, vol. LXXIII (1967), p. 421.
60. Nolte, *Der Faschismus in seiner Epoche* (Munich, 1963), p. 397. See also Lyttelton, *The Seizure of Power*, pp. 40, 118.
61. Heinrich August Winkler, in *Vierteljahrshefte für Zeitgeschichte*, vol. XX (1972), p. 190; very similarly the same, *Mittelstand, Demokratie und Nationalsozialismus* (Cologne, 1972), p. 180.
62. Reinhard Kühnl, *Formen bürgerlicher Herrschaft – Liberalismus-Faschismus*, p. 138.
63. John Weiss, *Nazis and Fascists in Europe* (Chicago, 1969), pp. 15-16.
64. Zibordi, *Critica socialista del fascismo* (1922), quoted by Nolte, *Theorien über den Faschismus*, pp. 83-4.
65. Hermann Rauschning, *Die Revolution des Nihilismus* (Zurich, 1938), quoted ibid., p. 343.
66. Paul Sering (Richard Löwenthal), 'Der Faschismus', *Zeitschrift für Sozialismus*, nos 24-5 (September-October 1935), p. 787.
67. George L. Mosse, in *Journal of Contemporary History*, vol. I, no. 1 (1966), pp. 14, 22.

68. Wolfgang Sauer, in *American Historical Review*, vol. LXXIII (December 1967), p. 412.
69. Karl Dietrich Bracher, *Die deutsche Diktatur* (Cologne-Berlin, 1969), p. 9.
70. John Weiss, *Nazis and Fascists in Europe*, p. 21.
71. Kurt Gossweiler, in Kurt Gossweiler, Reinhard Kühnl and Reinhard Opitz, *Entstehung und Verhinderung – Materialien zur Faschismus-Diskussion* (Frankfurt, 1972), p. 35.
72. Bracher, *Die deutsche Diktatur*, p. 9.
73. Kühnl, *Formen bürgerlicher Herrschaft – Liberalismus – Faschismus*, p. 122.
74. J. Solé-Tura, in S. J. Woolf, ed., *The Nature of Fascism*, p. 57:'Corporativism, the fascist ideology *par excellence*, was not a modern, but a traditional ideology in Spain.'
75. The opposite has been maintained by Martin Broszat, 'Soziale und psychologische Grundlagen des Nationalsozialismus', in E. J. Feuchtwanger, ed., *Deutschland – Wandel und Bestand* (Munich, 1973), pp. 166–7.
76. R. H. S. Crossman, *Government and the Governed* (London, 1939), p. 276.
77. Historikus (Arthur Rosenberg), *Der Faschismus als Massenbewegung* (Karlsbad, 1934), p. 7.
78. Thus the 13th Plenum of the Executive Committee of the Comintern in December 1933, quoted by Nolte, 'Zur Phänomenologie des Faschismus', *Vierteljahrshefte für Zeitgeschichte*, vol. X, no. 20 (1962), p. 384.
79. Reinhard Opitz, 'Wie bekämpft man den Faschismus?', in Gossweiler, Kühnl and Opitz, *Entstehung und Verhinderung – Materialien zur Faschismus-Diskussion*, p. 46.
80. Kühnl, ibid., p. 41. For financial support of Italian fascism, see Lyttelton, op. cit., pp. 142, 208–11.
81. This is the formulation of S. J. Woolf, in the Introduction to his *European Fascism*, p. 12. Professor Vierhaus uses the term 'a new "ruling class" '; ibid., p. 627.
82. This emerges very clearly from an important thesis which, however, does not make any comparison with Italy: A. J. Caplan, 'The Civil Servant in the Third Reich' (Ph.D. diss., Oxford University, 1973).
83. Leonard Schapiro, *Totalitarianism* (London, 1972), pp. 66–7. Cf. N. Kogan, in S. J. Woolf, ed., *The Nature of Fascism*, p. 16: 'I have serious doubts whether the Fascist Party was ever a ruling party as such. Mussolini ruled as *Capo del Governo* . . . rather than as *Duce del Fascismo*'; and Lyttelton, op. cit., pp. 158–66, 200–201, 293.
84. *Historische Perspektiven* no. 3 (Hamburg, 1976). I am referring in particular to the essays by Michael H. Kater, 'Sozialer Wandel in der NSDAP im Zuge der nationalsozialistischen Machtergreifung', pp. 25–67; Hans Mommsen, 'Zur Verschränkung traditioneller und faschistischer Führungsgruppen in Deutschland beim Übergang von der Bewegungs- zur System-

phase', pp. 157–81; and Wolfgang Schieder, 'Der Strukturwandel der faschistischen Partei Italiens in der Phase der Herrschaftsstabilisierung', pp. 69–96.

85. Thomas Childers, 'The Social Bases of the National Socialist Vote', *Journal of Contemporary History*, vol. X, no. 4 (1976), pp. 17–42.

86. Henry Ashby Turner, Jr, *Faschismus und Kapitalismus in Deutschland – Studien zum Verhältnis zwischen Nationalsozialismus und Wirtschaft* (Göttingen, 1972).

87. Wolfgang Wippermann, *Faschismustheorien – Zum Stand der gegenwärtigen Forschung*, 2nd ed. (Darmstadt, 1975), p. 176.

88. 'These questions remain unresolved'; the essay was originally published in *World Politics*, vol. XXIV, no. 4 (July 1972), pp. 547–64; reprinted in Henry A. Turner (ed.), *Reappraisals of Fascism* (New York, 1975), pp. 117–39: see especially p. 125.

89. Alan Cassels, 'Janus: The Two Faces of Fascism', ibid., pp. 69–92; the quotation on p. 78. Similarly, Alan Cassels, *Fascism* (New York, 1975), p. 347. Cf. the distinction made by Otto-Ernst Schüddekopf, *Fascism* (London, 1973), p. 132.

90. Wippermann, op. cit., pp. 90–91.

91. Ralf Dahrendorf, *Gesellschaft und Demokratie in Deutschland* (Munich, 1965).

92. David Schoenbaum, *Hitler's Social Revolution – Class and Status in Germany, 1933–1939* (New York, 1966).

93. Piero Melograni, 'The Cult of the Duce in Mussolini's Italy', *Journal of Contemporary History*, vol. XI, no. 4 (October 1976), pp. 221–2; Schieder, op. cit., p. 87.

94. Schieder, op. cit., pp. 87, 90.

95. The assertion was made by Michael Ledeen, in *The Times Literary Supplement*, 9 January 1976, p. 36.

96. Thus Wippermann, op. cit., p. 136.

97. Thus Jost Dülffer, 'Bonapartism, Fascism and National Socialism', *Journal of Contemporary History*, vol. XI, no. 4 (October 1976), p. 123.

98. Thus Turner, 'Fascism and Modernization', op. cit., p. 133. In a recent paper which this writer was privileged to attend, Professor Klaus Hildebrand of the University of Frankfurt in general opposed the use of the term 'fascism', and suggested that for Germany the term 'Hitlerism' should be used.

INDEX

Aachen, town, 101
Adler, Victor, 253-4, 255
Action Française, the, 325
Aichach, town, 77
Aitzema, Lieuwe van, 83, 85-88
Albert V, duke of Bavaria, 121, 124
Albrecht Achilles, margrave and elector of Brandenburg, 56
Albrecht, first duke of Prussia, 63, 66-72
Albrecht the Bear, margrave, 4
Alexander the Great, 296
Alexander I, czar, 182
Alsace, 91; towns of, 101
Alsace-Lorraine, 189, 221, 247
Alvensleben, noble family, 156, 237
Amandus, Dr., preacher, 61
Amsterdam, 87-88, 132
Anhalt, principality, 134
Anklam, town, 33, 52, 54-5, 56
Ansbach, principality, 183
Anti-Semitic League, the, in Austria, 264-5, 266
Anti-Semitism, 137, 221-8, 256-9, 263-7, 269-70, 304, 312-14
Antonescu, Ion, marshal, 342
Arndt, Ernst Moritz, poet, 220-1, 229
Arrow Cross movement, in Hungary, 342, 348
Augsburg, 74, 95-6, 100-1
Augustus the Strong, elector of Saxony, 130, 134
Aulic Council, the, 107, 110, 116-17, 124
Ausgleich, the (1867), 255
Austria, 95-6, 179, 184, 187, 201, 222, 235, 238, 255-70, 275, 283, 293, 344
—, Jews in, 127, 141, 222, 225, 256-8, 263-6
—, National Socialists in, 226, 261-3, 266-70, 329
—, Parliament of, 257, 262;
—, war with (1866), 242-3, 246-7
—, war with Serbia (1914), 275
Axelrod, Paul, politician, 252-4

Baden-Durlach, margraviate, 116, 118
—, margraves of, 116
—, Estates of, 116, 119 n. 2
Ballenstedt, counts of, 4
Barbu, Z., sociologist, 335
Barnekow, noble family, 55
Barnim, district, 45-7, 50

Barnim, duke of Pomerania, 4
Barnim X, duke of Pomerania, 40
Barten, town, 68
Bartenstein, town, 68
Barth, town, 55
Bauer, Max, colonel, 267
Bauer, Otto, politician, 227, 263, 290, 332, 339
Bavaria, 75-9, 92, 95, 98, 113, 183, 293
—, electors of, 102, 105, 108-9, 110-11, 113-14
—, Estates of, 75-6, 78, 113-14, 120-1, 125
—, government of, 206, 342
—, nobility of, 96-7
—, Protestants in, 75, 124
—, peasants of, 97, 293
—, taxation in, 76-9, 125, 143
Bayreuth, principality, 183
Bebel, August, SPD leader, 245-54, 274
Becher, Johann Joachim, writer, 95
Beck, Ludwig, general, 194, 219, 317, 319, 321
Beer, brewing of, 34-5, 37-8, 76, 78
Bennigsen, Rudolf von, politician, 243
Berg, duchy, 81, 92, 112, 173
—, dukes of, 110
—, Estates of, 83, 103
Berlin, 23, 34, 96, 112, 133, 146, 171-3, 181, 184, 188, 190, 237, 243, 245, 261, 295-7, 317
—, Communists in, 280
—, Jews in, 133, 139, 141, 226-7
—, revolution in (1918), 280, 284, 301
—, University of, 223, 295-6, 305
Bernstein, Eduard, SPD leader, 252, 272, 276
Bethmann Hollweg, Theobald von, 203
Bismarck, noble family, 156
—, Otto von, 177, 186-92, 193, 199, 201-2, 218, 229, 241-4, 246, 248, 271
Black Death, the, 32
Blanqui, Auguste, politician, 276-7
Blaskowitz, Johannes, colonel, 211
Blücher, Leberecht von, general, 182-3, 184
Böckel, Otto, politician, 223
Boer War, the (1899-1902), 310, 312
Boers, the, 310, 312-13
Bogislav X, duke of Pomerania, 35, 40, 56-7
Bohemia, 93-5, 96, 98, 102, 201, 222, 226, 256-7, 260-2

(Bohemia, continued)
—, elector of, 105-6
—, nobility of, 98
—, National Socialists in, 226
Bolshevism, 217, 263, 269, 276-9, 288, 305, 307
—, fear of, 227, 230, 263, 266, 270, 289, 290, 332
Bolshevists, the, 252-4, 286, 293, 297, 305
—, Workers' Opposition to, 297
Borcke, Baron, Prussian Minister in London, 174-5, 177
—, noble family, 10
Borkenau, Franz, political scientist, 338-9
Boyen, Leopold Hermann Ludwig von, general, 183, 238, 321
Bracher, Karl Dietrich, historian, 217, 343-4
Brandenburg, town, 5, 96
Brandenburg Mark, the, 1, 4-11, 15, 17, 19, 20, 22-4, 29, 31, 34, 39-40, 81-2, 91, 94, 96-8, 102-3, 107, 160-1, 220
—, electors of, 106-9, 114, 121
—, Estates of, 107, 121-22, 154
—, margraves of, 4-6, 21, 24, 33
—, nobility of, 24, 32-3, 37, 39, 145, 156, 158, 160, 193
—, towns of, 96, 169
Brandler, Heinrich, KPD leader, 297
Bremen, free city, 91-2, 96, 101, 158
—, duchy, 91
Breslau, town, 133, 141
British Empire, the, 177, 181, 184, 312
British navy, the, 212
Broszat, Martin, historian, 328
Brüning, Dr. Heinrich, chancellor, 209-11, 305, 306
Brunswick, dukes of, 56, 92, 103, 117, 131, 134
—, 103, 133, 140-1
Buckow, monastery, 2
Budapest, 342
—, Soviet Republic in (1919), 227, 263, 291-3
Bund, the (Jewish Socialist Party), 252-3
Burghausen, town, 77
Burschenschaften, the (in Austria), 256-7, 259
Butler, Rohan, historian, 218

Caesar, Julius, 179
Calcar, town, 82-3, 84
Calvinism, 94
Calvinist princes, 93-4, 125, 137
Calvinists, the, 113, 141

Cammin, bishopric, 2
Caporetto, battle of (1917), 336
Carlyle, Thomas, historian, 191
Carmarthen, Francis Osborne, Earl of, 181
Cassels, Alan, historian, 349
Castlereagh, Robert Stewart, Viscount, 182
Catherine the Great, Czarina, 169
Catholic Church, the, 259, 300
Centre Party, the, 200, 298, 300
Chamberlain, Houston Stewart, racialist writer, 218, 224
Charles II, king of England, 112
Charles VI, Emperor, 93, 117, 131, 171
Charles Alexander, duke of Württemberg, 134-5, 136
Charles Leopold, duke of Mecklenburg, 117
Charles Louis, Elector Palatine, 112, 119 n. 2
Childers, Thomas, historian, 348
China, civil war in, 303-4
Chorin, monastery, 7, 23
Christian Albrecht, duke of Holstein, 116
Christburg, district, 28
Christina, queen of Sweden, 138
Christian Social Party, the, in Austria, 259, 264-6, 284
Cistercian monasteries, 22-3
Clarendon, George William Frederick Villiers, Earl of, 185-7
Class, Heinrich, politician, 224
Cleves, duchy, 81-9, 104, 132, 134, 139, 155
—, dukes of, 81
—, Estates of, 82-8, 104, 119, 122-4, 139, 154-5
—, government of, 155
—, royal chamber of, 149
—, towns of, 81, 88, 103
Cleves, town, 84
Clothdealers, guild, 11
Cocceji, Samuel von, 158-9, 160
Codreanu, Corneliu Zelea, Romanian Fascist, 338
Cologne, archbishop of, 92, 105, 107-8, 111, 130
—, city of, 101, 140
—, Estates of, 107
Comintern (Communist International), the, 295, 297-8, 303-4, 345
Commune of Paris, the (1871), 248
Communist Party, German (KPD), 227, 229, 276, 279-81, 289, 295-303, 306
—, Austrian (KPÖ), 291
Conservative Party, the, in Prussia, 223, 240, 243
Constitutional Conflict, in Prussia, 177, 185-6, 197-9, 237-43
Cornwallis, Charles, Earl, 181-2
Corvey, monastery, 7
Cottagers, 8, 13

Index

Counter-Reformation, the, 93-4, 113, 121
Craig, Gordon, historian, 194, 212
Cromwell, Oliver, 178
Crossman, Richard, politician, 345
Culmerland, district, 28
Cuno, Heinrich, chancellor, 306
Czechoslovakia, 219, 262
Czechs, the, 218, 221-2, 226, 255-6, 260-1

Dahrendorf, Ralf, sociologist, 349
D'Annunzio, Gabriele, writer, 336
Danzig, town, 37, 162, 302
de Felice, Renzo, historian, 293, 332
Degrelle, Léon, Belgian Fascist, 338
de Jonge, Moses Jacobsen, merchant, 104, 132-3
Delbrück, Hans, historian, 304
Demmin, town, 52, 55-6
Denmark, kings of, 54, 57, 92, 116, 221
–, fleet of, 54, 57, 62
–, war with, 54, 57, 62, 186, 196, 202, 242
Depopulation, 29, 31-2, 41, 95-7
Deserted holdings, 24-5, 27, 29-33, 97
Deutsch, Julius, politician, 227, 263, 265
Deutschlandlied, the, 256
Deutschvölkischer Schutz- und Trutzbund, the, 227
Dickens, Guy, British Minister in Berlin, 173, 175-8
Diesdorf, monastery, 6, 8
Dinslaken, town, 82
Dollfuss, Engelbert, Austrian chancellor, 269-70
Dresden, town, 115, 140
Düsseldorf, town, 140
Duisburg, town, 82

East Prussia, 154-7, 160-1, 231
–, government of, 148, 159, 163
Ebert, Friedrich, President, 204, 206, 208, 230, 254, 265, 287-8
Eckart, Dietrich, writer, 341
Ehrhardt Brigade, the, 228
Einem, Karl von, general, 200
Eisenkolb, Dr. Anton, politician, 259
Eisner, Kurt, politician, 227-8
Elbing, district, 28
Eldena, monastery, 2, 22-3
Emmerich, town, 81, 83
Engels, Frederick, 245, 248, 256, 274-5, 307, 313
England, 40-2, 87, 98, 185-92, 201, 321
–, Parliament of, 84, 100, 119, 125, 128, 184, 239
–, nobility of, 100
–, towns of, 41-2
–, urban middle classes of, 42, 128

English trade, 74, 101, 201
Erfurt, town, 103
Eric, duke of Pomerania, 56
Ernest Augustus, Elector of Hanover, 115
Ermland (Warmia), bishop of, 69
–, bishopric, 14, 20, 26
–, chapter, 26
Erzberger, Matthias, politician, 228
Etherege, Sir George, 100, 106-8
Excise, the, 102-3, 125, 145
Eylau, castle, 68

Fascism, 306-7, 325-55
–, in Germany, 315
–, in Italy, 268, 283, 292-3, 325-7, 336, 341, 344, 348, 350, 354 n. 83
–, rise of, 293
Fascist movements, the, 331, 343-5
Ferdinand II, Emperor, duke of Styria, 121
Ferdinand III, Emperor, 85, 92-3, 106-7
Ferdinand Maria, Elector of Bavaria, 113-14
Finland, fascist movements in, 329, 331-2
First International, the, 246-7
First World War, the, 203-4, 209, 212, 260, 272-3, 283, 293, 295-6, 310, 315, 331, 333, 337
–, ex-servicemen of, 328-9
Fischer, Ruth (Elfriede Eisler), KPD leader, 297-8
Fischhausen, town, 66
Fiume, expedition to (1919), 336
Flanders, Fascists in, 329
Forckenbeck, Max von, politician, 239, 242
France, 88, 94, 98, 105, 123-5, 127-8, 133, 163-5, 180, 182-3, 195, 207, 220, 247
–, crown of, 74, 92
–, gains of in 1648, 91, 93, 101
–, power of, 92, 105, 108-9, 129
–, religious wars in, 73, 75
Franco-Prussian war, the, 188-91, 202, 223, 247
Frankfurt on Main, 74, 95, 100-1, 141, 180, 187-8, 297
–, National Assembly at, 235
Frankfurt on Oder, 102
Frederick II, margrave and elector of Brandenburg, 34, 56
Frederick III, margrave and elector of Brandenburg, 134, 138
Frederick II, king of Prussia, 91, 132-4, 139, 142, 161-2, 176-81, 191-2, 193, 195, 304
–, as crown prince, 147, 150-1, 178, 192
–, army of, 179-81
Frederick Augustus, Elector of Saxony, king of Poland, 115, 130, 134

Frederick Charles, duke of Württemberg, 117
—, prince of Prussia, 196-8, 202
Frederick William, the Great Elector, 81-2, 84, 86-8, 92, 102-4, 109, 111-12, 114, 122-5, 133, 139, 145, 154, 162-3, 179
—, army of, 82-6, 101, 109, 123, 145
Frederick William I, king of Prussia, 104, 132-3, 138, 143, 145-62, 166, 168, 171-3, 175-8, 193
—, giant grenadiers of, 149, 151, 171-8
Frederick William III, king of Prussia, 182-3, 195-6
Frederick William IV, king of Prussia, 184, 235-6
Frederick William, Prussian crown prince, 185, 187, 190-1, 241
Free Corps, the, 205-6, 228-9, 289-90, 329, 331, 336
Free Imperial Cities, the, 74-5, 101, 106, 217
Free Imperial Knights, the, 105, 110, 117
Freemasons, the, 222
French bourgeoisie, 128, 164-5
—, nobility, 164-5, 167
—, *Parlement*, 135
—, Republic, 247
—, Revolution, the, 127, 182, 195
Friesack, lords of, 5
Friesland, States of, 86
Fromm, Erich, psychologist, 327, 333-4
Fuggers, the, banking house, 101, 129

Galen, Bishop Christopher Bernard von, 103
Gans von Putlitz, the, 5
Gennep, town, 81
Gentry, the, in England, 40-2
George Louis, Elector of Hanover (later George I, king of Britain), 115, 117, 172
George II, king of Britain, 147, 175-6
George III, king of Britain, 181
George, duke of Pomerania, 61
Gerdauen, district, 68
Gericke, Hans, peasant leader, 65-6, 69
Gerlach, Helmuth von, writer, 254
German Empire, the (1871), 242-3, 256-7, 260, 271, 302-3
—, constitution of, 247
German medieval colonisation, 1-16, 19, 21-2, 31, 51
German nationalism, 219-22, 225, 229, 256-7, 270, 313, 315, 323
German peasants, 1-3, 6-8, 10-11, 13, 20
German race, the, 312
German racialism, 312, 345

German Nationalist Party, the, 229, 298, 301, 306, 342
—, in Austria (Grossdeutsche), 259, 264, 266, 269-70, 284
German Workers' Party, the, in Bohemia, 226, 260-2
Germani, G., political scientist, 333
Germanisation, 2, 7, 10-12, 15-16, 19, 222
Gestapo, the, 321
Giolitti, Giovanni, prime minister, 292
Gisevius, Hans Bernd, writer, 321
Gladstone, William Ewart, 188-9
Gneisenau, Neithardt von, general, 182, 321
Gobineau, Comte Arthur de, racialist writer, 218
Goerdeler, Carl, politician, 317, 319-21
Goldsmith, Oliver, writer, 181
Gomperz, Jewish merchant family, 104, 132, 137, 139
—, Moses Levin, 138-9, 142-3
—, Ruben Elias, 104
Goschen, George, politician, 188
Granville, George Leveson-Gower, Earl, 189-90
Greifswald, town, 52, 54-7, 60, 62
Grimm, Hans, writer, 309-15
—, *Volk ohne Raum*, 309-13
Grimmen, town, 55
Grundherrschaft, the, 17-19, 38
Groener, Wilhelm, general, 208-10, 215 n. 83, 287-8
Grumbkow, Friedrich Wilhelm von, general, 175
Güntersberg, noble family, 10
Gützkow, county, 5
Guchkov, A.I., minister, 285
Gustavus Adolphus, king of Sweden, 179-80
Gutsherrschaft, the, 17, 19-21, 26, 29, 36-8, 97

Haase, Dr. Hugo, politician, 227
Habicht, Theo, politician, 268
Habsburgs, the, 91-3, 128, 130-1, 283
—, state of, 222, 226-7, 255-9, 262, 284
Halberstadt, town, 134, 139-40
Halle, town, 140
Hamburg, 54, 74, 96, 100-1, 103, 138, 172, 301
—, Jews in, 138
Hammerstein-Equord, Kurt von, general, 208, 210-11
Hanover, principality, 98, 117, 133, 195
—, Electorate, 106, 115-16
—, army of, 115, 195
—, Estates of, 116, 119
—, Jews in, 140-1
Hanseatic League, the, 34-5, 51, 54-5, 57,

(Hanseatic League, continued)
  62, 218
—, decline of, 62, 73-4, 102
—, towns of, 217
Harden, Maximilian, writer, 313
Hardenberg, Karl August Freiherr von, 195
Hardwicke, Philip Yorke, Earl, 179-80
Harrington, Wm. Stanhope, Earl, 173, 175
Hassel, Ulrich von, diplomat, 317
Havelberg, bishop of, 31
Havelland, district, 43-5, 50
Heidelberg, town, 113
Heimwehren, the, in Austria, 259, 266-9
—, in Styria, 266, 268-9
Heine, Heinrich, 142
Henry VIII, king of England, 121, 128
Herder, Johann Gottfried, writer, 218
Hess, Moses, writer, 313
Hesse-Cassel, principality, 92, 94, 123
—, Estates of, 125 & n. 6
Heye, Wilhelm, general, 208
Hilferding, Rudolf, SPD leader, 304
Himmelpfort, monastery, 23
Hindenburg, Paul von, general and president, 203, 208-9, 211, 231, 274, 319, 342
Hinrichsens, Jewish merchant family, 134, 137
Hirsch, Paul, politician, 227
Hitler, Adolf, 194, 211, 218-19, 225-7, 229 231, 267-70, 289, 314-15, 317, 322 334, 338-9, 341
—, government of, 334
—, *Mein Kampf*, 222, 226
—, Putsch in Munich (1923), 229, 267, 342
—, resistance to, 245, 317-20
Hohenzollerns, the, 34-5, 39-40, 56, 114, 118, 133, 169, 235, 241, 283-4, 300, 319
—, army of, 101
—, state of, 89, 103, 107, 114, 119, 123, 135, 137, 141, 145, 201, 204, 227, 289, 321; *see also* Prussia, kingdom
Holland, 87-8, 133, 141
—, States of, 86-7, 88
Hollanders, 11
Holstein, duchy, 116
—, Estates of, 116, 119 n. 2
Holy Roman Empire, the, 91, 93-5, 124, 260
—, army of, 109
—, Circles of, 109
—, Diet of, 92-3, 105-9, 111, 124
—, Estates of, 93-5, 105
—, High Court of, 105, 110

Horthy, Miklós, Hungarian regent, 342
Huguenots, the, admission of, 178
Hungarians, the, 255
Hungary, 222, 255-6, 268, 284, 292-3, 328, 336, 342, 344, 348
—, Soviet Republic in (1919), 227, 263, 291-2
—, Communists in, 292, 332
—, Fascists in, 328, 331, 342, 348-9
Hussites, the, 31, 54

Iconoclasm, 59
Imperialism, 272-3, 275
Imperialism, the Highest Stage of Capitalism, 273
Independent Social Democratic Party (USPD), 276, 284, 288, 290, 296, 300-1
Ingolstadt, town, 77
Innsbruck, town, 265, 267
Iron Guard, the, in Romania, 329, 342, 348
Ius teuthonicum, 2, 12

Jacoby, Johann, radical politician, 189, 313
Jahn, Friedrich Ludwig, 220-1, 229
Jena, battle of (1806), 142, 145, 193
Jews, the, 94, 104, 127-43, 222-7, 256, 258, 262-3, 265, 270, 349
—, emancipation of, 221
—, World Conspiracy of, 314
Joachim I, margrave and elector of Brandenburg, 40
Joachim Frederick, margrave and elector of Brandenburg, 39
Jogiches, Leo, politician, 228, 272
John (Cicero), margrave and elector of Brandenburg, 34-5
John William, Elector Palatine, 113
Joseph I, Emperor, 93
Joseph Clemens, archbishop of Cologne, 130
Jünger, Ernst, writer, 323
Jülich, duchy, 81, 112, 173
—, dukes of, 81, 92, 110
—, Estates of, 83, 103
Jungdeutscher Orden, the, 229
Junkers, the, 17-42, 52, 68, 70-1, 99, 140, 154-9, 160-3, 164, 168, 192, 239, 245-6, 313
—, trade of, 37-8

Kantzow, Thomas, chronicler, 61
Károlyi, Count Mihály, 284, 292
Kapp Putsch, the (1920), 267, 289, 291
Kasimir, duke of Pomerania, 35
Katte, Lieutenant Hans Hermann von, 150-1, 153, 178

Kautsky, Karl, politician, 272, 276
Kehr, Eckart, historian, 295, 307
Kiel, revolutionary movement at (1918), 301
Kietze (fishing villages), 9
–, inhabitants of, 9, 10
Kleist, Heinrich von, poet, 219-20, 221, 225
–, noble family, 84
Knapp, Georg Friedrich, historian, 18
Knesebeck, noble family, 156
Knirsch, Hans, politician, 226, 261
Königsberg, town, 36, 64-9, 71, 102-3, 148, 150, 169, 189
–, castle of, 69
Köpenick, town, 33
Köslin, town, 35, 56
Kogan, N., political scientist, 327, 354n. 83
Kolbatz, monastery, 23
Kolberg, town, 60
Kreutz, noble family, 71
Kunschak, Leopold, politician, 264

Labour services, 23, 30, 37, 41, 64-6, 71, 97, 98-9, 163
–, commutation of, 23-4, 30
Lagarde, Paul de (Bötticher), racialist writer, 221-2, 227
Landauer, Gustav, writer, 228
Landbuch of Brandenburg (1375), 8, 22, 24, 42
–, of New Mark (1337), 29
Landsberg, town, 77
Landsberg, Dr. Otto, politician, 227
Landwehr, the, in Prussia, 186, 197, 237-9
Lapide, Hippolythus a, writer, 94
Lassalle, Ferdinand, 218, 244, 246, 274-5
Leader, the, of a Fascist party, 334, 337-8
League of Nations, the, 207, 229, 299
Leber, Julius, politician, 317
Lebus, bishopric, 10
Leibniz, Gottfried Wilhelm, philosopher, 115
Leipzig, 95, 103, 118, 141, 183, 246
–, battle of (1813), 182
–, officers' trial at (1930), 318-19
–, treason trial at (1872), 248, 250
Leitzkau, monastery, 6
Lenin, V.I., 253, 272-4, 276-8, 280-1, 292, 297
Leopold I, Emperor, 92-3, 107, 111, 115-16, 124, 131
Leubus, monastery, 23
Leuschner, Wilhelm, politician, 317
Levi, Dr. Paul, politician, 227, 279
Leviné, Eugen, politician, 228
Liebknecht, Karl, politician, 265, 279

–, murder of, 267
Liebknecht, Wilhelm, SPD leader, 247, 274, 3
Liebmann, Esther, jeweller and banker, 139
Lipset, Seymour Martin, sociologist, 327
Livonia, 97, 104, 132
Locarno, Treaty of (1925), 207-8, 311
Loen, Johann Michael von, writer, 100
Loftus, Lord, diplomat, 189
Louis XIV, king of France, 91-3, 95, 105, 108-9, 111-13, 115-16, 123, 130-1, 145, 158
–, wars of, 108, 116, 129
Louis, margrave of Baden, 131
Louis Ferdinand, Prince of Prussia, 319
Lower Saxony, 96-7
Lower middle classes, the, 326-9, 330, 333, 338, 347, 351 n. 14
Ludendorff, Erich, general, 203, 267, 296, 302
Lübeck, town, 54, 57, 62, 101
–, right of appeal to, 57
Lüneburg, duke of, 92
Lüttwitz, Walter Freiherr von, general, 205
Lueger, Dr. Karl, politician, 225-6, 257, 259
Lusatia, 74
Luther, Martin, 58, 124, 217
Lutheran princes, 94
Luxemburg, Rosa, 227-8, 252-3, 271-81
–, murder of, 267, 280
–, *The Accumulation of Capital*, 272-3
–, *The Crisis of Social Democracy*, 275
Lyttelton, Adrian, historian, 335-6

Macaulay, Thomas Babington, 180, 191-2
Mack Smith, Denis, historian, 293
Magdeburg, town, 96, 138
–, principality, 97-8, 156
Magyarization, Magyars, 255-6
Mainz, archbishop of, 92, 103, 105-6, 107-9
Mannheim, town, 138
Manteuffel, Otto von, minister, 236
–, noble family, 188, 237
Mark, county, 81, 104, 134, 139
–, Estates of, 83, 86, 119, 122, 139, 154-5
Marriott, J.A.R., historian, 191-2
Martov, Julius, politician, 274
Marwitz, Ludwig von der, 221
Marx, Karl, 245, 247, 256, 274-5, 278, 307, 313
Marxism, 262, 266, 269, 272, 304, 307, 325
Maslov, Arkadi, KPD leader, 297-8
Max Emanuel, Elector of Bavaria, 114
Maximilian I, Elector of Bavaria, 113, 119 n. 2, 121
Mayer, Gustav, historian, 295

Index

Mazarin, Jules, Cardinal, 92
Mecklenburg, 20, 40, 96-7, 118, 132-3, 134, 137-8
—, dukes of, 55-6, 110
—, Estates of, 116-18, 119, 124, 134
Meissen porcelain, 115
Memel, district, 68
—, town, 104, 132
Mendelssohn, Moses, 133
Menshevists, the, 252-4, 297
Metz, town, 189, 202
Middle Mark, the, 22, 24-6, 30, 36, 156
Mierendorff, Carlo, politician, 317
Milan, 293
—, occupation of factories, 292, 297, 331
Moltke, Helmuth von, general, 201-2, 321
Mommsen, Theodor, historian, 245
Morier, Sir Robert, diplomat, 185-6, 187, 189
Mosse, George L., historian, 325, 334, 343
Müller, Hermann, chancellor, 209
Münster, bishop of, 92, 103
—, town, 103
Müntzer, Thomas, 67
Munich, 76-7, 95-6, 101, 261, 301
—, National Socialists in, 228-9, 267
—, Soviet Republic in (1919), 227, 291, 293
Mussolini, Benito, 268, 293, 338, 341, 346, 349, 354 n. 83
Mutinies, in Austrian army and navy, 283
—, in German navy (1917), 283, 301

Napier, Lord, diplomat, 187
Napoleon I, 131, 145, 182-3, 193, 195, 219, 229, 241
Napoleon III, 188
Nassau, Count Georg Friedrich von, 85
—, Prince Johann Moritz von, 85-6, 138-9
Natangen, district, 67-8
National Committee for a Free Germany, the, 322
National Liberal Party, the, 223, 243
National Socialism, 217-18, 230-1, 260, 262, 268, 306, 315, 317-18, 325, 329, 338, 341, 346, 348, 350
National Socialist Party (NSDAP), 209-10, 228-9, 231, 262, 268, 299, 306, 315, 317-18, 323, 341
—, ideology of, 221, 327, 334, 349
—, propaganda of, 220, 314, 318, 348
—, in Austria, 261-3, 266-70
—, victory of, 317, 332, 334
Netherlands, the, 74, 87-8, 91, 98, 221, 257
—, garrisons of, 81-8

—, revolt of the, 73-4
—, States General of, 81-6
—, trade of, 81, 87-8, 101, 103-4
—, wars in, 75
New Left, the, 325, 333, 345
New Mark, the, 8, 10, 21, 29, 98, 159-60
Nibelungen, the, 260
Noblemen, Bavarian, 96-7, 101
—, English, 100
—, French, 164-5, 167
—, German, 99-101, 118, 230
—, Prussian, 193, 196, 199, 238-9
—, Russian, 167-8
—, Spanish, 100
Noblesse de robe, the, 164-5
Nolte, Ernst, historian, 325, 327, 340-1
Noreia, battle of (113 B.C.), 225, 258
North German Confederation, the, 242, 246
—, Reichstag of, 247
Northern War, the (1655-60), 86-7, 122, 129
Noske, Gustav, minister, 205
Nuremberg, 74, 96, 100-1, 180
Nymegen, Peace of (1679), 108

Oberland, Bavarian Free Corps, 229, 269
Old Mark, the, 5-8, 11, 22-4, 33, 37, 156
—, towns of, 34-5, 96
Oppenheimer, Samuel, banker, 131
—, Süss, 134-5, 138, 143
Orange, House of, 87
—, Louisa Henrietta of, 87
—, Prince William of, 87, 115, 241
Orel, Anton, journalist, 264
Orgesch (Organization Escherich), the, 267
Orsoy, town, 81
Otto, margrave of Brandenburg, 4, 6

Pabst, Waldemar, captain, 267
Palatinate, the, 112-13, 118, 125
—, devastation of, 113
—, Electors of, 94, 106-7, 112
—, Upper, 94, 113, 119 n. 2
Palatinate-Neuburg, principality, 81-2, 85, 111
—, count of, 81, 83, 92, 111-12
Paléologue, Maurice, diplomat, 285
Palmerston, Henry John Temple, Viscount, 184, 186-7
Pan-Germanism, 221-4
Pan-German League, the, 223-4, 227, 266
Pan-Germans, in Austria, 259-60, 262, 270
Papen, Franz von, chancellor, 210-11, 230, 305
Paris, bombardment of, 189

Pernerstorfer, Engelbert, 255
Peter the Great, Czar, 117, 153, 166-9, 171
Petrograd, 283-6
Pforzheim, town, 96
Pfrimer, Dr. Walter, politician, 268
Philip, duke of Pomerania, 62
Philip William, Count Palatine of Neuburg, 111
Pitt, William (elder), 179
Plaschka, Richard, historian, 283
Plekhanov, Georgii, politician, 276
Poland, 31, 33, 36-7, 38, 40-1, 95, 97, 104, 114-16, 132, 170, 207, 221-2, 226, 262, 271-2, 302, 315, 319
–, Estates of, 118
–, king of, 63, 69, 115, 130, 132
–, revolutionary movement in, 271-2
Poles, the, 218, 228, 255, 267, 302
Polentz, noble family, 63, 65
Polish independence, 271, 302
–, Jews, 222, 226-7, 263-4
–, throne, 130, 134
–, villages, 13
Polish Socialist Party (PPS), the, 252-3
Pomerania, duchy, 1-5, 7-8, 15, 22-3, 35, 38-9, 91, 96-8, 149, 156, 160, 220, 240
–, dukes of, 52-7, 59-62
–, Estates of, 55, 57
–, inhabitants of, 8, 99
–, nobility of, 24, 53-6, 61-2, 145, 157-8, 193
–, towns of, 35, 51-62
Pomerania-Wolgast, dukes of, 54-5
Pomesanien, bishop of, 27
Popitz, Johannes, minister, 317
Posnania, district, 302
Potsdam, town, 96, 133, 145, 151-2, 174
–, Day of (1933), 231
–, garrison of, 318
Prenzlau, town, 4
Pribislav, prince of Brandenburg, 4
Primo de Rivera, José Antonio, Spanish Fascist, 338
Pritzwalk, district, 8
Progressive Party, the, 239-44
Protestant princes, 93
–, sects, 94
Protestantism, 94
Provisional Government of Russia (1917), 284-6, 290, 292-3
Prussia, duchy, 17, 63, 82, 97-8, 104, 120-1, 122, 132
–, duke of, 63, 71
–, Estates of, 27, 32, 104, 122, 154

–, ports of, 87
–, principality of Teutonic Order, 1, 12-15, 20, 26-9, 31, 34, 38, 40, 63
Prussia, kingdom, 19, 42, 99, 117-18, 131, 133, 136, 143, 171, 177-92, 193-9, 220, 230-1, 235-7, 246, 287, 313
–, army of, 101, 136, 148, 166, 171, 182, 187, 194-9, 205, 212, 236, 241, 321
–, bureaucracy of, 163, 165
–, constitution of, 235, 242
–, general directory of, 146, 150, 152, 162
–, industry in, 133, 178, 237
–, militarism of, 145, 177, 192, 231, 314
–, military officers in, 140, 148, 157, 165, 173, 189, 193-203, 236
Prussian Freemen, 12, 14, 20, 70-1
–, mayors, 13-14
–, noblemen, 12, 29, 32, 69-72
–, peasants, 14-15, 16, 20, 64, 70-2
–, serfs, 13, 20, 70
–, traditions, 321, 323
Pufendorf, Samuel, writer, 94
Puritanism, in England, 125

Rathenau, Walther, 228
Ratisbon, town, 100-1, 105, 107-8, 124
Rauschning, Hermann, politician, 342
Rauter, Hanns, Heimwehr leader, 268
Ravensberg, county, 81
–, Estates of, 83
Rees, town, 81, 83
Reformation, the, 37, 57-9, 63, 120, 128, 300
Reich, Wilhelm, psychologist, 327, 334
Reichsbanner Schwarz-Rot-Gold, 319
Reichswehr, the, 205-6, 209-10, 211, 231, 318, 341-2
–, officer corps of, 205-8, 318-19, 321
Reinl, Hans, politician, 265
Revolution of 1918-19, in Austria, 263, 284, 287, 290-1
–, in Germany, 219, 229, 248, 265, 275, 279-80, 284, 287, 289-90, 295, 301-2, 319, 323
–, workers' and soldiers' councils in, 287-9, 290-1, 301-2
Rhenish Alliance, the (1658), 92, 103
Rhine, the, 183, 236
–, trade on, 74, 103
Rhineland, the, 96, 105, 183
Richau, Nicolaus, mayor of Königsberg, 66, 69, 70-1
Riehl, Dr. Walter, politician, 262-4
Rippe, noble family, 64-5, 68
Ritter, Gerhard, historian, 321
Robertson, C. Grant, historian, 191-2
Rode, Paulus vom, preacher, 61

Romania, 328, 344, 348-9
—, army of, 342, 348
—, government of, 342
—, Iron Guard in, 342, 348
Rome, march on (1922), 292-3, 336
Roon, Albrecht von, general, 193, 198-9, 238, 240-1, 321
Rosenberg, Arthur, historian, 295-307, 345
—, in first world war, 296
—, joins KPD, 296
—, in the Reichstag, 298-303
—, leaves KPD, 303
—, emigration, 305
—, works of, 302, 304-7
Rossbach, battle of (1757), 179-80, 229
Rostock, town, 51, 54, 56, 57, 117
Rotterdam, 88
Rothschilds, the, bankers, 256
Rubenow, mayor of Greifswald, 56
Rudolf II, Emperor, 81
Rügen, island, 3-4, 55, 57, 220
—, princes of, 3
—, principality, 1, 4, 52
Ruhr, the, 236, 310
—, industrial development at, 237
—, occupation of (1923), 228-9
—, rising in (1920), 289
Russell, John, Earl, 187
—, Odo, diplomat, 190-1
Russia, 33, 38, 127, 153, 166, 169-70, 192, 207, 222, 271, 276, 283-6, 344
—, army of, 117, 166-7, 205, 212, 230, 250, 283, 285, 290
—, fleet of, 187
—, *Narodniki* in, 344-5
—, nobility of, 167-9
—, peasants of, 277-8, 286-7, 290
—, serfdom in, 168-9
—, war against?, 201-2
Russian revolution of 1905, 250, 272
—, of 1917, 276-7, 280, 283-7, 289-90, 293, 305

SA, stormtroopers, 228, 269
Sadowa, battle of (1866), 242
St. Petersburg, 168
Salvatorelli, Luigi, historian, 326, 338
Salzburg, archbishop of, 108
Salzwedel, town, 5, 11, 34
Samland, bishop of, 14, 63
—, bishopric, 14
—, district, 14-15, 64-5, 67-70, 149
Sarnow, Karsten, mayor of Stralsund, 53
Sauer, Wolfgang, historian, 329, 330, 343

Saxony, 97-8, 102, 118, 132, 183, 284, 289
—, army of, 115
—, Electors of, 94, 106-7, 109-10, 112, 114-16, 123, 125
—, Estates of, 102, 114-15, 116, 118-19, 125 & n. 6
—, gains of 1648, 114
—, government of, 206
Schapiro, Leonard, historian, 346
Scharnhorst, Gerhard Johann David, general, 193, 195-6, 197, 321
Scheüch, Heinrich, general, 287
Schlageter, Albert Leo, Free Corps officer, 228
Schleicher, Kurt von, general, 193-4, 209-11, 305
Schlochau, district, 26
Schnee, Heinrich, historian, 127, 141-3
Schoenbaum, David, historian, 349
Schönerer, Georg Ritter von, 225-6, 256-61, 269-70
—, anti-Catholicism of, 225, 259, 270
—, racial anti-Semitism of, 256-8, 270
Scholem, Werner, KPD leader, 298
Schulenburg, noble family, 156
Schwerin, bishop of, 54
Schwerin, noble family, 33
Second World War, the, 327, 331, 348
Sedan, battle of (1870), 229
Seeckt, Hans von, general, 204-8, 321
Seipel, Dr. Ignaz, politician, 265-6
Serfdom, serfs, 19, 37, 97-9, 162-3, 169-70, 304
—, sale of, 169
Sering, Paul (Richard Löwenthal), political scientist, 330, 352 n. 24
Seton-Watson, Hugh, historian, 338
Sevenaer, town, 82, 84
Seven Years' War, the, 132, 179-80, 182
Silesia, 74, 91, 96, 98-9, 102, 180, 220, 222
—, linen from, 103
—, Upper, 228, 267
Silesian wars, the, 178
Sima, Horia, Romanian Fascist, 342
Slavonic law, 19-20
—, noblemen, 4-6, 10, 21
Slavonic peasants, 1-4, 6-8, 16, 19
—, peoples, 218, 220, 255
—, princes, 1
—, taxes, 6
—, villages, 2-3, 6-10
Slavs, the, 220, 225, 255, 260-1, 270
Sleswig and Holstein, duchies, 186-7

Smiterlow, Klaus, mayor of Stralsund, 60, 62
Social Democratic Party (SPD), the, 200, 230-1, 245, 248-52, 271-5, 284, 289-90, 292, 298-300, 301, 305, 313-15
–, in Austria, 226, 230, 255, 259, 261, 284, 290-1
–, in Bavaria, 251
–, of the Kingdom of Poland and Lithuania, 252, 271-2
Social Democrats opposing Hitler, 317, 320, 322
Socialist International, the, 273-4
Socialist-Revolutionaries, the (in Russia), 252-3, 277, 286, 292
Solé-Tura, J., political scientist, 327, 339
Sombart, Werner, historian, 141
Sophia Dorothea, queen of Prussia, 147, 172
South Africa, British, 309-10, 312
South-West Africa, former German colony, 310, 313
–, Herero War in (1908), 313
Soviets, the, in Russia, 284-6
Soviet Union, the, 299, 301, 321
Spaen, Jacob von, 85
Spain, 127-8, 329, 344
–, Jews of, 128
–, kings of, 129
–, throne of, 131
Spandau, town, 23, 96, 102
–, fortress of, 151
Spanish Netherlands, the, 81, 88, 108
Spanish Succession, war of, 114, 131
Spartacus League, the, 274, 276, 281, 301
–, rising (January 1919), 280, 290, 293
Speyer, town, 95, 110
Stab-in-the-back legend, the, 219, 288, 300, 302
Stahlhelm, the, 229
Stalin, J.V., 278
Stanhope, James, Earl, 172
Starhemberg, Ernst Rüdiger von, politician, 267
Stauffenberg, Claus Count Schenk von, 317-23
–, political views of, 320-2
Steidle, Dr. Richard, politician, 267-8
Stein, Freiherr Heinrich Friedrich Karl vom, 119, 195-6
Stendal, town, 11, 34, 96
Stern-Taeubler, Selma, historian, 127, 136-7
Stettin, town, 35, 56-7, 60-2, 91
Stewart, Charles, general, 182-3
Stieff, Helmuth, army officer, 318-19, 322

Stolp, town, 61
Stralsund, town, 35, 51-60, 62
–, Reformation in, 58-9
Stresemann, Gustav, chancellor and foreign minister, 206-7, 229
Stuart, House of, 87
Sukhanov, N.N., writer, 284-6
Swastika, the, 228, 267
Sweden, 87-8, 114, 129
–, acquisitions of in 1648, 91-3
–, army of, 91, 114
–, Empire of, 93
–, kings of, 92
Switzerland, 91, 96, 133, 221, 257
Sybel, Heinrich, historian, 239, 241, 244
Szálasi, Ferencz, Hungarian Fascist, 338, 342

Tasca, Angelo, writer, 327
Tauroggen, convention of (1812), 196
Taxation, 102-3, 181
–, of the Empire, 105-6
Taylor, A.J.P., historian, 212, 218
Teltow, district, 47-8, 50
Teutonic Order, 1, 12-15, 20, 26-9, 34, 36, 40, 63, 156, 218, 260
–, dissolution of, 63
–, Grand Master of, 32, 63
Teutonic race, the, 180, 189, 224, 260, 312
Teutonicus deus, 16
Thälmann, Ernst, KPD leader, 298
Thalheimer, August, politician, 330
The Hague, 83-5, 86-8
Third Reich, the, 314-15, 335
Thirty Years' War, the, 40, 73, 81, 98, 101-2, 103-4, 113-14, 121, 129-30
–, consequences of, 104-5, 112, 116, 123-5, 141
Tiefenau, noble family, 27
Tilsit, district, 68, 148
Togliatti, Palmiro, politician, 327
Treitschke, Heinrich von, historian, 223-4, 244, 304
Tresckow, Henning von, army officer, 318
Trevor-Roper, H.R., historian, 332
Tribsees, district, 1
–, town, 52
Trier, archbishop of, 92, 105, 107, 109
Trotsky, Leo, 278
Turati, Filippo, politician, 337
Turks, the, 91, 93, 100, 105, 107, 115, 124, 131
–, siege of Vienna by, 93, 105
Turner, Henry A., historian, 348-9

Index

Ucker Mark, the, 8, 22-3, 29, 156
Ulm, town, 96, 100-1
United Provinces, the, 92, 95, 117, 119, 128
University students, 256-7, 259, 328-9, 331
Ursin, Dr. Josef, politician, 264
Utrecht, States of, 88

Vansittart, Sir Robert, civil servant, 217-18
Versailles, court of, 112, 129
–, government at, 248
–, Treaty of (1919), 207, 209, 219, 229, 266, 309, 311, 317-18
Victoria, queen, 184-90
Victoria (Vicky), Prussian crown princess, 185-6, 189-91
Vienna, 131, 141, 256, 258, 261-4, 269, 291, 293
–, anti-semitism in, 225-7, 264, 266
–, Jews in, 256, 263-4
–, 'red' Vienna, 230, 266, 291
–, riots in, 267
–, University of, 256
Vierhaus, Rudolf, historian, 337-8, 354 n. 81
Vizlav, prince of Rügen, 3, 52
Völkisch ideology, the, 260, 267, 269-70
–, organizations, 261-4, 266
Voge, Otto, mayor of Stralsund, 55-6
Volkmann, Erich Otto, historian, 301
Volkswehr, the, in Austria, 291
Vollmar, Georg von, politician, 251

Wagner, Richard, 223-4
Waldersee, Count Alfred von, 196, 199-201, 203
Walpole, Horace, 178
Wandruszka, Adam, historian, 260
War of Liberation (1813-14), 195-6, 221, 229, 238, 318, 321
Warsaw, 271
Wartislaw, duke of Pomerania, 55
Waterloo, battle of (1815), 182-3, 184
Weber, Max, 18, 141
Wedel, noble family, 10
Wehrmacht, the, 221
Weimar Republic, the, 230, 232, 245, 315, 319, 322, 346
Wellington, Arthur Wellesley, Duke, 182, 184

Wels, Otto, SPD leader, 254
Welsers, the, banking house, 101, 129
Wendish language, 4, 6, 9
Wends, the, 4, 7, 10
Wertheimer, Samson, banker, 131
Wesel, town, 81-3, 85-6, 103, 139
Westminster, Treaty of (1756), 179
Westphalia, 96, 183
–, Peace of (1648), 88, 91-3, 94
West Prussia, 302
Wettin, House of, 114, 118, 300
Whitworth, Sir Charles, ambassador to Berlin, 171-3
Wilhelm, Prince of Prussia, 319
William I, king of Prussia, German Emperor, 185, 187, 191, 235-7, 239-42
William II, German Emperor, 191-2, 200, 202-3, 218-19
Wippermann, Wolfgang, historian, 349
Wismar, town, 54
Wittelsbachs, the, 118, 300
Wolgast, town, 55, 57, 59, 60
Woolf, Stuart J., historian, 328
Württemburg, duchy, 96, 98, 112, 117, 134, 136
–, dukes of, 110, 123, 134
–, Estates of, 112, 117-18, 119, 124-5 & n. 6, 134-6
–, house of, 300
Würzburg, bishop of, 134-5
Wulflam, mayor of Stralsund, 52-3
Wullenweber, Jürgen, mayor of Lübeck, 62

Xanten, Treaty of (1614), 81, 85, 88

Yorck, Hans David Ludwig von, general, 196
Yorck von Wartenburg, Peter Count, lieutenant, 320
Young Plan, the, 229
Yugoslavia, Partisans of, 283

Zauche, district, 4, 49-50
Zeeland, States of, 88
Zetkin, Clara, politician, 330
Zibordi, Giovanni, historian, 326, 328, 332, 342
Zürich, political émigrés, in, 271